NO OTHER PL

Visions of utopia – some hopeful, others fearful – have become increasingly prevalent in recent times. This groundbreaking, timely book examines expressions of the utopian imagination with a focus on the pressing challenge of how to inhabit a climate-changed world. Forms of social dreaming are tracked across two domains: political theory and speculative fiction. The analysis aims to both uncover the key utopian and dystopian tendencies in contemporary debates around the Anthropocene as well as to develop a political theory of radical transformation that avoids not only debilitating fatalism but also wishful thinking. This book juxtaposes theoretical interventions, from Bruno Latour to the members of the Dark Mountain collective, with fantasy and science fiction texts by N. K. Jemisin, Kim Stanley Robinson and Margaret Atwood, debating viable futures for a world that will look and feel very different from the one we live in right now.

Mathias Thaler teaches political theory at the University of Edinburgh.

NO OTHER PLANET

Utopian Visions for a Climate-Changed World

Mathias Thaler

University of Edinburgh

CAMBRIDGE
UNIVERSITY PRESS

CAMBRIDGE
UNIVERSITY PRESS

University Printing House, Cambridge CB2 8BS, United Kingdom

One Liberty Plaza, 20th Floor, New York, NY 10006, USA

477 Williamstown Road, Port Melbourne, VIC 3207, Australia

314–321, 3rd Floor, Plot 3, Splendor Forum, Jasola District Centre, New Delhi – 110025, India

103 Penang Road, #05–06/07, Visioncrest Commercial, Singapore 238467

Cambridge University Press is part of the University of Cambridge.

It furthers the University's mission by disseminating knowledge in the pursuit of education, learning, and research at the highest international levels of excellence.

www.cambridge.org
Information on this title: www.cambridge.org/9781316516478
DOI: 10.1017/9781009030250

First published 2022

A catalogue record for this publication is available from the British Library.

Library of Congress Cataloging-in-Publication Data
Names: Thaler, Mathias, 1978- author.
Title: No other planet : utopian visions for a climate-changed world / Mathias Thaler, University of Edinburgh.
Description: Cambridge, United Kingdom ; New York, NY : Cambridge University Press, 2021. | Includes bibliographical references and index.
Identifiers: LCCN 2022003221 (print) | LCCN 2022003222 (ebook) | ISBN 9781316516478 (hardback) | ISBN 9781009015653 (paperback) | ISBN 9781009030250 (epub)
Subjects: LCSH: Human beings–Effect of climate on. | Climatic changes–Social aspects. | Utopias in literature. | Geology, Stratigraphic–Anthropocene.
Classification: LCC GF71 .T43 2021 (print) | LCC GF71 (ebook) | DDC 304.2/5–dc23/eng20220321
LC record available at https://lccn.loc.gov/2022003221
LC ebook record available at https://lccn.loc.gov/2022003222

ISBN 978-1-316-51647-8 Hardback
ISBN 978-1-009-01565-3 Paperback

Contents

Acknowledgements

Apparently, it was not Isaac Newton who first observed that, whenever we strive to make intellectual progress, we cannot but stand on the shoulders of giants; it was Bernard of Chartres or perhaps William of Conches in the twelfth century.[1] No matter its true origins, the dictum always struck me as only partially compelling. For, while all scholarly work, in the humanities and social sciences at least, involves an incessant conversation with the past, the plan to climb on someone's back just to see a bit better, even if they are long gone and you prove to be a lightweight, does seem rather self-serving.[2]

This is why I prefer another image to account for the debts accrued in the process of writing this book: that of moving forward, together with others, in the comradely pursuit of a shared intellectual passion. Learning with and from a great many colleagues made this endeavour possible. It is a tribute to their stature, and to the solidary bonds between us, that none of them ever made me feel small.

Duncan Bell, Davina Cooper, Liz Cripps, Toby Kelly, Tony Lang, Vassilios Paipais, Paul Raekstad and Steve Yearley have commented on various chapters and offered incisive feedback. A panel at the University of Edinburgh including Elizabeth Bomberg, Andy Hom and Neil Walker steered an early draft in the right direction at a critical juncture. My home political theory crowd – Philip Cook, Liz Cripps, Mihaela Mihai

[1] Merton, *On the Shoulders of Giants*; Jeauneau, "Nani gigantum humeris insidentes."
[2] Moreover, who is to say that things could not turn awry, with the giants suddenly deciding it was now their time to crush our dwarfish bodies? On this point, see: Eco, *On the Shoulders of Giants*, chap. 1.

and Kieran Oberman – as well as the PhD and postdoc community (in particular Camilo Ardila Arévalo, Benedikt Büchel, Louis Fletcher, Maša Mrovlje, Lukas Slothuus and Gisli Vogler) and other colleagues across the School of Social and Political Science (especially Jamie Allinson, Janet Carsten, Claire Duncanson, Oliver Escobar, Andrew Neal, Nicola Perugini and Jonathan Spencer) have nurtured and stimulated my curiosity during the research phase for this book. A huge thanks to all of them.

While I was working on this project, Elizabeth Bomberg, Luke March and Wilfried Swenden led the Politics and International Relations Department and kindly supported me in the pursuit of my interests. Moreover, for invaluable mentorship over many years, I wish to thank Rainer Bauböck, Christina Boswell, Alessandro Ferrara, Kim Hutchings and Tony Lang.

Several stints away from my usual workplace shaped my thinking about the topic of utopianism. In 2019, on a sabbatical leave granted by the University of Edinburgh, I spent valuable time at Edinburgh's Institute for Advanced Studies in the Humanities, the Institute of Philosophy (RIPPLE) at KU Leuven and at the University of Sydney's Social Sciences and Humanities Advanced Research Centre. I am grateful to my hosts, Steve Yearley, Tim Heysse, Helder De Schutter and Dany Celermajer, for their hospitality, curiosity and financial support.

I am also thankful to the wider group of scholars leading and orbiting around Sydney's Environment Institute – Dany Celermajer, David Schlosberg, Lauren Rickards, Makere Stewart-Harawira, Petra Tschakert, Blanche Verlie and Christine Winter – for introducing me to their scholarship around multispecies justice. I have given talks in Cambridge, Leiden, Leuven, Glasgow, Norwich, Oxford, Sydney, Vienna and York and am grateful to the audiences for their helpful comments.

My biggest debt, however, is to Mihaela Mihai, with whom I have mulled over every single idea in this book at least once. It is hard for me to express in words how endlessly rewarding it is to be on the receiving end of her patience, acumen and care.

The final stage of writing this book would not have been possible without funding from the Leverhulme Trust, through a Research Fellowship (RF-2020-445). At Cambridge University Press (CUP), I owe gratitude first and foremost to Robert Dreesen, who expressed confidence in the project from the start. The manuscript benefitted from the substantial and constructive feedback provided by CUP's two anonymous referees. During the production phase, I wish to thank Catherine Rae for copy-editing the book, Erika Walsh for helping me with the publicizing materials and Jane Bowbrick, Jessica Norman and Niranjana Harikrishnan for coordinating the whole process.

Last but not least, special thanks are due to Ahmet Öğüt for granting me permission to use an image of his installation *The Castle of Vooruit* as the book's cover. Öğüt's project, originally exhibited in 2012, demonstrates with great acuity what I want to explore in this book. The installation consists of a balloon hovering high in the sky above Ghent, with the Vooruit building, a beacon of the Belgian working-class movement, levitating on top of a giant rock formation. Öğüt's artwork references René Magritte's surrealist painting *Le Chateau des Pyrénées* (1961), while supplanting the old castle with the replica of a concrete building that stores the social memory of past struggles for freedom and emancipation. Importantly, the dream behind the Vooruit cooperative still remains alive today, more than 100 years after it was inaugurated, in the form of a vibrant cultural centre that caters to the citizens of Ghent.

Öğüt's decision to transpose this iconic architecture onto a floating mountain reflects the profoundly paradoxical nature of the utopian imagination: On the one hand, the audience experiences the installation as agile and nimble, lighter than air in fact, so that even the most compact structures, such as rocks and castles, appear to be quickly carried away with grace and joy. Call this its future-oriented dimension. On the other hand, upon looking more closely, Öğüt prompts us to redirect our gaze from the bright sky to the rough ground beneath it and interrogate what it actually represents: a building with a tortuous history that tells of both progress and decay; of a time in the interwar period when workers could escape the misery of their impoverished lives; and of a period when the Nazi occupiers transformed the magnificent Festivities Hall into a mundane restaurant. Through this process, the artwork's focus on the past and the present is revealed. Just as when the utopian imagination is engaged, *The Castle of Vooruit* thus summons us to envisage both aspects in parallel – the fantastical weightlessness of a floating mountain and the compact robustness of the built environment – in a sort of double vision that might at first seem rather disconcerting, but turns out to be highly instructive. It is this peculiar way of seeing the world, and our place within it, that my book hopes to examine as well.

CHAPTER 1

Solid Frames and Open Doors

To pass freely through open doors, it is necessary to respect the fact that they have solid frames. This principle, by which the old professor had always lived, is simply a requisite of the sense of reality. But if there is a sense of reality, and no one will doubt that it has its justification for existing, then there must also be something we can call a sense of possibility.

Whoever has it does not say, for instance: Here this or that has happened, will happen, must happen; but he invents: Here this or that might, could, or ought to happen. If he is told that something is the way it is, he will think: Well, it could probably just as well be otherwise. So the sense of possibility could be defined outright as the ability to conceive of everything there might be just as well, and to attach no more importance to what is than to what is not.[1]

THE OPENING PARAGRAPHS OF ROBERT MUSIL'S *The Man without Qualities* speak of two contradictory senses that provide guidance to our being in the world: the sense of reality and the sense of possibility. Both depend on and influence each other, as Musil's protagonist, Ulrich, soon comes to appreciate. This is the case because one cannot expect to cultivate a sense of reality, of what is necessarily so-and-so, without simultaneously exploring a sense of possibility, of what could, due to its contingency, always be otherwise.[2]

---

[1] Musil, *The Man without Qualities*, para. 8.3–8.4. Throughout this book, I cite from e-books (in epub-format) by referring to the paragraph from which quotes are taken. To determine the paragraph, I use the cross-platform, open-source application Calibre (https://calibre-ebook.com).

[2] See: Sattler, "Contingency and Necessity." This attention to both the sense of reality and the sense of possibility also influences Musil's strategy of narration. On this aspect, see: Weissberg, "Versuch einer Sprache des Möglichen."

In this book, I pay heed to both the solid frames that structure our existence and to the open doors that enable us to change our lives. More concretely, I follow up on Musil's lead by looking at various and sometimes competing expressions of the utopian imagination.

This certainly seems to be an opportune moment to direct attention to utopias. Today, utopias are everywhere: from popular TV series telling post-apocalyptic stories, to revolutionary plans for the built environment; from philosophical treatises on the technological enhancement of *Homo sapiens*, to intimate settings created by counter-hegemonic communities. Our collective appetite to conjure and inhabit other worlds appears to be insatiable.

How can we explain this, given that only a few decades ago utopias were either derided as lofty castles in the sky or denounced as dangerous schemes for social engineering? And what should we make of the growing number of rival utopias that circulate in the public sphere? Are they merely the by-product of a craving for escapist fantasies in an era when alternatives to the status quo are increasingly elusive, or do they genuinely articulate empowering visions of the future?

Answers to these questions are not easy to discover. Important findings in the humanities and social sciences notwithstanding, we do not yet possess a satisfactory account of utopian visions in and for our times. This book aims to fill this lacuna, by analyzing what is the biggest challenge the world presently faces: anthropogenic climate change, a challenge for which, due to its multi-causality and scope, no straightforward solutions present themselves. The ongoing ecological crisis, which imperils our survival as a species, accelerates the extinction of the Earth's biota and significantly affects the planetary ecosphere, makes it imperative to critically reflect on how we could salvage our sense of reality while at the same time extending our sense of possibility.

It is one of the book's underlying assumptions that we do not have much chance of survival unless we take the task of figuring out better ways of being and living very seriously indeed. Utopias, conveyed through social and political theory and speculative fiction, can help in this process. Properly conceived, they are as much concerned with disclosing radically new perspectives as they are about illuminating the material and ideological circumstances that shape our lives. Precisely because the future is uncertain and risky, we cannot but conjure alternative scenarios – some hopeful, others fearful – of what is yet to come.[3] Since there is, in spite of delusions of interstellar escape, no other planet for our species to dwell on, we have no choice but to imaginatively explore better ways of being and living here on Earth.[4]

Against this backdrop, we may ask ourselves what modes of imagining a climate-changed world are prevalent today. And why should we turn to theory building and storytelling in particular when so much is practically at stake? These queries are central to reckoning with the current predicament, for coming to terms with the effects of climate change is not only a matter of acquiring the correct kind of scientific knowledge and of taking appropriate mitigating and adaptive action; it is also a matter of debating viable futures for a world that will look and feel very different from the one we are living in right now, as the COVID-19 pandemic has already been teaching us.[5]

Since "utopia" and "utopianism" can mean so many things, it will be helpful to start with an exploratory definition. With Miguel Abensour, I understand utopianism broadly as the *education of a desire for being and living otherwise.* This utopian pedagogy can take multiple forms, depending on the historical context wherein the underlying desire arises, but there are three key mechanisms on which it relies: estranging, galvanizing and cautioning. As will become evident on the following pages, it is through estranging, galvanizing and cautioning that social dreaming proceeds.

This definition is perhaps not commonly accepted in the public, but it equips us with the best framework for capturing a great variety of proposals to envisage a climate-changed world. Utopianism, thus

---

[3] On the centrality of imaginaries for debates around climate change, see: Milkoreit, "Imaginary Politics."

[4] The emancipatory potential of such acts of picturing alternatives has been acknowledged by many advocates of Critical Theory, but it is Iris Marion Young who put it most succinctly: "Imagination is the faculty of transforming the experience of what is into a projection of what could be, the faculty that frees thought to form ideals and norms" (*Justice and the Politics of Difference*, 6).

[5] For a discussion of the intersections between the COVID-19 pandemic and climate change, see: Malm, *Corona, Climate, Chronic Emergency*.

understood, is not exclusively directed at the idealizing construction of wholly other worlds. Rather, it consists in a specific form of creative and transformative reflection that breaks the spell of the status quo, a demonstration – in thought and in practice – that things could be otherwise: better (*eu*-topia) or worse (*dys*-topia), but different nonetheless.

Throughout this book, I follow Lucy Sargisson in holding "utopianism" apart from "utopia": utopianism describes a wide phenomenon that can be reconstructed in different cultural contexts and historical eras, and whose essence will be fleshed out shortly in terms of a desire for being and living otherwise, or in terms of social dreaming. Utopias, by contrast, are concrete manifestations of said phenomenon – they instantiate what utopianism aspires to be.[6] Hence, while my overall goal is to improve our understanding of *utopianism* in and for our times, the way to achieve this is via an in-depth engagement with manifold and sometimes conflicting *utopias*, formulated across a range of media and genres.

By way of creative and transformative reflection, utopias perform various functions, from offering relief to those who have to endure oppressive and violent conditions to the propagation of revolutionary agendas that aim to overthrow the hegemonic order of things. These tasks can be initially approached through the juxtaposition of two extremes: daydreaming (for the sake of coping with an unbearable situation) and worldbuilding (for the sake of creating a different order). Both represent forms of utopianism, but they play very different roles for the individual or collective undertaking them.

In the first case, utopia is there to console us in a situation that appears overbearing and beyond our control. In the second case, utopia is supposed to aid us in modifying the fundamental circumstances of our existence. While daydreaming can have important, if somewhat inchoate, repercussions – just think how the unofficial slogan of the *soixante-huitards* "Be realistic – demand the impossible!" keeps on invigorating counter-hegemonic struggles – it is worldbuilding that usually gets associated with the transformative potential of utopianism.[7]

---

[6] Sargisson, *Fool's Gold?*, 8.

[7] On the delayed yet real impact of the revolutions of the 1960s see: Graeber, *The Democracy Project*, chap. 5: Breaking the Spell. On the revolutionary appeal of the 1968 generation,

In her recent work, Donna Haraway has uncovered the biggest impediment that any vindication of utopianism in and for our times faces: that of avoiding both the "position that the game is over, it's too late, there's no sense trying to make anything any better" and, on the other side, "the comic faith in technofixes."[8] The still unexplored space between these two positions is where the most fruitful conversations around the future of our species, the Earth's biota and the planetary ecosphere are to be had. Only if we manage to liberate ourselves simultaneously from the incapacitating grip of ecological grief and from the delusional obsession with what I will later call "solutionism," can we grapple in earnest with the present moment.

Not everyone welcomes the resurgence of utopian thinking and acting, though. In fact, aversion to utopianism possesses an impressive pedigree in the history of political ideas. Traditionally, two objections have been levelled against it. The first accuses utopias of being useless, because the proverbial "castles in the sky" do not furnish us with protective shelter in the here and now. In this case, the charge entails that utopianism-as-daydreaming propagates nothing but wishful thinking. It ultimately collapses into escapism, dressed up in the shiny garb of sophisticated theory or high literature.

According to the second objection, utopias are not merely impractical but dangerous, for they frequently become, perhaps even against the best intentions of their creators, vehicles for domination. Here, the future fabricated by utopianism-as-worldbuilding is condemned as a manipulative smokescreen, rendering invisible the many sacrifices that would have to be made to reach the preferred ideal state.

Both of these criticisms will receive attention in Chapter 2, but note that they take off from diametrically opposed premises. In the first case, utopianism's problematic side is blamed on its presumed failure to come to terms with what Musil calls the "solid frame" of our shared reality. Daydreaming can become harmful when it distracts us from what should

---

and its continuing relevance for political theory, see: Rossi, "Being Realistic and Demanding the Impossible."

[8] Haraway, *Staying with the Trouble*, 3.

matter most – remedying the dire situation we currently find ourselves in.

In the second case, the concern is, by contrast, that utopianism can have profoundly negative consequences, precisely because people might actually want to create the alternative world that a specific utopian vision conjures. The perniciousness of worldbuilding, on this account, stems from its propensity to seduce an audience into believing in utopia's realizability. In this view, Musil's "open door" is nothing but a trap.

The ambition behind this book is to respond to these criticisms and to rehabilitate utopia's potential for our times. Put simply, my rejoinder to the challenges of utopianism-as-daydreaming and utopianism-as-world-building is not so much that they completely miss the point – there is an important truth to these worries that should not be ignored – but rather, that they overemphasize the risks and dangers of utopianism while discounting its tremendous benefits. The crux of my argument is therefore that we urgently require utopias to identify ways out of our current predicament, the ongoing ecological crisis; yet, at the same time, we also need to comprehend which utopias will be useful for engaging the imagination in productive ways, and which utopias might lead us astray.[9]

Accordingly, the project I pursue here delivers a systematic account of those utopias that assist us in dealing with real-world problems. These problems, I contend, are the result of an extraordinary dearth of genuine alternatives to the status quo. In addressing this lack, the book hopes to accomplish two objectives: to reconstruct the main eutopian and dystopian tendencies in contemporary discussions about climate change; and to provide orientation for our planetary future on the basis of which a political theory of radical transformation – avoiding both fatalism and wishful thinking – can emerge.

The remainder of this introduction lays the foundation for the more detailed analyses in the rest of the book by doing several things: first, I will elaborate on the wide-ranging concept of utopianism that undergirds my approach. In a second step, my goal is to say something more specific about the context in which I discuss contemporary

---

[9] Benjamin Kunkel thus seems right to suggest that today's existential choice is really between "utopia or bust." See: Kunkel, *Utopia or Bust.*

utopianism – ways of seeing a climate-changed world that are often associated with the Anthropocene. Third, I discuss the disciplinary perspectives that inform this scholarly project. The following section explains the book's methodological approach, by introducing two key terms for my case selection: constellation and plot line. In the fifth and final section, I provide a synopsis of the ensuing chapters.

1.1 A PRIMER FOR STUDYING UTOPIAS

In order to chart the space between defeatism and self-aggrandizement, we require a capacious framework that covers a great variety of utopias. Even though Chapter 2 will be devoted to examining this framework in more detail, this section includes a primer for how I propose to study utopias in the Anthropocene.

When approaching utopianism, we need to attend to at least three interrelated issues; first, the *dimensions* of utopianism: utopianism contains both *eu*-topian and *dys*-topian elements.[10] This view contravenes everyday linguistic conventions whereby the word "utopian" is usually reserved for positive visions that are meant to be significantly better than the status quo. However, the advantage of zeroing in on both eutopian and dystopian theories and narratives is that this allows us to better grasp the varying roles that hope and fear play in utopias: they can mobilize people to fundamentally change their behaviour by widening their horizon of expectation; or they can constrain their freedom, by imprisoning them in fatalistic stories.

Second, the *sites* of utopianism: utopianism manifests in three domains, which shape one another – political and social theory; fictional narratives in various genres and media (novels, films, paintings and even music); and social movements and experiments in communal living.[11] It is a central claim of this book that a holistic account of utopianism cannot materialize unless we scrutinize the intersections between these

---

[10] Although I employ a different terminology, this perspective resonates with Gregory Claeys' idea of a "composite definition" of utopianism. See: Claeys, "News from Somewhere."

[11] For the *locus classicus* of this taxonomy, see: Sargent, "The Three Faces of Utopianism Revisited."

three sites. We need to examine them in parallel and investigate where there are overlaps and divergences. The structure of this book reflects this insight by concentrating in particular on the storytelling and theory-building poles of utopianism.

Third, the *varieties* of utopianism: the utopian tradition is split between two rival strands – one that foregrounds the top–down construction of other worlds and one that conceives of utopian visions as more localized, modest, piecemeal interrogations of the hegemonic mainstream in society. Objections to utopianism often entail a critique of its tendency to generate static blueprints of the future. Human beings, the worry goes, are simply incapable of making systematic plans for transforming society as such. If they still try to do so, their wishes will inexorably pave the way for totalitarian domination, these critics deplore. Yet, once we envisage utopianism as internally varied and structurally ambiguous, the charge of utopianism's violent perfectionism becomes much less trenchant.

Based on this tripartite framework, I will argue that utopianism amounts to a flexible method, rather than the formulation of a fixed end goal, that can be applied to the anticipatory modelling of an uncertain and risky future. Where do the origins of this framework lie, given that up until recently utopianism seemed to be entirely discredited? The complex notion of utopianism springs from a rich discussion that emerged at a particular historical juncture. In the aftermath of the fall of communism, utopianism seemed to have been deposited on the ash heap of history. The triumphant victory of liberal democracy ostensibly signalled the end of history, to cite Francis Fukuyama's diagnosis.[12] In the New World Order, there would be no further appetite for utopias. The capitalist West appeared to have miraculously succeeded at what the most ambitious designs for a better future had only dreamed about: bringing into existence a global order where individuals could prosper in full liberty, without fear of oppression by the state.[13]

---

[12] *The End of History and the Last Man.*

[13] To be sure, I do not claim here that nobody pursued utopian ideas in the immediate aftermath of the Cold War. All I am suggesting is that the public mood after the demise of "actually existing socialism" was a decidedly anti-utopian one, due to the triumphalist

"Cold War liberals" – from Karl Popper to Isaiah Berlin, Judith Shklar and Leszek Kołakowski – had long warned that images of a better future would exert a detrimental impact on human freedom and societal pluralism. To hope too much, for instance by putting eschatological faith in a classless, egalitarian society, was condemned as the harbinger of extremism. The picturing of another world, just on the horizon and cleansed of all impurities, was so problematic, these commentators maintained, because it erased the inherently defective nature of human beings, perenially torn between impulses to do good and temptations to do bad. In promoting social and political arrangements that were ill fit for what Immanuel Kant described as "the crooked wood"[14] of humanity, utopian thinkers thus prepared the ground for widespread, eliminatory violence, unleashed by those who took it upon themselves to turn the perfect blueprint into harsh reality. A mature polity would be one, the Cold War liberals insisted, in which utopian impulses were either suppressed, circumscribed or transmuted into depoliticized aesthetics.

Over the past two decades, however, utopian thinking and acting has been resurrected from its temporary deathbed. This resurfacing can be observed in various social and cultural arenas. From global insurgencies against autocratic regimes to science fiction narratives, from radical pleas to transform the built environment to exhilarating experiments in communal living – today's public debate seems saturated with utopian ideas and practices. Just think of increasing enthusiasm around the World Social Forum, whose celebratory motto *Another World Is Possible* is unabashedly utopian.[15] This slogan points to the centrality of prefigurative forms of action and organization within the movement and beyond.[16] Put otherwise, since the goal of the alter-globalization camp is to demonstrate in practice that alternatives to the unjust status quo

rhetoric employed by defenders of Western liberalism and capitalism. For an overview of recent writings on anti-utopianism see: Skrimshire, "What Is Anti-Utopianism?"

[14] "Idea for a Universal History from a Cosmopolitan Perspective," 9.

[15] Santos, *The Rise of the Global Left*.

[16] Maeckelbergh, "Doing Is Believing"; Raekstad and Gradin, *Prefigurative Politics*; Sande, "Fighting with Tools."

already exist, the means to attain that goal need to abide by the underlying principles of a more equitable, dignified and non-violent society.[17]

Moreover, changes in local and workplace democracy have infused campaigns for wider civic participation with fresh energy.[18] Revolutionary occupations, too – from Tahrir Square to Occupy Wall Street – have been described as concerted attempts to carve out inspirational spaces for mounting resistance against the hegemonic mainstream of late capitalism. It is from within these utopian settings that protesters and activists have been trying to alter society at large.[19]

Once we move from the social sphere to the realm of culture, we quickly realize that utopias have undergone an astonishing renaissance in recent times. From the huge success of dystopian narratives in popular TV shows and adaptations (*Westworld, Handmaid's Tale, Black Mirror,* to name but a few) to the constant growth of climate change fiction, "other worlds" have become major sites of artistic expression.[20]

It is important to acknowledge that this resurgence of utopianism represents more than just a short-lived trend. As I will show, there are specific reasons why social dreaming has become so prevalent at this precise moment in time, to do with the circumstances of our precarious existence on planet Earth, at the beginning of the twenty-first century. It is, I argue, because we feel deeply disoriented, perhaps even paralyzed and terrified, when we contemplate an intrinsically uncertain and risky future, that we are drawn to utopian visions of what is to come.

Here is another reason for today's revival of utopianism: even though they frequently depict societies in the far future, utopias are always concerned with the present moment. The "not yet" and the "no place" alluded to in utopian projects necessarily hold up a mirror to the status quo.[21] Whether the future is imagined as foreordained, or whether it can

---

[17] Prefiguration is, at its core, a utopian practice. See: Kinna, "Utopianism and Prefiguration."

[18] Fung and Wright, *Deepening Democracy;* Wright, *Envisioning Real Utopias.*

[19] Butler, *Notes toward a Performative Theory of Assembly;* Graeber, *The Democracy Project.*

[20] On the recent turn to dystopianism in particular, see: Trotta, Platen and Sadri, *Broken Mirrors.*

[21] It was Ursula K. Le Guin who put this point best: "The thing about science fiction is, it isn't really about the future. It's about the present. But the future gives us great freedom

still be shaped through resistant thought and action is a vital issue that all utopias seek to address. In meshing together "explanatory-diagnostic and anticipatory-utopian moments,"[22] they cast a critical light on the contemporary condition, thereby opening the door to alternative ways of being and living.

Given the breadth of utopias that this capacious interpretation covers, can something more general be said about them? One way of responding to this question would be to focus on what utopias seek to achieve, rather than on an essential quality that they all share. Accordingly, prominent scholars within utopian studies, such as Ruth Levitas, have shown that utopias typically perform three functions, which often, but not always, overlap: compensation, critique and change.[23] Utopia as compensation is about consoling those who are suffering under the hegemonic order by offering them an alluring view of an alternative world. As critique, it is about setting up a juxtaposition between the status quo and an alternative world. Finally, utopia as change is about transforming the hegemonic order, by enacting forms of resistance that draw on the utopian imagination.

Naturally, these functions intersect. As I demonstrate shortly, utopian visions of a climate-changed world typically tend to combine critical with transformative functions – demonstrating that the status quo is unsustainable as well as insisting that urgent modifications need to be made. But other permutations are possible, too: dystopian narratives often weave together critique and consolation, interpellating their audience to become aware of the dangers inherent in the present moment, while at the same time denying the immediate availability of remedial action.

Each of these functions will be further explored, but notice here that this ecumenical framing of what utopias do lets us appreciate how difficult it is to nail down a singular drive behind them. This is the reason why influential scholars have chosen to define utopianism in broad terms,

---

of imagination. It's like a mirror. You can see the back of your own head" (Le Guin, "The Gift of Place," para. 5.3.).

[22] Allen, "Emancipation without Utopia," 514.

[23] Levitas, *Utopia as Method*, 4,107. This classification maps, to some degree, onto the spectrum between daydreaming and worldbuilding that I hinted at previously.

such as "social dreaming"[24] or as what Miguel Abensour calls the "education of desire."[25]

This desire should not be understood psychoanalytically, but rather as a cognitive as well as affective state that channels the aspirations of those who long for an alternative future. Utopianism, in this view, derives from humans' propensity to formulate wishes that a particular state of affairs be otherwise. Yearning for alternatives is more than merely the product of an individual's particular preferences, insulated from outside influence. Rather, the desire that Abensour invokes remains responsive to different types of external intervention, from the historical as well as contemporary archive of "real utopias"[26] to the artistic exploration of "green"[27] or "red"[28] planets.

Importantly, the utopian visions that we will be discovering in this book take the form of thought experiments that differ sharply from the abstract hypotheticals about unavoidable dilemmas sketched by analytical philosophers: (speculative) fiction in particular always seeks to make the reader feel – not only rationally contemplate – what it would be like to make difficult decisions.[29] In other words, utopias can be seen as fashioning our idiosyncratic wishes into concrete, shareable proposals for other ways of being and living. In so doing, they illuminate the historical specificity of the present moment.[30]

---

[24] Sargent, "The Three Faces of Utopianism Revisited."

[25] Abensour's definition arises from his engagement with William Morris. See: Abensour, "William Morris," 145. Amongst contemporary utopian studies scholars, Ruth Levitas is best known for her adoption of Abensour's definition: Levitas, *The Concept of Utopia,* 140–41. Abensour was first introduced into the Anglo-American debate through the following article: Thompson, "Romanticism, Utopianism and Moralism." For the wider context see: Nadir, "Utopian Studies, Environmental Literature, and the Legacy of an Idea"; Mazzocchi, "Excavating Abensour."

[26] Wright, *Envisioning Real Utopias.*

[27] Canavan and Robinson, *Green Planets.*

[28] Bould and Miéville, *Red Planets.*

[29] For a critique of the use of thought experiments in contemporary political theory see: Thaler, "Unhinged Frames."

[30] Behind these proposals lies not just any kind of hope for alternatives, but what Ernst Bloch, perhaps the most important voice in the discussion around utopianism of the twentieth century, named *docta spes,* or "educated hope." See: Bloch, *The Principle of Hope: Volume 1,* 7,9.

While the definition of utopianism as the education of desire is not uncontroversial, it captures an indelible component of all utopias: they arise in response to the perception of a lack or deficiency – something is to be desired – that in turn anchors demands for fulfilment and satisfaction. As Ernst Bloch observed in a conversation with Theodor W. Adorno, the starting point of all utopian projects can be condensed into a succinct formula, taken from Bertolt Brecht's libretto for Kurt Weill's opera *The Rise and Fall of the City of Mahagonny*: "But something's missing."[31] Utopias, then, aim to determine what that something entails and come up with strategies for responding to the emergent yearning for fulfilment and satisfaction. Even though the object of this desire, and the concomitant demand, varies greatly, a frequently desperate, sometimes joyful anticipation of a different world, of being and living otherwise, forms the backbone of all the manifestations of utopianism that interest me in this book.

1.2 WHAT DOES IT MEAN TO ORIENT ONESELF IN THE ANTHROPOCENE?

Rather than approaching the current resurgence of utopianism in the abstract, the book aims to situate it within a specific context: the Anthropocene. In the following, I investigate what it means to "desire otherwise"[32] in an age shaped by the realization that the relations between humans and their environment are shifting. The Anthropocene is one of the names we can give to this disorderly web of relations. As we shall see, the label "Anthropocene" itself remains highly contentious, but it has the virtue of bundling together insights into what seems distinctive about rival ways of imagining a climate-changed world.

In this section, my goal is to demonstrate that utopian visions seek to accomplish something specific in the present moment: to provide orientation around a landscape that is both unknown and unsettling. Figuring

---

[31] Bloch, "Something's Missing." For a musicological interpretation that reads the opera as a dystopia with insightful lessons for today, see: Hart, *Music and the Environment in Dystopian Narrative*, chap. 6: Sounding the Hurricane: Mahagonny.

[32] Abensour, "William Morris," 146.

out what it means to inhabit a climate-changed world can be a disconcerting and bewildering exercise. It is this cognitive and affective anxiety that explains the paramount relevance of utopias for our times. In a nutshell, my claim throughout this book will hence be that utopian maps of the Anthropocene are, for various reasons yet to be outlined, instrumental in navigating a climate-changed world.[33]

Before turning to the place of utopias in the Anthropocene debate, a short excursus into the meaning of this concept, and its contemporary applications, will be necessary. Geologists use the so-called Geologic Time Scale to divide periods in the genesis of our planet.[34] The word "Anthropocene" – a Greek neologism signifying "the age of the humans" – was introduced in 2000 by the chemist Paul Crutzen to challenge the existing periodization. Crutzen deemed the Holocene, which covers the past 12,000 years, from the last Ice Age onwards, simply unsuitable for describing the present moment.[35]

When the concept of the Anthropocene is deployed, it thus marks a literally world-changing break with the established periodization of planet Earth. Although the term itself originated in response to many different effects that humans have on the environment – from the loss of biodiversity[36] to the destruction of ecosystems on both land and sea[37] – it is human–induced climate change that has seized the public imagination the most.[38] The Anthropocene describes a rupture signalling the start of a new epoch in which humanity itself has become a geological force.

---

[33] I borrow the metaphor of utopias as mapping devices from: Tally, *Utopia in the Age of Globalization.*

[34] For a pictorial representation, see: The Geological Society of America, "GSA Geologic Time Scale (v. 5.0)."

[35] Falcon-Lang, "Anthropocene."

[36] This reduction in biodiversity is usually termed the "sixth extinction" event in geological history. See: Kolbert, *The Sixth Extinction.* On the historical emergence of discourses around biodiversity and extinction see: Sepkoski, *Catastrophic Thinking.* For critical discussions around extinction, see: Grusin, *After Extinction;* Rose, Van Dooren and Chrulew, *Extinction Studies.*

[37] There is a massive academic debate around this issue. For representative publications, see: Malhi et al., "Tropical Forests in the Anthropocene"; He and Silliman, "Climate Change, Human Impacts, and Coastal Ecosystems in the Anthropocene."

[38] This is the reason why I pragmatically use the phrase "a climate-changed world" to describe the Anthropocene epoch. Even though the concept of the Anthropocene has

We can convey the essential thought behind the Anthropocene through the notion of a "human-activity-induced geological time unit."[39] The impact of human societies on the planetary environment is, in this view, deemed so overwhelming that a new geological epoch beyond the Holocene needs inaugurating.

An important question within the Anthropocene debate concerns the starting date of this emergent period. When geologists examine transitions from one epoch to another, they use so-called golden spikes to identify the precise moments of fundamental shifts in the Earth system.[40] While the official organization for worldwide collaboration amongst geologists, the *International Union of Geological Sciences*, has not yet ratified the novel periodization, the scientific argument around the dating of the Anthropocene continues to evolve.[41]

Why is the issue of dating the Anthropocene so divisive? In their book *The Human Planet*, which contains a wide-ranging survey of the ongoing debate, Simon Lewis and Mark Maslin pinpoint the underlying tension:

> Since Buffon's first attempt at sketching Earth's history, when considering humans, geology often gets mixed up with how we want to view ourselves. Or put another way, geology plus humans equals politics. Whether you assert or deny that human activity has driven Earth into a new epoch undoubtedly has political implications. Such views, which are beyond a narrow, rational view of scientific evidence, are not welcome in modern-day scientific circles. Geologists who champion the Quaternary and Holocene today rationalize these choices by applying different criteria to define the final 0.1 per cent of Earth's history. They focus on climate, specifically glacial–interglacial cycles, rather than changes to life.[42]

---

much wider ramifications than climate change alone, this phrase captures something essential about our precarious life on the "human planet."

[39] Lewis and Maslin, "Defining the Anthropocene," 171.

[40] More precisely, a "golden spike" marks the physical place at which a global boundary between formal units of geological time can be stratigraphically detected. See: Walsh, Gradstein and Ogg, "History, Philosophy, and Application of the Global Stratotype Section and Point (GSSP)."

[41] Meyer, "Geology's Timekeepers Are Feuding"; Maslin and Lewis, "Anthropocene vs Meghalayan."

[42] Lewis and Maslin, *The Human Planet*, 73–4.

The task of periodizing the Anthropocene is a political one, for the idea of a post-Holocene epoch highlights the immense impact that human beings have already exerted on the planet. The explosiveness of the very notion of a "human planet" manifests itself in the competing claims around the Anthropocene's inception. The creator of the label "Anthropocene," Paul Crutzen, dates the origins of the new period back to the Industrial Revolution in the late eighteenth and early nineteenth century, and the concomitant increase in anthropogenic CO_2 emissions.[43] Others have gestured to the first nuclear bomb test in 1945 at Alamogordo, New Mexico, as the site of the Anthropocene's "golden spike."[44] In this perspective, the Anthropocene is essentially coeval with the nuclear age. Scholars have also pointed to the Great Acceleration – the recent phase of unprecedented population and economic growth starting in the mid-twentieth century – as the historical period wherein the boundary between the Holocene and the Anthropocene ought to be drawn.[45] Yet another attempt at dating identifies the genocidal colonization of the Americas as the event that eventually triggered the "Little Ice Age" of the seventeenth century.[46]

In each of these cases, a different catalyst of change is identified for bringing the age of the human planet into existence: industrial capitalism, Cold War politics and European imperialism. As this cursory review demonstrates, the Anthropocene continues to be hotly contested, not least because it – implicitly or explicitly – issues a judgment as to who should be held causally responsible for its beginnings and for the current phase of environmental disruptions.[47]

---

[43] Crutzen and Stoermer, "The 'Anthropocene.'"

[44] Waters et al., "Can Nuclear Weapons Fallout Mark the Beginning of the Anthropocene Epoch?"; Zalasiewicz et al., "When Did the Anthropocene Begin?"

[45] Steffen et al., "The Trajectory of the Anthropocene."

[46] Lewis and Maslin, "Defining the Anthropocene." For a comprehensive analysis of various proposals for dating the Anthropocene, see: Lewis and Maslin, "A Transparent Framework for Defining the Anthropocene Epoch"; Maslin and Lewis, "Anthropocene"; Oldfield, "When and How Did the Anthropocene Begin?"; Uhrqvist and Linnér, "Narratives of the Past for Future Earth"; Zalasiewicz et al., "Colonization of the Americas, 'Little Ice Age' Climate, and Bomb-Produced Carbon."

[47] Biermann and Lövbrand, "Encountering the 'Anthropocene.'" For a discussion of the emergence of Anthropocene scholarship see: Swanson, Bubandt and Tsing, "Less Than One but More Than Many."

The continuing struggles over the Anthropocene's inception thus bring into view the centrality of not only place and geology, but also of time and chronology for our understanding of a climate-changed world. There is a backward-looking dimension to this temporal dimension, as we saw in the controversy around who should bear responsibility for past actions that continue to influence the present state of the planet. But there is also a future-oriented aspect to it, insofar as the Anthropocene calls for forward-looking proposals that seek to reckon with the devastations wrought by anthropogenic climate change. This is where the utopian imagination comes into play.

The Anthropocene's power, Ursula Heise submits, "resides not in its scientific definition as a geological epoch, but in its capacity to cast the present as a future that has already arrived."[48] Conversations around the links between the past, the present and the future are always open-ended and pluralistic, full of polemicism and disagreement – a fact that will be consequential for our engagement with contemporary forms of social dreaming.[49]

Even though the notion of the Anthropocene has seen significant uptake in both the scientific and the public debate, there are also commentators who object to its prevalence. Perhaps the most common attack on the very idea of a human planet is that it tends to cover up socio-economic inequalities and differential responsibilities within and between diverse populations and societies. According to this perspective, a much closer link between the ecological crisis and the rise of capitalism would need to be established, leading to the competing nomenclature of the "Capitalocene."[50]

---

[48] Heise, *Imagining Extinction*, 203.

[49] See: Ellis, *Anthropocene*, 145; Szerszynski, "Getting Hitched and Unhitched with the Ecomodernists," 243. This view also chimes with an understanding of the Anthropocene not only in terms of a scientific proposition, but as "a cultural and political space where particular understandings of environmental problems, relations, places, and futures take form, stabilize, are contested, and are made anew" (Nikoleris, Stripple and Tenngart, "The 'Anthropocene' in Popular Culture," 67).

[50] Moore, *Anthropocene or Capitalocene?*; Moore, "The Capitalocene, Part I"; Moore, "The Capitalocene, Part II."

In a nutshell, not all humans are to the same degree blameworthy for the devastating effects of climate change, which is why it would be disingenuous to designate the current moment, in an undifferentiated manner, as the "Anthropocene."[51] Homogenizing talk of a human planet sidesteps the crucial question of "unequal human agency, unequal human impacts, and unequal human vulnerabilities"[52] in our climate-changed world.

Indigenous scholars in particular have insisted on the need to decolonize the concept of the Anthropocene, mostly by contesting its claim to relative newness. Since genocidal colonialism has already completely upended the living conditions of Indigenous populations around the world, it would be imperative to include their unique viewpoints about civilizational collapse in our reflections on the Anthropocene.[53] Moreover, students of gender politics have charged the notion of the Anthropocene with reinforcing "individualistic approaches to environmental and climate responsiveness, which stereotypically casts women in the roles of either vulnerable climate victims or hardy climate heroes."[54]

Others have maintained that naming a geological epoch after humans is a sure indication of our species' characteristic arrogance.[55] Donna Haraway, to refer to a further sceptic, suggests we should rather use the word "Chthulucene" to account for the web of relations holding together multispecies communities, something that the concept of the Anthropocene does not do with sufficient care.[56] A related worry says that, in its emphasis on our transformative impact on the Earth system,

---

[51] On this critique, see: Malm and Hornborg, "The Geology of Mankind?"

[52] Nixon, "The Great Acceleration and the Great Divergence."

[53] For presentational reasons, I am simplifying an immensely intricate controversy here, which we will encounter again at several junctures in this book. On this debate, see representatively: Whyte, "Indigenous Climate Change Studies"; Davis and Todd, "On the Importance of a Date, or, Decolonizing the Anthropocene"; Whyte, "Indigenous Science (Fiction) for the Anthropocene"; Whyte, "Our Ancestors' Dystopia Now."

[54] Chiro, "Welcome to the White (M)Anthropocene?," 489.

[55] Brannen, "The Anthropocene Is a Joke." On the tension between hubris and humility in the Anthropocene debate see: Mitman, "Hubris or Humility?"

[56] Davis et al., "Anthropocene, Capitalocene, ... Plantationocene?" Needless to say, the carousel of terminological innovations keeps on spinning. See: McBrien, "Accumulating Extinction"; Clark, *Between Earth and Empire*.

the Anthropocene erects an artificial divide between humans and nature, which is not warranted by a sound theory of environmentalism.[57] The discourse around the Anthropocene emerged, others observe, exclusively within "particular social, cultural, and political contexts (Euro-Australo-American academic environmental studies and environmental politics) and does *not* surface, nor has it gained any epistemic or political traction, in other contexts that are *equally* concerned with the social and ecological impacts of runaway climate change (environmental justice/climate justice organizations and social movements)."[58]

One aspect that remains divisive in the debate around this emerging nomenclature concerns the extent to which the periodization itself should be approached from a human-centred, or a planet-centred vantage point.[59] The social scientists and the humanities scholars partaking in the controversy grapple with the concept of the Anthropocene by relating it, one way or another, to historical time, as Dipesh Chakrabarty reminds us.[60] That is to say, in the discussion around naming and dating the human planet it is the history of our species – from the colonial intrusions of the Early Modern period to the deployment of nuclear weapons – that is investigated in view of its impact on the planet.

Geologists, by contrast, are innocent of such anthropocentrism. They are interested in studying stratigraphic transformations in the Earth system itself. This eventually leads them to adopt a planet-centred definition of the Anthropocene. From this perspective, talk of a "human epoch" is, at least to some degree, misguided insofar as the

> Anthropocene is here considered as an epoch of Earth time, just like all Earth's previous epochs. It so happens that its distinctive characteristics have up until now been driven largely by a variety of human actions. But if

---

[57] An interesting rejoinder to these challenges can be found in the work of Dipesh Chakrabarty. See: Chakrabarty, "The Climate of History"; Chakrabarty, "Postcolonial Studies and the Challenge of Climate Change." For an engagement with Chakrabarty's thinking on this issue, see: Meyer, "Politics in – but Not of – the Anthropocene."

[58] Chiro, "Environmental Justice and the Anthropocene Meme," 364.

[59] This distinction between human-centred and planet-centred ways of thinking about the Anthropocene is indebted to: Zalasiewicz, "The Extraordinary Strata of the Anthropocene," 126.

[60] Chakrabarty, "Anthropocene Time."

these characteristics (such as sharply increased atmospheric carbon dioxide levels, global carbon isotope and nitrogen isotope anomalies, a biosphere modified by species extinctions and invasions, and so on) were driven by any other means – such as by a meteorite impact, volcanic eruptions or the actions of another species – then they would have exactly the same importance geologically.[61]

A corollary of the aforementioned parting of human-centred and planet-centred viewpoints is that the unfathomable chasm between historical time and the Earth's "deep time" comes more forcefully into view. The extreme temporal scales of geological change do not only pose a challenge to students and practitioners of global governance;[62] they also force a rethink of what cultural reflection and dialogue, instigated through climate fiction for example, can accomplish.

Since I am not a geologist, I have little of substance to add to the ongoing discussions around the precise dating or naming of the epoch we are presently living through. But the basic intuition behind the Anthropocene strikes me, despite the challenges outlined before, as vital for a responsible engagement with the current crisis. This is the case because the "Anthropocene provides a framework for understanding the modern ecological catastrophe, rather than a prescription for resolving it. It is a way of seeing, not a manifesto."[63]

The Anthropocene, in this sense, has managed to stir the imagination of citizens and scientists alike. As an epochal marker of planetary alteration, the notion of a human planet has already rippled across society, influencing both policies to mitigate or adapt to climate change,[64] and

---

[61] Zalasiewicz et al., "A General Introduction to the Anthropocene," 3.

[62] Galaz, "Time and Politics in the Anthropocene."

[63] Davies, *The Birth of the Anthropocene*, 193. I do believe that, understood in terms of a malleable framework that shines a light on the ecological crisis, the notion of the Anthropocene can in fact accommodate the objections of Marxists, Indigenous scholars and students of gender politics. But if you still feel unpersuaded by the capacity of this concept to disclose what strikes you as distinct about the current moment, I suggest you call it whatever you find suitable ("Capitalocene," "Chthulucene," "Plantationocene," "Necrocene," etc.) and then try to engage with the substantive remainder of my argument.

[64] Biermann et al., "Navigating the Anthropocene"; Biermann, "The Anthropocene."

affecting our capacity to deliberate on a future in which humanity has finally taken account of its environmental footprint.[65]

Moreover, the Anthropocene has also thrown into sharp relief the massive obstacles that established political institutions as well as environmental justice movements will have to surpass in the coming years. Anthropogenic climate change summons us to reconsider some of the basic norms undergirding democratic practice and global governance.[66] This development will only accelerate in the foreseeable future.

It is important to note that the Anthropocene, as a discursive "framework for understanding the modern ecological catastrophe," leaves it open to further scrutiny whether we are about to enter an "epoch of the apotheosis, or of the erasure, of the human as the master and end of nature."[67] This indeterminacy results from the clash between human-centred and planet-centred ways of thinking about a climate-changed world. In other words, while the diagnosis of a human planet unmistakeably assigns responsibility for the dire state of affairs to (some agents amongst) our species, it is far from certain that humans will keep on playing the role of a geological force for a long time.[68] As we will remark in Chapter 5, social and political theorists as well as fiction writers have begun to take seriously the proposition that we have already passed the tipping point of our own extinction. Others, including the so-called ecomodernists we encounter in Chapter 4, vehemently rebuff this bleak assessment, accusing its proponents of baseless fearmongering and doomsaying.

Irrespective of where one stands on this question, it seems likely that the unresolved nature of the Anthropocene explains why so many competing visions of a climate-changed world are in circulation today. It is from within the tension between the confident reign of *Homo Deus* and the devastated, nostalgic universe of *Wall-E* that a great variety of today's

---

[65] Yusoff and Gabrys, "Climate Change and the Imagination."

[66] See: Kelly, *Politics and the Anthropocene*; Dryzek and Pickering, *The Politics of the Anthropocene*; Biermann, *Earth System Governance*; Biermann and Kim, *Architectures of Earth System Governance*.

[67] Szerszynski, "Reading and Writing the Weather," 16. See also: Dibley, "The Shape of Things to Come."

[68] On this point, see also: Nixon, "The Anthropocene."

utopias spring.[69] Social dreaming cannot provide us with unequivocal answers to the question of whether the "human planet" should be lauded as the apex of our species' achievements or whether it should be lamented as a period where the extinction of humanity becomes inevitable. Utopias probe different responses to the Anthropocene's unresolved nature. The ensuing chapters will therefore trace the ways in which utopian maps of a climate-changed world can be directed towards divergent objectives: democratic, technocratic or catastrophist ones.[70] Each of these need to be subjected to careful scrutiny and evaluated in light of the impact they exert on our thinking and acting.[71]

The basic intuition behind the Anthropocene invites us to face up to a challenge of gigantic proportions. A helpful way to make sense of that challenge would be to describe it, in Amitav Ghosh's words, as a time of "great derangement"; a historical epoch that forces us to contemplate how climate change is already permeating all facets of global politics, down to the everyday lives of vulnerable populations across the world. "The climate crisis," Ghosh observes, "is also a crisis of culture, and thus of the imagination."[72] This calls for new ways of orienting ourselves in a disconcerting, uncanny landscape where maps are being drawn not only by geologists and climatologists, but also by social and political theorists, novelists, filmmakers, activists and indeed citizens in variously affected regions around the globe.[73]

---

[69] On *Wall-E*, see: Canavan, "Unless Someone Like You Cares a Whole Awful Lot."

[70] Searle, "Three Anthopocenes."

[71] For an example of how this could be achieved, see: Dalby, "Framing the Anthropocene."

[72] Ghosh, *The Great Derangement*, para. 9.2. Environmental philosophers have made the same point for almost twenty years, as the following passage demonstrates: "If, as environmental philosophers contend, western metaphysics and ethics need revision before we can address today's environmental problem, then environmental crisis involves a crisis of the imagination, the amelioration of which depends on finding better ways of imagining nature and humanity's relation to it" (Buell, *The Environmental Imagination*, 2).

[73] Note, though, that Ghosh is deeply sceptical about the contemporary novel's ability to address the climate crisis. He also seems to think that science fiction inevitably slides into escapism, which would render it unsuitable, as a genre, to deal with the harsh realities of the Anthropocene. However, this argument is clearly based on a misunderstanding of science fiction's critical function, and of utopian literature more widely – a misunderstanding that this book seeks to clear up. On Ghosh's limitations, see: Heise, "Climate Stories."

I use the term "orientation" here not metaphorically, but rather in the illuminating manner Sara Ahmed has employed it. Applying a phenomenological lens to examine queer identity and the cultural politics of feelings, Ahmed posits that "orientations involve different ways of registering the proximity of objects and others. Orientations shape not only how we inhabit space, but how we apprehend this world of shared inhabitance, as well as 'who' or 'what' we direct our energy and attention to."[74] What Ahmed gestures at is that our relations to the environment, which can be composed of human as well as non-human beings, are always shaped by emotional and bodily investments: "To be affected by something, such that we move toward or away from that thing, is an orientation toward something."[75] There is nothing natural about how we cope with the experience of closeness, for example. Rather, feeling (too) close to someone or something is a sensation conditioned by social and political factors.

This notion of "orientation" seems productive for grasping what is at stake with the Anthropocene – not only the production of scientific knowledge, but also the cultivation of imaginative proposals that allow us to reassess, emotionally and bodily, how we should live in a "world of shared inhabitance." Our emotions and our bodies are paramount for exploring how we may not only survive, but flourish in this climate-changed world.[76]

Orientation in this sense is meshed together with the education of desire. If social and political factors have a bearing on how we move around the world, how we stand in relation to different objects, how we become (or fail to become) affected by those near to us, then we should reflect on the ways in which these factors can be transformed in light of specific objectives. As I show in the following pages, speculative fiction is particularly well attuned to this task. But social and political theory, too, can be said to be in the business of providing orientation. It is a crucial

---

[74] Ahmed, *Queer Phenomenology*, 3.

[75] Ahmed, *The Cultural Politics of Emotion*, 209.

[76] For a wide-ranging and informative collection of resources on the role of emotions in the ecological crisis, see: www.bbc.com/future/columns/climate-emotions.

feature of theorizing (on my account) that it seeks to practically guide action towards desirable goals.

A possible worry with this appropriation of Ahmed's concept of orientation might be that it is extracted from the context it was initially designed for. It is one thing to propose that sexual and racial politics ought to be scrutinized through the phenomenological lens of object relations. It is quite another to assert that our stance vis-à-vis a climate-changed world would be approachable by the same means. If the Anthropocene is clearly not an object like any other, how can the notion of "orientation" become generative for discussing utopias?

To answer this question, we need to pivot from a view of ordinary objects, which underpins Ahmed's account, to a rival one that focuses on another set of objects. As Timothy Morton has contended, climate change (or, in his preferred terminology, global warming) is akin to a "hyperobject" that is "massively distributed in time and space relative to humans."[77] Hyperobjects are multidimensional to such a degree that even the most sophisticated scientific models and philosophical approaches will fail to capture them in their entirety.

In essence, my claim throughout this book will be that it is the scale and intricacy of the Anthropocene, the immensity of imagining a climate-changed world, that makes it imperative for us to strive for orientation with the help of various utopian visions. The education of desire not only concerns the modelling of possible futures, but also channels our affects and reconfigures how we live with and through our bodies. Compressed into a pithy formula, we might therefore say that utopias provide orientation in situations where conventional maps around ordinary objects have forfeited their usefulness. This is their chief purpose in our greatly deranged age: to guide us, cognitively, emotionally and bodily, around hyperobjects.

Another way of expressing the same thought would be to propose that utopias work like maps. Orienting oneself in a landscape that is deeply unsettling necessitates, first of all, the disposal of outdated, inadequate maps. In a second step, orientation hinges on the creation, maintenance and adjustment of new maps that are better suited to the changing

---

[77] Morton, *Hyperobjects*, 1. See also: Boulton, "Climate Change as a 'Hyperobject.'"

circumstances. Utopias permit us to both gauge the utility of old maps for navigating a climate-changed world, and to draw new ones that guide our action as we move into a radically uncertain and risky future.

Note that orientation and mapping of this variety is not identical with the pursuit of quick fixes that attempt to patch up systemic pathologies. Much of today's public debate around the Anthropocene seems to be afflicted by what Evgeny Morozov has dubbed "solutionism"[78]: the consequential idea according to which intractable problems can always be broken down into smaller, manageable ones that existing technologies will be capable of comprehensively addressing.[79] The issue with this type of reflecting on global problems is that it completely misunderstands the nature of hyperobjects, or rather, that it mistakes a hyperobject, such as the Anthropocene, for an ordinary object.

Faced with the challenge of picturing a climate-changed world, the solutionist quest for quick fixes is not only ill-advised and myopic, it also distracts us from the actual task we have to confront – to devise ways of seeing the world anew that provide orientation in these disconcerting times.[80] The utopias I shall be analyzing all try to offer orientation in the sense of better understanding those social and political circumstances

---

[78] Morozov, *To Save Everything, Click Here.* On solutionist tendencies in the governance of the COVID-19 pandemic, see: Morozov, "The Tech 'Solutions' for Coronavirus Take the Surveillance State to the next Level."

[79] I am not claiming here that "solutionism" amounts to a universally held position in the current debate. Most scientists are, of course, fully aware that the Anthropocene creates multiple challenges for the Earth system that cannot be tackled with the help of innovative "silver bullets." On this point, see the recent report on biodiversity and climate change co-authored by the Intergovernmental Science-Policy Platform on Biodiversity and Ecosystem Services (IPBES) and the Intergovernmental Panel on Climate Change (IPCC): "Climate Change and Nature Loss Must Be Tackled Together, Says Report." Yet, the solutionist impulse remains deeply ingrained in the political imaginaries of global elites. This is why I believe that Morozov's diagnosis is, broadly speaking, correct when it comes to examining proposals for inhabiting a climate-changed world – as evidenced, for example, by Bill Gates' recent intervention into the debate. See: McKibben, "How Does Bill Gates Plan to Solve the Climate Crisis?"

[80] On the ways in which managerial solutionism affects mainstream environmental politics, and on potential rejoinders, see: Hammond, "Imagination and Critique in Environmental Politics."

that will allow us to move in one direction or another.[81] The essential task of charting the future can only be accomplished with the support of visions and projects that traffic between two of utopianism's domains: theory building and storytelling.[82]

The view of the Anthropocene as a hyperobject makes it clear that new forms of map-making are required. The added value that utopias bring to this endeavour is that they manage to account for the uncertainty, contingency and complexity of our climate-changed world. Utopias are far from static ideals. They formulate dynamic models for alternative possibilities that shatter ossified schemas of reality.

What all these visions and projects have in common is that they consider Earth to be the setting where the utopian desire for being and living otherwise needs to be educated. We might thus call them, perhaps paradoxically, "this-worldly" utopias, to stress that they disavow reveries of escaping from our home planet. In showing that other ways of being and living are possible, the theorists and the writers we will be conversing with on the following pages remind us that our species ultimately has nowhere to go: we must accept our fate as Earthbound creatures. Since the Anthropocene inaugurates an epoch moulded by humanity's impact on the planetary ecosphere, fantasizing about interstellar escape is as reactionary as it is pointless.[83]

Utopias in the Anthropocene hence commence with the recognition that there is no other planet for our species to thrive on. This acknowledgement of our eco-social grounding is shared amongst utopian visions and projects that are otherwise very different. N. K. Jemisin's far-future tale of a vengeful planet, which we will discuss in Chapter 3, as well as Kim Stanley Robinson's near-future narrative of Washington politics, the

---

[81] On the power of the idea of the Anthropocene to inspire utopian thinking and acting of this kind, see: Purdy, "Anthropocene Fever."

[82] This echoes what Mark Levene has said about the impact of the Anthropocene on the discipline of history: acknowledging the reality of the Anthropocene can stimulate outdated modes of thinking and facilitate novel patterns of ethical responsiveness. See: Levene, "Climate Blues."

[83] In his scathing review of Christopher Nolan's film *Interstellar*, which dramatizes the challenges that humanity might face when leaving its decaying habitat on Earth, George Monbiot makes this very point. See: Monbiot, "Interstellar."

topic of Chapter 4, channels the power of social dreaming "down to Earth," to reimagine what survival on this, rather than any other, planet, might require of us as a species.

This-worldly utopias have a tendency to trouble the distinction between human-centred and planet-centred thinking about our climate-changed world. That is so because speculative theory building and storytelling around the Anthropocene engages not only with how humanity manages (or fails) to prepare for an uncertain and risky future, but also attempts to shine a light on Earth's unique modes of self-organizing, along its own temporal scales that defy comparisons with historical time.[84]

To finish this section, a word on which utopias will be selected for closer scrutiny. Turning to the Anthropocene has the advantage of delimiting the temporal range of the utopias examined in this book. Given that the label only emerged in the early twenty-first century, the book primarily deals with utopian visions from 2001 onwards, while leaving further space for historical contextualization. Using the publication of Crutzen's seminal paper as a dividing line is obviously arbitrary, but it still supplies us with a pragmatic threshold for demarcating the remit of this investigation.[85]

1.3 DISCIPLINARY PILLARS

I now want to continue by reflecting on the disciplinary perspectives that inform this inquiry. In more narrowly academic terms, the book stands

---

[84] In fact, as Bronislaw Szerszynski holds, "just as the Anthropocene as an epoch-in-the-making disrupts the role of the human as the detached knower and coherer of the Earth, so it may also disrupt the very idea of the Earth as a singular body, and of the 'timeless', distanced understanding of geological time" (Szerszynski, "The Anthropocene Monument," 127).

[85] This tighter focus on utopias from the beginning of the twenty-first century also differentiates my project from preceding ones, such as Lisa Garforth's book *Green Utopias*. Garforth draws a much longer arc, from the emergence of environmental thinking in the 1960s to the current day. To be sure, her aim is, in many ways, similar to the one I have set for myself here: to trace and assess different utopian visions developed in response to environmental crises. However, while she uses a historical lens to accomplish this goal, reconstructing various ecological debates from the 1960s onwards, I choose a different structure and am committed to other objectives. Another prominent discussion of the same topic, which covers even more ground and charts various utopian projects from the sixteenth century onwards, can be found in: Geus, *Ecological Utopias*.

on three pillars of scholarship.[86] As a work in political theory, it promotes a view of practical philosophizing that is directly concerned with problems in the world today.[87] As an interpretive endeavour, political theory tries to make sense of a shared world marred by inequality, violence and oppression. In so doing, it caters to three objectives that are crucial for theorizing with a "practical intent":[88] understanding, evaluation and orientation.

As Raymond Geuss – a principal voice in the debate around realism and utopianism – observes, these tasks are entwined with one another.[89] In order to evaluate the current state of affairs, one first needs to grasp what is actually going on. Equally, in order to orient ourselves in the world, evaluative judgements about the direction of travel will be necessary. These judgements in turn guide us in the pursuit of understanding, and so a virtuous circle between understanding, evaluation and orientation is set in motion.

Political theory aims to discharge of these objectives in a systematic and coherent fashion so as to inform public debates about controversial issues.[90] What matters most, according to this view, is that we approach these issues with both a critical and a normative mindset.[91] The goal of a distinctly political-theoretical approach to utopias in the Anthropocene is not only to describe and explain their key components and historical

---

[86] Evidently, biophysical research on climate change matters to all discussions around the Anthropocene and hence also proves vital to the interests behind this book. Given my own professional background in the humanities and social sciences, however, I do not feel competent to directly intervene into these areas of research in the same way I do in discussions within and across political theory, utopian studies and the environmental humanities.

[87] Given the global range of the problems analyzed in this book, we might add that political theory always needs to be international in its focus. This is one of the key assumptions behind my reflections as well. For an introduction to this debate, see: Lang, *International Political Theory*.

[88] Young, *Intersecting Voices*, 5.

[89] See: Geuss, *Philosophy and Real Politics*, 37–55.

[90] On the relationship between political theory and public discourse see: Tully, "Public Philosophy as a Critical Activity."

[91] For a more comprehensive outline of my views on the ultimate purpose of political theory see: Thaler, *Naming Violence*, chap. 1. For an application of the same idea of orientation, see: McKean, *Disorienting Neoliberalism*.

trajectories, but also to subject them to evaluative scrutiny, in order to arrive at constructive proposals for navigating an uncertain and risky future.

Since all utopian visions need to be scrutinized against the material and ideological background in which they are formulated, it would be hard to say anything meaningful about these proposals in abstract terms. But towards the end of this book, I will develop a more general account, suggesting that we can test the reliability of competing utopian maps for our climate-changed world by the degree to which they are aware of, and constructed around, the predetermined fault lines along which they will break down. A conscious recognition of utopianism's inherent shortcomings thus delivers a criterion for assessing social dreaming today. It is this immanent and self-reflective critique that sets the kind of political theory I am embracing apart from the other two disciplinary pillars supporting this book – utopian studies and environmental humanities.

Second, this book engages with a diverse range of positions from utopian studies. Over the past thirty years, scholars across various academic disciplines have surveyed utopianism in many contexts. Academics such as Lyman Tower Sargent, Ruth Levitas and Tom Moylan have in great depth explored storytelling and social experiments, covering those aspects of utopianism that are also vital for tackling climate change. In articulating my own ideas on what is generative about utopianism, I therefore draw on findings from utopian studies, especially with regard to the critical turn that commentators have diagnosed in the late 1970s.[92]

What distinguishes utopian studies is the field's interest in the many settings in which the education of desire can be staged. As we will remark in Chapter 2, commentators have trained their eyes on such disparate phenomena as intentional communities in remote parts of the world,[93] the history of Black nationalism and Afrofuturism,[94] the practices of

---

[92] The novel that is usually credited with inaugurating this critical turn in utopian fiction is: Le Guin, *The Dispossessed*. On Le Guin's masterpiece, which has spawned a massive secondary literature, see exemplarily: Burns, *Political Theory, Science Fiction, and Utopian Literature*; Davis and Stillman, *The New Utopian Politics of Ursula K. Le Guin's The Dispossessed*.

[93] Sargisson and Sargent, *Living in Utopia*.

[94] Zamalin, *Black Utopia*.

queer futurity,[95] the racialized dreamworlds of Anglotopia[96] and human existence under conditions of widespread automation[97] to expand the horizon of what "utopia" usually signifies. This area of research is so illuminating because it allows one to detect cases of social dreaming where they would normally not be expected. Once we adopt a comprehensive framework, it becomes feasible to search for expressions of the yearning for alternative ways of being and living in many different domains and across many different genres.

Third and finally, the book turns to scholarship from the nascent discipline of environmental humanities.[98] Climate change is not only a topic of interest to the "hard sciences"; the humanities, too, have recently begun to pay heed to the cultural production around humanity's impact on the planetary ecosystem.[99] This becomes evident in the increasing fascination with what is known today as "climate fiction,"[100] which will be a focus of attention in the following chapters. Critics such as Adeline Johns-Putra[101], Antonia Mehnert[102] and Adam Trexler[103] have taken important steps to investigate the degree to which climate change poses a unique and exhilarating challenge to contemporary writers.

While the environmental humanities still represent a relatively recent addition to the scientific debate, they open up a valuable perspective on the problem I am interested in here. This is the case because scholars working within this field steer attention to how climate change creates both serious obstacles and extraordinary opportunities to traditional tropes and techniques of storytelling, not least due to the temporal scales of Earth's "deep time."

---

[95] Muñoz, *Cruising Utopia.*

[96] Bell, *Dreamworlds of Race.*

[97] Danaher, *Automation and Utopia.*

[98] For an influential programmatic statement about the purpose of the environmental humanities see: Rose et al., "Thinking through the Environment, Unsettling the Humanities."

[99] Arias-Maldonado, "The 'Anthropocene' in Philosophy."

[100] For an overview, see: Streeby, *Imagining the Future of Climate Change;* Tuhus-Dubrow, "Cli-Fi."

[101] Johns-Putra, *Climate Change and the Contemporary Novel.*

[102] Mehnert, *Climate Change Fictions.*

[103] Trexler, *Anthropocene Fictions.*

Methodologically, this book is therefore interdisciplinary in its out-look.[104] Anyone who wishes to pursue such an agenda – if it is to amount to more than a facile buzzword – will soon become aware that reaching beyond one's area of expertise is always a tricky undertaking, for it invites accusations of being "a jack of all trades, but a master of none." That risk is certainly one that I have felt acutely throughout the writing process, frequently grappling with specialized debates that are remote from my core qualifications. But, despite a nagging anxiety about amateurish dabbling, the risk is well worth it, not least because the problem I am interested in truly cuts across the three pillars of academic scholarship identified before. In fact, I am now convinced that one cannot even start to comprehend what is distinctive about utopias in the Anthropocene unless one becomes acquainted with findings from political theory, utopian studies and the environmental humanities.[105]

Part of what I hope to achieve on the following pages can thus be conveyed through the notion of "translational research." It remains a lamentable fact of the current academic landscape that initiatives in the humanities and social sciences are, more often than not, isolated from one another. This is especially blatant in the questions this book is animated by: political theorists, scholars within utopian studies and students of environmental humanities rarely speak to each other, despite

---

[104] Such an orientation has recently been recognized as absolutely paramount for dealing with problems such as the ones associated with the Anthropocene. See: Brown, Harris and Russell, *Tackling Wicked Problems through the Transdisciplinary Imagination.*

[105] This commitment to an interdisciplinary research agenda also grew out of a discontent with my own academic background. Even though the topic of utopianism has gained significant traction within political theory over the past ten years – notably in discussions around ideal and non-ideal theory, feasibility and realism, etc. – the debate almost always unfolds in a state of blissful ignorance about seminal findings by scholars actually studying utopias. The effect of this navel-gazing has been that political theorists frequently end up employing conceptions of utopia that are either superficial or unexamined (or both), such as "hopeless aspirational theory," for example. The problem with such a nomenclature is that it fails to interrogate the common-sense understanding of utopia as a "no place," which then produces a seriously limited picture of what utopianism actually entails. For a symptomatically narrow rendering of utopianism in recent political theory, which my approach seeks to counteract, see: Estlund, "Utopophobia," 2014. For a book-length treatment, see: Estlund, *Utopophobia,* 2020. I return to this methodological concern in Chapter 6.

a shared commitment to original scholarship, which ought to transgress disciplinary boundaries. The goal is hence to break through the walls of our comfortable silos, revealing points of contact and, where possible, exchange between distinct approaches to the Anthropocene and its utopian dreams.[106]

Beyond this bridge-building effort, I seek to combine empirical and normative considerations. This objective further sets my argument apart from allied accounts that also focus on green utopias. To explain, one ambition behind this book is to reconstruct the form and content of existing utopian visions in the Anthropocene. I take this to be an explanatory exercise that unpacks what exactly imagining a climate-changed world consists of.

A parallel aim is, however, to go beyond the charting of the current landscape. Since I subscribe to an understanding of political theory as critically and normatively geared towards real-world problems, I want to say something concrete about which kinds of utopian vision will be conducive for addressing the challenges arising today. If, as Ghosh reminds us, the current ecological crisis is also coupled with a crisis of the imagination, then efforts at intervening at the level of the imagination hopefully have a beneficial impact on practical action as well. The intersection between social and political theory on the one hand, and speculative fiction on the other, strikes me as an especially propitious site for identifying this-worldly utopias that can provide orientation in these greatly deranged times.[107]

As I shall argue in the book's final chapter, productive utopias can be identified by the extent to which they are aware of, and constructed around, the predetermined fault lines along which they will fail. To some

---

[106] Naturally, I am not suggesting here that there is no exchange at all between these three disciplines. A quick look at the editorial board of the journal *Environmental Humanities*, for example, reveals that it contains several political theorists. My claim is rather that learning across these disciplines still remains hampered by the widespread institutionalized mentality of inward-looking scholarship – what is aptly referred to as *Fachidiotentum* in German (see the prior footnote). Following in the footsteps of others, this book hopes to devise a remedy to this scholastic mentality.

[107] Although my book has a stronger affiliation with political theory, it shares this interest in speculative fiction with other recent publications. See in particular: Atchison and Shames, *Survive and Resist*; Wolf-Meyer, *Theory for the World to Come*.

degree, social dreaming is hence bound to go awry – due to its in-built propensity for indeterminacy, wishful thinking and defeatism. If that diagnosis is correct, then what matters most is how utopianism's susceptibility to failure gets adjusted through practices of self-reflective iteration – a process I explicate in the book's conclusion.

1.4 CONSTELLATIONS AND PLOT LINES

To conduct this analysis, I concentrate on three utopian constellations that are narrated through distinct plot lines. Since this terminology – "constellations" and "plot lines" – might sound fanciful, let me try to clarify what is meant here. In a nutshell, while the idea of a constellation is helpful in outlining the substantive content of my chosen cases (*what* a theory or story is about), the notion of a plot line foregrounds the formal characteristics of different forms of social dreaming (*how* a theory or story is construed).

I borrow the notion of a "constellation" from Walter Benjamin's philosophy of art. In *The Origin of German Tragic Drama*, Benjamin uses the metaphor of a constellation to analyze what kind of linkages exist between ideas and objects.[108] Just like a "star image" (*Sternbild*), an idea, for Benjamin, does not actually exist in the world – it is a figment of the imagination (a social, rather than a natural kind) that enables us, however, to describe the ways in which various objects stand in relation to one another, when viewed from a specific vantage point. A constellation therefore facilitates the organization of things in an intelligible manner: it embodies a heuristics for drawing out the interconnections between otherwise disparate phenomena.[109] Observed from a unique position, separate elements instantaneously cohere into a whole, akin to the star image that Benjamin adduces.[110]

---

[108] Benjamin, *The Origin of German Tragic Drama*, 34.

[109] As Fredric Jameson notes, "concepts represent aspects of empirical reality, while the Idea (and its philosophical notation) represents the relationships between them" (Jameson, *Late Marxism*, 54–5).

[110] See: Sahraoui and Sauter, "Introduction."

Even though Benjamin's historiographical approach need not interest us here in any detail,[111] the notion of a constellation helps explain
how this book's raw material of utopianism gets organized. Benjamin's
methodology makes it clear that thinking in and through constellations
is always relational, contingent on the viewers' vantage point and on their
capacity to communicate with discernment what they see in front of
them. Accordingly, I hope to persuade the reader that my way of
approaching utopias in the Anthropocene – my proposal for envisaging
otherwise unrelated texts as adding up to a perspicuous image – turns
out to be not only one amongst many possible accounts of our climate-
changed world, but a particularly lucid one.

Due to its declared reliance on the spectator's standpoint (its perspec-
tival character, we might say), this type of approach remains contestable,
of course. But perspectivism of this variety does not entail relativism.[112]
This is why the concept of a "constellation" opens up an original path for
elucidating how different sorts of intellectual and cultural production, in
terms of both theory building and storytelling, partake in the same
utopian project. Thinking in and through constellations allows for a
linking together of various kinds of vision that would normally be considered as not so easily comparable.[113]

The book thus extends an invitation to approach the aforementioned
ideas through the lens of a unified framework, sparking in the reader
what one might call "aspect change,"[114] the faculty of seeing something
as something: in this case, the ability to appreciate how a specific text in
social and political theory might relate to, and interact with, a book
written in the genre of speculative fiction. Once we realize that viewing

---

[111] For an introduction, see: Pensky, "Method and Time."

[112] This is one of the persistent concerns in the literature around Friedrich Nietzsche's
perspectivism, which becomes especially pronounced in: *On the Genealogy of Morality*, 87
(III/12). On the exegetical debate see exemplarily: Nehamas, *Nietzsche, Life as Literature*,
72–3; Gemes, "Life's Perspectives," 555.

[113] None of this is to imply that my specific selection of speculative fiction is the only
plausible one. As the burgeoning literature in the environmental humanities
demonstrates, there is a huge variety of artworks that one could engage with.

[114] See: Wittgenstein, *Philosophical Investigations*, 224e. On aspect-seeing and its relevance
for political theory, see: Gunnell, "Leaving Everything as It Is"; Thaler, "Political
Imagination and the Crime of Crimes."

planet Earth as an actor in its own right amounts to a distinct utopian constellation, it becomes feasible, for instance, to detect family resemblances between Bruno Latour's revitalization of the Gaia theory and N. K. Jemisin's far-future narrative in which our home planet is depicted as a vindictive agent waging permanent war on its human occupants – which is precisely what Chapter 3 claims.

Through the prism of constellational thinking, I suggest reading specific theoretical proposals in the debate around the Anthropocene in parallel with texts of speculative fiction for two interdependent reasons. First, I contend that these neighbouring sites of the utopian imagination – theory building and storytelling – can illuminate each other, revealing both strengths and weaknesses, fundamental insights and structural limitations. Whereas theorists tend to systematically address questions arising from the Anthropocene, fiction writers respond to climate change in a more poetic fashion, unravelling "the relationship between climate change and humanity in psychological and social terms, exploring how climate change occurs not just as a meteorological or ecological crisis 'out there' but as something filtered through our inner and outer lives."[115] In terms of providing orientation, a key driver behind today's climate fiction hence resides in the recovery and renegotiation of human as well as more-than-human agency, vulnerability and responsibility.[116]

By concentrating on the narrative development of characters inhabiting other worlds, artistic accounts add experiential texture and depth to debates that social and political theorists cannot properly touch upon.[117] What renders speculative fiction a valuable object of study, then, is its potential to produce novel frameworks for envisaging reality, coloured in either hopeful or fearful hues. Storytelling about climate change manages to stir the reader's imagination in ways that theory building does not even aspire to, thereby facilitating the drawing of original maps that are so pivotal to our greatly deranged times.[118] As expressions of a utopian

---

[115] Trexler and Johns-Putra, "Climate Change in Literature and Literary Criticism," 196.

[116] See: Cole, "At the Heart of Human Politics."

[117] On this aspect, see: Nikoleris, Stripple and Tenngart, "Narrating Climate Futures."

[118] The impact of fiction writing on readers' perception of climate change has also been empirically studied. See: Schneider-Mayerson, "The Influence of Climate Fiction";

desire surfacing from the same constellation, these contrasting approaches hence speak to each other via stimulating conversations that have not yet been fully appreciated in the scholarly debate.[119]

The second reason for turning to speculative fiction in conjunction with academic writing is that storytelling harbours resources of direct relevance to social and political theorists. In fact, literature can itself be read as promulgating a kind of theory, albeit one that traditional registers of interpretation are unable to unlock.[120] As Joan Haran expounds, the gain of "reading fiction as theory is due to the capacity of fiction to narrate multiple trajectories of social theory within a single text, and to reflect upon the potentials and foreclosures that specific trajectories enable and constrain."[121] Social and political theorists have consequently much to learn from the worlds conjured by authors such as Jemisin, Robinson and Atwood.

My claim here is not that zeroing in on such narratives should completely replace abstract theory building. Rather, the book starts from the more modest and more plausible supposition that speculative fiction can expand social and political theory's horizon of problematizations, and vice versa.[122] Thus, if the current moment demonstrates, amongst other things, that we are going through a profound crisis of the imagination, which in turn necessitates new modes of orienting ourselves vis-à-vis hyperobjects, then we simply cannot afford to disregard fictional representations of an uncertain and risky future.[123]

Schneider-Mayerson, "'Just as in the Book'?" Obviously, fictional accounts of our climate-changed world will not exert a uniform impact on all readers. Rather, the point here is that storytelling can disclose novel dimensions for studying the Anthropocene that theory building alone would not be able to reach.

[119] For a notable exception that emphasizes the seductive power of storytelling, see: Mihai, "Epistemic Marginalisation and the Seductive Power of Art."

[120] Nora Hämäläinen calls this approach the "open-ended use of literature in philosophy." See: Hämäläinen, "Sophie, Antigone, Elizabeth – Rethinking Ethics by Reading Literature."

[121] Haran, "Redefining Hope as Praxis," 394. See also: Haran, "Re-visioning Feminist Futures."

[122] For two applications of this framework see: Thaler, "Hope Abjuring Hope"; Thaler, "Bleak Dreams, Not Nightmares."

[123] Broadly speaking, this book hence subscribes to the "literary turn" in social and political thought. The most prominent voices in this philosophical debate range from Richard

How these deliberative processes across different genres of writing evolve concretely will vary from case to case, as I show in the analysis of my three constellations. But the methodological bet on which this book rides is that our comprehension of utopian visions in the Anthropocene can be enriched if we pay attention to the interfaces between theory building and storytelling.

The attentive reader will have noticed that I have consistently spoken of "speculative fiction" when underscoring the kind of storytelling I am interested in. What do I mean by this? It is not easy to give an answer to this question so long as the boundaries of the genre of speculative fiction remain hotly disputed. At various points in this book, I will return to the thorny issue of boundary setting and policing, be it in the controversy around the separation of science fiction from fantasy or in the argument around the peculiar features of near-future narratives. At this stage, though, let us commence with a broad categorization of "speculative fiction" in terms of

> all genres that deliberately depart from imitating "consensus reality" of everyday experience. In this ... sense, speculative fiction includes fantasy, science fiction, and horror, but also their derivatives, hybrids, and cognate genres like the gothic, dystopia, weird fiction, post-apocalyptic fiction, ghost stories, superhero tales, alternate history, steampunk, slipstream, magic realism, fractured fairy tales, and more.[124]

Another way of teasing out the same thought would be to say, with China Miéville, that the kind of literature I am drawn to in this book deals with "specific articulations of *alterity*."[125] The advantage of such a focus on otherness is that it manages to capture all kinds of utopian storytelling, while still leaving sufficient space for meaningful variations as to how far from the real world a text of speculative fiction might be creatively situated.[126]

Rorty, Martha Nussbaum and Judith Butler to Bonnie Honig. For a comprehensive survey, see: Stow, *Republic of Readers?*

[124] Oziewicz, "Speculative Fiction," 1.

[125] Miéville, "Cognition as Ideology," 244.

[126] Instead of realistic writing, the opposite of such a fiction of alterity could also be signified as "mimetic literature," the origins of which have been reconstructed in: Auerbach, *Mimesis.*

The authors discussed next conceptualize the alterity of their imagined worlds in interestingly varied ways: N. K. Jemisin conceives of the purpose of speculative fiction as assailing the "illusion that what you see is not actually what is happening."[127] Despite its commitment to otherness, her speculative fiction thus consciously reflects back on reality to demystify the obfuscation on which oppression and injustice always rely. Kim Stanley Robinson, on the other hand, calls his recent climate fiction "proleptic realism," an attempt to model the near future, which looks only slightly different than the current moment. By contrast, Margaret Atwood insists on her bleak stories of a world ravaged by catastrophe having nothing at all to do with science fiction – despite being frequently hailed as masterpieces of that genre. (Atwood instead elects to reserve the term "speculative fiction" for narratives of the future that have been sensibly extrapolated from what we know about the present.)

As a further structuring device, I employ a distinction that the science fiction author Octavia Butler made between three types of speculative fiction: the *What-If,* the *If-Only* and the *If-This-Goes-On.*[128] These are competing, and to some degree mutually exclusive, frames that shape specific modes of social dreaming. A useful way of understanding them would be as unique types of "emplotment."[129] "Emplotment" denotes a strategy for unpacking "the 'meaning' of a story by identifying the *kind of story* that has been told."[130]

---

[127] Bereola, "A True Utopia."

[128] Butler, "Devil Girl from Mars." I first came across Butler's taxonomy in an essay introducing the idea of "green planets." See: Canavan, "Introduction."

[129] If you prefer a musical metaphor instead, think of Butler's types of speculative fiction as rival expressions of a distinct *basso continuo* – the underlying harmonious scaffolding upon which various improvisations can be fixed.

[130] White, *Metahistory,* 7, italics in original. White applies this concept not to the exegesis of works of fiction, but to the ways in which historians have tended to frame their accounts of the past. This notion permits him to refine his interpretation of historiography, by shifting attention from how argumentative frameworks are constructed and what ideological positions are taken, to the specific styles in which histories are written. Looking at historiography through this lens reveals, for example, that one can separate out four major plot lines in nineteenth-century writing: romance (associated with Jules Michelet), tragedy (exemplified by Alexis de Tocqueville), comedy (linked to Leopold Ranke) and satire (connected with Jacob Burckhardt).

My suggestion is that this intuition about the significance of plot lines – of *how* a story is told, rather than *what* it tells – can be rewarding for the study of utopian visions. Although Butler herself has not elaborated on this schema, we can with relative ease flesh out its implications for our topic, applying each of her types of emplotment to my three constellations. Accordingly, the proposal to envisage planet Earth as a living being (my first utopian constellation) raises a *What-If* question: what would happen if we managed to reconceive our existence as deeply entangled with all kinds of planetary life forms? The ecomodernist wager in favour of a "good Anthropocene" (my second utopian constellation) urges us to declaim "If only!": what would happen if we were capable of taking on the current challenge, by harnessing science and technology to guide us through a climate-changed world? Finally, foregrounding collapse and apocalypse as likely consequences of our actions (my third utopian constellation) pushes the reader into the direction of an *If-This-Goes-On* inquiry: what would happen to our efforts in these greatly deranged times if our species' irresponsible behaviour did not change at all, or if mitigation and adaptation measures simply gained momentum too late?

It is not difficult to contemplate how these three plot lines spur the imagination in singular ways: the *What-If* evokes a type of speculation we would otherwise associate with philosophical thought experiments, often weaving together eutopian and dystopian themes. The *If-Only* will veer onto a more unambiguously eutopian track, whereas the *If-This-Goes-On* encourages visions that are shaped by dystopian reflections. Although they are always liable to rupture along discrete fault lines, these three kinds of emplotment illustrate how we might succeed in sidestepping the twin pitfalls that Haraway identified as serious risks to our imagination: nihilism and self-aggrandisement.

Two important clarifications need to be added here: first, even though they serve the objective of organizing the material surveyed in this book, I do not mean to intimate that specific utopias will always fit neatly into any one of these frames. To illustrate this, consider that, in some sense, all forms of social dreaming embark on a *What-If* inquiry.[131] That is, after all, the purpose of speculative fiction, and of speculation

---

[131] It might even be argued that "'What if?' is the question all fiction asks" (Burrow, "It's Not Jung's, It's Mine.").

more broadly – to confront the reader with theories and stories of other worlds that stand in more or less stark contrast to their ordinary perception of reality. Hence the emphasis on alterity. Similarly, all the fictional texts I discuss next contain, to certain degrees, not only eutopian but also dystopian motifs. Hopes and wishes, as well as fear and despair are, with varying intensity, marshalled in all the theories and stories that take centre stage in this book.

The point of Butler's tripartite schema is therefore to flesh out some general tendencies within my three constellations. Her distinction between *What-If*, the *If-Only* and *If-This-Goes-On* narratives has the virtue of equipping us with a conceptual platform that lends structure to the otherwise unruly utopias we can observe across different contexts.

Second, highlighting how a story is told privileges a text-immanent standpoint for the interpretation of utopias. The notion of emplotment directs attention to the rhetorical styles and atmospheric moods that prevail within specific texts, while putting less emphasis on how they are perceived by actual readers. This has important implications for one of the most challenging aspects of studying utopian ideas: their open reception. It is surely accurate that "one person's utopia is another's dystopia."[132] What might appear like an Arcadian future to some, will be experienced as an oppressive and violent vision by others.[133] In fact, dystopias often riff on this fact, when they deplore how the collective dream of a better society can morph into a hellish nightmare for some.[134]

---

[132] Claeys, "Three Variants on the Concept of Dystopia," 15.

[133] This point is central to the analysis of right-wing utopias, such as, for example, *The Turner Diaries*, William Luther Pierce's (pseudonym: Andrew Macdonald) infamous story of future race wars. Given that one's conjuring of a "worst place" crucially hinges on where one stands at the moment, it is undoubtedly true that some people consider *The Turner Diaries* visionary and empowering – in fact, many white supremacists, from Timothy McVeigh to the German terror cell NSU, have explicitly referred to Pierce's book to prop up their murderous plans. On the rise of right-wing utopias, see: Brodie, "The Aryan New Era"; Fitting, "Utopias beyond Our Ideals."

[134] As Samuel Delany remarks: "To the man who yearns after Arcadia, any movement to establish New Jerusalem will always look like a step toward Brave New World, that mechanized, dehumanized, and standardized environment, where the gaudy and meretricious alternate with the insufferably dull; where, if physical hardship is reduced, it is at the price of the most humiliating spiritual brutalization. In the same way, the man

To illustrate the openness of all interpretation, consider that even Margaret Atwood's *The Handmaid's Tale*, in spite of being lionized as a genre-defining exemplar of dystopian fiction, could be understood as a eutopian narrative. The basis for such a reading is that the ultra-violent patriarchy of Gilead might be thought to produce the salutary effect of erasing all the differences between groups of women who otherwise remain separated along lines of race, class and sexual orientation. While nobody will deny that the fate of women in *The Handmaid's Tale* is horrific, Gilead's reign of terror does shed light on what presumably unites all women – their subjugation to unfettered male power. In other words, Offred's fate is reimagined here as the portent of a peculiar type of homogenizing feminism that flattens hierarchies between women of various backgrounds.[135]

If we solely concentrate on how utopian visions are received, then we have no argument at our disposal to defuse such a reading of *The Handmaid's Tale*. The problem with unreservedly subscribing to the proposition that "one person's utopia is another's dystopia" is that it too quickly dissolves judgements as to the textual character of a specific theory or story into an undifferentiated, relativistic muddle. Separating *What-If*, *If-Only* and *If-This-Goes-On* narratives affords a counterpoint to the view that just because every theory or story can be read from different perspectives, there are no better or worse ways of interpreting them.

Attending to the plot lines that frame theories and stories helps clarify why it would be erroneous, or at least twisted, to conceive of the *The Handmaid's Tale* as a narrative that might sustain an affirmative vision of feminism. Although there are elements of eutopian promise in even the bleakest of dystopias, that does not render them positive visions of the future altogether. Like all *If-This-Goes-On* narratives, Offred's story contains a harrowing account of dangerous trends within the present that

---

or woman who dreams of New Jerusalem sees any serious attempt to establish an Arcadia as a retreat to the Land of Flies, that place of provincial ignorance, fear, disease, and death, where humans are prey to the untrammeled demons of our own superstitions as well as any caprice of nature: fire, flood, storm, or earthquake" (Delany, "Critical Methods/Speculative Fiction," 25).

[135] On this interpretation of Atwood, see: Lewis, "Dreams of Gilead"; Merteuil and Lewis, "Gestational Decrim."

might eventually have terrible effects on our lifeworlds. Although not impossible, reading Atwood's novel as a hopeful narrative is thus predicated on disregarding the cautionary pedagogy that inheres in all dystopias. Deciphering *The Handmaid's Tale* as heralding a peculiar type of feminism therefore strikes me as one of its less plausible interpretations.

With these two caveats in mind, once we look more closely into Butler's taxonomy, we will appreciate how utopias use various devices to fulfil their intended functions. I have already observed that social dreaming can cater to a multiplicity of goals, from the offering of consolation to the drafting of concrete plans for alternative worlds. On the basis of Butler's views on emplotment, one can further specify these goals by identifying three core mechanisms whereby utopias in the Anthropocene advance. These are estranging, galvanizing and cautioning.

Utopias written under the guise of a *What-If* question try to defamiliarize an audience from deeply held beliefs, to render unfamiliar what often appears to be entirely natural and normal. The effect of such an estrangement strategy is to interpellate the reader to see the world from new and unexpected angles. *If-Only* narratives play a different role: they seek mobilization when a situation appears too dire to permit any action at all. As a consequence, utopias can facilitate an overcoming of debilitating inertia in precisely those moments when no alternatives seem available. Finally, *If-This-Goes-On* stories aim to identify perils that are concealed within the status quo. Such warnings are especially salient when people fail to take current dangers seriously, either because they do not want to acknowledge them or because they cannot perceive them in the first place.

Already on this abstract level, it is obvious that these mechanisms – estranging, galvanizing and cautioning – can overlap with one another. I will probe these intersections in detail shortly, but note here that desires and hopes, and fear and despair play varied roles in all three constellations. A *What-If* plot line is premised on the longing for a certain state of affairs to be otherwise. Hence, defamiliarization amounts to a technique that tries to render the impossible thinkable.[136] In *If-Only*

---

[136] Jameson, "A New Reading of Capital," 13.

utopias, the rationale behind the propagation of a positive story is to insist that "another world is possible," to invoke the World Social Forum's motto once again. A plot line of this kind aspires to lift the audience out of its apathy and frustration, through the circulation of optimistic images of what might be just on the horizon. In *If-This-Goes-On* narratives, the drive behind a negative vision of the future is to establish that things could easily go awry, unless a radically different path is forged ahead. Even the bleakest of dystopias therefore always leave some residual room, however constrained, for oppositional agency. Without this hopeful perspective, a plot line of this type would collapse into fatalism.

While what I have proposed so far might appear rather anodyne, these constellations and plot lines will be scrutinized in more granular detail in the following chapters. There, I also explain how exactly theory building and storytelling set into motion the mechanisms I have associated with my three plot lines. My objective in this section has merely been to explicate on a conceptual level what the principles are on the basis of which the utopian visions of the Anthropocene have been selected.

1.5 SUMMARY OF THE ARGUMENT

In drawing this chapter to a close, I offer a synopsis of the rest of the book. Chapter 2 sets the stage for the substantive analysis of my three constellations by developing a robust account of utopianism that manages to withstand the charges laid out by anti-utopian critics, both from the left and the right. I hold that these detractors miss their target because they fail to acknowledge the intricacy of social dreaming. While utopias can, under specific circumstances, turn out to be impractical or dangerous, the standard objections are wrong to assume that this is necessarily and always the case. I hence claim that *anti-perfectionist utopias* embody forms of social dreaming that can educate our desire for things to be otherwise.

The chapter continues by investigating utopianism's chief function: the production of estrangement. By establishing critical distance from what is conventionally taken for granted, utopias teach us to perceive reality from surprising and illuminating angles. In short, they prompt us to see the world anew. This process has the effect of disrupting habitual patterns of lived experience that hold sway over our normal modes of existence.

In a further step, I scrutinize the other two purposes that utopian visions of the Anthropocene serve: galvanizing and cautioning. The chapter suggests that eutopias' main goal is to kick-start emancipatory action by outlining viable pathways into a future freed from the limitations of the past and the present. The risk that accompanies these positive visions is that they collapse into wishful thinking, downplaying or neglecting the obstacles that systemic transformations always have to surpass.

Dystopias, by contrast, operate under a different logic: their objective is to issue warnings about grave dangers that are located on society's horizon of expectations. Alerting an audience about existential perils remains a tricky endeavour, though. If the dystopian theorist or author paints too bleak a picture of the imminent catastrophe, the addressees of the narrative might be tempted to simply give up and adopt a fatalistic posture. What is needed, then, is a dystopia generating just the right level of despair – too much of it would hamper the audience, too little would banalize the threat.

I conclude Chapter 2 with a short intermezzo discussing utopian practices – experiments that organize social life "against the grain." Prefigurative communities transpose the desire for being and living otherwise from the realm of imagination to the real world. Even though the practical dimension of utopianism does not constitute a central preoccupation of this book, it still seems necessary to acquire at least a rudimentary sense of the diversity of such social experiments, from micro-level "everyday utopias" (Davina Cooper) that unfold oppositional spaces where bottom-up resistance to the mainstream can be launched, to macro-level "real utopias" (Erik Olin Wright) unearthing radical potentials from within the hegemonic order.

Chapter 3 moves on to our first constellation, the utopian vision of planet Earth as an actor in its own right. Rather than conceiving of humans as endowed with a special status that sets them ontologically, epistemically and ethically apart from both non-human animals and the planetary ecosphere, proponents of this idea outline a hypothetical

scenario that destabilizes entrenched modes of reflecting on our species'
place in the world.

I approach this utopian constellation, framed by a *What-If* plot line, via
two steps: first, by analyzing the Gaia hypothesis as recently revisited by
Bruno Latour. Here, I hold that Gaia should be deciphered as a critical
and normative framework that seeks to estrange us *for*, rather than *from*,
the world. While James Lovelock initially came up with the idea to
envisage Earth in terms of a self-regulating system, baptizing the entirety
of feedback loops of which the planet is composed with the mythological
name "Gaia," it is Bruno Latour's interpretation that interests me in
particular. Latour attempts to ground a political ecology that repudiates
the binary opposition of nature and culture, which underpins the
modern condition and ultimately obstructs a responsible engagement
with environmental issues. From this, an image of Earth emerges in
which agency is radically dispersed across different forms of being.

In a second step, the chapter directs attention to N. K. Jemisin's
Broken Earth trilogy, claiming that this science fiction text can further
draw out the contours of the Gaia figure. Through her subtle portrayal of
a group of survivors of environmental disaster, Jemisin underscores three
themes that are key to this constellation. The trilogy, first, describes our
home planet as a living, raging entity that enacts brutal retaliation for the
harm done to it. Second, Jemisin understands violence amongst humans
as well as between humans and other species as cyclical in character.
While rebellion must sometimes be pursued with brutal means, this will
bring about results that cannot be calculated and foreseen in advance.
A third insight that may be taken from Jemisin's fantasyland is that
interpersonal and interspecies solidarity provides an effective antidote
to the devastations wrought by oppressive institutions and structures. All
these motifs rebut simplistic conceptions of our climate-changed world,
for Jemisin's novels illustrate that humanity is internally too diverse and
too conflicted to be considered a homogenous actor. Only if we recognize the historical divisions within our own species will we be able to
foster new relationships with Earth and its myriad inhabitants.

Even though the champions of the Gaia hypothesis as well as the
author of the *Broken Earth* trilogy weigh up several options – from
Latour's manifesto for the "Earthbound" to Jemisin's embrace of a

fragile peace between our planet and its multiple occupants – their utopianism consists primarily in the opening up of novel possibilities for being and living otherwise. An ineradicable fault line running through the *What-If* frame is therefore its reluctance to forge concrete ways forward. My reading of this constellation thus reveals that this kind of utopia always oscillates between world-disclosing and world-negating estrangement.

This challenge is openly confronted in Chapter 4, which deals with one of the most prominent themes in contemporary utopianism: the notion that science and technology can somehow be harnessed to elevate humanity beyond the current impasse. My argument here is that ecomodernism – the tantalizing thought that scientific and technological progress will have a thoroughly constructive impact on the Anthropocene – should be understood as a unique type of social dreaming.

I analyze this constellation by, first, discussing various defences of ecomodernism. With regard to the theory pole of this *If-Only* plot line, my argument is that ecomodernism constitutes a broad movement in which both right- and left-wing defenders of scientific and technological progress have found ideological homes. Tracing the roots of this eutopian vision back to a programmatic statement by the American think tank The Breakthrough Institute, the chapter identifies a number of key commitments to which all ecomodernists subscribe. Chief amongst those is the plan to emancipate our species from its resource reliance on ecological processes. "Decoupling," which effectively turns Gaia's model of universal connectedness on its head, is supposed to be advantageous for both humanity and the environment.

Right- and left-wing ecomodernists seek to defuse the allegation that their eutopian vision of such decoupling is nothing but wishful thinking. They do so by celebrating actual discoveries and inventions, from carbon capture to geoengineering, that simply need to be optimized to turn the Anthropocene into a triumphant age of human attainment. At the heart of their proposals lies a worry about the debilitating effects that a catastrophist mindset can have. Only if we imaginatively explore realistic pathways into a positive future will we be able to reap the benefits of social dreaming.

In a second step, I embark on a reading of what is perhaps the most elaborate attempt at fictionally working through the material and ideological contradictions of a science-based response to climate change: Kim Stanley Robinson's *Science in the Capital* trilogy. Robinson's oeuvre examines how an optimistic state of affairs could grow organically from within the status quo, eschewing both revolutionary upheaval and an aggressive strike against "Gaia's revenge." The books are set in a near-future version of Washington, DC where a small group of scientists, politicians and spiritual leaders collaborates to confront the enormous challenges of a climate-changed world.

In over 1,200 pages, Robinson probes the utopian credentials of a scientific community that has become immunized against capitalist co-optation and willing to mount political struggles. Through a detailed study of the National Science Foundation (NSF), the *Science in the Capital* trilogy locates the motor behind progressive action in a state-sponsored organization that funds and coordinates technological innovations. Based on his sophisticated account of utopianism as a procedural, conflictual and open-ended exercise in modelling alternative futures, Robinson asks which changes on both the personal and the societal level would be required for our species to not only survive, but thrive in the Anthropocene.

Eutopian stories, such as the *Science in the Capital* trilogy, can shed light on the theoretical approaches of contemporary ecomodernists. In adding experiential and affective texture and narrative complication to the *If-Only* plot line, they invite the reader to acknowledge that the desire for being otherwise cannot be satisfied through scientific discoveries and technological innovations alone – Western lifestyles will have to undergo radical transformations as well, if there is to be any chance for our species to keep on living on this planet. Yet, just as is the case with both right- and left-wing ecomodernists, the danger of wishful thinking still looms large in Robinson's writings, as I demonstrate in the chapter's conclusion.

This is where our final constellation enters the stage. Chapter 5 turns to a much bleaker vision of the Anthropocene, based on the suspicion that the catastrophe is all but inevitable. In this part of the book, I attend to various dystopian visions of a climate-changed world, by first looking into contemporary expressions of apocalyptic thinking, which are then juxtaposed to a fictional narrative of what our planet might look like after the Anthropocene: Margaret Atwood's *MaddAddam* trilogy.

I begin the discussion of the *If-This-Goes-On* plot line with a historical overview, pointing out that we are currently witnessing a transformation of the ways in which the apocalypse is construed, not least since the outbreak of COVID-19 in 2020. Today, the environmental breakdown is not anymore imagined as an extraordinary event that will happen some-time in a far-away future. Rather, most people today are aware that climate change has already triggered a state of permanent crisis that cannot be reversed in any meaningful sense. The cataclysm, in other words, has become routinized, habitually integrated into our brittle lifeworlds.

Dystopias perform one major function in this context: to warn an audience about existential threats that are imminent, but whose true causes still remain hidden from public purview. In the case of climate change, I argue that we ought to separate narratives that either spin cautionary or post-cautionary tales. That is, on the one hand, we find analyses that use apocalyptic imaginaries to determine where the true origins of the ongoing breakdown might lie. In these dystopian visions, the future remains pliable, since we can still remedy the structural shortcomings in our current world that have exacerbated the ecological crisis.

Post-cautionary tales, on the other hand, contradict the proposition that the catastrophe may still be averted. The idea that climate change creates a state of constant cataclysm has been taken up by influential commentators. Their diagnoses culminate in a number of "palliative" verdicts on the future, from a philosophical inquiry into how we may learn to perish in the Anthropocene to the resigned withdrawal from all activism. What haunts these ideas is not only a waning of hope but also the spectre of defeatism – that the situation is in fact so dire that nothing we might do would ultimately make any difference.

Turning to the storytelling pole of this constellation, Margaret Atwood's *MaddAddam* trilogy navigates this rocky terrain by examining where grave dangers might emerge from within the status quo, without however suffocating the desire for alternative ways of being and living. The trilogy tells the story of a small group of humans who survived a global pandemic that has wiped out almost our entire species. Atwood's books move back and forth between a storyline that explains the unfolding catastrophe and another one that depicts how the surviving humans build a common future with other species.

My interpretation of the *MaddAddam* trilogy concentrates on two key features that are characteristic of Atwood's utopianism: first, the notion that eutopian and dystopian perspectives are always entangled with each other; and second, the observation that Atwood's writing grapples with fictional scenarios that might appear far-fetched but are meant to be eminently believable from the reader's point of view.

The trilogy visualizes the apocalypse not only as the catastrophic end of an era but also as an opportunity for pondering what might lie beyond the Anthropocene. Atwood's narrative thus troubles the arguments put forth by proponents of cautionary and post-cautionary tales. By summoning the reader to imagine what would come after the reign of our species, the trilogy exposes the contradictions and ambiguities of our climate-changed world that the utopian desire feeds on.

Chapter 6 concludes this book by exposing both the fault lines and the horizons of contemporary utopianism. Throughout the substantive chapters, I home in on what I consider the key mechanisms underpinning utopianism (estranging, galvanizing and cautioning), while also stressing the ways in which these mechanisms can misfire. Attentiveness to inherent tensions is essential for a balanced vindication of social dreaming in the Anthropocene. Based on a comparative reading of the three constellations, my argument is that utopianism remains pervaded by the following three fault lines: indeterminacy, wishful thinking and defeatism.

The *What-If* plot line aims to undo habitual patterns of experiencing the world, but it is susceptible to the charge of indeterminacy – what ought to follow concretely from the strange scenario conjured by these utopias is not always evident. The *If-Only* plot line, by contrast, seeks to mobilize people into action, yet its pedagogy of desire might come dangerously close to wishful thinking. Finally, although the *If-This-Goes-On* plot line intends to warn an audience about imminent risks, its depiction of a dire world to come can veer into fearmongering that incapacitates, rather than motivates, people.

Since these fault lines cannot be removed, the most auspicious manner of dealing with them would be to accept their pervasiveness and prepare for the eventual traps that any utopian project might fall into. If we conceive of social dreaming as the education of the desire for being and living otherwise, we need to remain constantly alert to the ways in which these pedagogical interventions can go awry. Critical self-reflexivity is therefore pivotal to the orientating function that all utopias perform in our climate-changed world. The book ends with a proposal for how such critical self-reflexivity could be cultivated. Ulrich, the anti-hero of *The Man without Qualities*, will offer valuable insights in this regard.

CHAPTER 2

Varieties of Utopian Thinking

Indeed, for those only too wary of the motives of its critics, yet no less conscious of Utopia's structural ambiguities, those mindful of the very real political function of the idea and the program of Utopia in our time, the slogan of anti-anti-Utopianism might well offer the best working strategy.[1]

I N THIS CHAPTER, I outline my understanding of utopianism, which lays the ground for the three constellations in the subsequent parts of the book. The goal here is to emphasize the internal diversity of utopianism and to motivate the thought that we urgently need utopias – of various kinds – to guide our conduct during the ongoing ecological crisis. To realize these objectives, I will propose a number of conceptual distinctions, such as the one between world-negating and world-disclosing estrangement, that can assist us in grasping why the standard objections to utopianism are misguided: duly conceived, utopianism is neither useless nor dangerous. Far from succumbing to escapist wishful thinking or totalitarian social engineering, utopianism sets into motion a critical and transformative interrogation of the present that bridges the imagination and action.

Drawing on a host of authors who have advanced the field of utopian studies over the past thirty years, from Lucy Sargisson to Ruth Levitas and Fredric Jameson, the chapter's overall purpose is to develop an account of utopianism that is suitable for grappling with the Anthropocene. In order to arrive at that account, I move through five phases: first, I reconstruct and evaluate a series of criticisms that have been levelled

---

[1] Jameson, *Archaeologies of the Future*, xvi.

against the very idea of utopianism. This will help us in acquiring a sense of what utopianism is *not* – before we continue to explore what it might yet become.[2] Second, I explain what construal of utopianism materializes once we remove perfectionism from the standard picture of social dreaming. The notion of an "education of desire for being otherwise," which will serve as the baseline reference for the rest of the book, takes centre stage then. These two sections define utopianism in broad analytical terms, by working through debates in political theory and utopian studies.

In the chapter's third section, I investigate the ways in which estrangement informs utopianism. The crux of my argument is that estrangement can either lead to a problematic withdrawal from the world or it can open the door – as per Musil's metaphor from the book's start – to new forms of being and living together. At its heart, estrangement therefore involves a dialectical process. The fourth part deals with the other mechanisms that undergird utopianism, galvanizing and cautioning. I show that the logic behind each of these is completely different: while galvanizing hinges on an inflationary critique that projects positive developments from the present into the future, cautioning operates in the opposite direction, deploying a deflationary critique that exposes dangers hidden from public purview.

Finally, the chapter's last part homes in on the relationship between imagination and action. Despite the widespread impression that utopianism only pertains to the fictional construction of other worlds (via both theory building and storytelling), it is useful to conceive of certain forms of real-world action as utopian. Here I stress that the education of desire is always directed at the praxis of collective action. The aim is to underline that imagination and action depend on each other, so much so that we might even speak of "imaginaction"[3] – action facilitated through imagination, imagination stirred by action.

[2] The importance of entering into a dialogue with detractors of utopianism is already prefigured in the epigraph to this chapter: Fredric Jameson suggests that a defensible account of utopianism emerges from a dialectical process whereby the final synthesis ("utopianism") is the outcome of a double negation ("anti-anti-utopianism").

[3] In the process of writing this book, I naively assumed I had come up with the neologism "imaginaction" by myself. Alas, a routine check of the relevant databases to assure myself

Before proceeding, a caveat: in this chapter, my ambition is to clarify the conceptual foundations on which the analyses of my three utopian constellations rests. This implies that I will be mainly concentrating on the general processes at work behind the education of desire, from the dialectics of estrangement to the mechanisms of galvanizing and cautioning. With Ruth Levitas, we might call this the methodological part of utopianism, its capacity to not only formulate an ideal end goal for society, but to supply us with a hermeneutics for better grasping the present moment. As a consequence, the content of specific utopian visions receives little attention in this part of the book. This substantive aspect will come more into focus once we shift to the *What-If*, the *If-Only* and the *If-This-Goes-On* plot lines in the following chapters.

2.1 THE CASE AGAINST UTOPIANISM: FUTILE OR DANGEROUS?

In Chapter 1, I stipulated which definition of utopianism I shall be applying in this book. But what I have not done yet is vindicate the proposition that Abensour's "education of desire" supplies us with the best framework for thinking about utopias. In this and the following section, I grapple with this task by defending an account of utopianism that can illuminate various, and sometimes contradictory, ways of imagining and inhabiting our climate-changed world.

Going back to the initial framing of the utopian tradition, let us recall the origins of the literary genre. Ever since Thomas More coined the term in his eponymous novel from 1516, utopia contained a witty pun, signifying at the same time a non-existent place (*ou-topos*) and an Arcadian place (*eu-topos*). The wordplay, oscillating between a simple absence and an alluring alternative, tells us something important about the structure of social dreaming, as Paul Ricœur notes:

> [A] place which exists in no real place, a ghost city; a river with no water; a prince with no people, and so on. What must be emphasized is the benefit of this special extraterritoriality. From this "no place" an exterior glance is

of the originality of this term (un)fortunately revealed it was a Swiss sociologist and student of utopianism who had first introduced that concept. See: Willener, *The Action-Image of Society*, 286–98.

cast on our reality. The field of the possible is now open beyond that of the actual; it is a field, therefore, for alternative ways of living.[4]

This passage reveals the procedural side of utopian thinking. By unfolding a space for "alternative ways of living," often through satire and hyperbole, utopias enable the reader to gain distance vis-à-vis the status quo – to perceive the solid frames of reality as opening up new possibilities.[5] While early utopias were normally set on far-away, isolated territories, from the eighteenth century onwards, they became temporalized, projecting the alternative worlds into the future and inaugurating the proto-genre of science fiction.[6]

This temporal turn is essential for understanding the multiple roles that utopias can perform in the Anthropocene. As Reinhart Koselleck reminds us, the "onset of the future in utopia"[7] deeply affected social dreaming. Originally, the geographically distant utopia embodied a static ideal that was remotely situated from the author's life world. In More's *Utopia*, the island's topography is the result of a decision by King Utopos to dig a deep channel that would separate his realm from the mainland. Moreover, the island's capital Amaurot is surrounded on three sides by a "dry ditch, broad and deep and filled with thorn hedges; on its fourth side the river itself serves as a moat."[8]

Contrast this image of physical extraterritoriality with utopias set in the future – *uchronias*, duly termed:[9] they are situated on a historical trajectory leading from the current moment into a made-up reality. It is therefore not surprising that utopias became temporalized during the period in European history most strongly geared towards universal progress – the Enlightenment.[10]

---

[4] Ricœur, *Lectures on Ideology and Utopia*, 16.

[5] For a reading of More's *Utopia* along these lines, see: Storey, "The Happy Place That Exists Nowhere."

[6] See: Vieira, "The Concept of Utopia," 9–15.

[7] Koselleck, "The Temporalization of Utopia," 85.

[8] More, *Utopia*, 45–6.

[9] For a reconstruction of this temporal turn, see: Alkon, *Origins of Futuristic Fiction*, chap. 4: From Utopia to Uchronia: L'An 2440 and Napoleon apocryphe.

[10] On this aspect, see: Collier, "Mercier's Enlightenment Utopia."

I will return to the issue of how the future is concretely envisioned at several junctures in this book, but note here that utopianism's mapping of multiple possibilities depends on a dynamic conception of historical time. Utopias tell us: the future is open; it can be shaped in positive or negative ways. At a minimum, this implies that fatalism about where we are heading needs to be rejected, or at least carefully negotiated. As we shall see in Chapter 5, even the most pitiless champions of the thought that we are already occupying an uninhabitable planet must make space for a limited, yet vivid form of hope. They simply cannot deny the undecided character of historical time.

We can clarify this observation via another route as well. In spite of the recent surge in "climate reductionism" (the method of elevating the climate to the all-dominant variable in explanations of the interactions between societies and their environments), no scientific approach – including those rooted in the "hard sciences" – can accurately predict the future of the planetary ecosphere and of the human and non-human communities within it.[11] This is precisely why utopian speculation, promulgated through both theory building and storytelling, remains pivotal for the wider discussion around our climate-changed world.[12]

The flexibility of the education of desire is not only a product of the open-endedness of historical time and of the shortcomings of "predictive science"; it also manifests itself in the change of perspective that any utopia set in the future triggers. All the utopian visions examined in this

---

[11] On this point, see: Hulme, "Reducing the Future to Climate." None of this is to say, of course, that science has no role whatsoever to play in the modelling of climate futures. Rather, the point here is about the inaccessibility of predictive frameworks when it comes to climate change – a fact that even the Intergovernmental Panel on Climate Change (IPCC) now fully accepts, as evidenced by its consistent use of the language of "pathways." On different forms of scenario-making, see: Tyszczuk and Smith, "Culture and Climate Change Scenarios."

[12] Throughout her oeuvre, Le Guin made this point, forcefully objecting to the notion that science fiction would have predictive powers: "The purpose of a thought-experiment, as the term was used by Schrödinger and other physicists, is not to predict the future – indeed Schrödinger's most famous thought-experiment goes to show that the 'future,' on the quantum level, cannot be predicted – but to describe reality, the present world. Science fiction is not predictive; it is descriptive" (Le Guin, "Author's Note," paras. 5.6–5.7).

book generate an effect that is central to social dreaming: "they trans-form our own present into the determinate past of something yet to come."[13] This casting of the world we are living in as the "determinate past of something yet to come" accentuates the uncertainty, contingency and complexity of all human action – a fact that becomes especially pertinent in debates around the Anthropocene.

Before delving into these debates, however, I want to take a step back and explore why so many commentators have denounced utopianism as either pointless or pernicious. How could it be that authors with vastly different intellectual backgrounds have expressed scorn for the quest for better ways of being and living? What might be wrong with the impulse to conjure non-existent places that enable the critique of the status quo?

We have already encountered one criticism that became especially prominent during the Cold War. The Cold War liberal position remains influential today, but it articulates, in fact, only one amongst several charges levelled against utopianism.[14] For the purpose of systematicity, we may hold apart two macro-critiques: first, that utopianism encapsu-lates a flight from reality that distracts us from the actual challenges we are presently facing; and second, that utopianism involves a dangerous kind of imagining that paves the way for social engineering and, even more worryingly, widespread violence. In a nutshell, the first objection states that utopianism is not practical enough, while the second one holds that it is somehow too practical, too seductive in its modelling of alternative futures.

At the risk of turning both objections into caricatures, we might say that the first macro-critique characteristically emerges from the left, while the second one emanates from the right side of the political spectrum.[15] Any vindication of utopianism for our times will have to

---

[13] Jameson, "Progress versus Utopia; Or, Can We Imagine the Future?," 152.

[14] As Ruth Levitas puts it: "Where utopia is concerned, the Cold War is still with us" (*Utopia as Method,* 176).

[15] Theodor W. Adorno's objection to utopianism complicates this picture considerably, since he criticized the very act of positively picturing an alternative to the status quo: "The materialist longing to grasp the thing aims at the opposite: it is only in the absence of images that the full object could be conceived. Such absence concurs with the theological ban on images. Materialism brought that ban into secular form by not

reckon with these two charges. For, although we can clearly witness a revival of utopianism across different media today, a generalized suspicion of social dreaming remains palpable in the public sphere.

Let us thus start with the allegation that utopianism is idle daydreaming, a wishful thinking that renders understanding the real world impossible. Perhaps the best expression of this thought can be uncovered in the Marxist aversion to utopianism, which has its roots in Marx's and Engels' attack on their close rivals, the utopian socialists.[16] In the *Communist Manifesto*, Marx and Engels take issue with authors such as Robert Owen and Charles Fourier, whom they accuse of being politically naive and philosophically incoherent.[17] The reason for their misguided standpoint, the authors of the *Communist Manifesto* declare, stems from the utopian socialists' affinity for exhaustively describing the society that they hope to create in the future. The problem is that their dreamy disposition comes at the expense of a strategic reflection on the revolutionary means by which a desirable society could be brought into existence.

In other words, Marx and Engels do not dispute the attractiveness of the utopian ideal *per se* – after all, both Owen and Fourier are fellow socialists – but they contest their construal of social change. The utopian socialists cannot but "deaden the class struggle and ... reconcile the class antagonisms,"[18] which evinces for Marx and Engels that their vision of the future has become decoupled from the emancipatory mission of the revolutionary subject. Since the proletariat is largely absent from the utopian socialists' plans for the egalitarian society to come, Owen and Fourier remain stuck in an account of social change that ignores the working class' capacity for self-organization. Later on, Engels would

permitting Utopia to be positively pictured; this is the substance of its negativity" (Adorno, *Negative Dialectics*, 207).

[16] The question of how Marxism relates to utopianism is a rather complicated one, so it suffices here to highlight only some relevant publications: Geoghegan, *Utopianism and Marxism*; Smith, "Reflections on Aspects of Marxist Anti-utopianism"; Paden, "Marx's Critique of the Utopian Socialists"; Fischbach, "Marx and Utopia"; Leopold, "On Marxian Utopophobia." Note that the designation "utopian socialism" in fact precedes Marx's and Engels' usage. See: Stedman Jones, "Utopian Socialism."

[17] Marx and Engels, "The Communist Manifesto," 268–70.

[18] Marx and Engels, 269.

throw this position into even starker relief, by proclaiming an unbridge-able gulf between two kinds of socialism: utopian and scientific.[19] It is evident which kind of Marxism Engels preferred – the scientific one.

This invective notwithstanding, it would be an error, however, to identify in Marxism *tout court* a hostile attitude towards utopianism. Not only is it the case that some of the most vocal advocates of utopianism in the twentieth century have been Marxists (of sorts) – from Ernst Bloch to Fredric Jameson and Ruth Levitas – but Marx's own wrestling with his socialist predecessors might betray a vacillating attitude towards utopian-ism, perhaps even bordering on inconsistency.[20] As Steven Lukes puts it, Marx's views on this topic amount to an "anti-utopian utopianism," a paradoxical standpoint that Engels' insistence on socialism's scientific character obscures.[21]

Be this as it may, on the standard Marxist reading, the wishful think-ing inherent in utopianism is not innocuous – it serves the purpose of obfuscation. By channelling energy towards an ideal society to come, rather than focusing on the task of overthrowing the bourgeoisie's hegemony, it draws attention away from the revolutionary subject and its historical mission.[22]

While the Marxist critique of utopianism has faded in recent years, the basic structure of the argument will be familiar from contemporary controversies around radical transformation. As we shall see in Chapter 3, where Bruno Latour's Gaia figure is shown to disavow any association with utopianism, it is a common feature of debates around climate change that they stand in a somewhat uneasy relationship to social dreaming. The origins of this unease can, I believe, be traced back to a point that both Marx and Engels have made: that utopias offer us pictures of an attractive future, and as such they are to be welcomed; but

---

[19] Engels, *Socialism, Utopian and Scientific.*
[20] For a useful reconstruction of Marx's views on communism along these lines, see: Ollman, "Marx's Vision of Communism."
[21] Lukes, "Marxism and Utopianism."
[22] Russell Jacoby associates the prohibition on conjuring a positive vision of an ideal future with an iconoclastic variety of "anti-utopian utopianism," rooted in the Jewish tradition. See: Jacoby, *Picture Imperfect.*

they are also problematic, due to the allure of that picture sapping away intellectual resources.[23]

Turning now to the second class of objections, utopianism has also been blamed for spreading totalitarian plots to forcefully create another world: the view from nowhere as harbinger of violent upheaval. On this account, utopias can become vehicles for domination when the world, here and now, is exposed as corrupt and in need of repair. Numerous critics have concluded that utopias represent not only fantasies that distract their audience but become schemes for legitimizing social engineering. Philosophers such as Karl Popper, Isaiah Berlin,[24] Judith Shklar[25] and Leszek Kołakowski[26] all suspected that utopias were pernicious, for they advanced visions of society that appeared to be without flaws and contradictions. The conjuring of another world, just on the horizon and cleansed of all impurities, was so dangerous, these commentators maintained, because it erased the intrinsically defective and indefinite nature of human beings, forever torn between impulses to do good and temptations to do bad.

In designing social and political arrangements that are ill fit for what Immanuel Kant described as "the crooked wood"[27] of humanity, utopian thinkers thus prepare the ground for widespread, eliminatory violence. Here, the anticipation of a different world is itself manipulative insofar as it discounts the sacrifices that would have to be endured for a prosperous future. Totalitarian societies depend, according to this view, on blueprints for an alternative reality that redeems the hardship experienced in the here and now. This millenarianism brings into existence, in the words of the Russian revolutionary Valerian Osinsky, a "world of insatiable utopia," where the "simplest ethical rules become real and free from exceptions and contradictions."[28]

---

[23] Raymond Geuss calls these utopian projects "form-based" to highlight that they fail to provide guidance for how we may transition to a desirable future. See: Geuss, "Realism and the Relativity of Judgement."

[24] Berlin, "The Pursuit of the Ideal."

[25] Shklar, *After Utopia*; Shklar, "The Political Theory of Utopia."

[26] Kołakowski, "The Death of Utopia Reconsidered."

[27] Kant, "Idea for a Universal History from a Cosmopolitan Perspective," 9.

[28] Cited in: Slezkine, *The House of Government*, 67.

It is Karl Popper who voiced the most stringent objection to this voracious view of the world. Popper's critique is based on a peculiar epistemology that centres human fallibility. The following quotation summarizes this account:

> Since we cannot determine the ultimate ends of political actions scientific-ally, or by purely rational methods, differences of opinion concerning what the ideal state should be like cannot always be smoothed out by the method of argument. They will at least partly have the character of reli-gious differences. And there can be no tolerance between these different Utopian religions. Utopian aims are designed to serve as a basis for rational political action and discussion, and such action appears to be possible only if the aim is definitely decided upon. Thus the Utopianist must win over, or else crush, his Utopianist competitors who do not share his own Utopianism and who do no profess his own Utopianist religion. But he has to do more. He has to be very thorough in eliminating and stamping out all heretical competing views. For the way to the Utopian goal is long.[29]

The main point here is that violence results directly from the perfect blueprint that Popper detects in all utopias. Because utopias hinge on the construction of an ideal state whose consolidation is projected into the future, they resort to social engineering, which is then justified by the goal of building a homogenous and conflict-free community.[30] Since it seeks to remove human fallibility, utopianism is totalitarian in nature. Human beings, Popper thought, will never know what the ideal state of any political organization will look like; nor can they fathom what con-crete steps might be necessary to establish a fundamentally new order.

---

[29] Popper, "Utopia and Violence," 6.

[30] See: Popper, *The Open Society and Its Enemies*, chap. 9. In this regard, Popper's philosophy is quite close to Michael Oakeshott's critique of rationalism in politics, which culminates in his famous definition of what it means to be a conservative: "to prefer the familiar to the unknown, to prefer the tried to the untried, fact to mystery, the actual to the possible, the limited to the unbounded, the near to the distant, the convenient sufficient to the superabundant, the perfect, present laughter to utopian bliss" ("On Being Conservative," 169). On the debate between Popper and Oakeshott, which also revolved around the bonds between rationalism and utopianism, see: Jacobs and Tregenza, "Rationalism and Tradition."

Utopianism, in short, succumbs to an epistemic fallacy with practical repercussions; it denies the limitations of our cognitive capacities and thereby paves the way for the demiurgic arrival of the "new man."[31] The desire to legislate a rational method for attaining an ideal state gives rise to the subjugation of those who do not share in the utopian dream or disagree on the best way to realize it. While social engineering is for Popper deeply flawed, piecemeal reform, with its pragmatic process of trial and error, is grounded in the right sort of epistemology – one that does not displace human fallibility.[32]

Popper, Berlin, Shklar and Kołakowski have collectively been labelled "Cold War liberals."[33] Maybe this label is a bit heavy-handed, but there is truth to it, because all these critics of utopianism grounded their objections in a staunch anti-Communism. While they were also concerned with the epochal evil of Nazism, a central incentive for their theorizing was hostility to socialist ideas. Communism was faulted for annihilating freedom and pluralism by subjecting individuals to unfettered state control.[34]

Notice that, for these authors, the deterioration of actually existing socialist states into totalitarianism was not just an accident of history that could have been avoided if, for example, Stalin had not become general secretary of the Bolshevik Party in 1922. Rather, their attack on these regimes was a thoroughly philosophical one that traced communism's violence and oppression back to a defect in Marxism's redemptive promise of an emancipated working class. For violent and oppressive states, the anti-totalitarian contention goes, utopias play a paramount role: they legitimize the hardship that collectives need to withstand to rid themselves of prevailing injustices and exclusions.[35]

---

[31] On the history of the idea of a "new Soviet man," see: Bergman, "The Idea of Individual Liberation in Bolshevik Visions of the New Soviet Man."

[32] For a reconstruction and rebuttal of Popper's views, see: Goodwin, "Utopia Defended against the Liberals"; Sargent, "Authority & Utopia."

[33] See: Müller, "Fear and Freedom: On 'Cold War Liberalism.'"

[34] Shorten, *Modernism and Totalitarianism*, 109–23.

[35] In later years, French thinkers such as François Furet, Marcel Gauchet, Claude Lefort and other members of Raymond Aron's circle would continue this line of argumentation by developing anti-totalitarian accounts of the perils of revolution. On this debate, see: Sawyer and Stewart, *In Search of the Liberal Moment.*

This critique of utopianism has received sustained attention in recent years. John Gray, to name but one prominent voice, claims that the perfectionism integral to utopian projects has extremely deleterious effects.[36] This is so because social dreaming feeds on an aspiration that Gray considers fatal: the yearning for complete harmony. Gray's analysis thus elaborates on an argument that we have already come across before, namely that utopia's longing for concord imperils freedom and plural-ism. Yet, a life without conflict is simply beyond humanity's reach. So, the demands articulated by utopians prepare, once again, the ground for violent oppression.

Summing up these two objections, we can clearly see how the case against utopianism is at the same time about the kind of knowledge about the real world that we possess and about the sort of actions we should be taking on the basis of that knowledge. Critics from the left as well as from the right stress that the focus on positive visions of the future is either futile or dangerous. Utopianism's uselessness is normally associ-ated with the failure of its proponents to explain in concrete terms how the blueprint of a desirable alternative to the status quo could be turned into reality. In other words, it is precisely due to their focus on a perfect state that utopians lose sight of the necessity to ponder how we may get there. Utopianism's threat is related to its failure to admit contradictions and ambiguities in the anticipation of an alternative future. Due to their reluctance to accommodate within their models the uncertainty, contin-gency and complexity of all human action, utopians are prone to push through their proposals by brutal means.

2.2 FROM PERFECTIONISM TO THE EDUCATION OF DESIRE

In response to this multipronged attack, it is imperative to appreciate that conceiving of utopias as otherworldly or hazardous relies on an intellectual shortcut. Utopias, properly construed, explore alternative ways of living that do not have to turn into rigid templates. They draw maps for navigating an uncertain and risky future, but their cartography can be flexible and adaptative. The most effective rejoinder to the

---

[36] Gray, *Black Mass.*

objections just outlined is, hence, that critics tend to underestimate the internal diversity of utopianism.

My argument in this section is that not all utopian visions fall prey to the accusation of being futile or dangerous, because at least some manage to let go of perfectionism. The defence of utopianism that I pursue thus proceeds via two steps: first, by disarming the aforementioned lines of attack, and second, by developing a positive account of utopianism.

While a few advocates of utopianism continue to embrace the idea that utopias are by default dedicated to the building of perfect worlds,[37] others have sketched a different picture of utopianism. In *Fool's Gold*, Lucy Sargisson advances this project by asserting that "utopias *should not* seek to create a perfect world."[38] She begins her argument by acknowledging that the anti-utopian suspicion of blueprints is, to some extent, warranted. The image of a perfect world can be both alluring and manipulative. Due to their rigidity, blueprints may seduce people into uncritically accepting sacrifices in the name of a brighter future.

If utopianism only involved the construction of perfect worlds, then the anti-utopian critique would be devastating. But Sargisson shows that we can, and indeed must, hold perfectionist and non-perfectionist utopias apart. The inadequacy of the anti-utopian canon is therefore that it misrepresents social dreaming, which becomes evident once we foreground the multiple functions that utopias perform:

> Utopias have many different functions: for example, they engage with contemporary debates and comment critically on their time, they can be used as hermeneutic texts and reading the utopias of a given age can illuminate contemporaneous concerns and issues. They can also perform heuristic functions and this applies both to textual utopias (fiction and/or theory) and practical utopian experiments: they can function as real or imaginary spaces in which to test and explore alternative ways of

---

[37] For prominent examples, see: Davis, *Utopia and the Ideal Society*; Kumar, *Utopia and Anti-utopia in Modern Times*; Kumar, *Utopianism*. For Davis and Kumar, it is the fictional portrayal of perfect societies that sets utopias apart from other types of idealizing thought.

[38] Sargisson, *Fool's Gold?*, 14, italics in original.

organizing our lives. Utopias are almost always radical in content, going to the roots of their present social and political norms and challenging or questioning core assumptions.[39]

Sargisson's claim, which she defends through studies of various projects, from feminist science fiction to Dubai's "fantastic" architecture, is that associating utopias with blueprints alone is misleading. A balanced account would have to conclude that perfectionism does not represent a necessary condition of utopianism. This insight marks one of the cornerstones of my reflections on utopianism in the Anthropocene, too. If we envisage utopias solely through the lens of blueprints, we miss a great deal of what social dreaming can accomplish. The kind of utopian visions I shall be investigating in the following chapters all disavow perfectionism, substituting it instead with provisional and often conflict-ridden interrogations of an uncertain and risky future – social dreaming as a struggle that never ceases.

To get a sense of how widespread this rejoinder is to the critique of utopianism, consider the following three standpoints: first, Jay Winter distinguishes between *major* and *minor* utopias. *Minor utopias* – a term deployed in his historical sketch of peace initiatives during the twentieth century – are cultural and social projects whose aim is the fractional, rather than comprehensive, renewal of the world. Unlike major utopias, which Winter associates with social engineering, their objective is to become incubators of change on a local, not a global, scale. Since they necessarily react to particular formations of power, minor utopias cannot but reflect the material and ideological conditions from which they emerge. Winter thus detects a tension within social dreaming: as a "narrative about discontinuity," it is still "written by men and women rooted in contemporary conditions and language."[40]

He then goes on to examine this tension in a number of contexts, from the rise of human rights discourse in the aftermath of World War II to the ascendancy of liberation theology in the 1960s. Winter's intuition is that minor utopias disavow perfectionism, gesturing instead towards

[39] Sargisson, 29.
[40] Winter, *Dreams of Peace and Freedom*, 3.

endeavours, "which aim not at the total eradication of social conflict or the construction of an ideal city, but at partial transformations, steps on the way to a less violent and unjust society."[41]

Second, in a similar fashion, Elise Boulding, the feminist peace scholar, attempts to hold *micro-* and *macro-level* utopias apart. These can be separated by looking into the catalyst behind change:

> As we look in turn at macrolevel and microlevel utopian efforts to design and implement utopias, we will see how differently various experimental groups have dealt with the tension between the rage for order and the longing for the spontaneity of organic processes; between the desire for central control, and the recognition that locality has its own competence; between the desire to destroy all traces of oppressive structures and wipe the slate clean before beginning anew, and the impulse to nurture the seeds of the new within the shell of old, trusting that gentleness, not violence, will free the goodness in humans; and finally the tension between structural redesign and trying to produce new kinds of human beings to achieve the new society.[42]

Boulding's approach is interesting due to its account of how utopian projects are implemented. While the Cold War liberals and their contemporary heirs disapprove of macro-level efforts of social engineering, Boulding hints at bottom-up initiatives that invest hope in prefigurative practices. As we shall see shortly, these practices are essential to intentional communities and other types of "everyday utopias."[43] Micro-level initiatives circumvent, as much as possible, the problems that Popper, Berlin, Shklar and Kołakowski associate with state-sponsored plans for creating a "new man."

Third, let us look at Miguel Abensour, whose definition of utopias as promoting the "education of desire" we have already encountered. Abensour cleaves the *persistent* utopia from the *eternal* one. "Persistence" here describes the attempt of social dreaming to shatter an audience's "acceptance of the established order they take for granted." Refusing to

---

[41] Winter, 208.

[42] Boulding, "Utopianism," 353.

[43] Cooper, *Everyday Utopias.*

identify utopia with perfectionism, Abensour juxtaposes this emancipatory function with the eternal utopia:

> "Eternal utopia" is a conservative motif, probably born with the bloody repression of the revolution of June 1848. According to the counter-revolutionary publicists who used it, there is an "eternal utopia" from Plato to Fourier by way of More that is, unbeknownst to its authors, always one and the same, impermeable to history and always affected by the same failings. The eternal utopian text would invariably produce a closed, static, authoritarian society that negates temporality and does violence to plurality and individual singularity.[44]

In attending to Sargisson, Winter, Boulding and Abensour, I have so far followed a reactive path: to demonstrate why perfectionism, which remains the boon of the anti-utopian critique, does not constitute a central component of all utopian visions. When utopias offer orientation around systemic challenges, such as imagining a climate-changed world, they can do so without the kind of blueprint that troubles critics from both the left and the right. But what exactly is involved in the anti-perfectionist strand of utopianism?

To answer that question, I want to revisit a number of conceptual clarifications that Ruth Levitas proposed. This will get us closer to an affirmative account of utopianism. Levitas' book *The Concept of Utopia*[45] remains to this day the most coherent engagement with the topic of utopianism. Levitas begins by remarking that, in the absence of a sound theory of utopianism, the scholarly debate will be stuck in a limbo, for different commentators tend to speak past each other or, worse, undermine each other's legitimacy.[46] This is an especially serious conundrum for those who want to defend utopia against the critics introduced in the previous section. Without a clear sense of where the conceptual boundaries of utopia lie, there is a risk of overstretching the notion.

Levitas' review of extant definitions of social dreaming focuses on three issues: their content, their form and their function. Definitions that

---

[44] Abensour, "Persistent Utopia," 407.
[45] Levitas, *The Concept of Utopia.*
[46] Levitas, 208.

home in on the content of utopia are usually "evaluative and normative, specifying what the good society would be, rather than reflecting on how it may be perceived."[47] While this is a common strategy for capturing utopia, Levitas suggests that a focus on what utopias contain diminishes the explanatory potential of the definition. Commentators who define utopianism based on its content cannot but smuggle in value judgments that tarnish their analytical framework. Levitas hence maintains that an evaluative or normative notion of utopia will inevitably be too narrow to cover utopias in all their diversity.

By contrast, definitions that concentrate on utopia's form are descriptive in character: unburdened by value-laden bias, they emphasize the various shapes that utopias can take, from literary fiction to movies, the built environment and social and political theory. The mutability of utopianism according to specific historical circumstances is strongly foregrounded in this definitional strand. Levitas connects this attempt to define utopia with the liberal-humanist tradition, whose main concern lies with describing "an ideal common-wealth, an imaginary ideal society; and one which is more or less completely couched in fictional terms."[48]

Finally, the function that utopia performs can also become the foundation of a definition. The central issue here concerns what utopias are set up to achieve, rather than which values they promote or through which media they are conveyed. As we have seen already, Levitas maintains that we should separate three such functions: compensation, critique and change. She also argues that any definition that narrowly concentrates on only one or two aspects (content, form or function) of utopia is doomed to fail, giving the following example to illustrate this thought:

> Intuitively, most people are unwilling to include in the category of utopia prognoses or plans as morally offensive as Nazism, although we would no doubt draw the line in different places. There is a normative element in many definitions which excludes evil utopias and regards them as contradictions in terms. Conversely, such a normative element implies that some

---

[47] Levitas, 5.
[48] Levitas, 38.

utopias are objectively better than others. While such judgments are politically and morally necessary, they are not properly part of utopia as an analytic category and indeed produce misleading results.[49]

Defining away Nazi utopias, such as the fantasy of a racially pure community or Adolf Hitler's megalomaniac plans for the new capital *Germania*, by reasoning that specific values (like freedom and equality, for example) need to be incorporated in all utopias, amounts to a slight of hand that confirms the worries of the anti-utopians we came across in the prior section. Levitas thus wants to shield the definition of utopia from evaluative and normative contamination.

What about the other two dimensions of utopia's definition, form and function? Form-based definitions are beset by a weakness: if the form of utopias is liable to change, it becomes difficult to identify expressions of social dreaming across different historical periods and within varied cultural contexts. Levitas therefore believes that form-based definitions, just as content-based ones, are too restrictive.

This brings us to the last approach: Levitas' analysis of function-based definitions is especially illuminating, because it shines a light on the impact that utopias exert, at specific moments in time and for specific audiences. Yearning for consolation, for example, becomes urgent in situations of extreme hardship and deprivation. To explain this, consider the medieval parable of the *Land of Cockaigne*, in which the longing for elemental and luxury goods is fully satiated. Living in a place like *Cockaigne* is clearly not within our reach, and the people who listened to the tales about a country where all human needs are perennially and utterly satisfied were, it appears, well aware of *Cockaigne's* fantastical nature.[50]

What happens when social dreaming goes beyond consolation? The issue of *feasibility* then becomes more prominent. Utopias do not only respond to a dearth of material resources by providing escapist fantasies, but also open up perspectives for criticizing and transforming the current state of affairs. This marks the domain of what Ernst Bloch glossed

---

[49] Levitas, 212.
[50] Pleij, *Dreaming of Cockaigne*, 273.

as "concrete utopia," "an anticipatory kind which by no means coincides with abstract utopian dreaminess, nor is directed by the immaturity of merely abstract utopian socialism."[51] Bloch and other Marxist champions of utopianism insist that positive change depends on collective wishes that are shaped by proposals for other ways of being and living. As I remarked in Chapter 1, behind these proposals lies not just any kind of yearning for alternatives, but what Bloch named *docta spes*, or "educated hope."[52]

Despite her sympathies for Bloch's oeuvre, Levitas still remains sceptical of function-based definitions of utopia, which tend to focus on critique and transformation, while rebuffing escapist fantasies as unproductive.[53] Here is why. When utopia's function shifts from compensation to critique and transformation, hope becomes paramount. In other words, Levitas claims we can only hope for something that we believe is realistically achievable. Otherwise, we end up, once again, in the *Land of Cockaigne*, a beautiful place to be sure, but one that we will unfortunately never manage to reach. Centring hope in our understanding of utopia presupposes a blending together of *willing* something and *wishing* it into existence:

> The problem of limiting utopia to the "possible world" is that it conflates the categories of hope and desire. It limits utopia to the question "what may I hope?" and refuses the question "what may I dream?" It implies also that the function of utopia is necessarily that of change ... When the function of utopia is to catalyse change, then of course the issue of practical possibility becomes salient. But even here, utopia does not need to *be* practically possible; it merely needs to be believed to be so to mobilise people to political action ... Utopia expresses and explores what is desired; under certain conditions it also contains hope that these desires may be met in reality, rather than merely in fantasy. The essential element in utopia is not hope, but desire – the desire for a better way of living.[54]

---

[51] Bloch, *The Principle of Hope: Volume 1*, 146. For an introduction to Bloch's oeuvre, see: Moir, "Ernst Bloch."

[52] Bloch, *The Principle of Hope: Volume 1*, 7, 9.

[53] Levitas, "Educated Hope."

[54] Levitas, *The Concept of Utopia*, 219–21.

The notion of desire ("what may I dream?") invoked here is directly borrowed from Miguel Abensour. Whereas hope constrains social dreaming, due to its orientation towards the realistically achievable, desire furnishes us with a much more stable foundation. Without tethering utopia to what is feasible, a great diversity of utopian projects finally comes into view. The upside of this wide framing is that it allows us to investigate how various alternatives to the status quo can be imagined as well as enacted.

Consider, though, that Levitas' argument hangs on a sharp contrast between hope, which she thinks can only be directed at ideas and proposals that are in principle within our reach, and desire, which can be channelled at all kinds of visions of the future – independent of whether acting on the basis of such visions will make a difference at all. In sum, *The Concept of Utopia* defines utopia as the "desire for a better way of being and living,"[55] thereby opting for an analytical framework that is maximally ecumenical.

In her later work, Levitas slightly modified this account, by linking up her definition of utopia with reflections on how society could effectively be altered. This includes an approach that Levitas calls the "Imaginary Reconstitution of Society."[56] Levitas thus pursues an analysis of social dreaming as a multifaceted method:

> Utopia as method has three modes. The first is an archaeological mode, piecing together the images of the good society that are embedded in political programmes and social and economic policies. The second is an ontological mode which addresses the question of what kind of people particular societies develop and encourage. What is understood as human flourishing, what capabilities are valued, encouraged and genuinely enabled, or blocked and suppressed, by specific existing or potential social arrangements: we are concerned here with the historical and social determination of human nature ... The third is an architectural mode – that is, the imagination of potential alternative scenarios for the future, acknowledging the assumptions about and consequences for the people who

[55] Levitas, 8.
[56] Levitas, *Utopia as Method*, xi.

might inhabit them. These in turn must be subject to archaeological critique, addressing the silences and inconsistencies all such images must contain, as well as the political steps forward that they imply.[57]

The most widely recognized of these three modes is utopia-as-architecture, which covers much of the utopian theorizing and fiction that will interest us in the following. But the other modes are of equal relevance to Levitas' and my approach. The archaeological mode seeks to recoup potentials for better ways of being and living that remain latent in the status quo.[58] As such, it delivers crucial material for alternatives to the status quo. The ontological mode, on the other hand, pertains to the idea that deliberations about who we are, as human beings, and who we should strive to become, are integral to any utopian project.

In essence, *Utopia as Method* thus makes explicit "a method that is already in use whenever and wherever people individually or collectively consider what the future might bring and how humans might choose to shape it."[59] This view has the advantage of avoiding many of the problematic issues that the anti-utopian critics identified. Conceiving of utopianism in terms of a provisional heuristics that shapes our desire for being and living otherwise is different from idle daydreaming or totalitarian social engineering. It amounts to a procedure of modelling possible futures that remains open to contestation and debate.

I have dedicated ample space to Levitas' analytical apparatus for a specific reason: given the scope, originality and sophistication of her thinking, Levitas' writings offer an excellent stepping stone for the vindication of utopianism. Before I continue to apply her account to the analysis of ways of imagining a climate-changed world, I still need to clarify a matter that seems vital to Levitas' thinking – the preference of desire at the expense of hope, in the defence of social dreaming.

Recall why Levitas is sceptical of hope as the defining feature of utopia: hope is, on her account, about fixing aspirations and yearnings onto achievable visions of the future. In some sense, then, hope

---

[57] Levitas, 153.

[58] This conceptualization reverberates with Laurence Davis' distinction between "transcendent" and "grounded" utopias. See: Davis, "History, Politics, and Utopia."

[59] Levitas, *Utopia as Method*, 218.

presupposes a prior judgement as to the range of options we can reasonably aim for.[60] While Levitas appreciates the attractiveness of this idea, she finds it too limiting. Wishing is for her not the same as willing, precisely because one can wish for something to happen while being conscious of the impossibility of that wish ever materializing. Consequently, the desire that Levitas locates at the heart of utopianism's pedagogical efforts derives from our capacity to wish, not from our ability to will.

I do not think, however, that the distinction between hope and desire needs to be as stringent as Levitas makes it appear. The porosity of the boundary between hope and desire emerges once we grasp that what counts as possible or impossible at any given moment is itself up for debate. Nowhere is this truer than in politics. There simply is no way to objectively determine the limits of what is possible or impossible in the political realm.

Although I will discuss this issue in Chapter 5, when scrutinizing the so-called Atwood principle – Gregory Claeys' label for Margaret Atwood's preferred criterion to distinguish speculative fiction – let us quickly turn to struggles over the presumably superior character of capitalist societies. The suspicion of utopias as perfectionist, and hence problematic, has from the 1960s onwards seeped into the cultural mainstream, culminating in the unofficial slogan of the neo-liberal Thatcher/Reagan era: TINA, or *There Is No Alternative.*[61] Faced with the intransigence of

---

[60] This account corresponds to what Adrienne Martin has named the "orthodox view" of hope. Martin contrasts this view with her idea of hope as a syndrome. See: Martin, *How We Hope.*

[61] While it is surely the case that TINA expresses an anti-utopian sentiment, it would be mistaken to view the market society revered by both Reagan and Thatcher as a project devoid of any utopian aspirations. As Vincent Geoghegan observes, "Thatcherite conservatism is a glaring example of right-wing utopianism, with its summoning up of the supposed glories of Victorian Britain as a model and its underlying, far-fetched beliefs that, for example, the market is essentially a benign institution and that brutalizing youngsters with short, sharp shocks somehow improves them" (*Utopianism and Marxism,* 18). Part of neoliberalism's ideological power derives precisely from its ability to obfuscate the utopian aspirations on which it feeds, by presenting its unique vision of society as the outcome of a natural process of selection amongst a variety of competing worldviews and economic systems.

"capitalist realism,"[62] many sought to recuperate the critical and transformative aspects of social dreaming, distilling the radical impetus of the alterglobalization movement into a catchy formula – *Another World Is Possible*. We can infer from this clash that politics always revolves around the limits of what is deemed possible or impossible at a given historical juncture.

That (wilful) hope and (wishful) desire are not easy to hold apart can be rendered even more transparent by attending to Jonathan Lear's notion of "radical hope."[63] Lear develops this concept through a reading of the pronouncements of the last great chief of the Crow Nation, Plenty Coups. Radical hope designates the anticipation of a "good for which those who have the hope as yet lack the appropriate concepts with which to understand it."[64] I will engage with this conceptualization in the chapter on dystopian visions, but note here that Lear's notion allows us to redescribe utopianism in such a way as to loosen the constraint of feasibility in the act of hoping. Central to radical hope is a commitment, visible in Plenty Coup's reckoning with the Crow tribe's existential collapse, to "the bare idea that *something good will emerge*."[65]

The chief's stance when everything seems lost can be reconstructed as simultaneously wilful and wishful, encompassing both a yearning for collective survival and a diffuse, but efficacious faith in the potential of a risky and uncertain future. This is why we must depart from Levitas' overly strict distinction between hope and desire. In a strange echo of Brecht's and Bloch's exhortation that "something's missing," marking the outset of any utopian project, the object of Plenty Coup's radical hope remains entirely undecided. Radical hope merely carves out a blank space, however limited it may be, on which the education of desire can be projected. The hope at work in utopias is hence much closer to

[62] Fisher, *Capitalist Realism*.
[63] Although I do not engage with her work in this context, it would also be worthwhile to gesture towards Sara Ahmed's original treatment of wilfulness. Her understanding of wilfulness as "a diagnosis of the failure to comply with those whose authority is given" (*Willful Subjects*, 1) especially speaks to my argument, because it foregrounds the impact of power relations on the stubborn desire to act otherwise.
[64] Lear, *Radical Hope*, 103.
[65] Lear, 94, italics in original.

the one examined by Lear – not so much about what is realistically achievable (as Levitas suggests), but more about the conditions that make it conceivable to go on, even under extremely adverse circumstances.

2.3 ON THE DIALECTIC OF ESTRANGEMENT AND REALISM

If utopianism involves a flexible and adaptative practice of mapping possible futures, how can this cartography remain sensitive to contestation and debate? In raising this question, we want to better comprehend the mechanisms whereby the desire for other ways of being and living is given shape. Put differently, we are now shifting from the abstract analysis of utopianism as the education of desire to an investigation into the processes that social dreaming sets in motion.

In this section, I suggest differentiating between utopianism's basic functions (compensation, critique and change) and the particular mechanisms underpinning them. Compensation, critique and change are the external effects that utopias aim to generate in their addressees. *The Land of Cockaigne*, for example, is intended as an uplifting tale that affectively consoles its readers about dwelling in a harsh world where both elemental and luxury goods are lacking. Once we shift attention to how the *The Land of Cockaigne* discharges of this function, it becomes imperative to study the mechanisms with which this fantasy of utmost abundance operates.

Let us kick-start the investigation by concentrating on what many consider the principal means through which compensation, critique and transformation get activated: estrangement or defamiliarization (I will use those terms synonymously). Utopias always aim to extend their readers' sense of the possible. If we remain under the impression that the present state of affairs cannot be changed for the better at all – as the neoliberal mantra *There Is No Alternative* seeks to impress on us – then resignation, depression and mourning become the only options available.[66] Such negative feelings have seen an enormous rise in recent

---

[66] For an analysis of the Left's melancholic vision of history, animated by its hurtful experience of persistent losses, see: Traverso, *Left-Wing Melancholia.* Traverso, to be sure,

years. "Ecological grief," for example, turns out to be an entirely expectable reaction to the helplessness and hopelessness that many of us experience when bearing witness to the utter destruction of natural habitats, such as the Great Barrier Reef, for example.[67] Clinical evidence suggests that especially the mental health of younger people is more and more perturbed by anxieties about climate change.[68]

Utopias supply us with an antidote to the crippling sensation that the "game is over," by demonstrating that things could be otherwise and by restoring a sense of self-reflective orientation. In this process, the importance of estrangement cannot be overestimated. Estrangement takes a first step towards changing the status quo: once the taken-for-grantedness of reality has been shattered, it becomes feasible, in principle and in practice, to contemplate how one may improve the current order.

In order to unpack this idea, I begin with an exposition of what is the best-known interpretation of estrangement within utopian studies. My argument entails that we need to acknowledge the fundamental *paradox* behind the education of our desire, permanently torn between estrangement and realism.

Darko Suvin is usually credited with delivering the first comprehensive account of the role of estrangement within utopian studies. From the 1970s onwards, Suvin has been working on a theory of science fiction that he describes as a systematic "poetics." This project, with its Aristotelian undertones, indicates that Suvin is especially concerned with the formal and structural aspects of science fiction. At the core of this framework lies a definition of science fiction as the "a literary genre whose necessary and sufficient conditions are the presence and interaction of estrangement and cognition, and whose main formal device is an imaginative framework alternative to the author's empirical

---

diagnoses a widespread decline of utopianism after the end of "actually existing socialism." As should be evident, I do not concur with this assessment.

[67] See: Marshall et al., "Reef Grief"; Conroy, "'Ecological Grief' Grips Scientists Witnessing Great Barrier Reef's Decline." On the relationship between feelings of guilt and grief in the Anthropocene, see: Jensen, *Ecologies of Guilt in Environmental Rhetorics*, chap. 5: Guilty Grief and Ecological Mourning.

[68] See: Majeed and Lee, "The Impact of Climate Change on Youth Depression and Mental Health"; Doherty and Clayton, "The Psychological Impacts of Global Climate Change."

environment."[69] The obvious contrast here is with realistic – or, what Suvin calls "naturalistic" – fiction, which seeks to mirror nature and shuns the use of defamiliarizing tropes.

What sets science fiction apart from fantasy and fairy tales is, according to Suvin, the appeal to cognition, its attempt to draw on quasi-scientific knowledge. In fact, Suvin claims (at least in his earlier writings) that *only* science fiction generates knowledge of this kind – fantasy, fairy tales as well as the whole genre of realistic fiction fail to do so.[70] Science fiction, in other words, estranges us from the status quo, but it does so in such a way as to stimulate cognitive processes that are relevant to the real world. Knowledge is produced when the readers recognize that what they accept in an unquestioned manner is in fact the result of ideological and material conditions that shape their existence.[71]

Estrangement is effected through the introduction of a *novum*. Suvin appropriates this concept from Ernst Bloch, who highlighted the power of radically new experiences and insights to expand our horizon of expectations.[72] Against this background, Suvin insists on the strictly scientific credentials of the *novum*:

> The novum is postulated on and validated by the post-Cartesian and post-Baconian scientific method ... Science in this wider sense of methodically systematic cognition cannot be disjoined from the SF innovation, in spite of fashionable currents in SF criticism of the last 15 years ... Indeed, a very useful distinction between "naturalistic" fiction, fantasy and SF ... is that

---

[69] Suvin, *Metamorphoses of Science Fiction*, 7–8.

[70] For a later revision of the cognitivist framework see: Suvin, Positions and Presuppositions in Science Fiction, chap. 13: SF as Metaphor, Parable and Chronotope (with the Bad Conscience of Reaganism). Suvin's narrow interpretation of the cognitive content of various genres has been criticized. See: Parrinder, "Revisiting Suvin's Poetics of Science Fiction"; Renault, "Science Fiction as Cognitive Estrangement."

[71] Csicsery-Ronay, "Marxist Theory and Science Fiction," 118–19.

[72] Bloch, *The Principle of Hope: Volume 1*, 124–30. Moreover, Suvin's conceptualization is also indebted to H. G. Wells' account of what he labelled as "scientific romances": the inclusion of a "fantastic element, the strange property or the strange world" (Wells, "Preface to The Scientific Romances," 13). On Wells' perspective, time travel is the paradigmatic case of a *novum*. See also: Suvin, "Wells as the Turning Point of the SF Tradition."

naturalistic fiction does not require scientific explanation, fantasy does not allow it, and SF both requires and allows it.[73]

As we can glean from this passage, in Suvin's view, a high threshold exists for when science fiction generates cognitive estrangement: it must be strictly methodical and internally consistent, emulating scientific inquiry. Speculative fiction, which does not pass this threshold, should not be considered science fiction at all.

These views have been strongly debated in utopian studies. Today, the notion of "cognitive estrangement" is widely recognized as a milestone in the scholarly discussion, for Suvin was the first commentator to systematically explore and taxonomize science fiction.[74] His theory has undergone an especially enthusiastic reception within Marxist circles.[75]

While Suvin and his followers have done much to clarify this technique, I now wish to continue with an observation that departs from the framework discussed so far. The crux of my argument is that we should distinguish between estrangement *from*, and estrangement *for* the world, if we want to understand the critical and transformational functions of utopianism.[76] Put otherwise, only utopias that manage to defamiliarize their audience *for* the world are capable of providing orientation around hyperobjects. World-negating utopias, by contrast, are liable to succumb to escapism.

To make this argument, I propose revisiting the origins of the idea of estrangement. This approach differs from Suvin's in that it abandons the ambition to elevate estrangement to a genre-defining characteristic of science fiction or indeed any other type of literature. Instead, we should

---

[73] Suvin, *Metamorphoses of Science Fiction*, 54–66.

[74] Together with R. D. Mullen, Suvin was also the co-founder of the journal *Science Fiction Studies* in 1973.

[75] Carl Freedman, for example, amended Suvin's framework by relaxing its firm bond with quasi-scientific knowledge, which he thinks excessively restricts what should count as science fiction. Instead, Freedman foregrounds the notion of a "cognition effect" that comes into play in specific literary texts. Here, the basic criterion of distinction between science fiction and fantasy or fairy tales is that science fiction makes a *rhetorical appeal* to cognition; an appeal that falls short, however, of scientific inquiry in the fuller sense intended by Suvin. See: Freedman, *Critical Theory and Science Fiction*, 18–19.

[76] For an application of this distinction to the politics of agonistic reconciliation see: Thaler, "Reconciliation through Estrangement."

envision defamiliarization as an operation that can be put to use in various artistic and political contexts.

The concept of estrangement that I am interested in has roots in literary theory, dating back to the Russian formalist Viktor Shklovsky, with even deeper pedigrees reaching into Hegel's and Marx's philosophy (at least).[77] Shklovsky first developed the concept of *ostranenie* (translated into English either as defamiliarization or estrangement) in an article from 1917 called "Art, as Device."[78] As Suvin himself points out, *ostranenie* captures a specific technique whereby things that we habitually consider ordinary and common are presented from new and surprising angles.[79] Instead of realistically depicting a scene or character, the estranging technique makes visible the process through which art works are made:

> And so this thing we call art exists in order to restore the sensation of life, in order to make us feel things, in order to make a stone stony. The goal of art is to create the sensation of seeing, and not merely recognizing, things; the device of art is the "estrangement" of things and the complication of the form, which increases the duration and complexity of perception, as the process of perception is, in art, an end in itself and must be prolonged. Art is the means to live through the making of a thing; what has been made does not matter in art.[80]

The application of this technique within literature is widespread, disproving Suvin's assertion that only some narrowly conceived genres (science fiction, fantasy and fairy tales) utilize estrangement .[81] For instance, Tolstoy's writings – usually classified as masterpieces of *realist*

---

[77] Ginzburg, "Making Things Strange."

[78] Shklovsky, "Art, as Device." For a recently published collection of Shklovsky's writings in English, see: Shklovsky, *Viktor Shklovsky*. This book also contains a helpful introduction to Shklovsky's thinking. On the wider context, see: Robinson, *Estrangement and the Somatics of Literature*. On formalism in literary theory see: Rivkin and Ryan, *Literary Theory*, pt. 1: Formalisms: Russian Formalism and New Criticism; Steiner, *Russian Formalism*.

[79] Suvin, *Metamorphoses of Science Fiction*, 6. See also: Cuddon, "Defamiliarization."

[80] Shklovsky, "Art, as Device," 162.

[81] This assessment marks one of the major divergences between Suvin's and Shklovsky's uses of the notion of estrangement. See: Parrinder, "Revisiting Suvin's Poetics of Science Fiction," 37; Spiegel, "Things Made Strange."

literature – capture that which is normally perceived as familiar with a shocking naivety, "describing it as if seen for the first time, as if happening for the first time."[82] Defamiliarization of this kind is always sparked by a stubborn refusal to take settled meanings and conventional understandings for granted.[83]

The idea of estrangement has undergone an astonishing career. Looking back at his own conceptual innovation fifty years earlier, Shklovsky noted with amazement how far it had travelled.[84] Certainly the most influential way in which the notion of *ostranenie* later evolved was through Bertolt Brecht's theory and practice of epic theatre.[85] What Brecht calls *Verfremdung* (translated into English as either estrangement, alienation or distanciation) is closely related to Shklovsky's concept.[86] For Brecht, however, the effect of *Verfremdung* exceeds that of "making things strange": on stage, it unravels a process whereby the audience becomes cognizant of the unbridgeable gulf between its own idiosyncratic, ideologically imbricated standpoints and the scene on stage. Like Shklovsky, Brecht sought to lay bare the mechanisms with which art is being crafted, anticipating that the theatre visitors would draw their own conclusions from what is being shown. In Brecht's view, critical and transformative thinking can only gain momentum once the members of the audience see through the artificiality of what is being staged.[87]

To comprehend the impact of estrangement within utopias, we need to investigate the linkages between aesthetics and politics. While it is relatively straightforward to grasp how Brecht conceived of these

---

[82] Shklovsky, "Art, as Device," 163. Miguel de Cervantes and Lawrence Sterne are further examples of authors who frequently employ the technique of *ostranenie*. See: Shklovsky, *Theory of Prose.*

[83] Christoyannopoulos, "The Subversive Potential of Leo Tolstoy's 'Defamiliarisation'"; Knapp, "The Development of Style and Theme in Tolstoy."

[84] Robinson, *Estrangement and the Somatics of Literature,* 79.

[85] Brecht, "A Short Organum for the Theatre."

[86] Mitchell, "From Shklovsky to Brecht." Another important source of inspiration for Brecht was the Chinese theatre tradition. See: Brecht, "On Chinese Acting"; Bai, "Dances with Mei Lanfang."

[87] As Jameson observes with respect to Brecht's approach, "the spectacle as a whole should try to demonstrate to the audience that we are all actors, and that acting is an inescapable dimension of social and everyday life" (Jameson, *Brecht and Method,* 25). For an exhaustive analysis of theatre-making and political judgement see: Arjomand, *Staged.*

bonds – his stagecraft was, after all, highly didactical and geared toward emancipation[88] – Shklovsky's case requires a little more unpacking; for it is the case that *ostranenie* was primarily understood as a literary method, with restricted reach beyond the world of novels. In what ways, then, does defamiliarization also serve as a primer for critique and change?

To answer this question, let us pay attention to the issue of estrangement's relation to the real world. Svetlana Boym detects a profound, yet largely unappreciated, resonance between Shklovsky's reflections and Hannah Arendt's notion of world-disclosure[89]. Boym's central claim is that "*ostranenie* was never an estrangement from the world, but estrangement for the sake of the world's renewal."[90] It would hence be wrong to conceive of estrangement solely in terms of an imaginative turning away from reality. World-negating estrangement – estrangement *from* the world, in Boym's terminology – is the result of a fading attachment to what is commonly shared, triggering apathy, distrust and anxiety amongst citizens. By contrast, estrangement *for* the world is predicated on a passionate commitment to worldly affairs that counteracts the alienating effects of withdrawal and introspection:

> [E]strangement for the world is an acknowledgment of the integral human plurality that we must recognize within us and within others. This is a way of seeing the world anew, a possibility of a new beginning that is fundamental for aesthetic experience, critical judgment, and political action.[91]

It is this construal of estrangement, as opening up a "way of seeing the world anew," that seems most conducive for illuminating utopias in the Anthropocene. Boym's distinction between two types of estrangement allows us to recognize the basic dynamic underpinning utopianism. Estrangement *for*, rather than *from*, the world is the mechanism whereby

---

[88] Jestrovic, *Theatre of Estrangement*, chap. 3: Epic Theatre in the Age of Mechanical Reproduction.

[89] See: Arendt, *The Human Condition*. From the plentiful secondary literature, see representatively: Lara, "Reflective Judgment as World Disclosure"; Zerilli, "We Feel Our Freedom."

[90] Boym, "Poetics and Politics of Estrangement," 599.

[91] Boym, 602.

social dreaming strives to gain distance to reality in the right manner. What Boym shows is that utopias necessarily maintain a connection with the real world: they break with some elements of the status quo, while affirming others. It is through this movement that critique is exercised, and transformation anticipated.

We can dig deeper into this paradoxical operation by turning to another stalwart of utopian studies. If utopias are not necessarily perfectionist and if their critical and transformative function is premised on estrangement *for*, rather than *from*, the world, then we need to look more closely into how utopias simultaneously disrupt the status quo and remain under its continuous spell. The author who has done more than anyone else over the past forty years to elucidate this process is Fredric Jameson.

Jameson's oeuvre is extremely diverse in interests, harnessing a peculiar brand of Marxism to interrogate a variety of cultural artefacts and social phenomena.[92] Given the breadth and depth of his work, I will in the following exclusively focus on his engagement with utopianism, which remains embedded, however, in his project of critical analysis.[93] The crux of this engagement can be detected in an early interpretation of Herbert Marcuse:

> The Utopian idea, on the contrary, keeps alive the possibility of a world qualitatively distinct from this one and takes the form of a stubborn negation of all that is ... For Utopian thinking may be said to unite both the philosophical and the artistic impulses, at the same time that it transcends both: it is philosophy become concrete, it is art which takes as its object not products and works but life itself. The impulse of fantasy ... now negates the existing real world, the "realistic" world, and prepares for that world a future.[94]

---

[92] For critical overviews of Jameson's writings, see: Helmling, *The Success and Failure of Fredric Jameson*; Kellner and Homer, *Fredric Jameson*; Roberts, *Fredric Jameson*; Tally, *Fredric Jameson*.

[93] My main guide for navigating Jameson's thought will be: Fitting, "The Concept of Utopia in the Work of Fredric Jameson." For further useful discussions, see: Alexander, "Jameson's Adorno and the Problem of Utopia"; Boeckmann, "Marxism, Morality, and the Politics of Desire"; Buchanan, "Metacommentary on Utopia, or Jameson's Dialectic of Hope"; Wegner, "Horizons, Figures, and Machines."

[94] Jameson, *Marxism and Form*, 111.

In this passage, we find the two key components of Jameson's understanding of utopianism: dialectics and negation. Jameson insists that social dreaming finds itself in a bind with the real world. This becomes visible when the utopian impulse fails to break free from the strictures of the status quo. Fictional representations of other worlds "bring home, in local and determinate ways, and with a fullness of concrete detail, our constitutional inability to imagine Utopia itself, and this, not owing to any individual failure of imagination but as the result of the systemic, cultural, and ideological closure of which we are all in one way or another prisoners."[95]

This passage points to a tension at the core of utopianism, forever wavering between its drive towards estrangement and the mesmerizing force of reality. Since our capacity to conjure alternatives to the status quo is affected by the material and ideological conditions of the present, this diagnosis appears to indicate that Jameson is rather cautious about utopianism's promise to critique and transform the world as we know it. Picking up earlier concerns by Frankfurt School scholars such as Marcuse, Horkheimer and Adorno, he is acutely aware that all artworks can be reinserted into, and domesticated by, the very system that they rebel against. Even the most radical challenges to the status quo frequently get transformed into consumable products, such as when a counterculture ends up "selling out."[96]

Does this imply that no space is left for critical and transformative interventions? Jameson's answer is a resounding no. Despite the impossibility of inducing a complete break with the status quo, artistic representations of other worlds exercise a reflective function that can unsettle a stable order whose continued existence hinges on barring the prospect of systemic alternatives.

"At best," Jameson notes, "Utopia can serve the negative purpose of making us more aware of our mental and ideological imprisonment ... and that therefore the best Utopias are those that fail the most comprehensively."[97] Failure here testifies to our powerlessness to liberate

---

[95] Jameson, "Progress versus Utopia; Or, Can We Imagine the Future?," 153.

[96] This late-capitalist form of reification is dissected in: Heath and Potter, *The Rebel Sell.*

[97] Jameson, *Archaeologies of the Future*, xiii.

ourselves entirely from the shackles that capitalist realism puts on our imagination and action. Attending to the ways in which utopian visions fall short can bring about a clearheaded reckoning with our complicity in the very processes of closure that social dreaming attempts to dismantle. Through this often-painful process of disillusionment, we acquire a "better sense of what it is about the future that we are unwilling or unable to imagine."[98]

So, if a complete unravelling of the status quo must remain a chimera, how do utopias subvert what is usually taken for granted? What remains of estrangement *for* the world, on this account? For Jameson, utopias necessarily target the ideological illusion of the unchangeability of the status quo:

> Disruption is, then, the name for a new discursive strategy, and Utopia is the form such disruption necessarily takes. And this is now the temporal situation in which the Utopian form proper ... has its political role to play, and in fact becomes a new kind of content in its own right. For it is the very principle of the radical break as such, its possibility, which is reinforced by the Utopian form, which insists that its radical difference is possible and that a break is necessary. The Utopian form itself is the answer to the universal ideological conviction that no alternative is possible, that there is no alternative to the system. But it asserts this by forcing us to think the break itself, and not by offering a more traditional picture of what things would be like after the break.[99]

Importantly, utopias have a negative thrust: they "dissolve" and "neutralize" the world from which they depart.[100] In his interpretation of Le Guin's *The Dispossessed*, Jameson identifies the novel's narrative device as "world reduction."[101] To reduce the world involves a transgression of society's common sense. As we have already observed, the fictional dissolution and neutralization of reality relies on a paradoxical operation, for the utopian impulse is by default ideologically imbricated, moulded by material conflicts here and now. Jameson insists on this point, by

---

[98] Jameson, "Utopia and Failure."
[99] Jameson, *Archaeologies of the Future*, 231–32.
[100] See: Jameson, "Of Islands and Trenches."
[101] Jameson, *Archaeologies of the Future*, 271.

underscoring the "inescapable situatedness in class, race and gender, in nationality, in history"[102] of all human beings. Here, again, it becomes apparent how the education of desire remains enmeshed with the sensations of lack and deprivation that give rise to social dreaming in the first place.

2.4 GALVANIZING AND CAUTIONING: TWO DEVICES OF UTOPIANISM

Let us now move from estrangement to utopianism's other mechanisms: galvanizing and cautioning. As we shall observe in the chapter on eco-modernism, the purpose of eutopias is, crudely, to mobilize an audience into resistant action when a situation seems particularly dire; in fact, so dire that people tend to give up all hope for seeing the world anew. The way mobilization works differs from story to story, but the overall argumentative and rhetorical strategy is always the same. By charting pathways out of the current crisis, eutopias radiate with positive, infectious energy. At the same time, these optimistic pictures also expose an inherent weakness of all eutopias: their tendency to collapse into wishful thinking.

The purpose of dystopias, by contrast, is completely different: to issue as clear a warning as possible. This admonition is supposed to shake an audience out of its apathy when coping with an existentially threatening situation. In the chapter on apocalyptic visions of a climate-changed world, I maintain that this cautionary pedagogy is precarious, for the bleak depiction of the future always runs the risk of paralyzing its addressees. If what is on the horizon is indeed so terrible, why should we even bother to fight back against the looming catastrophe? In short, defeatism accompanies dystopia as its constant shadow.

Understanding the precise nature of dystopias is so important because of the suspicion that they are not only engaged in a pessimistic form of social dreaming, but that they are anti-utopian altogether. I shall argue that this identification of dystopian thinking with anti-utopianism is misguided insofar as it ignores the ways in which its cautionary

---

[102] Jameson, 170.

pedagogy communicates anxiety about the future *in the right dosage*: dystopias leave space for the cultivation of a radical sort of hope (in Lear's sense) that banishes the shadow of defeatism. In other words, they do not stifle the basic dynamic from which all utopias spring; they only direct it in a direction that is very different from eutopias.

To buttress this claim, we first have to reconstruct the mainstream picture of dystopian thinking. Judith Shklar's position illustrates the identification of dystopias with anti-utopianism best.[103] Shklar, together with the other Cold War liberals we have already encountered, delivered one of the most acerbic indictments against utopianism in the twentieth century. Her plea for a "liberalism of fear," whose main characteristic lies in avoiding the "summum malum"[104] of cruelty, underpins this position. According to Shklar's view, utopian projects, with their promise of future redemption, embody a form of idealism that needs to be kept in check by bearing witness to, and actively remembering, historical instances of evil.

This "preoccupation with political evil"[105] has a further repercussion, though: despite her suspicion of utopianism, Shklar was convinced that depictions of totalitarian regimes may serve a productive goal – they alert people to the grave risks of social engineering.[106] That is why it is not surprising to learn that Shklar was an ardent admirer of George Orwell's *1984*, a genre-defining stalwart of the classical dystopian canon.[107] To put the wider links between dystopian thinking and the (Cold War) liberal mindset in a nutshell, "dystopias do fictionally what Popper, Hayek, Oakeshott, Dahrendorf, and other liberal thinkers do philosophically."[108]

---

[103] Note, though, that by focusing mostly on Shklar's late work, I am sketching a simplified version of the full story. As Katrina Forrester has demonstrated, Shklar's account of utopianism is more variegated than usually suspected. However, for presentational reasons it seems appropriate to foreground Shklar's anti-utopianism in this context. For it is surely true that Shklar and other Cold War liberals strongly influenced the dominant perception of realism as anti-utopian. See: Forrester, "Hope and Memory in the Thought of Judith Shklar." See also: Ashenden and Hess, *Between Utopia and Realism*.

[104] Shklar, "Liberalism of Fear," 29.

[105] Shklar, "Obligation, Loyalty, Exile," 181.

[106] See: Benhabib, "Judith Shklar's Dystopic Liberalism"; Rengger, "Realism Tamed or Liberalism Betrayed?"

[107] Shklar, "Nineteen Eighty-Four."

[108] Donskis, "The End of Utopia?," 197.

Given the emergence of Shklar's account from within a specific anti-totalitarian framework, it seems necessary, however, to unpick the straightforward equation of dystopias with anti-utopianism. So, what is it that dystopias do with the education of desire when they issue warnings about imminent dangers to society? To answer this question, we need to leave the Cold War liberal position behind and attend again to the contrast between eutopias and dystopias. If eutopias instigate social dreaming by casting a geographically or temporally distant society in a distinctively positive light, then dystopias do something else: they describe a "non-existent society ... in considerable detail and normally located in time and space that the author intended a contemporaneous reader to view as considerably worse than the society in which that reader lived."[109]

Gregory Claeys helpfully excavates the origins of dystopianism during two separate periods in European history, the first one in the aftermath of the French Revolution and the second one towards the end of the nineteenth century, when eugenics and socialism became predominant topics for authors such as Samuel Butler and William Morris.[110] Each of these epochs was characterized by social upheaval and technological innovation, which these writers made sense of by conjuring alternative worlds that were different from their historical background, yet recognizably derived from it.

The dystopian genre only came to full fruition when H. G. Wells, and later Aldous Huxley and George Orwell, started to pen their accounts of what the future of humanity might look like.[111] Their seminal additions to the twentieth-century canon – *Brave New World*[112] and *Nineteen*

---

[109] Sargent, "The Three Faces of Utopianism Revisited," 9.

[110] Claeys, "The Origins of Dystopia."

[111] As a "utopian pessimist," Wells was an especially interesting figure because he wrote both utopian – for example *A Modern Utopia* – and dystopian – for example *The Island of Dr. Moreau* – "scientific romances." Wells also played a crucial role in the dissemination of socialist ideas around the globe. See: Partington, *Building Cosmopolis*; Parrinder and Partington, *The Reception of H. G. Wells in Europe*; Bell, "Pragmatism and Prophecy"; Planinc, "Catching Up with Wells." It should be noted that Huxley, too, wrote a novel that clearly falls into the utopian genre: *Island*

[112] Huxley, *Brave New World.*

Eighty-Four[113] – exemplify that dystopias indeed frequently contain anti-utopian elements. The worlds imagined by Huxley and Orwell do not only portray societies marred by tremendous levels of oppression, they also put forth comprehensive critiques of utopianism itself. Their novels causally link the rise of state surveillance to organized plans for improving human nature through visions of an ideal, or even perfect society. As such, these narratives are, at least to some degree, anti-utopian by design, denouncing positive visions of the future as detrimental to collective welfare: the flawless society invented by utopians is disparaged as a nightmare from which nobody would escape. What we might call "classical" dystopias are, thus, suffused with a deep-seated anxiety about "technological modernity and psychological manipulation."[114] That is precisely why they appealed so intensely to Cold War liberals like Shklar.

Not all dystopias are saturated with such an anti-utopian animus, though.[115] This becomes evident once we devote attention to speculative fiction from the past thirty years. While the twentieth-century canon of dystopian writing is rather well known, recent developments within the genre have received less consideration. Tom Moylan's book *Scraps of the Untainted Sky* filled this lacuna by scrutinizing in detail the "maps of hell" that science fiction authors sketched in the 1980s. Moylan's contention is that the latest wave of dystopian writing rejects the anti-utopian impulse:

> From works such as Robinson's *Gold Coast* (1988) to Piercy's *He, She and It* (1991) and the series begun by Octavia Butler in *The Parable of the Sower* (1993), a discernible and critical dystopian movement emerged within contemporary science fiction and film that at its best reached toward Utopia not by delineation of fully detailed better places but by dropping in on decidedly worse places and tracking the moves of a dystopian citizen as she or he becomes aware of the social hell and – in one way or another, and not always successfully – contends with that diabolical place while moving toward a better alternative, which is often found in the recesses of memory or the margins of the dominant culture.[116]

---

[113] Orwell, *Nineteen Eighty-Four.*
[114] Claeys, *Dystopia,* 389.
[115] Sargent, "Utopia—The Problem of Definition," 138.
[116] Moylan, *Scraps of the Untainted Sky,* 106. The term "critical dystopia" was coined in an earlier work, however: Moylan, *Demand the Impossible,* chap. 1: Introduction: The Critical Dystopia.

This description conveys the strategic combination of hope and despair in these narratives. Critical dystopias construct alternative worlds in which human beings are subjected to severe adversity, but they leave room for the nurturing of hope. To appreciate the weaving together of hopeful and fearful motifs, let us recall the political moment during which critical dystopias first materialized.[117] The principal contributors to this sub-genre of speculative fiction, from Marge Piercy to Octavia Butler, all wrote in the shadow of Ronald Reagan's and Margaret Thatcher's reigns. In this context, the classical dystopian position, with its "militant pessimism"[118] and almost complete negation of hope, would have been self-defeating: when the semi-official slogan of a hegemonic worldview bars the prospect of a different order altogether, as *There Is No Alternative* does, dystopias that frustrate the yearning for a better future are at risk of deteriorating into a "fiction of helplessness and hopelessness."[119]

In order to eschew complicity with the neoliberal project, critical dystopias hence problematize naive forms of social dreaming that come close to wishful thinking. These narratives mine the "dystopian tradition in order to bring utopian and dystopian tendencies to bear on their exposés of the present moment and their explorations of new forms of oppositional agency."[120] We can envisage classical and critical dystopias in terms of a spectrum of standpoints: from an all-embracing denial of hope at one extreme to a more flexible negotiation of optimistic and pessimistic themes at the other.

If we look at contemporary debates around the Anthropocene, what we witness is, in fact, an analogous intermingling of hopeful and fearful motifs that reverberates with the scholarly diagnosis of a critical turn. While most visions of a climate-changed world tend to highlight one facet more than the other through their unique plot lines – ecomodernism contains eutopian ideals, while apocalyptic stories deploy dystopian tropes – they usually display elements of both hopeful and fearful

---

[117] Baccolini and Moylan, "Introduction: Dystopia and Histories."
[118] Moylan, *Scraps of the Untainted Sky*, 157.
[119] Lepore, "A Golden Age for Dystopian Fiction."
[120] Moylan, *Scraps of the Untainted Sky*, 198–99.

projections of the future. As a consequence, rather than conceiving of hope and despair as polar opposites, one of the intuitions behind this book is that we have to carefully study the shifting interfaces between them.

In abstract terms, we can begin this investigation by sketching a taxonomy of four ideal-typical imaginaries that reinforce utopian visions. Samuel R. Delany, himself a highly regarded author and prolific essayist, avers that speculative fiction can be divided, on the one hand, into positive stories set within a cityscape and those located in the country-side, from a *New Jerusalem* that "is the technological super-city where everything is bright and shiny and clean, and all problems have been solved by the beneficent application of science" to *Arcadia*, a "wonderful place where everyone eats natural foods and no machine larger than one person can fix in an hour is allowed in."[121]

On the other hand, both high-tech *New Jerusalem* and *Arcadia* comprise within themselves the seeds of their own disintegration. The dark mirror of the high-tech cityscape is *Brave New World*, where collective life is regimented and restricted. In *Brave New World*, machines have taken over control, and nature has been completely devastated. The foil of the bucolic countryside consists in the *Land of the Flies*, a space where nature strikes back with utter cruelty, punishing humanity through the sort of extreme weather events that we will encounter in the next chapter.

This taxonomy is helpful for placing within an instructive matrix various proposals for imagining a climate-changed world. To give just two examples that will continue to interest us: in the controversy around ecomodernism, the dichotomy between cityscape and countryside is foundational to the plea for a "good Anthropocene." While many ecomodernists conceive of a densely populated urban environment as a desirable *New Jerusalem*, their critics object that the blueprint for a humanity "decoupled" from nature will end up creating a *Brave New World*.

A similar logic is at play in Margaret Atwood's *MaddAddam* trilogy, and in (post-)apocalyptic narratives more widely, where an intentional community (the "God's Gardeners") organized around principles of sustainability yearns for the pastoral charm of *Arcadia*; but after the civilizational

---

[121] Delany and RMP, "On 'Triton' and Other Matters," 303.

Table 2.1 A taxonomy of utopianism

	Key Mechanism	Paradigmatic Example	Mode of Critique
Eutopia *If-Only*	Galvanizing	*New Jerusalem* *Arcadia*	Inflationary
Dystopia *If-This-Goes-On*	Cautioning	*Brave New World* *Land of the Flies*	Deflationary

breakdown, the plot moves into the murky territory of the *Land of the Flies*, a much bleaker vision for a disfigured humanity. Both these cases demonstrate that eutopian and dystopian motifs are not always easy to disentangle.

While it is important to note that hopeful and fearful perspectives are tied up with one another, it is equally necessary to comprehend how eutopias and dystopias exercise critique. Adapting Carl Freedman's thoughts on this matter, we might say that eutopian visions are *inflationary* in their outlook on the world, while dystopian visions are *deflationary*.[122]

What makes *New Jerusalem* and *Arcadia* paradigmatic cases of inflationary critique is that they explore ways of being and living otherwise that expand the material and ideological constraints of the status quo. Their hopeful aspect manifests itself in the assertion that things can be positively different, if only systemic modifications were undertaken. This is why I have spoken of the galvanizing appeal of eutopias – they interpellate us to acknowledge that the current order is not all that there is to our common world; another, better future can be imagined and thus enacted.

Dystopian narratives turn this picture upside down, by demolishing the assurances that the status quo still holds. *Brave New World* and the *Land of the Flies* thus embark on a deflationary critique. An important target of all dystopias is our investment in *false hope*, or what I will call, with Lauren Berlant, "cruel optimism" – a naive belief in redemption that makes the actual occurrence of catastrophic failure more, rather than less, likely.

---

[122] To be clear, Freedman does not distinguish between eutopian and dystopian visions but between film noir and science fiction. However, I utilize his framework for explaining the critical impact of both eutopian and dystopian stories. See: Freedman, "Marxism, Cinema and Some Dialectics of Science Fiction and Film Noir."

Let us close this section with a historical map. The so-called Hunt-Lenox globe from ca. 1500 CE contains a famous inscription: *HC SVNT DRACONES* – "here be dragons."[123] The makers of the globe also added visual cues as to what would await anyone foolish enough to disregard the warning and venture into this hazardous zone – monstrous creatures roam this haunted territory.[124]

For the early modern traveller and explorer, the cipher was primarily supposed to demarcate the limits of geographical knowledge. The mythological dragons served as an admonition that the cartographers simply did not know enough about that specific area. Anyone who ignored the globe's counsel would proceed at their own peril.[125] Metaphorically, "here be dragons" signifies with great precision how dystopias work. They pinpoint dangers and instruct their readers to change course and move in a different direction. They provide orientation, in other words.

2.5 WHY UTOPIAN PRACTICES MATTER

In the last two sections, I have zoomed in on the idea that utopias demystify the spell of the status quo's unchangeability. I now want to shift perspective and direct attention to the practical side of social dreaming. Both social movements, such as the World Social Forum alluded to previously and experiments in communal living, can be described as utopian. Even though they will not play a great role in the following reflections, due to my focus on only two facets of the utopianism (theory building and storytelling), we still need to acquire a rudimentary sense of the ways in which the education of desire can be put into practice.

We have already established that utopias employ estrangement so as to unsettle habitual patterns of thought and affect, galvanize an audience

---

[123] For an interpretation of that inscription in the context of utopianism, which deviates from mine, however, see: Tally, *Utopia in the Age of Globalization,* chap. Conclusion: Hic Sunt Dracones.

[124] On the historical use of monsters in maps see: Duzer, "Hic Sunt Dracones: The Geography and Cartography of Monsters."

[125] On this point see: Elahi, "Here Be Dragons ... Exploring the 'Unknown Unknowns.'"

to facilitate transformative action or caution readers about risks concealed from public purview. But, at least at first sight, this raises perplexing questions for utopias in practice: how can communities engage in utopian experiments without breaking up? In what ways do their actions disrupt the status quo without completely antagonizing wider society?

In trying to answer these questions, we should commence with an important clarification: utopian practices have always existed alongside, and in exchange with, theory building and storytelling.[126] They contest some of the core values of the society wherein they are enacted – a basic disposition that these experiments share with fictional texts negating and dissolving the status quo. The most prevalent form that these practical experiments have historically taken is in so-called intentional communities.[127] Sargent defines an intentional community "as a group of five or more adults and their children, if any, who come from more than one nuclear family and who have chosen to live together to enhance their shared values or for some other mutually agreed upon purpose."[128] Retreating from mainstream society is another key feature of intentional communities. Sargisson explains that

> intentional communities are at once inside and outside the wider community. They are embedded. They stem from it. They are part of it. However, they exist because they are deeply critical of dominant norms, values, and practices … Intentional communities necessarily operate at a normative and spatial distance from the wider community. This distance creates self-marginalisation, which permits them to function as Utopian spaces inside which members may explore visions of the good life. This self-marginalisation is necessary and difficult to endure because intentional communities pertain to the real: they are Utopian but not outopic; they contain real people who need sustainable relationships inside and beyond their chosen communities.[129]

---

[126] Sargent, *Utopianism*, chap. 2: Utopian Practice.

[127] For representative publications from different disciplines, see: Brown, *Intentional Community*; Sargisson and Sargent, *Living in Utopia*; Kozakavich and Nassaney, *The Archaeology of Utopian and Intentional Communities*.

[128] Sargent, "The Three Faces of Utopianism Revisited," 14–15.

[129] Sargisson, "Strange Places," 411.

This passage shows that shifting between insider and outsider perspectives is pivotal for how intentional communities produce and negotiate estrangement. Moreover, Sargisson shows that inhabiting such sites is an often painful experience that strains interpersonal bonds and puts pressure on individual identity. Self-marginalization is hard to sustain over long periods of time.[130]

So, experiments in communal living, epitomized by intentional communities, are grounded in the quotidian experiences of those who enact utopian visions through embodied forms of resistance and dissidence.[131] Two examples will help us see how this can be accomplished: Davina Cooper's observations on "everyday utopias" and Erik Olin Wright's account of "real utopias." Instead of merely scrutinizing abstract ideas, Cooper demonstrates how particular milieus can be turned into spaces for emancipatory practices. Her book *Everyday Utopias* examines utopias through the lens of ordinary encounters in settings designed for communal promise and hope. She defines these sites as everyday utopias,

> networks and spaces that ... perform regular daily life in a radically
> different fashion. Everyday utopias don't focus on campaigning or advo-
> cacy. They don't place their energy on pressuring mainstream institutions
> to change, on winning votes, or on taking over dominant social structures.
> Rather they work by creating the change they wish to encounter, building
> and forging new ways of experiencing social and political life.[132]

Far from being figments of the imagination, these practical utopias thus strive to actualize the utopian desire for change in the here and now. This drives them beyond the realm of imaginative processes into the sphere of contentious politics, albeit on a small scale. While social transformation might be an ulterior ambition of utopias such as the ones examined by Cooper, their chief objective is to salvage, through "alternative ways of living," emancipatory potentials from within existing

---

[130] This experience of hardship also seems to resonate with what we know about prefigurative politics. On the psychological processes at play in prefigurative projects, see: Lin et al., "Engendering the Prefigurative"; Trott, "Constructing Alternatives"; Wallin-Ruschman and Patka, "Learning From Critical Collective Spaces."

[131] Davis, "History, Politics, and Utopia."

[132] Cooper, *Everyday Utopias*, 2.

power structures. Cooper demonstrates this through a detailed analysis of various case studies, ranging from local exchange trading schemes in the United Kingdom to spaces for casual sex for women in Toronto.

This project of excavating emancipatory purposes – to refer back to Levitas' notion of utopianism's archaeological mode – has also been pursued by scholars outside utopian studies. Perhaps the most elaborate proposal to this effect can be found in Erik Olin Wright's *Real Utopias Project*. In collaboration with a group of political economists and philosophers, Wright endeavoured to recuperate counter-hegemonic practices and institutions from within the capitalist system. The underlying research agenda affirms the

> tension between dreams and practice. It is grounded in the belief that what is pragmatically possible is not fixed independently of our imaginations, but is itself shaped by our visions ... What we need, then, is "real utopias": utopian ideals that are grounded in the real potentials of humanity, utopian destinations that have accessible waystations, utopian designs of institutions that can inform our practical tasks of navigating a world of imperfect conditions for social change.[133]

Wright and his associates embrace the concept of a "real utopia" in order to explore the potential of actually existing practices and institutions that embody ideals of emancipation.[134] Examples of what they deem real utopias deviate from Cooper's everyday experiments and comprise worker cooperatives, such as the Mondragón Corporation in the Basque country, participatory budgeting in the Global South or proposals for a universal basic income.

The *Real Utopias Project* appears to be animated by a yearning for reconciliation, for its "point is to sustain our deepest aspirations for a just and humane world that does not exist, while also pursuing the practical task of building real-world alternatives."[135] Thus, Wright's plea for a "real utopianism" is driven by the wish to spur progressive action in a world that bears the hallmarks of injustices and exclusions. Wright's

[133] Wright, *Envisioning Real Utopias*, 6.
[134] Wright, "Transforming Capitalism through Real Utopias."
[135] Wright, "How to Be an Anticapitalist Today."

thoughts on the recalcitrance of capitalism are symptomatic of this wish: transformation can only occur if progressive actors creatively combine anarchist ("interstitial") with social-democratic ("symbiotic") techniques of upsetting the current order.[136] Capitalism is so entrenched that nothing can seriously jeopardize its stability. Revolutionary action, which Wright associates with "ruptural" transformation, is bound to failure due to the fixity of the state apparatuses protecting the economy. Real utopias, however, reveal that the hope for a different future can be kept alive, even if the option of a radical break with the status quo needs to be relinquished, or at least suspended for the time being.

What we can learn from both Cooper's analysis of different spaces of communal hope and Wright's engagement with experiments in alternative economy is that the desire for other ways of being and living is not only educated through interventions by social and political theorists or authors of speculative fiction, but also by activists and citizens. Their initiatives aim to prove that another world is indeed possible, to once again cite the evocative and powerful slogan of the World Social Forum. While compromising with mainstream society is common in these utopias, they still play a crucial role in debunking the assertion that there is no meaningful and viable alternative to the way we live right now.[137]

Looking into the praxis of collective action, performed on different scales and with varying intensities, discloses that imagination and action are much harder to disentangle than one might initially presume. When Kim Stanley Robinson, the fiction writer I will be discussing in Chapter 4, remarks that "we're going to have to imagine our way out of"[138] the ecological crisis, he puts the finger on the nexus between imagination and action. Action without the input from estranging, galvanizing and cautioning theories and stories remains hampered by the bric-a-brac of routine politics, whose solutionist reflexes cannot provide orientation in these greatly deranged times. Conversely, figuring out novel ways of being and living in the Anthropocene without the expectation of critical and transformative action easily deteriorates into soliloquy. This implies

---

[136] Wright, *Envisioning Real Utopias*, chap. 8.

[137] For an argument to this effect, see: Thaler, "Peace as a Minor, Grounded Utopia."

[138] Robinson, *Sixty Days and Counting*, para. 58.11.

that, in the context of debates around utopianism, we should conceive of imagination and action as two sides of the same medal – "imaginaction," which requires us to "unite in one word what is indistinguishable in reality."[139]

To wrap up this chapter, we have seen how intricate the notion of utopianism as the education of desire actually is. In stark opposition to the anti-utopian critics, it seems plausible to recover an understanding of utopianism that does not rely on the idea of a perfect blueprint. Once this more refined picture emerges, we can also start appreciating the diverse mechanisms behind utopian projects. Estranging, galvanizing and cautioning are all key devices that empower social dreaming. But none of these mechanisms is without its own contradictions: estrangement, a dialectical process as we have observed, comes in at least two varieties – *for*, and *from*, the world; the wish to galvanize an audience into action always runs the risk of downplaying the obstacles lying ahead; and, finally, the stark warnings that dystopias issue can easily engender feelings of helplessness and hopelessness, thereby extinguishing the flame that must be kept ablaze in all utopian projects.

The following three chapters attempt to operationalize this multifaceted notion of utopianism. How exactly do *What-If* utopias generate estrangement? In what ways do *If-Only* utopias draw on galvanizing appeals? And are the warnings that *If-This-Goes-On* utopias administer always straightforward? Debates around climate change offer us propitious opportunities to answer these vexing questions.

---

[139] Willener, *The Action-Image of Society*, 134. For an application of the same idea, albeit taken in a different direction, see: Haran, "Instantiating Imaginactivism."

CHAPTER 3

What If

Planet Earth as an Actor

THE GOAL OF THIS CHAPTER IS TO FLESH out my first utopian constellation: the notion that our planet is alive, an actor in its own right, capable of mounting resistance against humanity's destructive inclinations. As outlined in Chapter 1, the plot line framing this type of utopia is the *What-If*, a meditation on the present and future that assumes the form of a thought experiment. Its purpose is to transform how we see the world, its narrative device is estrangement. In one way or another, all the writers discussed here, through their fascination with what are often far-fetched scenarios, embark on a *What-If* inquiry that throws new and surprising light on our world, here and now.

The aim of this speculative exercise is not escapism, even though this accusation has been frequently levelled against utopian projects. Rather, it is to estrange us *for*, not *from* the world. The idea is that we acquire a better sense of reality once we perceive its hegemonic articulations as what they are: constructs that have a history and are hence amenable to comprehensive change. In the case of climate change, this mechanism of first distancing us from the status quo, through imaginative theories and stories, before forcing us "back to Earth," is crucial for demonstrating that things could be otherwise. Such defamiliarization is sparked by what we have glossed before as "planet-centred," as opposed to human-centred thinking about the Anthropocene.

Like the other two cases, this utopian constellation meshes together eutopian and dystopian motifs. My interlocutors in this chapter brand unambiguously positive visions of the future as naive and misguided; at the same time, they refuse to endorse catastrophist perspectives on a climate-changed world. This ambiguity turns *What-If* inquiries into sites of vivid debate, but it also leaves them open to an objection about indeterminacy. What ought to follow in terms of practical action from these chronicles of estrangement is a question that requires careful unpacking.

I have already hinted at the internal structure the substantive chapters: my approach is to juxtapose theory building and storytelling in such a way as to allow for mutually illuminating insights. To achieve this goal, I will bring together one of today's most prolific social theorists (Bruno Latour) with a rising star of science fiction and fantasy writing (N. K. Jemisin).

3.1 EARTHBOUND UTOPIANISM: REVISITING THE GAIA HYPOTHESIS

I have no utopia to propose, no critical denunciation to proffer, no revolution to hope for: the most ordinary common sense suffices for us to take hold, without a minute of apprenticeship, of all the tools that are right here at hand.[1]

If, as the old maxim maintains, "politics is the art of the possible," there still need to be arts to multiply the possibles.[2]

Do we continue to nourish dreams of escaping, or do we start seeking a territory that we and our children can inhabit?[3]

In this section, my objective is to reconstruct the so-called Gaia hypothesis as a distinctly utopian project, focusing in particular on its recent appropriation by Bruno Latour. The Gaia hypothesis is one of several ideas that foreground the connectedness, and indeed interpenetration, of human culture with the natural environment. This existential entanglement in which our species finds itself has been captured through different philosophical vocabularies and on the basis of various research agendas: from Donna Haraway's notions of "becoming-with" and "kin-making" in the Chthulucene[4] to Jane Bennett's study of thing-

---

[1] Latour, *Politics of Nature*, 163.
[2] Latour, *Facing Gaia*, para. 14.4.
[3] Latour, *Down to Earth*, 5.
[4] Haraway, *When Species Meet*; Haraway, *Staying with the Trouble*.

power,[5] the current discussion is rife with positions that unsettle anthro-pocentric frameworks. The kind of critique that these approaches mobil-ize is also, I shall argue, the central driver behind the Gaia hypothesis. In order to vindicate this idea, I begin with an account of the origins of the hypothesis, which will then be followed by a reconstruction of Latour's interpretation. The section's final part is dedicated to explaining why it might be illuminating to signify Latour's Gaia as utopian in character.

Before I continue, a caveat: in some sense, it might seem curious to portray Latour's project in this manner: *Facing Gaia* and *Down to Earth*, as well as his earlier writings, contain merely a few scattered references to the idea of utopianism, and almost all of them appear to be dismissive. The resounding plea one can detect in all of Latour's writings is for more realism and more common sense, for us to finally get back "down to Earth," to stop hallucinating of escape, to once and for all jettison the quest for other worlds.

Despite this, my contention in the following is that Latour's *New Climate Regime* amounts to a utopian enterprise. This claim can be fleshed out with the support of the theoretical apparatus outlined in Chapter 2. I will thus read Latour against the grain, positing that his account of politics in the Anthropocene entails a commitment to educate our desire for being and living otherwise. Latour thus falls into the same trap as many anti-totalitarian critics when he assimilates social dreaming to wishful thinking.

3.1.1 THE GAIA HYPOTHESIS: ORIGINS AND APPROPRIATIONS.

Before turning to Latour, we need to acquire a sense of the wider controversy into which his account intervenes. The Gaia hypothesis was first formulated in the late 1960s by the inventor and chemist James Lovelock.[6] Lovelock himself had been inspired by the writer William Golding – of *The Lord of the Flies* fame – to name his theory of planetary

---

[5] Bennett, *Vibrant Matter*.

[6] For a book-length treatment of the idea, see: Ruse, *The Gaia Hypothesis*. For a biography, see: Gribbin and Gribbin, *He Knew He Was Right*. Lovelock also wrote an autobiography: Lovelock, *Homage to Gaia*.

self-regulation after a Greek goddess.[7] The hypothesis' intellectual background is thus entwined with Western images of humanity and nature.

In ancient mythology, Gaia embodies Earth as one of the four primal forces, together with Tartaros, Chaos and Eros.[8] Hesiod's *Theogony* tells the story of how Gaia gave birth to hills and the sea, and how, with Ouranos (Sky/Heaven), she conceived the Titans.[9] Since Zeus is the son of Kronos, Gaia's and Ouranus' youngest son, Gaia stands at the very beginning of the Olympian Gods' genealogy. Lovelock therefore tapped into a deep well of mythical imagery – a decision that would influence the scientific and public uptake of the hypothesis.

The Gaia hypothesis emerged from an intuition that first dawned on Lovelock when he was working at the NASA laboratory in Pasadena, studying whether there could be life on Mars. Lovelock turned this puzzle on its head and asked how a Martian would go about ascertaining whether Earth was full of life. The answer, for Lovelock, comes down to the observation that our planetary atmosphere remains in a permanent state of disequilibrium, which can only be explained by the continued existence of biological organisms. The physical detection of life on Mars would hence have to isolate a similar kind of chemical imbalance – which was simply not warranted by experimental observation of the planet's atmospheric composition.[10]

What, then, explains the fact that Earth's atmosphere is alive? Lovelock's thought, which he kept on elaborating in a career spanning more than fifty years, revolves around the "hypothesis that the entire

---

[7] Lovelock himself recalls the moment the Gaia figure was proposed to him: "It came about in the 1960s when the author William Golding, who subsequently won the Nobel and many other prizes, was a near neighbor and friend. We both lived in the village of Bowerchalke, twelve miles southwest of Salisbury in southern England. We would often talk on scientific topics on walks around the village or in the village pub, the Bell Inn. In 1968 or 1969, during a walk, I tried out my hypothesis on him; he was receptive because, unlike most literary figures, he had taken physics while at Oxford as an undergraduate and fully understood the science of my argument. He grew enthusiastic and said, 'If you are intending to come out with a large idea like that, I suggest that you give it a proper name: I propose "Gaia"'" (Lovelock, *The Vanishing Face of Gaia*, 196).

[8] Hard, *The Routledge Handbook of Greek Mythology*, 24.

[9] Hesiod, *Theogony*, 27. The youngest titan, Kronos, then uses a sickle to castrate his own father, finalizing the separation of Earth and Sky/Heaven.

[10] Lovelock, "A Physical Basis for Life Detection Experiments."

range of living matter on Earth, from whales to viruses, and from oaks to algae, could be regarded as constituting a single living entity, capable of manipulating the Earth's atmosphere to suit its overall needs and endowed with faculties and powers far beyond those of its constituent parts."[11] This view of our planet as composed of myriad organisms, which are entangled in feedback loops with their environment, has implications for our understanding of life itself. This is why Lovelock has ever since been so vehemently lambasted by rival biologists, especially by neo-Darwinians who object to the Gaia hypothesis on the grounds that the planet itself cannot figure as a unit for natural selection processes.[12]

If the Earth's organisms regulate their environment in such a way as to establish homeostatic conditions for making life possible, then we must conclude that our planet itself is, in some sense, alive. Gaia might thus be defined "as a complex entity involving the Earth's biosphere, atmosphere, oceans, and soil; the totality constituting a feedback or cybernetic system which seeks an optimal physical and chemical environment for life on this planet."[13]

This diagnosis of a living planet, encompassing feedback loops between organisms and their environment, has given rise to accusations of Lovelock being a neo-pagan mystic whose deep ecology would make a mockery of scientific methods.[14] Lovelock sought to respond to these allegations by constructing theoretical models, such as *Daisyworld*, to prove that planetary self-regulation through looping mechanisms between organisms was feasible in the absence of teleology.[15] Via simulations, he thus aimed to demonstrate why and how a planet's system of life – its biosphere – can establish long-term homeostasis through natural selection. In other words, no intentional design, no master plan, would

---

[11] Lovelock, *Gaia*, 9.

[12] This critique is prominently put forth by Richard Dawkins in: *The Extended Phenotype*, 234–36.

[13] Lovelock, *Gaia*, 10.

[14] Ruse, "Earth's Holy Fool?"

[15] Watson and Lovelock, "Biological Homeostasis of the Global Environment." For later reformulations, see: Lenton and Lovelock, "Daisyworld Is Darwinian"; Lenton and Lovelock, "Daisyworld Revisited." On the model's epistemological assumptions, see: Dutreuil, "What Good Are Abstract and What-If Models?"

be necessary for self-regulation on a planetary level to succeed, because biotic communities manage to adjust and regulate their environment's chemical processes.[16]

Lovelock went on to expand his framework by collaborating with the microbiologist Lynn Margulis.[17] Sharing Lovelock's aversion to the animist connotations of the name-giving mythological figure, Margulis tried in her own research to correct the impression that their shared project conceived of Earth as a single organism, preferring instead to capture Gaia in terms of "an emergent property of interaction among organisms, the spherical planet on which they reside, and an energy source, the sun."[18]

Before turning to Latour's engagement with the Gaia figure, a quick word on Lovelock's later reception. Throughout his career, Lovelock has been stressing his commitment to a "mechanistic, reductionistic tradition of Western science."[19] The invention Lovelock is still most famous for is a device for producing and capturing electrons, which he developed in the 1950s.[20] It allowed the detection of very small particles, including pesticides in the environment. In fact, Lovelock's *Electron Capture Detector* was instrumental in launching the early phase of modern environmentalism: Rachel Carson's book *Silent Spring* would not have had such a momentous impact, had it not been based on reliable data regarding the harmful chemical compounds used in industrial agriculture.[21] That data was collected with the help of Lovelock's device.

And yet, the scientific dispute around the plausibility of the Gaia hypothesis keeps on evolving.[22] Lovelock himself has done his bit to stoke controversy as well: in recent years, he attempted to update the original theory, predicting that humanity is facing a cataclysmic showdown with Gaia. Climate change, according to Lovelock, has already

---

[16] Downing and Zvirinsky, "The Simulated Evolution of Biochemical Guilds."
[17] Lovelock and Margulis, "Atmospheric Homeostasis by and for the Biosphere."
[18] Margulis, *The Symbiotic Planet*, 149.
[19] Ruse, *The Gaia Hypothesis*, 180.
[20] Lovelock, "A Sensitive Detector for Gas Chromatography"; Lovelock, "The Electron-Capture Detector."
[21] Sella, "Lovelock's Detector."
[22] For the latest invective, see: Tyrrell, *On Gaia.*

reached a tipping point, making it all but inevitable that our planet will switch into a new geological phase, "one that could easily be described as Hell: so hot, so deadly that only a handful of the teeming billions now alive will survive."[23] Mankind is here portrayed as a deadly disease ravaging Gaia; a pathogen that our planet will defeat by eradicating its cause.

It is possible to observe a shift in the way Lovelock thought about Gaia throughout his long life: from a largely benign force that embodies the splendour of planetary self-regulation to a vengeful and vicious entity that fights for survival. In *The Vanishing Face of Gaia*, his final discussion of the Gaia motif (up until today), Lovelock strikes a similarly apocalyptic tone, prophesying that increasing temperatures will render the demise of vast swathes of the human population very likely. Given that "the hot Earth Gaia's metabolic needs can be met with a mere million or so humans, enough for the recycling of life's constituent elements,"[24] he forecasts that the majority of our species will not survive the imminent shock of accelerating climate disruptions.[25]

In his public statements since the 2000s, Lovelock has unfailingly taken issue with current designs for ecological sustainability, disputing, for example, the usefulness of established recycling schemes and praising the gains of nuclear energy.[26] Despite ongoing discussions around the Gaia hypothesis, there can be little doubt that Lovelock is more than merely an eccentric "maverick," as a major exhibition from 2015 in London's *Science Museum* suggested.[27] His ideas continue to inspire and provoke debate, including in fields of research for which the Gaia hypothesis was initially not intended.

---

[23] Lovelock, *The Revenge of Gaia*, 189.

[24] Lovelock, *The Vanishing Face of Gaia*, 249.

[25] Lovelock has in the meantime softened his stance. See: Harrabin, "Gaia Creator Rows Back on Climate."

[26] Aitkenhead, "James Lovelock"; Vaughan, "James Lovelock"; Lovelock, "We Need Nuclear Power, Says the Man Who Inspired the Greens." Lovelock also appears to be a supporter of Brexit and of some of its most dubitable advocates. See: Delingpole, "James Lovelock on Voting Brexit, 'Wicked' Renewables and Why He Changed His Mind on Climate Change."

[27] The exhibition was entitled "Unlocking Lovelock: Scientist, Inventor, Maverick." See: "Unlocking Lovelock."

3.1.2 LATOUR'S NEW CLIMATE REGIME. The lasting productivity of Lovelock's reflections can be seen in Bruno Latour's interpretation of the Gaia hypothesis. Latour is one of the most original and provocative sociologists today. His oeuvre spans fifteen monographs that have been translated into close to thirty languages. As one of the founders of so-called Actor Network Theory (ANT), Latour is widely considered a stalwart of Science and Technology Studies.[28] Given the enormous breadth of Latour's interests, ranging from ethnographic studies of laboratory life[29] to methodological reflections on scientific inquiry,[30] the purpose of this section cannot be to exhaustively summarize all his works.[31] To complicate matters further, Latour can hardly be classified as a scholastic academic: over the past twenty years he has maintained close contact with the arts, curating three exhibitions in Karlsruhe's ZKM, for example.[32] My goal is therefore to clarify how Latour appropriated the Gaia hypothesis and what status it occupies in his theorizing about politics more generally.

We have already seen that Lovelock's basic intuition of a living planet is amenable to competing appropriations, some of which assimilate the Gaia hypothesis to New Age obscurantism, while others underscore its explanatory potential in terms of rigorous hypothesizing. Latour takes a very pronounced stance on these issues: for him, Lovelock must be recognized as our age's Galileo, a free-thinking revolutionary whose visionary insights have been unfairly ostracized by the scientific community.[33]

---

[28] For a paradigmatic statement of ANT see: Latour, "On Actor-Network Theory." On the historical evolution of STS see: Jasanoff, "Genealogies of STS"; Law, "STS as Method."

[29] Latour and Woolgar, *Laboratory Life.*

[30] Latour, *We Have Never Been Modern.*

[31] For an introduction to Latour's oeuvre that strikes a helpful balance between in-depth explanation and broad surveys, see: Gertenbach and Laux, *Zur Aktualität von Bruno Latour.* For an outline of Latour's political stance, see: Harman, *Bruno Latour.*

[32] For the exhibition catalogues see: Latour and Weibel, *Iconoclash*; Latour and Weibel, *Making Things Public*; Latour and Leclercq, *Reset Modernity!* Latour was also appointed to co-curate the 2020 Taipei Biennale: Durón, "Taipei Biennial Names Bruno Latour and Martin Guinard-Terrin Curators for 2020 Edition." For a recent interview around Latour's relevance in the era of COVID-19, see: Watts, "Bruno Latour."

[33] Latour, "Bruno Latour Tracks Down Gaia."

Why is Lovelock so misrecognized within academia, even though the Gaia hypothesis has had a steep career in the wider public? An answer to this question depends, Latour posits, on comprehending what is actually at stake in this debate – a wholly different way of seeing the planet, with far-reaching repercussions for how we should live our lives.

To explain this, one first has to understand that Latour's approach to the Gaia hypothesis grew out of a long-term interest in the politics of nature. A key motif in his sociological thinking concerns the distinction between culture and nature. Where and how we draw the border between (human) culture and (non-human) nature is foundational to what we call "modernity," whose current transformation is "taken as a chance to assemble 'parliaments of things.'"[34] Latour suggests that, once we acknowledge that a separation of culture and nature cannot be consistently sustained, novel forms of doing politics will become available to us.

This opportunity is especially palpable in the context of environmental politics. Against prevailing mantras, Latour maintains that "political ecology has nothing to do, or rather, *finally no longer* has anything to do with nature, still less with its conservation, protection, or defense."[35] Conserving, protecting and defending nature is elusive, Latour maintains, because nature simply does not exist anymore. There is no such thing as a natural sphere that could be observed in isolation from human interference.

As a romantic invention, the idea of pristine nature serves to stabilize and reify the opposing idea of human culture; it thus cannot supply a basis for humanity's reckoning with its environment. In repudiating the nature/culture dyad, Latour positions his project systematically "after nature."[36] A political ecology "after nature" demands that we stop viewing nature as valuable in itself.[37] As a consequence, deep ecology

[34] Latour, "Is Re-modernization Occurring – And If So, How to Prove It?," 44.

[35] Latour, *Politics of Nature*, 19, italics in original.

[36] The phrase "after nature" has become a mainstay in reflections around the Anthropocene. For early explorations of the idea see: Cronon, "The Trouble with Wilderness; or, Getting Back to the Wrong Nature"; McKibben, *The End of Nature*.

[37] Jedediah Purdy expresses the underlying intuition succinctly: "The Anthropocene finds its most radical expression in our acknowledgment that the familiar divide between

amounts to a dead end for Latour because it remains committed to the untenable opposition between culture and nature.[38]

In order to re-politicize humanity's engagement with nature, a fundamental rethink is required. This is where the Gaia figure comes to the fore, as a thought experiment that advances what Latour labels the *New Climate Regime*. A first step in that direction can be found in Latour's proposal for a "parliament of things," in which the conventional institutions of politics are adapted to stage productive interactions between humans and non-humans.[39] Importantly, and despite the metaphor of a parliament, this plan goes beyond humans merely representing the interests of voiceless non-human beings, for the sake of safeguarding their welfare.[40] Latour wants to break with this caretaker model of proxy representation in a dramatic fashion, by foregrounding the integral agency of what would normally be considered the apolitical "natural sphere."

people and the natural world is no longer useful or accurate. Because we shape everything, from the upper atmosphere to the deep seas, there is no more nature that stands apart from human beings. There is no place or living thing that we haven't changed. Our mark is on the cycle of weather and seasons, the global map of bioregions, and the DNA that organizes matter into life. It makes no sense now to honor and preserve a nature that is defined by being not human, that is purest in wilderness, rain forests, and the ocean. Instead, in a world we can't help shaping, the question is what we will shape" (*After Nature*, para. 6.6).

[38] In response to Latour's diatribe against more traditional ecological models, one could point to forms of protecting and defending nature that are not premised on the idealization of nature at the expense of culture. Indeed, it seems possible to establish a commitment to conserving "wild nature" that remains thoroughly political: as an environmentalist strategy for resisting the logic of mastering the planet. Latour believes that such a strategy would be inescapably tarnished by the contradictions of modernity. But this need not be the case. For a recent vindication of this perspective, which critiques the proposal of collapsing the nature/culture dichotomy, see: Maris, *La part sauvage du monde*. For a similar argument in defence of "naturalness" see: Hettinger, "Naturalness, Wild-Animal Suffering, and Palmer on Laissez-Faire."

[39] On this issue, see: Simons, "The Parliament of Things and the Anthropocene."

[40] For a defence of such "proxy representation" for animals, see: Donaldson and Kymlicka, *Zoopolis*. For the wider debate see: Cochrane, *An Introduction to Animals and Political Theory*; Cochrane, *Sentientist Politics*; Wissenburg and Schlosberg, *Political Animals and Animal Politics*; Tănăsescu, *Environment, Political Representation, and the Challenge of Rights*.

Lovelock's ideas enabled Latour to take further steps towards a wholesale "redefinition of the political."[41] The 2013 Gifford Lectures at the University of Edinburgh provided a welcome opportunity to subject the Gaia hypothesis to closer scrutiny, deepening his engagement with questions of political ecology. *Facing Gaia*, published four years after the talks, contains a systematic analysis of Lovelock's oeuvre. Right from the start, Latour gives short shrift to the misinterpretation of Gaia as a harmonious figure, reasoning that there is "nothing maternal about her – or else we have to revise completely what we mean by 'Mother'! If she needed rituals, these were surely not the nice New Age dances invented later to celebrate the postmodern Gaia."[42]

In dispensing with the caring image of Gaia, Latour unearths a tension within Lovelock's reflections on planetary self-regulation. Putting a name on the complex web of feedback loops between organisms and their environment makes it appear as if the planet were constituted as a whole, standing above the tangled connections beneath it. However, this rendering of Gaia is based on a misunderstanding, as Latour points out:

> The whole originality ... of Lovelock's enterprise is that he plunges head first into an impossible question: how to obtain effects of connection among agencies without relying on an untenable conception of the whole. He sensed that extending the metaphor of organism to the Earth was senseless, and that micro-organisms were nevertheless indeed conspiring by sustaining the long-term existence of this critical zone within which all living entities are combined. If he contradicts himself, it is because he is fighting with all his might to avoid the two pitfalls while trying to trace the connections without taking the Totality route.[43]

Dismantling the notion of Gaia as a totality becomes possible because Lovelock extends the ability of shaping their environment to not only non-human animals, but also to "trees, mushrooms, algae, bacteria, and

---

[41] Latour, *Politics of Nature*, 6.
[42] Latour, *Facing Gaia*, para. 9.18.
[43] Latour, para. 9.64.

viruses."[44] Latour argues that "the capacity of humans to rearrange everything around themselves is a *general property of living things*. On this Earth, no one is passive."[45]

Agency is, in other words, much more broadly distributed than either evolutionary biologists or social scientists, philosophical ethicists and political theorists would normally assume.[46] Such a comprehensive dispersal of the ability to act also affects the notion of subjectivity: "To be a subject is not to act autonomously in front of an objective background, but to share agency with other subjects that have also lost their autonomy. It is because we are now confronted with those subjects – or rather quasi-subjects – that we have to shift away from dreams of mastery as well as from the threat of being fully naturalized."[47]

What is so puzzling about this view of globally dispersed agency is that it immediately arouses accusations of animism: the Gaia figure, with its mythological origins, spurs these allegations, even though Latour attempts to hold them at bay. Boiled down to a succinct formula, the essence of Latour's understanding of Gaia can hence be summarized as "*connectivity without holism.*"[48]

Letting go of "dreams of mastery" does not only affect the modern notion of nature, but also demolishes the metaphor of Gaia as a well-oiled machine, which remains operative in cybernetic accounts of the Earth system:

> Understanding the entanglements of the contradictory and conflictual connections is not a job that can be accomplished by leaping up to a higher "global" level to see them act like a single whole; one can only make their potential paths cross with as many instruments as possible in order to have a chance to detect the ways in which these agencies are connected among themselves.[49]

---

[44] Latour, para. 9.70.

[45] Latour, para. 9.70, italics in original.

[46] Despite diverging from Latour's account in various respects, Jane Bennett develops a similar account of the "agency of assemblages." See: Bennett, *Vibrant Matter.*

[47] Latour, "Agency at the Time of the Anthropocene," 5.

[48] Latour, "Why Gaia Is Not a God of Totality," 75, italics in original. Indeed, this slogan could even stand in for all of ANT. See: Gertenbach and Laux, *Zur Aktualität von Bruno Latour,* 248.

[49] Latour, *Facing Gaia,* para. 10.90.

This perspective allows Latour to shed new light on the concept of the Anthropocene. As remarked in Chapter 1, our climate-changed world can be interpreted in radically divergent ways: either in terms of a triumphalist proclamation of humanity's control over nature, or as mankind's humbling absorption into the realm of nature. Both of these readings fall short, according to Latour, because they remain indebted to the modern understanding of nature as the polar opposite of human culture.

Importantly, Latour rejects the thought that there is such a thing as a unified humanity, which should be held jointly responsible for climate change: humans are much too unequally endowed with the power to harm the ecosphere to be treated as a collective agent with equal liability.[50] Latour is especially scathing in his critique of those who trust that Gaia can be subdued, for instance through geoengineering projects. We will encounter these proposals in more detail in Chapter 4, which discusses eutopian dreams of mastering a climate-changed world. An "optimistic version of the Anthropocene"[51] is delusional, for it elevates humanity to a position of absolute dominion over nature. This project is doomed to failure. Since Gaia is no machine, it cannot be manipulated or optimized. Realizing this has important consequences:

> Facing the Anthropocene, once the temptation to see it simply as a new avatar of the schema "Man facing Nature" has been set aside, there is probably no better solution than to work at disaggregating the customary characterizations until we arrive at a new distribution of the agents of geohistory – new peoples for whom the term human is not necessarily

---

[50] "Speaking of the 'anthropic origin' of global warming is meaningless, in fact, if by 'anthropic' we mean something like 'the human species.' Who can claim to speak for the human in general without arousing a thousand protests at once? Indignant voices will be raised to say that they do not hold themselves responsible in any way for these actions on the geological scale – and they will be right! The Indian nations deep in the Amazonian forest have nothing to do with the 'anthropic origin' of climate change – at least so long as politicians running for election haven't given them chain saws. The same can be said of the poor residents in Bombay's shantytowns, who can only dream of having a carbon footprint more significant than the one left by the soot from their makeshift stoves" (Latour, para. 11.31).

[51] Davis and Latour, "Diplomacy in the Face of Gaia," 49.

meaningful and whose scale, form, territory, and cosmology all have to be redrawn. To live in the epoch of the Anthropocene is to force oneself to redefine the political task par excellence: what people are you forming, with what cosmology, and on what territory?[52]

The Anthropocene, duly understood, thus heralds the beginning of a *New Climate Regime*, shaping social identities and humans' relations to one another and to the non-human world. This novel kind of ecology is political in the sense that it acknowledges the conflictual encounters between humanity and its environment.[53] In the *New Climate Regime*, our species may suddenly find itself in an asymmetrical confrontation with Gaia, in a war "that we can only lose: if we win, we lose; if we lose, we still lose."[54]

Towards the end of *Facing Gaia*, Latour paints a multifaceted picture of Gaia that stresses humanity's responsibility to react to planetary changes with care and consideration. At this stage, he also introduces a distinction between two kinds of actors engaging with the environment: humans and Earthbound.

> Every conception of the new geopolitics has to take into account the fact that the way the Earthbound are attached to Gaia is totally different from the way humans were attached to Nature. Gaia is no longer *indifferent* to our actions. Unlike the Humans in Nature, the Earthbound know that they are contending with Gaia. They can neither treat it as an inert and mute object nor as supreme judge and final arbiter. It is in this sense that they no longer enter into an infantile mother–child relation with Gaia. The Earthbound and the Earth have grown up. Both parties share the same fragility, the same cruelty, the same uncertainty about their fate. They are powers that cannot be dominated and cannot dominate. As Gaia is neither external nor indisputable, it cannot remain indifferent to politics. Gaia can treat us as enemies. We can respond in kind.[55]

---

[52] Latour, *Facing Gaia*, para. 11.98.

[53] This fact also explains Latour's turn to Carl Schmitt. On Latour's fascination with Schmitt, which predates his interest in the Gaia hypothesis, see: Harman, *Bruno Latour*, chap. 6: "An Interesting Reactionary": Latour's Right Flank.

[54] Latour, *An Inquiry into Modes of Existence*, 485. For a discussion, see: Danowski and Castro, *The Ends of the World*, chap. 7: Humans and Terrans in the Gaia War.

[55] Latour, *Facing Gaia*, para. 14.60.

A shift from the old to the *New Climate Regime* entails, for Latour, relin-quishing fantasies of mastering Gaia. In Donna Haraway's terminology, being bound to and by Earth is a condition shared by all species, human as well as non-human.[56] Latour further expands on this thought in his latest book, *Down to Earth*. Where *Facing Gaia* analyzes how a political ecology after nature might look like, *Down to Earth* resembles a manifesto whose objective is narrower: to replace the Gaia figure with a new concept, the *terrestrial*, which for Latour represents a "new *political actor*."[57] *Down to Earth* thus spells out some of the lessons that the Gaia hypothesis has in store.[58]

The concept of the *terrestrial* helps Latour make sense of a cleavage that runs through contemporary politics: between the local and the global. The local and the global are the two main "attractors" of the current moment, pulling our societies in opposing directions. While the global encapsulates modernity in its expansionist drive, the local is the site wherein pushbacks against globalization occur. Latour explains the rise of populist movements, for example, as the result of transform-ations within the *New Climate Regime*. A return to the local, to the soil, is the promise that nativist populists offer their constituencies, yearning for a retreat into an imaginary, nostalgic realm that would shield them from the unwanted intrusions of globalization.

The *terrestrial* represents for Latour an idea that shows a way out of the impasse between the global and the local, by combining the most attract-ive dimensions of both: "The soil allows us to attach ourselves; the world allows detachment. Attachment allows us to get away from the illusion of a Great Outside; detachment allows us to escape the illusion of borders. Such is the balancing act to be refined."[59] So, simultaneously paying heed to soil as well as the world creates the basis for a responsible politics in the Anthropocene; one that accepts the entanglement of humans – or, more accurately, the Earthbound – with their environment.

---

[56] Haraway, *Staying with the Trouble*, 55.
[57] Latour, *Down to Earth*, para. 18.6, italics in original.
[58] On this point, see: Delbourgo, "No More EasyJet."
[59] Latour, *Down to Earth*, para. 28.11.

Latour also speaks of a fourth attractor in the present moment, the *Out-of-This-World*, the "horizon of people who no longer belong to the realities of an Earth that would react to their actions."[60] Climate change denial is a clear symptom of this condition, where the physical make-up of the real world is simply wished away. Latour considers both the global, the local and the *Out-of-This-World* as utopias, "places with no *topos*, without earth and without land."[61] Only by becoming terrestrial, by recognizing Gaia's immense clout over us, will we be able to establish more constructive relationships with the planet.

Although *Down to Earth* does not answer all the questions left open by Latour's appropriation of the Gaia hypothesis, it clearly demonstrates how not to proceed: neither the comforting return to the soil nor a speeding up of de-territorialized globalization will do.

So, what should we make of Latour's preferred alternative? In the following, I shall claim that, *pace* Latour's own pronouncements, the terrestrial, as well as its earlier incarnation, Gaia, are distinctly utopian visions. Interpreting Latour's reflections in this way uncovers a chief preoccupation of his entire project: the production of estrangement.

3.1.3 RE-TERRESTRIALIZE THIS! EARTHBOUND LIFE AS A UTOPIAN PROJECT.

In my reading of Latour's oeuvre, I will foreground three components: first, his peculiar anti-utopian utopianism; second, the centrality of estrangement for the Gaia figure; and third, the inter-mingling of hope and fear in Latour's modelling of an uncertain and risky future. Together, these features bring out two insights: they let us rectify a widespread error in the application of the label "utopia" and envisage Gaia and the terrestrial as utopian maps for the Anthropocene.

The first point to emphasize is that Latour's account echoes some of the anti-totalitarian objections we encountered in Chapter 2. The very terminology of being Earthbound is supposed to signal that the rival "attractors" of the global and the local are lacking an appropriate con-nection with a place that anchors sustainable relations between humans and their environment. In line with this conceptualization, the idea of

---

[60] Latour, para. 17.5.
[61] Latour, para. 20.21.

utopia possesses, throughout Latour's work, predominantly negative connotations.

Evidence for this sceptical appraisal is easy to find. In *Politics of Nature*, for example, he exhorts the virtues of common sense and contrasts the conjuring of other worlds with his own allegedly reconstructive effort to convene a "parliament of things." "Far from designing a world to come," Latour notes, "I have only made up for lost time by putting words to alliances, congregations, synergies that already exist everywhere and that only the ancient prejudices kept us from seeing."[62]

Put differently, the world right now is already governed by the sort of agents that his version of ANT seeks to explain; all that is needed is a coherent framework that makes those agents more amenable to scientific inquiry and political intervention. The revisited Gaia hypothesis, together with the notion of the terrestrial, supplies such a framework.

Facing Gaia and *Down to Earth* are therefore simultaneously premised on disenchanting fantasies of fleeing from planet Earth and on resisting the temptation of a homecoming to Mother Nature. Tellingly, the Earthbounds' motto should be *plus intra* (further inside), rather than the progressive and modern *plus ultra* (further ahead).[63] What transpires, then, is a plea for an interpretative model that politicizes ecological thinking and acting. "We shall try to rematerialize our existence," Latour pleads, "which means first of all reterritorializing it or, better, though the word does not exist, reterrestrializing it."[64] This proposal is meant as an alternative to social dreaming: "Gaia is the great figure opposed to utopia and uchronia."[65]

Given the evidence of Latour's aversion to utopianism, why would it still make sense to portray Gaia as a utopian figure, to conceive of

---

[62] Latour, *Politics of Nature*, 163.

[63] Latour, "Telling Friends from Foes in the Time of the Anthropocene."

[64] Latour, *Facing Gaia*, para. 14.60.

[65] Latour, para. 14.79. See also Latour's interpretation of being grounded on Earth: "Paradoxically, in view of determining their limits, the Earthbound have to pull themselves away from the limits of what they used to consider space: the narrow countryside they were so eager to leave behind, as well as the utopia of indefinite space they were so eager to reach. Geohistory requires a change in the very definition of what it means to have, hold, or occupy a space, of what it means to be appropriated by an Earth" (Latour, para. 14.83).

Earthbound life as a utopian experience? As I remarked in Chapter 2, it is a dominant trope of the anti-utopian canon to identify utopias with either daydreaming or social engineering. Latour seems to waver between these two positions, but he certainly does not take seriously the proposition that utopias could be conceptualized differently, for example along the lines of an education of the desire for other ways of being and living.

If we subscribe to this broader understanding of social dreaming, however, we manage to flesh out what exactly is distinctive about this "anti-utopian utopia."[66] For Latour clearly wants his engagement with Gaia to deliver more than just a factual report on the planetary condition. Any reflection on the Anthropocene will be sustained by evaluative judgements about what *should* be done about the ecological crisis. This is fully acknowledged by Latour himself:

> It is very, very difficult now to maintain the old idea of a division between statement of fact and statement of value when you say that "there is now 440 parts per million of CO2 in the atmosphere." Even if you say it as coldly as possible, it sends a message that you should do something. So, the division between fact and value, which is the traditional way of handling these questions, is weakened.[67]

Once we accept that the Gaia figure, as a framework for envisaging our climate-changed world, aims to educate the desire for being and living otherwise, we can explore the mechanisms whereby Latour hopes to achieve this goal. This brings us to the second aspect: that Gaia should be interpreted as a speculative exercise whose main purpose lies in disrupting conventional representations of the planet and our place within it. The crux of revisiting Lovelock is to alter how humans perceive themselves and their bonds with the environment.

Latour suggests that viewing Earth as deeply entangled gives rise to an entirely new kind of politics. Hence, he poses a typical *What-If* question, summoning us to imagine planet Earth as possessing agential powers:

---

[66] I borrow this idea from Lisa Garforth, who applies it to another of Latour's books. See: Garforth, "Book Review Symposium," 140–41.

[67] Davis and Latour, "Diplomacy in the Face of Gaia," 44.

how would we have to redescribe ourselves, as members of the human species, if we realized that the planetary ecosphere is more than just a resource to be consumed and destroyed?[68]

The Gaia hypothesis thus furnishes us with the means to dismantle deeply entrenched ideas about the world we share with others. The very thought of a living planet extends an invitation to change course in the most radical way possible. Through the stress on universal connectivity, human agency becomes constrained and encumbered in webs of intersecting feedback loops. Since Latour maintains that on this planet "no one is passive," our species must reckon with its own limitations.

Such a reorientation also denounces the hubris of techno-optimists. The Gaia figure serves as a bulwark against the ebullience of the ecomodernist proposals we will be analyzing in more detail in Chapter 4. This is why, throughout his oeuvre, Latour refrains from painting life under the *New Climate Regime* in rosy colours. In that sense, his vision of a political ecology "after nature" also confronts the hope that our planet might swiftly return to a state of comfortable inhabitability, once humans have reined in their environmentally destructive tendencies and developed cutting-edge technologies to mitigate and adapt to a climate-changed world.

Estrangement is therefore put to use with a very specific aim in mind: to thwart a conception of the Anthropocene that assigns humans a unique position that would be unattainable for other planetary actors. That is why Latour insists on Lovelock's insight into the self-regulatory capacity of life on Earth being as revolutionary for us today as Galileo's geocentric model was for astronomy in the seventeenth century.[69] Since we are locked into Gaia's "critical zone,"[70] everything we do – from the most mundane routines of everyday life to the higher strata of geopolitics – will have to be modified in light of our Earthbound existence. Visualizing the planet as a network of universal connections ignites a cognitive and affective spark to refashion our lifeworld's solid frames.

---

[68] I take the notion of "redescription" from: Vries, *Bruno Latour*, 199–200.

[69] Watts, "Bruno Latour."

[70] See: Latour and Lenton, "Extending the Domain of Freedom, or Why Gaia Is So Hard to Understand."

The disconcerting vista of an Earth where nobody and nothing is passive makes it imperative to think again what agency might mean for us humans. The utopia embedded in this account is thus profoundly relational. This is the practical upshot of Latour's defamiliarization strategy.

My third point concerns the intermingling of hope and fear in this portrayal of a living planet. As Latour's reflections on Gaia's vengeful side demonstrate, politics in the Anthropocene will continue to be conflictual and even deadly for some. Far from cementing a harmonious unity amongst all peoples, climate change has already exacerbated divisions within humanity, exposing fractures and liabilities in geopolitics. This is why Latour puts so much emphasis on diplomacy as the vehicle for fostering Earthbound relations.[71]

Given the prevalence of antagonism in Latour's account of Gaia, would it perhaps be more appropriate to label his project dystopian in character? Should we fear Gaia, as Lovelock counsels, rather than invest hope in the promise of a living planet? Both *Facing Gaia* and *Down to Earth* riff on dystopian themes, but Latour seems reticent to join those who see nothing but environmental apocalypse, civilizational breakdown and species extinction on the Anthropocene's horizon. Although the idea of a living planet punctures delusions of human exceptionalism, Latour also insists on its immense potentials: the notion of the Earthbound can provide orientation in this uncanny landscape, by unlocking a new space, somewhere between the local and the global, that satisfies our longing for an eco-social grounding.

We can sense in Latour's writings a leitmotif that will surface again at several points throughout this book. In many utopian projects, hope and fear are enmeshed with each other in ways that cannot be adequately captured if we conceive of them exclusively as either eutopias or dystopias. Gaia appears to be a figure on whom both inflationary and deflationary desires can be projected, weaving together prospects of great hope with fearful outlooks that are designed to admonish us about impending perils.

Drawing on Levitas' theorization of utopianism as a method, we can conclude that Latour primarily deploys an archaeological, rather than an

---

[71] Latour, "Why Gaia Is Not a God of Totality," chap. 5.

architectural, mode of exploring alternatives to the status quo, excavating what is already out there, albeit hidden from sight. The estrangement effect is central to the Gaia hypothesis: as a particular kind of imagining our climate-changed world, Gaia seeks to defamiliarize us from how we experience, both cognitively and affectively, our planetary existence. The upshot of this speculative exercise is a non-perfectionist recasting of humanity's place within the Anthropocene. The benefit of Latour's *What-If* plot line is that it renders unfamiliar what often appears to entirely natural and normal. When it comes to figuring out life in a climate-changed world, such a systemic interrogation of the status quo – such an anti-utopian utopianism – is urgently required.

The political implications of this process are uncertain, however. One of the downsides of utopias centred around estrangement (rather than galvanizing and cautioning) is that they are prone to indeterminacy; a tendency that affects the transformational aspect of utopianism. In other words, what exactly should be done once habitual patterns of seeing the planet have been undone, cannot be easily determined. This lack of concreteness is not incidental. Rather, it constitutes a structural feature that inheres in this particular constellation. As such, it cannot be avoided, only mediated through different theoretical and narrative moves, many of which are on full display in Latour's reflections.

Latour's thinking with and through Gaia symptomatically discloses the difficulties that *What-If* plot lines have to overcome. The indeterminacy of defamiliarization as a utopian mechanism, oscillating between estrangement *for* and estrangement *from* the world, manifests itself in Latour's stance vis-à-vis normativity and critique. Some commentators read Latour's diatribe against Critical Theory as emblematic of a general attitude of anti-normativity and anti-critique.[72] To be sure, there is plenty of fodder for their cannons.[73] As I have already remarked, Latour

---

[72] See, for example: Mills, "What Has Become of Critique?"; Noys, "The Discreet Charm of Bruno Latour."

[73] Such as when Latour provocatively notes that "[i]t might be time to put Marx's famous quote back on its feet: 'Social scientists have *transformed* the world in various ways; the point, however, is to *interpret* it'" (Latour, *Reassembling the Social*, 45). For the most comprehensive rebuttal of a critically oriented sociology, see: Latour, "Why Has Critique Run out of Steam?"

himself appears quite comfortable with his work on science and technology being categorized as "reconstructive," instead of "critical."[74] Others have answered that Latour's theory building needs to be evaluated in light of its unique normative and critical credentials.[75]

If my interpretation of the Gaia figure as utopian is accurate, then Latour's defenders are broadly on the right track: the panorama of a world in which agency is dispersed demands humanity to change direction. The questioning of the present that the Gaia figure instigates differs from the visions of the future we will be analyzing in the coming chapters. Neither galvanizing nor cautioning preoccupy Latour's project – even though both hope and fear do play roles in the development of another kind of political ecology. Rather, the thought experiment of a living planet is a speculative exercise that seeks to magnify our sense of the possible. It demonstrates why estrangement is so instrumental in educating the desire for being and living otherwise.

3.2 "BUILT ON A FAULT LINE OF PAIN, HELD UP BY NIGHTMARES": N. K. JEMISIN'S CHRONICLES OF ESTRANGEMENT

When a comm builds atop a fault line, do you blame its walls when they inevitably crush the people inside? No; you blame whoever was stupid enough to think they could defy the laws of nature forever. Well, some worlds are built on a fault line of pain, held up by nightmares. Don't lament when those worlds fall. Rage that they were built doomed in the first place.[76]

There's the idea that dystopia makes no sense when you're talking to people from certain marginalized groups. Because the society we live in is a dystopia to those people. To my ancestors who struggled to survive in a country that actively sabotaged them again and again and again and again and is still doing so, a country that claims to have gotten rid of slavery and yet snuck in a little clause in the Thirteenth Amendment to make it "teehee, still

---

[74] Katti, "Mediating Political 'Things,' and the Forked Tongue of Modern Culture," 98.
[75] See: McGee, *Bruno Latour.*
[76] Jemisin, *The Stone Sky*, para. 60.1.

possible," I mean, this society is and remains a dystopia. Dystopia is in the eye of the beholder.[77]

We have always had more than enough resources for everyone and we're capable of thinking up ways to come up with more. People who write science fiction do tend to be utopian thinkers. We do tend to think that we can achieve great things as a species. We just have to be willing to acknowledge what needs to be done to get there and sometimes the things that need to be done to get there are terrifying or can be terrifying to those in a position of privilege.[78]

How have science fiction and fantasy writers dealt with the utopian constellation of Earth as a living planet? Has climate fiction, broadly construed, come up with ideas and proposals that resonate with those we have come across in the Gaia hypothesis? To what extent, if at all, can utopian literature expand our understanding of the real world?

In this section, I shall approach these questions via a close reading of N. K. Jemisin's *Broken Earth* trilogy. To contextualize this reading, I begin with a discussion of fantasy literature and its relation to science fiction in general. This will be followed by a summary of the three books under scrutiny here. In my interpretation of Jemisin's novels, I home in on what I consider their central narrative object: not exactly Gaia, but something rather similar – an image of our planet as hostile and vindictive, yet also responsive to humanity's cautious negotiations and diplomatic efforts at reconciliation. Jemisin's fiction, I will show, can be seen as filling some of the gaps left open in Latour's theorizing. Conversely, the Gaia hypothesis can help us make sense of the *Broken Earth* trilogy. Thus, I contend that these two utopian visions of a climate-changed world can illuminate each other.

3.2.1 SHOULD THE SCIENCE FICTION/FANTASY DISTINCTION BE ABOLISHED?. Before delving into the text, let us take a step back and look at the genre of fantasy fiction. This will allow us to elucidate the storytelling-pole of this utopian constellation. N. K. Jemisin's *Broken Earth*

---

[77] Hurley and Jemisin, "An Apocalypse Is a Relative Thing," 471.
[78] Bereola, "A True Utopia."

trilogy is usually classified as a work of fantasy. Does such a classification matter? In some sense, it might seem irrelevant how we pigeonhole these award-winning books. What counts, from the point of view of an interdisciplinary investigation like this one, are their narrative and formal qualities as well as their ability to move the readers in specific directions.

But debates around genre boundaries are never only about scholarly labels. They also touch upon artistic sensibilities that are the result of power relations. So, it does matter how we categorize various narratives taking place on a far- or near-future Earth, for all such taxonomies shed light on what values we attach to specific kinds of storytelling.

In the following, I interrogate some of the existing genre conventions and ask whether we might want to abolish the science fiction/fantasy distinction altogether. My conclusion is ultimately that the distinction is much less stable than commonly assumed – which is not the same as saying that that it should not exist at all.

Fantasy, as a genre, possesses boundaries that are fuzzy. While common tropes and rhetorical techniques undoubtedly exist, they vary significantly across texts.[79] One definition of fantasy approximates it to both science fiction and utopia: "A fantasy text is a self-coherent narrative. When set in this world, it tells a story which is impossible in the world as we perceive it; when set in an otherworld, that otherworld will be impossible, though stories set there may be possible in its terms."[80]

A text's self-coherence can be established in different ways. A potential strategy for examining various types of fantasy would accordingly distinguish between "full fantasy" on the one hand, and stories that deploy fantastical elements in a more limited fashion, on the other hand. Full fantasy covers "stories of profound, all-transforming change."[81] As the archetypal example of such fantasy – J. R. R. Tolkien's *Lord of the Rings* – demonstrates, change always happens against the backdrop of an abundant fantasy land, an "otherworld" drawn with intricate details and immense depth.[82] What we typically find in full fantasy is an effort at

---

[79] On the porous borders around the fantasy genre, see: Attebery, *Strategies of Fantasy*, 10.
[80] Clute and Grant, "Fantasy," 338.
[81] Clute and Grant, "Fantasyland," 341.
[82] James, "Tolkien, Lewis and the Explosion of Genre Fantasy."

comprehensively building another world wherein the actual plot unfolds. When fantastical tropes are introduced in a more restricted manner, all-encompassing worldbuilding is usually absent. In such stories, elements of fantasy are presented in ways that do not depend on the existence of an elaborate fantasy land in the background.

In order to better comprehend what is distinctive about fantasy writing, let us return to a debate touched upon in Chapter 2. Recall how Darko Suvin parses science fiction from fantasy, despite granting that both occupy the realm of estrangement literature: the cognitive dimension integral to science fiction is missing in other sub-genres. Whereas science fiction generates knowledge and thus contributes to emancipatory efforts (from a Marxist point of view), fantasy lacks – for Suvin and his followers – the vital ingredients of believability and valid-ation, which are necessary for social change in the real world. Fantasy narratives are, on this account, so detached from reality that the readers cannot gain useful insights into how they might transform their own lifeworlds. Science fiction's cognitive element, by contrast, serves as a catalyst for progressive action – the *novum*'s alterity throws mundane experiences into a new light, precisely because its strangeness raises awareness of socially and politically relevant issues.

As a consequence, a hierarchy of respectability haunts the relation-ship between science fiction and fantasy. Although Suvin has slightly softened his position vis-à-vis fantasy over time,[83] his views on science fiction's superior status are broadly shared. Both Fredric Jameson and Carl Freedman, two of Suvin's followers, express a similar disdain for fantasy, calling it "technically reactionary"[84] and "irrationalist, theoretic-ally illegitimate."[85]

Given this antipathy, might it be possible to conceive of fantasy in a more affirmative manner? China Miéville, himself a highly prolific author,[86] has come up with an interesting response to this question. His main point is that focusing on "cognition" (in Suvin's terminology)

---

[83] Suvin, "Considering the Sense of 'Fantasy' or 'Fantastic Fiction.'"

[84] Jameson, *Archaeologies of the Future*, 60.

[85] Freedman, *Critical Theory and Science Fiction*, 17.

[86] For a representative list of some of his novels, see: Miéville, *King Rat*; *Perdido Street Station*; *Iron Council*; *The City & the City*; *Embassytown*.

as the criterion for identifying science fiction is much less helpful than initially anticipated. This is the case because there is no intrinsic component of science fiction texts that would once and for all establish their cognitive credentials. Who is to tell, after all, whether a specific rendering of ultra-fast travel, for example, corresponds to a representation of future technologies that could be scientifically validated? At best, in the sub-genre of so-called hard science fiction, authors aspire to operate with conjectures and inferences that are technologically informed, through extrapolations from current research.[87]

Miéville reasons that science fiction presupposes a playful encounter between author and reader, in which the reader provisionally assents – through the suspension of disbelief – to the claims to cognition advanced by the author:

> The cognition effect is a persuasion. Whatever tools are used for that persuasion (which may or may not include actually cognitively-logical claims), the effect, by the testimony of SF writers for generations and by the logic of the very theorists for whom cognition is key, is a function of (textual) charismatic authority. The reader surrenders to the cognition effect to the extent that he or she surrenders to the authority of the text and its author function.[88]

Despite Suvin's Marxist background, Miéville suspects that the wish to keep science fiction apart from fantasy betrays an "uncomfortably patrician and antidemocratic class politics."[89] It would be much more productive to accept that, while there are good reasons for distinguishing science fiction from fantasy – focusing on the use of magic, for instance – no unbridgeable gap separates them. Both fiction and fantasy deal with alterity and unreality, albeit to varying degrees that readers are sensitive and responsive to.[90]

If Miéville is right to cast doubt on the hierarchy between science fiction and fantasy, then utopianism's mechanisms of estranging,

---

[87] On "hard science fiction," see: Pierce, "The Literary Experience of Hard Science Fiction"; Samuelson, "Modes of Extrapolation"; Westfahl, "The Closely Reasoned Technological Story."

[88] Miéville, "Cognition as Ideology," 238.

[89] Miéville, 240.

[90] The label that comes closest to properly characterizing Miéville's own writing is "weird fiction." See: Miéville, "Weird Fiction."

galvanizing and cautioning might be exercised in fantasy novels as much as in science fiction and other genres of speculative writing.[91] The same argument that Jameson makes about utopia's dialectical nature – caught between the yearning for radical otherness and the impossibility of enacting an absolute break with the status quo – also applies to fantasy. Fantasy writing, just like any other cultural artefact, is rooted in concrete historical circumstances that shape its form and content.[92]

That said, fantasy texts are never merely reflections of the material and ideological structures within which they are produced and consumed; their alterity and unreality also provide opportunities for interrogating the way we experience the world's solid frames. This makes it imperative to pay attention to "the conditions of their production, to the particular constraints against which the fantasy protests and from which it is generated, for fantasy characteristically attempts to compensate for a lack resulting from cultural constraints: it is a literature of desire, which seeks that which is experienced as absence and loss."[93] Absence and loss are key markers of the novels I discuss in the next section. As we will observe, the desire behind that absence and loss is an eminently political one – to come to terms with a situation that keeps on devastating the lives of marginalized and oppressed populations.

3.2.2 CONTENDING WITH FATHER EARTH: THE *BROKEN EARTH* TRILOGY.

My aim in this section is to provide a compressed summary of N. K. Jemisin's books, which will then, in a further step, permit me to draw out major motifs running through the entire trilogy. The *Broken Earth* series consists of three novels published in quick succession: *The Fifth Season* (2015), *The Obelisk Gate* (2016) and *The Stone Sky* (2017). Its author, N. K. Jemisin, was the first to win the Hugo Award – the most prestigious prize for science fiction and fantasy writing – three times in a row.[94]

---

[91] For an illustration of this more ecumenical approach, see: Paik, *From Utopia to Apocalypse*.

[92] Bould and Vint, "Political Readings."

[93] Jackson, *Fantasy*, 2.

[94] Schaub, "N. K. Jemisin Makes History at the Hugo Awards with Third Win in a Row for Best Novel"; Barnett, "Hugo Awards." Jemisin was recently also awarded a MacArthur

Since the laureate is selected on the basis of readers' votes, Jemisin's success represented a powerful rebuke to right-wing insurgents within the science fiction and fantasy community, who had attempted to sabotage the diversification of the genre by manipulating the selection procedure.[95] As an African American woman, Jemisin has been consistently outspoken about the motivations behind her writing, denouncing racist and sexist practices both within the artistic field to which she belongs and within the wider US context.[96] Following in the footsteps of authors such as Octavia Butler and Samuel R. Delany, Jemisin's fiction aims to reinvent both the vocabulary and the grammar with which utopian texts are drafted.[97]

The world of the *Broken Earth* trilogy is set in a far-away future torn asunder by geological and meteorological turmoil: Stillness, the fantasy land where the story unfolds, is frequently ravaged by intense climate catastrophes that demolish the Earth's surface for long periods of time. These cataclysms are named Seasons, and they come and go in unexpected waves. The surviving humans are organized in so-called Comms, scattered around the Stillness amidst the ruins of disappeared civilizations.

Besides humans, other beings roam this strange world as well: there is a small number of people who possess extraordinary magical power to placate the geological fluctuations and eruptions during a Season. The gift of these "Orogenes" (named after their ability to create mountains) is extremely dangerous when left unchecked. Rather than quelling environmental mayhem, their magic can also instigate utter devastation and ruin. Due to their ability to annihilate everything around them,

grant, one of the highest American accolades across science and culture. See: Flood, "N. K. Jemisin Leads 2020 Round of MacArthur 'Genius Grants.'"

[95] Romano, "The Hugo Awards Just Made History – and Defied Alt-Right Extremists in the Process." On the origins of this movement, see: Flood, "Hugo Award Nominees Withdraw amid 'Puppygate' Storm." On how Jemisin's fiction has evolved, see: Flood, "N. K. Jemisin."

[96] Rivera, "N. K. Jemisin Is Trying to Keep the World From Ending."

[97] The *Broken Earth Trilogy* is not her first attempt at writing such genre-bending stories. For prior works, see especially the *Inheritance Trilogy*: Jemisin, *The Hundred Thousand Kingdoms*; *The Broken Kingdoms*; *The Kingdom of Gods*. For a collection of short stories that deals with political issues as well, see: Jemisin, *How Long 'til Black Future Month?*

Orogenes are feared and hated by humans. Lynching them has become a common practice.

To train young Orogenes in the proper use of their powers, they are snatched away from their parents and transported to the Fulcrum, where they are schooled by a caste of Guardians. These Guardians are in possession of superhuman strength and apply brutal means to subdue their disciples. In the event of an impending climate catastrophe, Orogenes must draw energy from the Earth's crust and mollify its fluctuations and eruptions. Apart from these human actors with far-reaching powers, the Stillness is also inhabited by Stone Eaters, mysterious figures who look like sculptures, but can ostensibly move through Earth itself.

The first book in the trilogy, *The Fifth Season*, tells the story of three women with magical abilities: Essun, an Orogene who lives amongst humans, disguised as a schoolteacher; Damaya, a child whose gift for magic has only just been discovered; and Syenite, a fully trained Orogene embarking on a mission to rescue a coastal Comm from ruin. After a short prologue, the saga starts with the outbreak of a new Season, triggered by a massive energy burst that splits the whole continent in two.

At the beginning of the trilogy, we witness the end of the world, or rather, *an* end of *a* world. Essun finds the body of her son, killed by her husband Jija, an ordinary human with no magical powers. Eventually, she has to flee from her home as well and sets off in search of her remaining daughter, Nassun, who has been kidnapped by Jija. On her trek through the Stillness, Essun is accompanied by a shadowy Stone Eater named Hoa. After being rejected by her family, Damaya, the protagonist of the second storyline, is being trained at the Fulcrum to become an industrious and docile Orogene. Her teacher is a Guardian by the name of Schaffa. Finally, Syenite, the third storyline's lead character, is ordered by the Fulcrum to conceive a child with Alabaster, the most powerful Orogene across the Stillness. As they are asked to clean up the harbour of a small fishing village, Syenite realizes that it is not a reef that is blocking the entrance to it, but rather a massive ancient relic, an obelisk lying on the bed of the sea. When Syenite connects to the obelisk in the same way she normally harnesses the Earth's energy, Guardians are sent to murder both Alabaster and her.

Through a lucky escape, both eventually arrive on an island inhabited by Orogenes, who live freely beyond the reach of the Fulcrum. On this island, Syenite gives birth to a boy. The Guardians notice their hideout, attack the community and obliterate the island. Syenite is confronted by her old teacher, Schaffa, who wants to abduct her child to enter the Fulcrum. Rather than permitting Schaffa to inflict on her boy what had been done to herself, Syenite suffocates her own child and mobilizes her magic to destroy everything around her.

While the three plots proceed in isolation from one another, it slowly dawns on the reader that Essun, Damaya and Syenite are in fact the same person. We hence acquire a sense of why and how Essun became who she is.

Accordingly, the trilogy's second part changes tack. *The Obelisk Gate* traces just two plots running in parallel, one focused on Essun and the other on Nassun, her daughter. Essun's quest for her child brings her to an underground Comm, where Orogenes and humans live in relative harmony. To her great surprise, Essun is there reunited with Alabaster, her ex-lover, who she thought had been killed when Guardians assailed the island.

It is then revealed that Alabaster was in fact the force behind the inception of the Fifth Season. His motive for causing the continental rift have to do with an astronomical anomaly: the moon cannot any longer be seen from Earth, its orbit having been dislocated more than 1,000 years ago. In an attempt to restore the cosmic balance and to correct the moon's elliptical trajectory, Alabaster sought to harness the planet's geological energy, thereby inaugurating the Fifth Season. After some time together, they are once again lambasted by a rival Comm. During the prolonged siege, tensions between Orogenes and humans flare up and Alabaster finally passes away. But Essun ultimately manages to save the members of her new Comm. Her opening of the title-giving Obelisk Gate emits uncontrollable energy and leads to Essun almost dying.

Apart from Essun's storyline, we also follow her daughter, Nassun. Nassun was abducted by her father, upon realizing that his offspring possessed potentially lethal powers. Travelling together through a landscape riven by Alabaster's triggering of a Fifth Season, the two finally arrive at a settlement that promises respite: Found Moon, a town under the control of a group of Guardians who have relinquished the Fulcrum. These Guardians pretend to offer a cure to orogeny, but in reality, they set up an alternative school for children with a talent for magic. The leader of that town is Schaffa, whom we last encountered as the erstwhile teacher of Damaya/Syenite/Essun. Schaffa, sensing in her the same power as in her mother, takes Nassun under his wing. *The Obelisk Gate* thus follows both mother and daughter on their respective paths.

The fusion of these separate narratives occurs in the third volume, *The Stone Sky*. Essun's tale continues with her being severely injured by the opening of the Obelisk Gate. Her daughter, Nassun, wants to open the Obelisk Gate as well, but for entirely different reasons: to make the moon crash into Earth. These destructive urges are caused by the recognition that life on this planet has become unbearable, both due the climatic cataclysms and due to the oppression that Orogenes experience in human societies. There is but one place on Earth where Essun and Nassun can grasp for the moon: a city called Corepoint that in earlier days served as a scientific hub of sorts. Essun travels there with the help of a Stone Eater, Hoa, who manages to carry her through the Earth's crust.

Hoa's story is central to the entire saga, for it contains within it the background to the geological turmoil befalling Earth. Originally, thousands of years ago, Hoa belonged to a genetically modified species whose sole purpose was to operate the obelisks. The aim of this operation would have been the generation of limitless energy, by tapping directly into the Earth's core. Yet, when Hoa became aware that his species' sole raison d'être amounted to powering the Obelisk Gate, he decided to disobey the orders of his human masters. This immediately set in motion a chain reaction whereby the obelisks started the Seasons. In the aftermath of this series of cataclysmic events, Hoa and the other tuners were turned into Stone Eaters – nearly immortal creatures that wander the world in search for redemption.

During Essun's and Hoa's voyage through the planet's core, Earth's true nature is disclosed, as a living being that harbours anger and resentment at humanity for trying to tame it and for stealing its "child," the moon. Once both Essun and Nassun arrive at Corepoint, the trilogy approaches its grand finale. While Essun is trying to utilize her magic to restore the moon's trajectory, Nassun fights back and thwarts her mother's plans. Towards the end, Essun lets go and releases her grip on the obelisks. This immediately kills her, turning her to stone. Upon witnessing her mother's death, Nassun changes her mind and fulfils Essun's lasting dream: uniting Earth and moon once again. The saga ends with an outlook on life after the Seasons, when the planet's inhabitants can begin anew to build viable and thriving civilizations.

As my summary surely demonstrates, the story told by Jemisin is of epic proportions – a typical feature of fantasy fiction.[98] What I want to do now is to draw out some key motifs that run through the meandering narrative: first, the notion of Earth as a living being; second, the role of cyclical violence in human and multispecies relations; and third, the place of altruism and solidarity in apocalyptic moments. In a further step, I shall delineate how these motifs coalesce around a utopian vision, one that thoroughly unravels models of the future centred around white male power.

3.2.3 A LIVING PLANET, CYCLICAL VIOLENCE AND SOLIDARY RELATIONS. To begin with our first theme, the image of our planet as a living, raging being looms large in Jemisin's story. Earth is depicted not as an inert fantasy land through which the plot meanders, but rather plays a part in the narrative itself. One way of making sense of its representation would be in terms of "planetary weirding," a mode of thinking through the Anthropocene that underscores "its persistent imagining of geological confrontations, unsettlings, and hauntings."[99] Far from postulating the harmonious unity of our species in this climate-changed world, planetary weirding highlights deep-seated conflicts both within humanity and between humans and the environment.

On a basic level, this aspect becomes palpable in how Earth's inhabitants designate their home planet, addressing it consistently as "Father Earth." Jemisin's use of the paternal epithet signals a departure from allegories of Earth as a caring, nurturing figure.[100] Whereas Mother

---

[98] Attebery, "Introduction."

[99] Ingwersen, "Geological Insurrections," 74.

[100] Evidently, this spiritual image also bears resemblance to the Gaia figure, but not in the sense endorsed by Latour. On the metaphor of "Mother Earth," which is both gendered and spiritually loaded, see: Swanson, "A Feminist Ethic That Binds Us to Mother Earth";

Earth can be relied upon for guaranteeing the peaceful coexistence of all the species on the planet, Father Earth has a much more antagonistic role: to defend itself against the intrusions of humanity.

This view echoes Latour's insight that "Earth has become ... an active, local, limited, sensitive, fragile, quaking, and easily tickled envelope."[101] The charging of Earth with agentic powers also brings with it a shift in how humans perceive themselves, as Jemisin observes: "But human beings, too, are ephemeral things in the planetary scale. The number of things that they do not notice are literally astronomical."[102]

In explaining how the Earth's vengeful character was formed, Jemisin supplies a background narrative that assigns responsibility for the ongoing Seasons to only some human beings and their insatiable longing for control and supremacy.[103] Two passages from the trilogy's first volume summarize the origins of this clash between humanity and Father Earth:

> There was an age before the Seasons, when life and Earth, its father, thrived alike ... Earth our father knew He would need clever life, so He used the Seasons to shape us out of animals: clever hands for making things and clever minds for solving problems and clever tongues for working together and clever sessapinae to warn us of danger. The people became what Father Earth needed, and then more than He needed. Then we turned on Him, and He has burned with hatred for us ever since.[104]

> In fact ... once upon a time Earth did everything he could to facilitate the strange emergence of life on his surface. He crafted even, predictable seasons; kept changes of wind and wave and temperature slow enough that every living being could adapt, evolve; summoned waters that purified themselves, skies that always cleared after a storm. He did not create life – that was happenstance – but he was pleased and fascinated by it, and

---

Gaard, "Ecofeminism Revisited." On the intersections between religion and environmentalism more widely, see: Taylor, "Earth and Nature-Based Spirituality (Part I)"; Taylor, "Earth and Nature-Based Spirituality (Part II)"; Tomalin, *Biodivinity and Biodiversity.*

[101] Latour, "Agency at the Time of the Anthropocene," 3.

[102] Jemisin, *The Fifth Season,* para. 14.2.

[103] See: Iles, "Repairing the Broken Earth."

[104] Jemisin, *The Fifth Season,* para. 12.69.

proud to nurture such strange wild beauty upon his surface. Then people began to do horrible things to Father Earth. They poisoned waters beyond even his ability to cleanse, and killed much of the other life that lived on his surface. They drilled through the crust of his skin, past the blood of his mantle, to get at the sweet marrow of his bones. And at the height of human hubris and might, it was the orogenes who did something that even Earth could not forgive: They destroyed his only child.[105]

By inflicting environmental damage and ejecting the moon from its trajectory, humans have thus aroused the planet's ire and provoked it into becoming a formidable opponent. Father Earth's fury is reactive, rather than aggressive. Kick-starting the age of recurring Seasons signals the end of historical time as we know it. The apocalypse, in the *Broken Earth* trilogy, is not a one-off event, but rather keeps on happening again and again. Rolling climate catastrophes are embedded in a wider panorama of cataclysms that span from the breakdown caused by the opening of the Obelisk Gate to recurring smaller disasters that are the new normal. Nassun's intention to destroy the planet once and for all would have produced the definitive calamity from which Father Earth could not have recovered. The fact that her plan eventually falters is vital for my claim that Jemisin's novels ought to be read as utopian texts.

What counts as truly devastating amongst those different apocalyptic scenarios is a matter of perspective. "An apocalypse," Jemisin writes in *The Stone Sky*, "is a relative thing, isn't it? When the earth shatters, it is a disaster to the life that depends on it – but nothing much to Father Earth ... When we say that 'the world has ended,' remember – it is usually a lie. The planet is just fine."[106]

The very idea of deep time, so central to the entire series, stresses that climatic catastrophes do not carry the same weight for human beings as they do for other species or indeed the planet itself. Geological and historical timescales are of entirely different magnitudes, as we have already remarked in Chapter 1. By assigning Father Earth a stance of equal importance to humanity, Jemisin unsettles the human-centred

---

[105] Jemisin, paras. 27.104–27.105.
[106] Jemisin, *The Stone Sky*, paras. 59.1, 40.1.

cosmology underpinning mainstream approaches to our climate-changed world.[107] Her planet-centred thinking sets into motion a defamiliarization strategy whose purpose is to make us envisage ourselves and our place in this world from a new and surprising angle. In these greatly deranged times, such re-visioning amounts to "an act of survival"[108] because the Anthropocene aggravates divisions between differently positioned members of our species as well as between human and non-human beings.

How is Earth imagined in the novels, then? This is such a difficult question because Jemisin refrains from personalizing the planet's qualities. In fact, just like the image of Gaia, the *Broken Earth* trilogy deploys various metaphors, such as that of a paternal figure, to adumbrate how connectivity without holism might be represented. In a passage reminiscent of Latour's thoughts on the self-regulatory functioning of planet Earth, Jemisin draws on the metaphor of an open network, rather than a closed system of command and control:

> The stuff underneath orogeny, which is made by things that live or once lived. This silver deep within Father Earth wends between the mountainous fragments of his substance in exactly the same way that they twine among the cells of a living, breathing thing. And that is because *a planet* is a living, breathing thing; she knows this now with the certainty of instinct. All the stories about Father Earth being alive are real.[109]

Turning now to our second motif, to understand the rupture leading to the "fifth season" we need to situate it in the wider context of cyclical violence. The lust for domination over Father Earth is related to oppression amongst humans and other species. Recall the reason why the disasters ravaging the planet have started in the first place. Father Earth resolves to retaliate only because an experiment goes fatally wrong: humans' attempt to genetically engineer and subjugate a breed of technologically enhanced beings (the latter Stone Eaters) kicks off a series of

---

[107] For an analysis of the importance of deep time to the idea of the Anthropocene, see: Heringman, "Deep Time at the Dawn of the Anthropocene."

[108] Rich, "When We Dead Awaken," 18.

[109] Jemisin, *The Stone Sky*, para. 1333.1.

disastrous events that later on cannot be halted anymore. The rebellion of the Stone Eaters, which seems justified given the servitude and imprisonment that humans had in store for them, stands at the inception of a chain of suffering across the planet.

This point has relevance for how the Anthropocene is usually perceived. As we observed in Chapter 1, one of the chief objections to simplistic understandings of the Anthropocene is that the universal category of humankind is problematic, due to the different levels of vulnerability to which populations and societies across the globe are exposed. Kathryn Yusoff homes in on this point when she remarks:

> If the Anthropocene proclaims a sudden concern with the exposures of environmental harm to white liberal communities, it does so in the wake of histories in which these harms have been knowingly exported to black and brown communities under the rubric of civilization, progress, modernization, and capitalism. The Anthropocene might seem to offer a dystopic future that laments the end of the world, but imperialism and ongoing (settler) colonialisms have been ending worlds for as long as they have been in existence.[110]

Echoing this observation, Jemisin's trilogy traces the many ways in which worlds can be undone and remade – through human intervention and through planetary upheaval. Capitalism and colonialism have produced a system of violent dispossession and exploitation from which marginalized people around the world have not yet broken free.[111] And yet, the story's protagonists, from Damaya/Syenite/Essun to her daughter Nassun and teacher Alabaster, are all embroiled in revolts against oppressive institutions and structures. The de facto enslavement of Orogenes represents only the most blatant type of subjugation in the novels, but we can also detect other kinds of domination that disfigure the enduring communities. The planet itself seems to be driven by a

---

[110] Yusoff, *A Billion Black Anthropocenes or None*, 11.

[111] For a discussion of the ways in which the vexed history of capitalism and colonialism provides the background to the *Broken Earth* trilogy's representation of the natural world, see: Bastiaansen, "The Entanglement of Climate Change, Capitalism and Oppression in The Broken Earth Trilogy by N. K. Jemisin."

desire for revenge, fired up by its defencelessness at the hands of humanity.

The universe of the *Broken Earth* trilogy is tarnished by violence, leaving its inhabitants with the heavy legacy of making peace for and with themselves. While searching for justice is one motivating factor in that quest, mere survival is another one:

> For some crimes, there is no fitting justice – only reparation. So for every iota of life siphoned from beneath the Earth's skin, the Earth has dragged a million human remnants into its heart. Bodies rot in soil, after all – and soil sits upon tectonic plates, plates eventually subduct into the fire under the Earth's crust, which convect endlessly through the mantle ... and there within itself, the Earth eats everything they were. This is only fair, it reasons – coldly, with an anger that still shudders up from the depths to crack the world's skin and touch off Season after Season. It is only right. The Earth did not start this cycle of hostilities, it did not steal the Moon, it did not burrow into anyone else's skin and snatch bits of its still-living flesh to keep as trophies and tools, it did not plot to enslave humans in an unending nightmare.[112]

The dynamic interplay between domination and rebellion forms the crucible wherein the trilogy's various narrative strands are forged together. Attested by her fascination with the Haitian Revolution, Jemisin does not believe violence per se can have redemptive effects, even when it is directed at institutions and structures that are oppressive.[113]

The ways in which subjugated people liberate themselves are always fraught with risk and imperilled by backlash from their adversaries. This becomes particularly salient in the novels' focus on the unintended consequences of revolutionary uprisings. One of the key insights of the *Broken Earth* trilogy is that social change brings with it costs that the oppressed are rarely aware of in their legitimate resistance against domination.

---

[112] Jemisin, *The Stone Sky*, para. 1364.1.
[113] Jemisin, "The Effluent Machine."

Indeed, amongst the principles upholding collective life in the Stillness is one that stipulates: "necessity is the only law."[114] This twist on the Roman proverb *necessitas non habet legem* ("necessity knows no law") evinces that declaring a state of exception, which is only supposed to be temporary and reversible, becomes obsolete in the Fifth Season. When the planet is in turmoil, positive transformation will require extreme measures, shaking up what is taken to be immutable. A return to a mode of cooperative existence calls for more than slow reformism. As Jemisin notes in an interview, insurgent action always needs to be assessed in light of the suffering it will cause, often as a side effect of good intentions:

> There are those who believe in incremental change as the only safe way to make the world a better place. I don't believe in that. Incremental change means a lot of people suffering for a very long time, mostly so that the people in the status quo can be comfortable longer. The people pushing incremental change aren't the ones who are suffering. And sometimes a revolution is necessary; sometimes you do have to burn it all down. I wanted to depict realistically what that'd be like. If you burn it all down, a whole lot of people get hurt. If you're going to advocate for burning it all down, I'm going to show you what burning it all down looks like.[115]

While the series culminates without the total destruction of the planet, it is far from assured that the future on the Stillness will remain devoid of violence. The novels' open ending underlines that reconstruction in the aftermath of long-term and systemic oppression will not necessarily be straightforward. Reaching for a *New Jerusalem* is as useless a goal for this utopian project as is the hope that we could ever turn *Arcadia* into reality.

This issue brings us to the third thread running through the trilogy: the importance of altruism and solidarity in the face of adversity. It is commonplace in science fiction and fantasy writing to portray the surviving of the apocalypse as a lonely business, typically attained by a White heroic loner.[116] Jemisin deconstructs this gendered and racialized

---

[114] Jemisin, *The Fifth Season*, para. 24.56; Jemisin, *The Stone Sky*, para. 383.1.

[115] Hurley and Jemisin, "An Apocalypse Is a Relative Thing," 473.

[116] For the most notorious example of openly racist and misogynistic speculative fiction, see: Heinlein, *Farnham's Freehold*. On the centrality of race and ethnicity in science fiction narratives, see: Leonard, "Race and Ethnicity in Science Fiction"; James, "Yellow,

stereotype, not only by selecting a Black middle–aged woman as her protagonist, but also by overturning the "controlling image"[117] of the solitary hero who overcomes all the hardship by himself. While Essun's life is characterized by terrible sacrifices, including the tragic killing of her own child, she is also nurtured, cared for and sustained by a group of friends. "In real situations of disaster," Jemisin observes, "it's people who cooperate who survive. It's people who look out for each other. Altruism and community are what help you get through, not being Mad Max."[118]

This statement is supported by research into the aftermath of real-world catastrophes. Rebecca Solnit has shown that responses to disasters are typically driven by both self-preservation and by a concern for the welfare of others. Examining events such as hurricane Katrina, 9/11 or the 2004 tsunami in the Indian Ocean, she holds that "most people are altruistic, urgently engaged in caring for themselves and those around them, strangers and neighbors as well as friends and loved ones. The image of the selfish, panicky, or regressively savage human being in times of disaster has little truth to it."[119]

Solnit describes the emergent solidarity in the wake of calamities under the banner of "disaster utopias." Disaster utopias are usually short-lived, surfacing when the ashes of an old order are still in the air and fading away once a more regular course of life – a new normal – has been restored. Such utopias do not involve grand schemes for social engineering or amount to full-fledged expressions of social dreaming, but rather spring up almost automatically:

Black, Metal, and Tentacled." On the ways in which African American artists have sought to dismantle this politics of race, see: Carrington, *Speculative Blackness*.

[117] I take the notion of a "controlling image," which describes how some ideas "make racism, sexism, poverty, and other forms of social injustice appear to be natural, normal, and inevitable parts of everyday life," from Patricia Hill Collins. See: *Black Feminist Thought*, 69.

[118] Hurley and Jemisin, "An Apocalypse Is a Relative Thing," 470.

[119] Solnit, *A Paradise Built in Hell*, para. 1.63. For an illuminating reading of Solnit's thesis in the context of climate change debates, see: Fiskio, "Apocalypse and Ecotopia." Solnit has also extended her thesis to the COVID-19 pandemic. See: Solnit, "The Way We Get Through This Is Together."

> [D]isaster throws us into the temporary utopia of a transformed human
> nature and society, one that is bolder, freer, less attached and divided than
> in ordinary times, not blank, but not tied down ... You don't have to
> subscribe to a political ideology, move to a commune, or join the guerrillas
> in the mountains; you wake up in a society suddenly transformed, and
> chances are good you will be part of that transformation in what you do, in
> whom you connect to, in how you feel.[120]

This inquiry into disaster utopias dovetails with Jemisin's account of how group improvisation can aid those who grapple with the catastrophic consequences of the Fifth Season. Their patterns of empathy and collaboration could also be glossed as "disaster communism."[121] A complementary explanation of the ways in which altruism and solidarity materialize in extreme situations would be via decolonial scholarship around the links between survival and resistance.[122] Faced with the wholesale destruction of their cultures, Indigenous writers have long emphasized the centrality of storytelling for individual and collective flourishing. The practical objective of stories, then, is to repair and reinforce the social fabric holding together past, present and future generations. Besides, their narratives also affirm how human thriving is always tied up with caring about and for Earth.[123]

What Vanessa Watts calls "Place-Thought" captures the non-anthropocentric cosmology behind Jemisin's fantasy land, where care extends not only to interpersonal and multispecies relations, but to the planetary ecosphere more generally: "Place-Thought is based upon the premise that land is alive and thinking and that humans and non-humans derive agency through the extensions of these thoughts."[124] As

---

[120] Solnit, *A Paradise Built in Hell*, paras. 1.105, 1.108.

[121] Out of the Woods, "The Uses of Disaster." Along the same lines, Andreas Malm suggests recovering the concept of "war communism," which signifies a specific period of the Bolsheviks' reign during the Russian Civil War. See: Malm, *Corona, Climate, Chronic Emergency*.

[122] On this point, see: Ingwersen, "Geological Insurrections," 84–6. I also take the next reference to "Place-Thought" from this text.

[123] See: Sium and Ritskes, "Speaking Truth to Power"; Whiteduck, "But It's Our Story. Read It."

[124] Watts, "Indigenous Place-Thought & Agency amongst Humans and Non-humans (First Woman and Sky Woman Go on a European World Tour!)," 21.

we have seen, the ability of the Orogenes to marshal their powers stems from their existential entanglement with the Earth's infrastructure. Orogenes are quite literally "Earth-makers," whose gift of geoengineering turns out to be an extremely hazardous one: used diligently, it expediates pacific relations between humans and planet Earth; used inconsiderately, it exerts a devastating impact on both humanity and the environment.

The ambivalent magic of the Orogenes thus facilitates a deeper appreciation of the links that bind humans to the more-than-human world. As a consequence, the kind of disaster communism we find at work in the *Broken Earth* trilogy goes beyond the human sphere, inaugurating instead new types of human–planet relations. This process depends on novel forms of altruism and solidarity, both between humans of different backgrounds and between humans and the more-than-human world.[125]

Taken together, these three motifs – Earth as a living being, the role of cyclical violence and the centrality of altruism and solidarity – inform a comprehensive rebuttal of speculative fiction structured around White male power. In sharp contrast to gendered and racialized controlling images of heroic masculinity, Jemisin demonstrates that individual rebellion is likely to falter and that violent upheaval will not automatically lead to liberation. On this level, the trilogy's utopian dimension is fairly easy to discern – as the celebration of alternative avenues for survival and resistance that do not rest on the ruinous assurances of White male power.

Are there other ways in which the text could be read as politically generative? What should we make of the unsettling image of Father Earth as an agent in its own right? In order to answer these questions, we may be guided by two hermeneutical strategies: either pursuing a *strong* allegorical reading that interprets the world of the *Broken Earth* trilogy principally as a defamiliarizing critique of White male power; or employing a *weak* allegorical reading that embeds the trilogy's planetary weirding within broader debates about environmental degradation and

---

[125] On the importance of providing a physical infrastructure for such solidarity, see: Kearse, "The Worldmaking of N. K. Jemisin."

human hubris in the Anthropocene. Let us unpack each of these and weigh their respective virtues.

The strong allegorical interpretation submits that the calamities of the *Broken Earth* trilogy should be read as symbolizing the painful experiences of oppressed people when their struggles for emancipation are repeatedly thwarted. On this reading, Father Earth's irascible outbursts are mere ciphers for what happens when the just order of things – one in which the good life is accessible to everyone and in equal measure – has been severely disturbed.

An advantage of this interpretation is that we can with relative ease identify real-world equivalents of the novels' oppressive institutions and structures: the Guardians may hence be understood as the repressive police apparatus, while the violence exerted by the Orogenes may correspond to brutal clashes amongst subjugated groups, etc.[126] This appears to be the hermeneutical strategy favoured by the author herself, as the following passage shows:

> So it wasn't that I was trying to write an apocalyptic story, it was that I was trying to depict a society that had the emotional impact of the society that I live in now where there have been, not Fifth Seasons, but where there have been the equivalent of pogroms and holocausts and all of these disasters happening to a people again and again and again. And I wasn't specifically depicting just the African-American experience; I was drawing a lot of material from a number of different experiences of oppression, like being closeted from queerness, or drawing from the Holocaust, which you see a lot in the third book. When you look at human history, it's full of Fifth Seasons, full of apocalypses, quiet ones in many cases, but just as devastating to its people. I wanted to draw a world that felt realistic.[127]

What is distinctive about the *Broken Earth* trilogy is the extent to which the planet in its entirety is depicted as marred and constituted by violence. This is how our actual world looks when viewed from the vantage point of the oppressed, Jemisin reminds us, confirming once again that in utopian projects estrangement and realism are enmeshed with each

---

[126] Hepplewhite, "The Stone Sky by N. K. Jemisin."
[127] Hurley and Jemisin, "An Apocalypse Is a Relative Thing," 472.

other.[128] Her main sources of inspiration during the drafting process were movements, such as *Black Lives Matter*, that channel their anger at systemic domination via solidary self-empowerment, but also findings into the deprivations of Indigenous children, who were forcibly removed from their families to expunge their native culture in so-called residential schools.[129]

Following this line of thought, the Stillness effectively embodies a defamiliarized version of the brutal, unequal world we inhabit right now, a world where "breathing doesn't always mean living."[130] The destructive Seasons can be interpreted as embodying what Christina Sharpe calls the "weather that produces a pervasive climate of anti-blackness."[131] Tellingly, the verb "weathering" is also used in medical discourse to capture the pervasive effects that racism has on health inequalities, independent of variations in socio-economic status.[132] On this account, extreme meteorological events stand for the totality of social relations scarred by enslavement and its aftermath. As a parable, the image of a living planet highlights, in an Afropessimist vein, that fighting White supremacy means nothing less than completely obliterating the oppressive institutions and structures that uphold White supremacy.[133]

---

[128] Before publishing the *Broken Earth* trilogy, Jemisin elaborated on this point on her personal blog: "That's the whole point of speculative fiction for me, really – playing the 'what-if' game. What if, all other things being equal and people being people, the apocalypse happened every few hundred years? What if, all other things being equal and people being people, gods lived among us, and were sometimes real assholes? Those what-ifs don't work without the *people being* people part. Which means I need to understand people, in the real world, in all their glory and grotesquerie" (Jemisin, "Why I Talk So Damn Much about Non-writing Stuff").

[129] "Black Lives Matter Inspired This Chilling Fantasy Novel."

[130] Jemisin, *The Stone Sky*, para. 1004.1.

[131] Sharpe, *In the Wake*, para. 11.16.

[132] On "weathering" and health inequalities, see: Geronimus et al., "'Weathering' and Age Patterns of Allostatic Load Scores among Blacks and Whites in the United States"; Phelan and Link, "Is Racism a Fundamental Cause of Inequalities in Health?"; Williams, Lawrence, and Davis, "Racism and Health."

[133] This picture reverberates with the thought that the "afterlife of slavery" generates a permanent state of "social death," which cannot be overcome through practices of emancipation alone. See: Hartman, *Lose Your Mother*; Patterson, *Slavery and Social Death*. The idea that the continuous experience of social death renders any form of optimism

While this approach strikes me as intuitively persuasive and confirmed by Jemisin's own explanations, it has one downside: it relegates the figure of Father Earth to the secondary status of a mere cipher, symbolically standing in for real-world violence and oppression. If we read Jemisin's oeuvre in this way, we risk losing sight of the trilogy's troubling of the contested distinction between culture and nature, which strikes me as vital for the novel's political implications.

Let us hence pursue a different hermeneutical strategy that accentuates the text's environmental facets. While this weak allegorical interpretation would still accept the estranged character of the fantastical story, it refrains from treating Father Earth as a metaphor for the just order of things. On this alternative reading, Jemisin promotes a "radical Black ecology," vigorously debunking the notion that "capitalism, the state, heteropatriarchy, and the domination of more-than-human nature are the means and ends of justice and freedom."[134]

We have already observed that the image of our planet as a living, raging being evokes how Latour conceives of the Gaia figure. Just like Latour's *New Climate Regime*, Jemisin's universe, too, is premised on the existence of irradicable and ongoing conflicts between various parties that have a stake in a planetary existence. Even Earth itself is caught up in these altercations. The antagonisms of the *Broken Earth* trilogy force a rethink of the modern idea of nature as a neutral background against which human culture evolves. Latour captures this thought in his discussion of how wars will unfold in the future:

> We have reached the point when we should make no mistake about the role of Gaia in the return to the situation of war. Gaia no longer occupies in any sense the position of arbiter that Nature occupied during the modern period. Such is the tipping point between unified, indifferent, impartial, global "nature" whose laws are determined in advance by the principle of causality, and Gaia, which is not unified, whose feedback loops have to be discovered one by one, and which can no longer be said to be

frivolous plays a paramount, if contested, role in the current debate around Afropessimism. See: Gordon et al., "Afro Pessimism"; Sexton, "Afro-Pessimism"; Wilderson, *Red, White & Black*.

[134] Opperman, "We Need Histories of Radical Black Ecology Now."

neutral toward our actions, now that we are obliged to define the Anthropocene as the multiform reaction of the Earth to our enterprises. Gaia is no longer "unconcerned" by what we do. Far from being "disinterested" with respect to our actions, it now has *interests* in ours.[135]

This theoretical framework allows us to approximate Jemisin's representation of a living planet bent on warfare to Latour's conception of a political ecology that disavows romantic conceptions of pristine nature. Conserving, protecting and defending nature is not an option for the inhabitants of the Stillness, because Father Earth does not require tutelage of any kind. Rather, what the *Broken Earth* trilogy narrates is the process whereby the planet and its occupants negotiate a mutually agreeable settlement in the wake of an ecological crisis. Interestingly, this settlement does not result from the shared interests of a unified humanity. On the contrary, Jemisin's fantasy land shows us a fractured universe in which different human as we all more-than-human communities contend with one another.

A major objection to the idea of a "human planet" involves, as already stated, that it exaggerates the degree to which humanity amounts to a unified actor when it comes to assessing the impact our species has on the planetary ecosphere. Jemisin's narrative takes full account of this fact, notably through her portrayal of humanity as internally split: between ordinary human beings and their magical counterparts. In fact, the origins of Father Earth's vengeful attitude can be tracked down to intense divisions amongst humans. This perspective allows us to more clearly identify who bears primary responsibility for environmental damage and pollution – a question that is inseparable from the issue of how violence ripples through human and multispecies communities.

Both the dystopian vision of recurrent catastrophes and the eutopian promise of disaster-proof communities are part of the same stubborn struggle for a world beyond oppressive institutions and structures. Without attending to the planet's direct participation in these struggles, we could not comprehend the full ramifications of Jemisin's fantastical yet this-worldly utopia.

---

[135] Latour, *Facing Gaia*, para. 13.52.

3.3 ESTRANGEMENT AND ITS DISCONTENTS

As discussed in Chapter 1, the utopian education of desire is so urgently needed right now because we find ourselves in the midst of a crisis of the imagination. The champions of the Gaia hypothesis and N. K. Jemisin are proponents of a particular type of mapping our climate-changed world that disabuses its readers of outdated ways of experiencing the world. Their visions of the future remain pervaded, however, by a fundamental tension between the two modes of defamiliarization just identified: estrangement *from* and estrangement *for* the world. Reading together the theory-building and the storytelling pole of this utopian constellation reveals how difficult it is to gain distance to reality in the right manner.

Raising a *What-If* question is integral to all kinds of social dreaming: to once again invoke Fredric Jameson, utopias strive to "dissolve" and "neutralize" the status quo, prompting us to let go of, or at least provisionally bracket, deeply held convictions about the real world. One such conviction, I have suggested, pertains to the view that our planet merely provides the passive background against which humanity's sovereign actions play out. The utopian vision of our planetary habitat as an actor in its own right assaults this anthropocentric view, by formulating a theory of universal connectedness and by foregrounding the conflicts between an internally divided mankind and "Father Earth."

At the end of this chapter, it is time to take stock and ask which features cut across this first constellation. Juxtaposing the champions of the Gaia hypothesis with N. K. Jemisin's narrative lays bare a number of overlapping preoccupations that can help us identify what is distinctive about the utopian vision of a living planet. The first of these is the refutation of Earth as a caring, nurturing figure. There simply is no place for such a benevolent character in a world ravaged by climatic disruptions.

The second idea shared by proponents of this constellation has to do with the antagonistic dimension of both human and multispecies relations. The emphasis on persistent enmity can be explained as an endeavour to re-politicize ecology in a comprehensive manner: not as the "slow, strong drilling through hard boards,"[136] in Max Weber's words, but as the simple, yet consequential fact of being exposed to constant dangers that need careful mediating and negotiating.

This affects our understanding of what it means to be human on a living planet, demonstrating that questions of what Levitas calls the "ontological" mode of utopianism are central to this constellation: how we may thrive, as members of a rapacious and hubristic species, cannot be divorced from the ways in which we inhabit a climate-changed world. Since conflicts result from this diagnosis of *Homo sapiens* as destructive, the proponents of this *What-If* plot line experiment with new ways of processing and experiencing our place in the world.

A third point concerns what should happen next, once the notion of a planet on which nobody and nothing is passive has been established. Neither the champions of the Gaia hypothesis nor Jemisin are fatalistic about the future. Although they do not offer a detailed escape route out of the current impasse, they supply us with a sense of how oppositional agency may gather traction, especially through the solidary bonds that the *Broken Earth* trilogy discovers in resistance movements.

Given these disparate characteristics, why might it still be useful to call their visions utopian? An initial observation is that the idea of planet Earth as a living being does not in any meaningful sense translate into a perfect plan for how a climate-changed world should evolve in the near or even the far future. Neither Latour nor Jemisin deliver blueprints for what needs to be done to improve the relationships between humans and the environment. But they convey imaginative constructs that defamiliarize the reader from the way Earth and its inhabitants are conventionally viewed, and that is an important part of the critique that this planet-centred utopianism exercises.

What clearly emerges is that both Latour's *New Climate Regime* and Jemisin's *Broken Earth* trilogy seek to educate a desire for other ways of being and living. This desire springs from the acknowledgement that the current state of affairs is deeply problematic, locking our species into a trajectory towards likely destruction: in Latour's case, the origins of the ecological crisis are traced back to a modern misconception of our

---

[136] Weber, "The Profession and Vocation of Politics," 369.

planetary habitat itself. The Gaia hypothesis constructs a lens for envisioning the interface between nature and culture – not as diametrically opposed spheres of interaction between humans and non-humans, but as a critical zone, a shifting borderland, where various types of agency collide with each other.

Jemisin's conjuring of the Stillness serves a comparable purpose: to summon the reader to see the real world anew. Her narrative opens a strange perspective through which anthropocentric worldviews become unsettled. Differently positioned humans, in this world full of magic, are but marginal players who have to struggle to preserve their place within a landscape occupied by a variety of hostile actors.

This clash of standpoints demonstrates that utopian storytelling can address similar issues as theory building. The *Broken Earth* trilogy never fully personalizes Father Earth, but it does invite the reader to imagine what it would be like to inhabit an irascible planet whose geology turns out to be not as amenable to *Homo sapiens* as Earth's Goldilocks zone. Jemisin's description of a period in time when our species has completely lost control over the "human planet" provides us with a useful variation on the Gaia hypothesis. Investigating the deep time of fantasy adds experiential texture and depth to the claim of universal connectedness. In that sense, the *Broken Earth* trilogy does more than simply illustrate the approach adopted by Lovelock, Latour and others. It explores how our planetary existence might be altered if the Gaia hypothesis were to become reality.

Naturally, this shift from the realm of social and political theory to the domain of speculative fiction brings with it a departure from scientific inquiry as we know it. Due to its explicit embrace of magic, Jemisin's fantasy land is much more disengaged from present epistemological practices than the other narratives discussed in this book. But this renders her work more, rather than less, instructive from the point of view of the education of desire. Attending to the complex manners of what life might feel like in a post-Anthropocene world sheds light on our greatly deranged times.

As I have already stated, both Latour and Jemisin refrain from specifying in detail how we could counteract the perils of the present. A shortcoming of their defamiliarizing utopianism might hence be that the estrangement technique ends up eclipsing reflections about what should be done concretely, here and now. I have dubbed this the fault line of indeterminacy: the tendency of all adherents to a *What-If* frame to prioritize estrangement over concreteness. This is a development that our next constellation aspires to avoid at all costs, through its singling out of viable pathways out of the ecological crisis.

CHAPTER 4

If Only

Eutopias of Scientific Progress between Techno-Optimism and Anti-capitalism

I N THIS CHAPTER, I switch perspective and direct attention to a utopian constellation in which the desire for being otherwise is incited through appeals to scientific and technological progress. The tone here changes dramatically compared to our first case. Against a worry about catastrophic events and in contrast with the thought that human and non-human actors are fundamentally entangled with one another, champions of so-called ecomodernism invest hope in a gradual but steady resolution of the ecological crisis through groundbreaking innovations in science and technology.

As such, their proposals are not directed at far-away horizons, but rather at a nearby future, a present almost in our grasp that merely operates as an optimistic extension of where we stand right now. Hence, many ecomodernists assert that we already possess the basic know-how – from carbon capture to geoengineering – that is going to allow us to bring a "good Anthropocene" into existence. All that is needed for successfully addressing the immense dangers inherent in a climate-changed world, they argue, is an answer to collective action problems that have plagued humanity throughout history. Democracy, science, the economic system as well as individual morality play different, yet interrelated roles in coping with those problems.

This utopian constellation is based on an *If-Only* plot line. The speculative question that animates ecomodernists is therefore: what would happen if science and technology were capable of developing solutions to the conundrum of climate change? Through its galvanizing appeals, the eutopian dimension in this vision of the future might appear obvious, but it is, in fact, shaped in many different ways that frequently clash with one another. The chapter's overall purpose is to reconstruct and evaluate these diverse proposals as unique forms of social dreaming.

To accomplish this goal, I start by analyzing the theory pole of this utopian constellation, focusing in particular on the recent development of ecomodernist discourse. Ecomodernists typically advance the proposition that human welfare ought to become completely "decoupled" from natural resource systems. This move, which contravenes the basic intuition behind the Gaia hypothesis, can only be accomplished with the support of cutting-edge technologies whose aim is to radically reduce humanity's environmental footprint.

While this proposal has seen enthusiastic uptake amongst many market-friendly liberals, there are also left-wing ecomodernists who embrace scientific and technological progress on entirely different grounds: not as a means to surpass humanity's existential dependency on nature, but as emancipatory tools that throw a spanner into the dominative logic of market-based capitalism. How ecomodernism relates to the market and whether it stands in an affirmative or hostile relation to capitalism are therefore just two of the key questions that deeply divide the current debate. I conclude my discussion of the social and political theory of ecomodernism with an analysis of the pitfalls of this *What-If* frame.

The second part of this chapter is devoted to interpreting Kim Stanley Robinson's *Science in the Capital* trilogy as a meditation on the promise of science and technology to save our species from itself. Robinson is an inspiring author who combines reflections on the purpose of utopianism with a literary oeuvre that is always politically inflected. His *Science in the Capital* trilogy provides us with a rich example of speculative fiction: its representation of the ecological crisis, refracted through the lives and experiences of a diverse range of stakeholders, expands on the positions of theorists such as Steven Pinker or the contributors to *Jacobin* magazine. At the same time, Robinson's version of ecomodernism complicates the picture painted by contemporary ecomodernists, by carefully probing the tensions arising from within modernity itself. This facet will be further fleshed out in the chapter's conclusion, where I examine what kind of orientation ecomodernism seeks to provide.

4.1 DREAMING OF A "GOOD ANTHROPOCENE"

We need stories about the future that paint a realistic and optimistic vision of what the world can be. A good Anthropocene is likely to be radically different from the world of today, involving fundamental change in human-environment relationships, changes in values, cultures, worldviews, and even the power and gender relations influencing social norms and behaviour. But envisioning a future so different from the world of today, while obviously appealing, is also incredibly difficult.[1]

An anecdote is not a trend. Remember your history: The fact that something is bad today doesn't mean it was better in the past. Keep some perspective. Not every problem is a crisis, plague, epidemic, or existential threat, and not every change is the End of This, the Death of That, or the Dawn of a Post-Something Era. Don't confuse pessimism with profundity: Problems are inevitable, but problems are solvable, and diagnosing every setback as a symptom of a sick society is a cheap grab for gravitas.[2]

After the realm of speculation, we draw upon the world as it is, or rather as it is becoming. Here we examine seemingly disparate technologies – in automation, energy, resources, health and food – before concluding that the foundations are cohering for a society beyond both scarcity and work. Nothing is certain about where these technologies will end, nor whose benefit they will serve. What is discernible, however, is that a disposition can be drawn from them – if only they are allied to a political project of collective solidarity and individual happiness.[3]

In reconstructing the theory pole of this utopian constellation, my objective is to account for an array of positions that all revolve around one essential lesson – that the Anthropocene, despite its obvious perils, can be turned into an opportunity for the wonderous augmentation of human welfare. As we shall see shortly, envisaging the idea of a "human planet" with a hopeful, rather than fearful, mindset can be accomplished in different ways, linking up with either right-wing or left-wing political agendas.

---

[1] "Planting Seeds of the Future."

[2] King, "Steven Pinker on the Past, Present, and Future of Optimism."

[3] Bastani, *Fully Automated Luxury Communism*, 12.

Unsurprisingly, the very idea of a "good Anthropocene" has also received its fair share of criticism, which I will unpack as well. Ultimately, my aim in this section is therefore to demonstrate that ecomodernism, as a utopian project, constitutes a broad church composed of warring sects: it can garner support from opposing sides of the political spectrum, depending on how the linkages between science, technology and capitalism are construed. Its shared purpose, however, is the galvanization of collective action in catastrophic times.

Given the fault lines pervading social dreaming, I will highlight how this orientation towards a positive goal is always liable to collapse into wishful thinking. The reason for this is straightforward. In order to mobilize an audience, ecomodernists need to tell emphatic stories about human ingenuity and empowerment. Such stories run the risk of downplaying the existential threats of inhabiting a climate-changed world. The ecomodernist education of our desire for being otherwise is thus imperilled by a tendency to discount the solid frames of our planetary existence.

4.1.1 HOW TO DECOUPLE HUMANITY FROM THE ENVIRONMENT. While it is unclear who first came up with the slogan "good Anthropocene" – both Erle C. Ellis and Andrew Revkin appear to be candidates[4] – its general features are relatively easy to set out. These contrast sharply with the constellation identified in Chapter 3, with its focus on principles of universal connectedness governing a world wherein humans have vacated their place at the centre of the moral universe.

The notion that science and technology can be harnessed so as to enhance the human planet feeds on a desire for our species' unique power to turn things around, evading the cataclysmic effects of climate change and mass extinction. The maps that ecomodernists draw to guide us into the planetary future are therefore anchored in an optimistic bedrock. Their wager sounds both simple and daring: if only people

---

[4] See: "A Man-Made World"; Ellis, "Neither Good nor Bad"; Revkin, "A Darker View of the Age of Us – the Anthropocene"; Revkin, "Building a 'Good' Anthropocene from the Bottom Up"; Revkin, "Natural Resources and the Environment."

began to appreciate what incredible opportunities lay ahead for humanity, the doom and gloom of the present moment would instantly
wither away.

Chief amongst ecomodernism's commitments are four ideas, as
Jonathan Symons expounds: first, the identification of excessive pollution, not growth per se, as the key driver behind global warming; second,
a belief in the importance of economic security (and hence consumption) as the basis of all environmental action; third, an endorsement of
development policies that are supposed to alleviate global poverty, even
if this brings with it a higher rate of overall fossil fuel use; and fourth, the
employment of metaphors, such as "decoupling," that are meant to
signal humanity's supremacy over nature.[5]

Although these are crucial components of this kind of social dreaming, not all versions of ecomodernism give equal weight to all four ideas –
commentators from the right of the political spectrum typically emphasize the effectiveness of market mechanisms more strongly, while those
from the left tend to foreground the authority of the state to inaugurate
a "good Anthropocene."

An emblematic manifestation of this utopian constellation can be
found in a document co-authored by eighteen self-professed ecomodernists.[6] Their agenda-setting manifesto from 2015 remains one of the
most powerful attempts to add a eutopian angle to the Anthropocene.[7]
The assumption behind this programmatic document is that a "good
Anthropocene demands that humans use their growing social, economic, and technological powers to make life better for people, stabilize
the climate, and protect the natural world."[8] How can this be achieved in

---

[5] Symons, *Ecomodernism*, chap. Defining Ecomodernism. Symons' book contains a
comprehensive overview of both the history and the politics of
contemporary ecomodernism.

[6] Many of these authors are affiliated with the aforementioned *Breakthrough Institute*, a US-
based think tank dedicated to identifying and promoting "technological solutions to
environmental and human development challenges." See: "The Breakthrough Institute."

[7] This seems true even though the intellectual origins of ecomodernism can be traced back
to the early 1970s. See: Huebner, "Tackling Climate Change, Air Pollution, and
Ecosystem Destruction." For an anthropological analysis see: Isenhour, "Unearthing
Human Progress?"

[8] Asafu-Adjaye, et al., "An Ecomodernist Manifesto," 6.

an evermore integrated, fossil fuel–based, globally stratified economy? The manifesto's chief response entails that a "decoupling" of environmental and human development is vital for our species' survival. Science and technology are the main vehicles for such decoupling: their purpose is to drastically diminish the extent to which humanity relies on the planetary ecosystem.

Crucially, transforming socio-economic structures within the most developed countries is not considered central for this project. Rather, ecomodernism remains wedded to the idea that science and technology will facilitate an energy revolution that moves humanity closer to a zero-carbon future; a future that will be simultaneously more prosperous and more sustainable. For this comprehensive separation of human needs from the planetary ecosystem to succeed, "next-generation solar, advanced nuclear fission, and nuclear fusion"[9] must become viable sources of energy production. Defying the assumption that there are physical boundaries to safe human development,[10] the authors endorse a much more positive assessment of where the limits to growth may lie:

> To the degree to which there are fixed physical boundaries to human consumption, they are so theoretical as to be functionally irrelevant ... Human civilization can flourish for centuries and millennia on energy delivered from a closed uranium or thorium fuel cycle, or from hydrogen-deuterium fusion. With proper management, humans are at no risk of lacking sufficient agricultural land for food.[11]

Is this wishful thinking, driven by a naive confidence in our capacity as a species to master planet Earth? The manifesto answers with a firm "no." Decoupling environmental from human development is already happening, in the form of a steady process underpinned by "both technological and demographic trends."[12] In an effort to dispel the accusation of wishful thinking, the authors assert that we have by now reached a tipping point in history where the growth rate of the human

---

[9] Asafu-Adjaye, et al., 23.

[10] Rockström et al., "A Safe Operating Space for Humanity"; Steffen et al., "Planetary Boundaries."

[11] Asafu-Adjaye, et al., "An Ecomodernist Manifesto," 10.

[12] Asafu-Adjaye, et al., 11.

population has peaked and where cities are by far the most common sites of habitation. All these developments indicate that decoupling is well under way, but they also show that more needs to be done to shrink humanity's environmental footprint: "Decoupling human well-being from the destruction of nature requires the conscious acceleration of emergent decoupling processes ... Urbanization, agricultural intensification, nuclear power, aquaculture, and desalination are all processes with a demonstrated potential to reduce human demands on the environment, allowing more room for non-human species."[13]

So, decoupling of the sort propagated by the manifesto is not only advantageous for humans, as we should subsequently become less dependent on natural resource systems; it also benefits the ecosystem at large, insofar as more space will become available for the rewilding of nature.[14] The authors clearly state that any rewilding project will have to be the result of human decisions with regard to what part of nature ought to be protected and conserved. Decoupling in the Anthropocene implies that there can be no return to a bucolic time when Earth remained unperturbed by humanity's footprint.

Sensibly, the ecomodernists allow for different degrees of decoupling according to local priorities, opening up the possibility for democratic control over climate mitigation and adaptation strategies: "People may choose to have some services — like water purification and flood protection — provided for by natural systems, such as forested watersheds, reefs, marshes, and wetlands, even if those natural systems are more expensive than simply building water treatment plants, seawalls, and levees. There will be no one-size-fits-all solution."[15]

A crucial feature of these proposals concerns the relationship between modernization and capitalism. The manifesto straightforwardly discards the conflation of modernization with capitalism, positing instead that modernity designates a much wider arc of human emancipation spanning social, economic and political reforms, such as the

---

[13] Asafu-Adjaye, et al., 18.

[14] On rewilding as a conservation strategy see: Lorimer et al., "Rewilding"; Nogués-Bravo et al., "Rewilding Is the New Pandora's Box in Conservation"; Jørgensen, "Rethinking Rewilding."

[15] Asafu-Adjaye, et al., "An Ecomodernist Manifesto," 27.

abolition of slavery and the institution of legitimate government. Any advancement of scientific and technological measures to tackle climate change would have to be closely aligned with those broader efforts to foster human freedom.

Given this rendering of modernization, the authors appear to take an accommodationist, broadly social-democratic view of the market, incorporating arguments from the anti-utopian canon: "While we reject the planning fallacy of the 1950s, we continue to embrace a strong public role in addressing environmental problems and accelerating technological innovation, including research to develop better technologies, subsidies, and other measures to help bring them to market, and regulations to mitigate environmental hazards."[16] The manifesto concludes with the enthusiastic affirmation that a "*great* Anthropocene" is just on the horizon, inviting the reader to conceive of "human prosperity and an ecologically vibrant planet"[17] as bound up with one another. The crux of the ecomodernist manifesto, as an agenda-setting paper, is therefore that our species will only be able to attain the twin goals of prosperity and sustainability if we unshackle the pursuit of collective welfare from its destructive dependency on natural resources. Science and technology represent our best hope for accelerating already existing trends of this decoupling process.

What the ecomodernist manifesto leaves open, however, is the pivotal issue of authoritative agency: who will be in charge of enacting the decoupling process and who will be held accountable if it fails, for whatever reason? Given the extraordinary investments that would have to be made into highly risky technologies, this question touches upon a key dimension of the ecomodernist wager. The technocratic aspect of the whole enterprise stands in considerable tension with the demand for democratic control by those affected by climate change. The rhetorical ingenuity of the manifesto lies in its gesture towards both the prospect of democratic control and the saving promise of science and technology. But the fact that this tension remains unresolved also gives rise to sharply

---

[16] Asafu-Adjaye, et al., 30.
[17] Asafu-Adjaye, et al., 31, italics in original.

divergent readings of the ecomodernist proposal, which we will explore in the next section.[18]

4.1.2 ECOMODERNISM, RIGHT AND LEFT. Before submitting this proposal for a "good Anthropocene" to critical scrutiny, I want to examine two opposing ways in which the intuitions behind the ecomodernist manifesto have been taken forward: one into the direction of a general progressivism that seeks to jettison the element of democratic control altogether; and another one attempting to reconcile ecomodernism with a specific type of socialist environmentalism.[19]

These two variants of the ecomodernist wager reveal that the basic idea identified in the previous section can be teased out in pronouncedly different ways: although all ecomodernists affirm, for example, that questions of socio-economic development must not be divorced from environmental considerations, there is deep disagreement around the desired drivers behind continuous growth. Whether it is the largely unregulated market or the interventionist state that is supposed to harness science and technology thus marks an essential dividing line in the ongoing debate.

To explain this, consider how the first extension strives to rehabilitate the Enlightenment project in a comprehensive fashion: progress, Steven Pinker claims, is undeniably real, yet its impact remains hidden in plain sight. According to this worldview, unless we unlock the potential of science and technology, we will unavoidably fail to tackle the challenge posed by climate change. In many ways, Pinker thus continues the line of argumentation instigated by the ecomodernist manifesto, while also adding more depth to the story. This theoretical sophistication springs from Pinker's explanation for why progress has been overlooked, and

---

[18] For further engagements with the manifesto, see: Crist, "The Reaches of Freedom"; Hamilton, "The Theodicy of the 'Good Anthropocene'"; Szerszynski, "Getting Hitched and Unhitched with the Ecomodernists."

[19] Apart from these two directions, ecomodernist ideas also seem to have taken hold in both architectural theory and practice. Evidence for this can be found, for example, in a recent exhibition at New York's Guggenheim Museum (*Countryside, The Future*), which reimagines the countryside in ways that resonate with the wider vision of ecomodernism. See: Heathcote, "Rem Koolhaas' Countryside at the Guggenheim Remakes Rural Life."

from his willingness to elaborate specific proposals for how the Anthropocene can be turned into an opportunity for prosperous and sustainable development.[20]

Pinker's defence of ecomodernism is part of a comprehensive research programme devoted to the rehabilitation of the Enlightenment heritage. While he was up until the early 2000s primarily renowned for his eclectic work in experimental psychology and cognitive science,[21] the publication of a monumental study on the history of violence considerably boosted Pinker's public status.[22] *The Better Angels of Our Nature* attacks the widely shared assumption that violence has been escalating throughout history, but especially in the twentieth century. All the available data, Pinker surmises, proves beyond any reasonable doubt that our times are much less violent than usually presumed. With the help of a vast array of biological, psychological, sociological and historical research, the author claims that violence is actually in decline, and has been so for quite some time.

A major motor behind this decline, albeit not the only one, has been the European Enlightenment, which triggered what Pinker terms the "humanitarian revolution."[23] This revolution had its origins in the rationalism of the seventeenth and eighteenth century: only during the Age of Reason, Pinker declares, did it become possible for people to overcome institutionalized violence that served no other purpose than spiteful and superstitious malice. Torture as well as cruel and unusual punishment, for example, were abolished partly because unexamined dogmas waned away and were replaced with a scientific spirit across society. Other forms of violence, such as slavery, lost their moral acceptability when Enlightenment humanism took roots in Western societies, according to Pinker's narrative.

---

[20] Pinker's views are clearly aligned with those of other "sceptical environmentalists" who seek to question the data behind the political agenda of ecological movements. Undoubtedly the most vocal of these critics is Bjørn Lomborg. See: Lomborg, *The Skeptical Environmentalist; Cool It.*

[21] For some of his earlier work see: Pinker, *Language Learnability and Language Development; The Language Instinct; The Blank Slate.*

[22] Pinker, *The Better Angels of Our Nature.*

[23] Pinker, chap. 4: The Humanitarian Revolution.

While this *grand récit* about the putative waning of violence does not need to directly interest us here,[24] Pinker's attempt at rescuing the Enlightenment from its detractors is integral to his vindication of the ecomodernist cause. In his latest book, *Enlightenment Now*, which expands on the chief contention of *The Better Angels of Our Nature*, Pinker seeks to again make the case for acknowledging the true success of Enlightenment reason, science and humanism.[25] Analyzing a variety of social settings, from public healthcare to the knowledge economy, Pinker claims that we tend to turn a blind eye to the immense advances Western societies have made over the past 200 years.

One chapter in this *apologia* of the Enlightenment is dedicated to the environment and to how contemporary societies should respond to sustainability concerns. In this part of the book, Pinker picks up where the ecomodernist manifesto stopped: in telling a story about how much progress has been made in the past and present, *Enlightenment Now* lays the ground for practical prescriptions regarding future solutions. Accordingly, Pinker's first undertaking is to delineate why current environmentalist discourse and politics are misguided, for they conceive of Earth as a "pristine ingénue which has been defiled by human rapacity."[26]

This image is pivotal to what Pinker signifies as the quasi-religious ideology of "greenism," embraced by people as different as "Al Gore, the Unabomber, and Pope Francis." "Greenism" is not only predicated on an unsound, romantic vision of our planet, it supposedly also contains deeply misanthropic views of humanity, "including an indifference to starvation, an indulgence in ghoulish fantasies of a depopulated planet, and Nazi-like comparisons of human beings to vermin, pathogens, and cancer."[27] By contrast, ecomodernism is wedded to a hope that Pinker dubs "conditional." His version of ecomodernism thus coincides with the project outlined in the manifesto:

---

[24] For a number of representative objections to Pinker's argument, see: Bhatt, "Book Review Symposium"; Lea, "Book Review Symposium"; Ray, "Book Review Symposium"; Rose, "Book Review Symposium"; Mitzen, "The Irony of Pinkerism."

[25] Pinker, *Enlightenment Now*.

[26] Pinker, para. 21.5.

[27] Pinker, para. 21.6.

We cannot be complacently optimistic about climate change, but we can be conditionally optimistic. We have some practicable ways to prevent the harms and we have the means to learn more. Problems are solvable. That does not mean that they will solve themselves, but it does mean that we can solve them *if* we sustain the benevolent forces of modernity that have allowed us to solve problems so far, including societal prosperity, wisely regulated markets, international governance, and investments in science and technology.[28]

What grounds are there for such optimism about a "good Anthropocene," propelled by the "benevolent forces of modernity"? Modernity's positive impact on humanity and the planet can be gauged by the degree to which environmental doomsday scenarios have in fact failed to materialize. A dislike of "eco-miserabilism" spurs Pinker's ambitions. Drawing on statistical data, Pinker points out that undeniable improvements in protecting and conserving nature have taken place over the past thirty years. Perhaps predictably given his aversion to religion in all its guises, *Enlightenment Now* also excoriates Pope Francis' encyclical *Laudato Si*"[29] for upholding the "vision of someone who has woken up thinking it's 1965, the era of belching smokestacks, waterfalls of sewage, rivers catching fire, and jokes about New Yorkers not liking to breathe air they can't see."[30] Reality is very different today, Pinker maintains, with much less pollution and much more efficient energy production now being the norm.

What looks like a massively improved scenario (at least from a New Yorker's perspective) results from the kind of decoupling encouraged by the members of the Breakthrough Institute. The push towards liberating human development from its reliance on the planetary ecosystem originates in the process of modernization itself. In line with his overall agenda, Pinker thus wants to demonstrate that modernity is completely self-guiding in its teleological determination to make the world a better place:

---

[28] Pinker, para. 21.102.
[29] Pope Francis, "Laudato Si'."
[30] Pinker, *Enlightenment Now*, para. 21.26.

These remarkable trends required no coercion, legislation, or moraliza-
tion; they spontaneously unfolded as people made choices about how to
live their lives. The trends certainly don't show that environmental legislation is dispensable—by all accounts, environmental protection agencies,
mandated energy standards, endangered species protection, and national
and international clean air and water acts have had enormously beneficial
effects. But they suggest that the tide of modernity does not sweep humanity headlong toward ever more unsustainable use of resources. Something
in the nature of technology, particularly information technology, works to
decouple human flourishing from the exploitation of physical stuff.[31]

Technology's inbuilt momentum towards reducing humanity's carbon
footprint contrasts with a radically different perspective on the kinds of
social, economic and political transformations that would be indispens-
able to successfully tackle climate change. Pinker opposes the climate
justice movement according to which the only way forward is to "abolish
free markets, restructure the global economy, and remake our political
system."[32] These proposals point in the wrong direction, he decries,
because any degrowth policy necessarily entails a reduction in global
prosperity, impoverishing both developed and developing countries.
A decrease in economic output, however, imperils the entire endeavour
of progressive modernization upon which the plea for an Enlightenment
project for the twenty-first century is built.

Like the ecomodernist manifesto, Pinker urges the reader to concede
that a decarbonization of the global economy is fully compatible with
constant, and indeed steadily rising, levels of wealth and welfare. While
Enlightenment Now hails the emancipatory properties of science and
technology, Pinker's proposal is, as a consequence, conservative in at
least one respect: it wants to leave the capitalist order completely intact,
militating against a root-and-branch overhaul of consumer society and
the market mechanisms governing global trade.[33] This attachment to the
socio–economic status quo is not accidental, for Pinker seems to believe

[31] Pinker, para. 21.47.
[32] Pinker, para. 21.55.
[33] Anthony, "Steven Pinker."

that the core set of Enlightenment values – reason, science and human-ism – hinges on the civilizing force of bourgeois virtues.[34]

The main catalysts for a decarbonized economy would accordingly consist in the introduction of a carbon tax as well as a massive investment in nuclear energy. While Pinker is cautious about the efficacy of taxing fossil fuels to offset their natural abundance and their negative external-ities, he is sanguine about groundbreaking technologies around nuclear energy. Deploring the unfairness of "crippling regulatory hurdles,"[35] Pinker identifies nuclear energy, due to its low cost, its density and cleanliness, as a remedy to our current predicament of carbon-based energy systems. Whereas technological breakthroughs will be necessary to further advance decarbonization, we are thus already on the right track towards minimizing humanity's dependence on natural resources.

A major hurdle remains, though: the "American squeamishness and political gridlock"[36] stymieing sustainable change. Competing nations, such as China and Russia, will accrue the benefits of modernization more quickly, presumably because they are capable of proceeding without the burdensome checks imposed by regulatory apparatuses. Pinker con-cludes his plea for an ecomodernist vision of the future with a pithy summary:

> An enlightened environmentalism recognizes that humans need to use energy to lift themselves out of the poverty to which entropy and evolution consign them. It seeks the means to do so with the least harm to the planet and the living world. History suggests that this modern, pragmatic, and humanistic environmentalism can work. As the world gets richer and more tech-savvy, it dematerializes, decarbonizes, and densifies, sparing land and species. As people get richer and better educated, they care more about the environment, figure out ways to protect it, and are better able to pay the costs. Many parts of the environment are rebounding, emboldening us to deal with the admittedly severe problems that remain.[37]

---

[34] See: Pinker, *Enlightenment Now*, para. 19.19.
[35] Pinker, para. 21.86.
[36] Pinker, para. 21.89.
[37] Pinker, para. 21.101.

Just like his prior claim about the constant decline in violence, Pinker's rehabilitation of the Enlightenment project for the twenty-first century has been met with sharp criticism. Commentators have accused the book as a whole of being "dogmatic,"[38] "complacent"[39] and "embarrassingly feeble."[40] It certainly seems fair to observe that Pinker's depiction of the Enlightenment appears rather one-sided and simplistic, for he imputes that a great variety of thinkers and positions partake in the same, coherent, and indisputably admirable project. Moreover, his ode to the Enlightenment completely obscures its violent and destructive underbelly, which can be best illuminated through a process of dialectical reasoning.[41] Likewise, Pinker's denunciation of who he considers to be the Enlightenment's most formidable *bête noire* – Friedrich Nietzsche – is cliché-ridden and unwarranted from the point of view of philosophical scholarship.[42]

Concerning his account of the decoupling strategy, critics have, moreover, raised a number of objections that expose the shortcomings of market-enthusiastic versions of ecomodernism. Amongst their concerns is one that harks back to Pinker's rather mechanistic worldview.[43] The relations between humanity and nature are, these critics suggest, much more entangled than the author of *Enlightenment Now* seems willing to accept. This renders the optimistic interpretation of science and technology's capacity to quickly shrink humanity's ecological footprint rather unrealistic. As we saw in Chapter 3, the Gaia idea formulates a hypothesis that is completely at odds with the practical prescriptions of ecomodernism. What Pinker consistently does is relegate models such as Lovelock's to the realm of childish fantasy and quasi-religious delusion. However, his sceptical take on "greenism" amounts to not much more than a crude

---

[38] Bell, "Waiting for Steven Pinker's Enlightenment."
[39] Moyn, "Hype for the Best."
[40] Gray, "Unenlightened Thinking." See also: Riskin, "Pinker's Pollyannish Philosophy and Its Perfidious Politics."
[41] The *locus classicus* for this kind of analysis is: Horkheimer and Adorno, *Dialectic of Enlightenment.*
[42] Pinker, *Enlightenment Now*, para. 36.111.
[43] Kolinjivadi, "The Enlightenment of Steven Pinker."

parody of debates that are in fact deeply scientific in their own right, as Latour's position makes clear.

Moreover, the celebration of the Enlightenment as a reliable motor of progress conveniently glosses over the West's own long history of exploitation and expropriation: both colonialism and imperialism are completely disregarded as structural elements that have historically conditioned the Enlightenment project.[44] The search for natural resources on an alleged *terra nullius*, boosted by the illusion of never-ending expansion, played a paramount role in all colonial and imperial conquests.[45] This multifaceted inheritance, from which the Enlightenment cannot easily unburden itself, does not receive the attention it would have merited in an even-handed appraisal of what human progress entails.

In sum, Pinker's version of the ecomodernist wager is wedded to the supposition that science and technology can deliver vital impulses to address the challenges caused by climate change. While *Enlightenment Now* makes room for state regulation, the best way to incentivize scientific and technological discoveries would be to let the market do its thing. This constitutes the essence of this right-wing defence of ecomodernism. Characteristically, politics is here portrayed as getting in the way of truly groundbreaking inventions (and their societal adoption), which is why *Enlightenment Now* contains such a rallying cry for the urgent need to master planet Earth – with or without democratic control.

In line with utopian visions from the eighteenth century, Pinker's depiction of our climate-changed world is reliant on the image of self-directed improvement towards an ideal state. What Reinhart Koselleck observed with regard to the foundational utopia of the Enlightenment period – Louis-Sébastien Mercier's *L'An 2440* – still rings true for Pinker and his adepts today:

> Mercier's utopia of the future is a variant of the philosophy of progress; its theoretical foundation is the temporalization of the *perfectio* ideal. The anticipation of the future was only redeemable as the cognitive

---

[44] Consider Immanuel Kant's writings on colonialism, which have recently received sustained attention. See: Flikschuh and Ypi, *Kant and Colonialism*.

[45] Grandin, *The End of the Myth*.

achievement of the author and writer ... The author is first of all no
historian or chronicler but is foremost the producer of the coming time,
executor of its aptitude for perfection. He is, so to speak, the incarnation
of the utopian dimension that inheres within every philosophy of history.[46]

Pinker's market-friendly defence of the ecomodernist wager can be
juxtaposed with an alternative one that approaches the same conundrum
from a left-wing perspective. A collection of articles in a recent issue of
Jacobin attempts to work towards a new socialist politics that joins up with
ecological activism and planning initiatives. The issue editor, Alyssa
Battistoni, sums up what is at stake with such a proposal. First, it must
accept the fact that the revolution is not simply around the corner:

> The Left's vision of radical transformation can seem like an obvious match
> for the climate challenge. But the Left remains historically weak and a
> return to real power on the scale required isn't likely anytime soon —
> certainly not on the timescale we need to start taking serious action. We
> can't shortcut the long-term project of building socialism — but nor can
> we sideline climate action along the way. Otherwise, even in the best-case
> scenario, the Left will win power only to manage a state of increasing
> climate breakdown. So no matter how necessary a break with capitalism is,
> for now we'll have to settle for addressing climate change as best we can
> within it. That means pushing hard to decarbonize as rapidly as possible in
> ways that set the stage for a sustainable socialist society.[47]

What is intriguing about the positions debated in *Jacobin* is how they all
try to carefully manoeuvre between a vision of the Anthropocene in
which the socialist agents of radical transformation seek to master planet
Earth, and a rival one where the emphasis lies much more on the
ecological underpinnings of socialism itself. Battistoni appears to be a
proponent of the latter standpoint, with her plea to inaugurate a "future
whose glory can last a lot longer than thirty years."[48] The only way to
promote this type of social dreaming is by taking account of the labour
movement in its plurality, including not only classical blue-collar

[46] Koselleck, "The Temporalization of Utopia," 90.
[47] Battistoni, "Within and against Capitalism."
[48] Battistoni, "Living, Not Just Surviving."

(productive), but also care and educational (socially reproductive) work. Waiting for the revolution to happen and wipe away capitalism, particularly in the current context of right-wing insurgencies around the globe, would be an indulgence that we simply cannot afford: the extreme urgency of the Anthropocene's many crises necessitates a rethink of socialism's temporal horizons.

In other words, what renders the current struggles around productive as well as socially reproductive labour so tenacious is the realization that climate change itself poses a challenge to how working-class movements organize themselves. Fighting for better workplaces is today simply insufficient for addressing the havoc that a fossil fuel–dependent economy has already been wreaking upon vulnerable people around the world. The collective struggle has therefore got to become both broader and more ambitious, creating transversal alliances that feed on utopian visions:

> Organizing reproduction in a new way means making the work of our daily survival less onerous and more pleasurable. It means creating and maintaining spaces of communal luxury and collective leisure – lush public parks and gardens, beautiful spaces for recreation and relaxation, art and culture accessible to all.[49]

While Battistoni makes the case for a socialist vision that is ecologically sensitive and democratically legitimate, other authors have embraced more technocratic solutions. As a consequence, some of the contributions to the *Jacobin* issue veer towards a version of ecomodernism that deviates from Battistoni's bottom-up approach.[50] The state, on this rival account, has to be much more ambitiously positioned as a sovereign agent of innovation so as to thwart the misguided trust many ecomodernists, such as Pinker and his followers, put in purely market-based solutions. The worry here is that the short-termism of venture capital might undermine technologies that offset the negative effects of anthropogenic

[49] Battistoni.

[50] The issue also contains a number of articles that historically contextualize contemporary environmentalism and analyze some of its antinomies. See for example: Aronoff, "The Eco-Right's One Simple Trick"; Billet, "Bono Kills the Planet"; Marcetic, "People Make the World Go Round"; Riofrancos, "Digging Free of Poverty."

climate change.[51] The state's involvement does not only pertain to the funding of science, it also affects ideas of accountability and popular control that bring us closer to the core of the left-wing plea for mastering planet Earth.[52]

Leigh Philipps and Michal Rogowski, for example, claim that efforts at regulating markets, such as the ones endorsed by the ecomodernist manifesto, are fundamentally unfit for the task of decarbonizing the economy in its entirety. The only meaningful alternative would be a "global, democratically planned economy,"[53] which the authors propose as a long-term goal whose pursuit should guide action in the immediate future. Expressing both exhilaration and anxiety about the Anthropocene, Philipps and Rogowski maintain that, rather than allowing global capital to monopolize humanity's "awesome capability" to interfere with atmospheric and geological processes on a planetary scale, our species needs to redirect its prowess so that it genuinely satisfies human needs. Embracing the notion of a "good Anthropocene" from a left-wing perspective, the authors press fellow travellers to

> accept our role as collective sovereign of Earth and begin influencing and coordinating planetary processes with purpose and direction, ever furthering human flourishing. We cannot reach this worthy goal without democratic planning and a steady overcoming of the market. The scale of what we must do – the biogeophysical processes we must understand, track, and master in order to prevent dangerous climate change and associated threats — is almost unfathomable. We cannot trust the irrational, unplanned market with its perverse incentives to coordinate ecosystems. Counteracting climate change and planning the economy are of comparable ambition: if we can manage the Earth system, with all its variables and myriad processes, we can also manage a global economy.[54]

---

[51] Tarnoff, "Bill Gates Won't Save Us."

[52] This idea about the central importance of the state will appear again in the next section where I discuss Kim Stanley Robinson's *Science in the Capital* trilogy. Just like the left ecomodernists, Robinson too is convinced that the state must play a crucial role in shoring up investment for science and technology.

[53] Phillips and Rozworski, "Planning the Good Anthropocene." For a more comprehensive elaboration of this argument see: Phillips, *Austerity Ecology & the Collapse-Porn Addicts.*

[54] Phillips and Rozworski, "Planning the Good Anthropocene."

The suggestion here, with its stress on mastering planet Earth, noticeably echoes what Pinker advocates as well: the sheer scale of the problem makes anything other than a confident assertion of human supremacy appear frivolous. The main difference between Pinker's and this plea for a "good Anthropocene" is that the *Jacobin* contributors are strongly invested in central planning mechanisms that they believe need to be democratically legitimated. Naturally, Pinker is entirely opposed to such top-down statism.

Pushing this socialist reading of ecomodernism even further, Peter Frase wants the Left to deliberate more frankly about the virtues of geoengineering. Geoengineering can be defined as the "deliberate large-scale manipulation of the planetary environment to counteract anthropogenic climate change."[55] Proponents of such manipulation usually argue that we are already influencing the planetary environment through our greenhouse gas emissions; we only do so in incredibly destructive ways. To counter these negative impacts, new measures are urgently required. Examples of positive interventions include carbon capture – the trapping and storing of CO_2 underground[56] – and the biological fertilization of the oceans, which is also thought to have a beneficial effect on the sequestering of atmospheric carbon.[57] Frase suggests that measures like these offer us a glimpse of a bright future that we can shape in our interests and according to our needs. As such, geoengineering disabuses the Left of its obsession with the siren songs of apocalypse and collapse. Constant lamentation of the imminent end of the world

> can encourage passivity and quiescence. This can take the pessimistic form of anticipating inevitable doom, or the optimistic conviction that the present system will necessarily fall and be replaced by something better. Neither version motivates political action. This is the purpose of raising the prospect of geoengineering in a left context – not as a substitute for

---

[55] The Royal Society, "Geoengineering the Climate," 1.

[56] For some of the mechanisms around carbon capture and sequestration see: Lal, "Carbon Sequestration"; Post and Kwon, "Soil Carbon Sequestration and Land-Use Change."

[57] Lampitt R.S. et al., "Ocean Fertilization." For a critique see: Strong et al., "Ocean Fertilization."

decarbonization, but as part of a larger portrait of eco-socialism. Drawing this portrait matters, because the Left has always motivated itself for the immediate struggle by looking to a vision of a better world in the future. And for that vision to appear both realistic and appealing today, it must encompass both the end of fossil fuels and active intervention in the climate. Otherwise we are left to imagine a future of hair-shirt austerity at best, and apocalyptic die-off at worst.[58]

Asserting humanity's sovereignty over nature is therefore an imperative for our survival in the Anthropocene. The scientific and technological means through which this "vision of a better world in the future" can be realized resemble the ones recommended by rival ecomodernists: nuclear as well as solar power are increasingly seen as playing a vital role in the Left's decoupling strategy. In sum, as another defender of this strategy has put it, "our mission as a species is not to retreat from, or to preserve, something called 'nature', but rather to become fully conscious environment makers. Extreme technology under public ownership will be central to a socialist project of civilizational rescue, or civilization will not last."[59]

Despite the overlaps between this conception of humans as "fully conscious environment makers" and Pinker's position, a chasm separates these two approaches: the left-wing appropriation of ecomodernism does not hang on an overarching story of progress that draws its theoretical legitimacy from the Enlightenment. The contributors to *Jacobin* recognize the importance of popular mobilization for transformative politics, whereas Pinker seems to think that we already have all the necessary instruments at our disposal to address the present challenge.

At the same time, the left-wing variety of ecomodernism remains rooted in an optimism about science and technology that venerates human ingenuity. This seems to be true despite variations within the Left's invocation of a "good Anthropocene": Battistoni's emphasis on bottom-up approaches obviously differs from the top-down measures favoured by Philipps, Rogowski and Frase. Nonetheless, both are keen

[58] Frase, "By Any Means Necessary." See also: Frase, *Four Futures*.
[59] Parenti, "If We Fail." See also: Parenti, *Tropic of Chaos*.

to assert our species' tremendous abilities, without which the ecomodernist wager would be nothing but wishful thinking.

It should not come as a surprise that this socialist dream has also received its fair amount of criticism. The main charge levelled against this left vision of a "good Anthropocene" revolves around the issue of growth. The very purpose of decoupling human from natural development is to forestall another proposal that has enjoyed heightened support within environmental movements since the 1970s: that the only effective and just response to the current crisis can be found in the pursuit of degrowth strategies. According to defenders of degrowth, an ever-expanding global economy will by necessity erode the material basis on which organized human life depends. Instead of untrammelled market mechanisms, degrowthers tend to gesture towards a radically different society that is sustained by care, reciprocity and simplicity.[60]

This is where the rift within the contemporary Left becomes visible. We have already observed that for some of the ecomodernists writing in *Jacobin*, degrowth proposals point in the wrong direction – central planning and innovative technologies should be mobilized for socially as well as environmentally desirable goals. Sustainability is for them a goal that can be achieved – for the time being – within the structures of actually existing capitalism. This conjecture has been lambasted for erasing a long tradition of socialism that keeps the prospect of a genuine alternative to the status quo alive. In the words of John Bellamy Foster,

> [w]hat is remarkable about the contributions *to Jacobin*'s special issue on the environment and related works by its writers and editors is how removed they are from genuine socialism—if this involves a revolution in social and ecological relations, aimed at the creation of a world of substantive equality and environmental sustainability. What we get instead is a mechanistic, technoutopian "solution" to the climate problem that ignores the social relations of science and technology, along with human needs and the wider environment ... The ecological crisis brought on by

---

[60] The literature on degrowth is too variegated to be covered in any sort of detail here. For introductory purposes, see: D'Alisa, Demaria, and Kallis, *Degrowth*; Liegey and Nelson, *Exploring Degrowth*; Hausknost, "Degrowth and Democracy"; Czech, "The Steady State Economy."

capitalism is used here to justify the setting aside of all genuine ecological values. The issue's contributors instead endorse a "Good Anthropocene," or a renewed conquest of nature, as a means of perpetuating the basic contours of present-day commodity society, including, most disastrously, its imperative for unlimited exponential growth. Socialism, conceived in these terms, becomes nearly indistinguishable from capitalism—not a movement to replace generalized commodity society, but homologous with the fundamental structure of capitalist modernity.[61]

Infinite growth is nothing but a chimera, critics like Foster surmise, that a socialist environmentalism must dismantle.[62] Simply put, the attempt to reconcile the ecomodernist promise of asserting human sovereignty over nature with a sincere commitment to equality and sustainability runs the risk of being self-contradictory. As Stefania Barca has convincingly argued concerning the history of Marxist thought on ecological crises, socialists have for a long time been facing a profound predicament with respect to environmental concerns: for the labour movement to gain traction and hold power, productive work needs to be sustained by constant industrial investment and technological innovation, which in turn threatens the material basis on which an alternative future can be built.[63] This dilemma continues to vex the Left's formulation of the ecomodernist wager.

4.1.3 THE DREAM TURNED NIGHTMARE: NEW JERUSALEM OR BRAVE NEW WORLD?. Having reviewed these competing versions of ecomodernism, we are now in a position to take stock and survey their rich utopian textures. In stark contrast with our first constellation, the Gaia figure and the notion of a living planet endowed with vengeful agency, defenders of ecomodernism invest hope in humanity's ingenuity to forge paths out of the current quandary. The maps that these utopians draw get illuminated by an unshakeable faith in science and technology.

---

[61] Foster, "The Long Ecological Revolution."

[62] Leonardi, "Reframing the Left Eco-modernism vs. Orthodox Eco-socialism Debate, or: Assessing the Transformation of the Value-Nature Nexus."

[63] Barca, "Labour and the Ecological Crisis."

Where the proponents of the Gaia hypothesis highlight the interconnectedness of human and non-human agents, many ecomodernists proclaim that such linkages have the unfortunate consequence of harming
both our species and the wider ecosystem. Recall how the purpose of the
Gaia figure is to furnish us with a lens for seeing planetary relations in a
new and surprising light, bringing about a change in perspective that is
supposed to pave the way for a *New Climate Regime* beyond
anthropocentric delusions.

Chapter 3 claimed that Latour's proposal is ultimately hampered by a
lack of precision as to which range of possibilities would be preferable in
the near future. When we ponder what climate change is doing to us and
what we may do about it, a *What-If* inquiry will ineluctably tend towards
the extreme hypothetical end of the utopian spectrum. This is why I have
suggested that the Gaia figure, as well as Jemisin's depiction of a climate-
changed world called the Stillness, resembles intricate thought experiments more than anything else. Their rhetorical clout resides in the
attempt to unsettle how we perceive and inhabit the real world, by setting
into motion estrangement devices that render problematic what we
habitually take for granted.

The absence of concrete plans exposes a lacuna in the *What-If* plot
line that the ecomodernists are trying to fill. The utopian dimension of
their endeavour surfaces most visibly once we pay heed to the ways in
which an alternative to the present moment's impasse is imagined. The
metaphor of "decoupling" human from environmental welfare allows
ecomodernists to simultaneously attain two objectives: to gesture towards
a human agency that affirms collective mastery; and to foreground our
responsibility to conserve, protect and defend nature by promoting
scientific and technological innovations that free our species from its
damaging dependency on a fragile, overburdened ecosystem.

While right- and left-wing advocates of ecomodernism remain divided
over the status of market mechanisms for instigating the desired
unlinking, they share a general attitude of optimism about the future.
Fearmongering and an obsession with impending catastrophe are poor
guides for an era where confusion and anxiety about what should be
done abound. This is why ecomodernists make use of an *If-Only* plot line,
charging their proposals with the emotional energy of a positive outlook

on the future. Their critique of the status quo is unabashedly inflationary, summoning us to recognize that our current outlook on the
Anthropocene remains hampered by needless humility vis-à-vis the
natural world.

One way of inoculating this optimistic stance against the unwanted
contagion with wishful thinking is to posit that we are, broadly speaking,
already in possession of the basic knowledge – both practical and moral –
that will enable us to emancipate ourselves from an over-reliance on
nature. This is, *in nuce*, Pinker's claim about the continuing relevance of
the Enlightenment project. Another way of picturing the transition to a
decoupled humanity is by proclaiming the need for democratic control
of the very processes that can move us into a bright future. This is the
essence of the socialist case for ecomodernism.[64]

In order to further explain the internal diversity of ecomodernist
utopianism, it might help to return to Samuel R. Delany's interpretation
of the different figures of cityscape and countryside that we encountered
in Chapter 2. Recall how Delany distinguishes between four ideal-typical
positions within science fiction: *New Jerusalem, Arcadia, Brave New World*
and *Land of the Flies.* How could we locate ecomodernism within the
matrix drawn by Delany?

As an essentially eutopian project, ecomodernism discards both *Brave
New World* and the *Land of the Flies* as future visions, for they fail to
galvanize action in the face of climate change. Dystopian motifs are,
consequently, largely absent from the ecomodernist imaginary. If they
appear at all, then either as nefarious fantasies that blind us to the
actually wonderous state of the world (as in Pinker) or as intermittent
warning signs that foreground the necessity of radical transformation (as
in the various *Jacobin* contributors).[65] The characteristic intermingling of

---

[64] Paul Mason has recently proposed an argument to this effect. See: Mason, *Clear Bright
Future.* For a similarly optimistic left-wing vision see: Bastani, *Fully Automated Luxury
Communism.*

[65] Another way of putting it would be to suggest that socialist ecomodernists adhere to what
Shinichiro Asayama calls "emancipatory catastrophism" – a way of envisaging climate
change that traces its origins back to capitalism's most destructive tendencies, while
allowing for radical imaginings of the future. See: Asayama, "Catastrophism toward
'Opening up' or 'Closing Down'?"

eutopian and dystopian motifs that we have observed in our first constellation is attenuated here.

Variations within the ecomodernist camp emerge once we attend more closely to how its members conceive of the porous borders between *New Jerusalem* and *Arcadia*. The authors of the ecomodernist manifesto as well as Pinker are staunch admirers of a *New Jerusalem*, revelling in the civilizing force of urbanization and hailing the miraculous properties of science. But the gleaming cityscape is not the only object of their eutopian desire. Many ecomodernists, especially from the left of the political spectrum, also suggest that *Arcadia* is just around the corner – not as a permanent site to inhabit, but as a beautiful place to visit and to enjoy from some distance. Decoupling, via emerging technologies that accelerate the shift to a decarbonized economy, turns wild nature into an enthralling prospect: in the absence of humanity's addiction to fossil fuels, environmental degradation will gradually subside, enabling our species to once again experience being in and with nature, rather than destroying it.

This is a perspective shared by some of the left voices we have heard in this chapter. Recall, for example, how Battistoni insists that "lush public parks and gardens, beautiful spaces for recreation and relaxation" (together with other low-carbon luxuries) must be included in any plan for an environmentally sensitive socialism. *Arcadia* is here construed as a convenient by-product of the concerted effort to move all of humanity into a *New Jerusalem*, a technologically advanced cityscape where the demand for much of the productive work being done right now is significantly reduced through automation.

An upshot of this generally optimistic outlook is that some elements of the ecomodernist wager, such as the faith in geoengineering to balance the climatic equilibrium, appear to downplay the risks and dangers of far-reaching interventions into the environment. Another objection to geoengineering is based on an analysis of the political economy undergirding it. Philip Mirowski, for example, has argued that geoengineering marks the last stage on neoliberalism's spectrum of responses to climate change. What starts off as barefaced denialism about scientific facts morphs into an enthusiastic endorsement of taxing carbon emissions, culminating finally in the ultimate techno-fix: geoengineering.[66]

The problem that surfaces in this context is that, by highlighting optimistic themes in their visions of the future, ecomodernists, especially of the market-friendly variety, tend to think about human ingenuity in a rather simplistic manner, as the sole font of unblemished progress. The violent and vicious side of our species is usually brushed away as an atavistic remainder of an age before the "humanitarian revolution."

This tendency to overemphasize our species' resourcefulness becomes rampant in the ecomodernists' treatment of cutting-edge technologies that are intrinsically ambivalent. As we have already seen, authors like Pinker and Frase conceive of geoengineering along the lines of a planetary ethics of care that ultimately benefit all of humanity. Fully buying into the Promethean aspects of this proposal, their eutopian desire is spurred through an enthusiastic willingness to "think big." Oliver Morton, one of the most outspoken defenders of geoengineering today, taps into this enthusiasm when he writes:

> There is much to criticize in such thinking. It can be horribly simplistic. It can feed on, and give rise to, ideas about 'the control of nature' that are neither plausible nor palatable. It can be used to justify inaction. But I believe it can also open up doors, doors both practical and utopian. I think there may be ways in which climate geoengineering could really reduce harm. I also think that imagining geoengineered worlds that might be good to live in, in which people could be safer and happier than they would otherwise be, is worth doing. A utopia does not need to be attainable – indeed, by definition it cannot be. But that is not a reason to reject utopian thought. It is part of the reason for embracing it.[67]

Even though theorists like Morton seek to account for both the potentials and the perils of geoengineering, this ambivalence is frequently flattened out in much of this discourse. Ecomodernists often fail to consider the social and political implications of their plea for

---

[66] See: Mirowski, *Never Let a Serious Crisis Go to Waste*, chap. 6: The Red Guide to the Neoliberal Playbook.

[67] Morton, *The Planet Remade*, para. 7.97.

geoengineering: their assumptions about feasibility and about what constitutes a "lesser evil" remain highly controversial.[68] Moreover, ecomodernists underrate the extent to which geoengineering fundamentally challenges democratic institutions in their capacity to check on, and reign in, market forces.[69] The fact that geoengineering as a techno-fix possesses undemocratic traits is an obstacle, especially for those on the Left who wish to turn the Anthropocene into a project of state-directed planning in the service of a global working class.[70] If a climate-changed world will be overseen by scientists and engineers, what is left of the promise of an Anthropocene governed by democratic processes that are responsive to the needs and claims of vulnerable and marginalized people? In sum, as Mike Hulme has shown,

> creating a thermostat for the planet through aerosols injected into the stratosphere – is *undesirable, ungovernable* and *unreliable*. It is *undesirable* because regulating global temperature is not the same thing as controlling local weather and climate. It is *ungovernable* because there is no plausible and legitimate process for deciding who sets the world's temperature. And it is *unreliable* because of the law of unintended consequences: deliberate intervention in the atmosphere on a global scale will lead to unpredictable, dangerous and contentious outcomes.[71]

Apart from these worries, we can also identify a further objection to the ecomodernist wager, which derives from ideas encountered in Chapter 3. Recall how Latour reasons that the core idea behind the Gaia figure can be summarized as *universal connectivity without holism*. As we have already seen, Donna Haraway, to name just one other voice, shares this intuition when she lauds "making kin" and "becoming-with" as rejoinders to an ecological crisis in response to which neither techno-fixes nor fatalism seem appropriate.

---

[68] This is the argument in: Gardiner, "Is 'Arming the Future' with Geoengineering Really the Lesser Evil?"

[69] Szerszynski et al., "Why Solar Radiation Management Geoengineering and Democracy Won't Mix."

[70] For a more fine-grained analysis of the potential of geoengineering, which homes in on the utopian potential of degrowth, see: Buck, *After Geoengineering,* chap. 6: Working.

[71] Hulme, *Can Science Fix Climate Change?*, para. 7.8.

At the heart of all these positions lies a commitment to an ontology, epistemology and ethics of relationality. Through its recognition of humanity as inextricably bound up with the planetary ecosystem, such a framework upends anthropocentric worldviews. In this context, the ecomodernists' resolve to liberate humanity from its reliance on natural resource systems might on the surface sound like an auspicious plan, but it presupposes an ideal of human separation and exceptionalism that jars with the kind of ontology, epistemology and ethics advocated by Latour, Haraway and others.

Both right- and left-wing ecomodernists locate the human at the centre of their utopian visions of a "good Anthropocene." As Earthmakers, they proclaim, we should be unabashedly proud of asserting our supremacy over ecological processes that ought to benefit humanity first. Implied in this proposal is a worldview that renounces the connectivity that Gaia, or indeed Jemisin's "Father Earth," embodies. In fact, ecomodernists perceive the sort of entanglements we encountered in Chapter 3 as part of the problem, rather than the solution. Dissolving relationships, unmaking kin is their professed goal. The question arising from this strategy, then, is not only where this leaves nature, but also what it does to us, as a distinct species.

In sum, ecomodernism's optimistic outlook makes it vulnerable to a criticism frequently raised against eutopian visions of all sorts: that they ultimately collapse into wishful thinking, a jubilant hopefulness that fails to take into account the risks and dangers that the current moment actually harbours.[72] I will return to this point shortly, when examining the connecting strands within this utopian constellation, but note here that it inversely mirrors the one aired in the prior chapter: ecomodernism's faith in its transformative potential in the short term – the suggestion that a Promethean type of science and technology can in fact redeem us from this ordeal of intersecting crises – might eclipse its effort to grapple with the deeper structures affecting the Anthropocene.

This fault line surfaces with particular acuity in controversies around the economic system behind ecomodernism. As the argument between

---

[72] On the charge of wishful thinking see: Monbiot, "Meet the Ecomodernists"; Vansintjan, "Decolonizing Nature, the Academy, and Europe."

traditional degrowthers and "alternative growthers" on the Left reminds us, science and technology cannot be easily dissociated from the biophysical conditions that underpin them. Pinker's liberal version of ecomodernism is even more ebullient about the positive feedback loop between capitalism, humanist values and our capacity to harness groundbreaking research for the purpose of mitigating climate change. To return to Stefania Barca's observation, ecomodernism might therefore end up in an impasse, stuck between the emancipatory potential of increased human welfare through socio-economic progress and the clear-headed acknowledgement of the destructive impact of this growth paradigm.

One way out of this dilemma is through another kind of decoupling: not of humanity from the ecosystems that sustain it, but of science and technology from market forces. This is the path taken by our next interlocutor: the novelist Kim Stanley Robinson. As we shall see, what is distinctive about his eutopian stance is that it sets into motion a fierce critique of the growth paradigm itself, without, however, relinquishing faith in the clout of science and technology to address the greatest challenges of the Anthropocene.

4.2 "THE PALAEOLITHIC PLUS GOOD DENTAL CARE": KIM STANLEY ROBINSON'S GALVANIZING APPEALS

Now the future is a kind of attenuating peninsula: As we move out on it, one side drops off to catastrophe; the other side, nowhere near as steep, moves down into various kinds of utopian futures. In other words, we have come to a moment of utopia or catastrophe; there is no middle ground; mediocrity will no longer succeed. So utopia is no longer a nice idea but, rather, a survival necessity.[73]

These days I tend to think of dystopias as being fashionable, perhaps lazy, maybe even complacent, because one pleasure of reading them is cozying into the feeling that however bad our present moment is, it's nowhere near as bad as the ones these poor characters are suffering through. Vicarious thrill of comfort as we witness/imagine/experience the heroic struggles of our

---

[73] Robinson, "Remarks on Utopia in the Age of Climate Change," 10.

afflicted protagonists—rinse and repeat. Is this catharsis? Possibly more like indulgence, and creation of a sense of comparative safety. A kind of late capitalist, advanced-nation schadenfreude about those unfortunate fictional citizens whose lives have been trashed by our own political inaction. If this is right, dystopia is part of our all-encompassing hopelessness.[74]

So look, the problem is capitalism. We've got the good tech, we've got a nice planet, we're fucking it up by way of stupid laws. That's what capitalism is, a set of stupid laws.[75]

Kim Stanley Robinson's writings over the past thirty years have spanned a wide range of topics, from swashbuckling accounts of the century-long colonization of Mars[76] to an unlikely dramatization of scientific exploration in Antarctica.[77] At the same time, his fiction has always dealt with profound socio-economic challenges that contemporary societies confront: environmental disaster as well as global inequality are perhaps the two most persistent preoccupations around which all of his novels revolve. Thus, to suggest that Robinson is America's greatest political novelist does not sound like a great exaggeration anymore.[78]

What is special about Robinson's fiction is that it remains in constant exchange with his scholarly interests: as a former PhD student of Fredric Jameson in the early 1970s, writing his dissertation on Philip K. Dick, he is animated by the historical development of utopianism, eruditely conversing with a large number of scholars across the humanities.[79] His writings are thus propelled by a fascination with the tropes and techniques of the utopian canon.

Robinson's intellectual trajectory evinces an "extremely productive artistic self-consciousness"[80] about both the form and the content of his fictional oeuvre. Moreover, he has over the past fifteen years emerged as

---

[74] Robinson, "Dystopias Now."
[75] Robinson, *New York 2140*, 5.
[76] Robinson, *Red Mars*; Robinson, *Green Mars*; Robinson, *Blue Mars*.
[77] Robinson, *Antarctica*, 1998.
[78] Kreider, "Our Greatest Political Novelist?"
[79] Lydon and Robinson, "Kim Stanley Robinson: We Have Come to a Bad Moment, and We Must Change"; Feder and Robinson, "The Realism of Our Time."
[80] Prettyman, "Living Thought," 183.

one of the most engaged writers working directly on climate change.[81] As we shall see, this interest in the Anthropocene has also led to a noticeable shift in his approach to the motors behind social dreaming – from radical-democratic types of self-governing communities to technocratic bureaucracies as harbingers of positive impact on society.

My contention in this chapter is that Kim Stanley Robinson adheres to a peculiar version of the ecomodernist wager that is at odds with competing utopian projects foregrounding scientific and technological innovations in the pursuit of a "good Anthropocene." Whereas he supports many facets of this kind of social dreaming, such as the faith in dense urbanization[82] and in geoengineering,[83] he completely refutes the market-friendly interpretations advanced by Pinker and others. What is more, Robinson's education of desire for alternative ways of being problematizes its own narrative mode of production, shedding light on the pitfalls of appealing to a "good Anthropocene."

As a consequence, Robinson traces the *If-Only* plot line in an ambivalent, but ultimately affirmative, fashion. His creative reimagining of how science and technology may be put to use for the sake of climate adaptation and mitigation puts forth an optimistic perspective on the multiple challenges of our age. Sometimes, this perspective comes perilously close to wishful thinking, but Robinson strives to avoid naive optimism by exploring a range of realistic pathways out of the ongoing ecological crisis.

Robinson's fiction thus opens up yet another perspective for how we may conceive of a "good Anthropocene." The title of this section already suggests what is unique about his stance: Robinson seeks to marry sweeping plans for socio-economic reform with a firm commitment to science and technology. As a eutopian vision, this proposal envisages the future through the lens of a "proleptic realism" that dramatizes climate change for the purpose of galvanizing collective action. Accordingly, Robinson throws into sharp relief climate change's abrupt effects so as to render the call for immediate, and in some sense depoliticized, responses more urgent.

---

[81] Trexler and Johns-Putra, "Climate Change in Literature and Literary Criticism," 187.

[82] Robinson, "Empty Half the Earth of Its Humans."

[83] Robinson, "Geoengineering Makes Everyone Uneasy, but It Shouldn't"; Kaufman, "The King of Climate Fiction Makes the Left's Case for Geoengineering."

The proposal's exceptional dimension comes to the fore in Robinson's analysis of two rival systems for making sense of a climate-changed world: science and capitalism. While his attack on capitalism puts Robinson firmly in the left-wing camp of ecomodernists, his reverence for science and technology gradually, yet undeniably sets the project up for a conflict with the promise of a democratically governed Anthropocene.

The upshot of this is that Robinson's variety of ecomodernism remains pervaded by a tension arising from his commitment to what is effectively a political order of anti-capitalist governance through science. What is meant here by "governance" will be explored in detail shortly, so suffice it to note that the technocratic bureaucracy favoured by Robinson enters into an almost symbiotic relationship with a new form of politics that mimics populist styles and tactics.

The remainder of this chapter proceeds as follows: after reconstructing Kim Stanley Robinson's understanding of utopianism, I continue with a close reading of his *Science in the Capital* trilogy. These three novels, a sort of "Victorian Triple-Decker,"[84] make an original case for a revised ecomodernism that merits our attention. The orientation that Robinson's prose provides is of particular relevance for our thinking through the Anthropocene: While clearly articulating a eutopian vision of various alternatives to the status quo, the *Science in the Capital* trilogy, with its modelling of multiple pathways into the future, rejects solutionist shortcuts. Some forms of wishful thinking, especially with regard to managerial techno-fixes, are thus successfully contained. But just like any other story written under the guise of a *What-If* plot line, Robinson's utopianism remains pervaded by an irradicable strain. The chapter's final step therefore leads me to an evaluation of Robinson's ecomodernism in light of its utopian credentials.

4.2.1 STRUGGLE FOREVER! KIM STANLEY ROBINSON'S UTOPIANISM.

Robinson's science fiction writing consistently engages with the history and theory of social dreaming.[85] In this section, I aim to describe,

---

[84] Robinson, *Imagining Abrupt Climate Change*, 16.

[85] One of the most systematic essays wherein Robinson elaborates on his understanding of utopianism is: Robinson, "Remarks on Utopia in the Age of Climate Change."

in broad strokes, Robinson's sophisticated understanding of the desire for alternative ways of being and living. My argument is that Robinson's utopianism can be characterized by three interrelated tenets: first, a commitment to proceduralism; second, the incorporation of conflict; and third, an endorsement of open-endedness. While these are the key characteristics of Robinson's utopianism, a prominent element in his oeuvre pertains to the interconnectedness of scientific and moral progress. This becomes especially germane in his later writings, from the *Mars* trilogy onwards, and manifests itself most vividly in the *Science in the Capital* series, our main concern in this chapter.

A good place to start examining the nexus between Robinson's prose and his account of utopianism is in his early work, the *Three Californias* trilogy, published in the 1980s. *The Wild Shore*, *The Gold Coast* and *Pacific Edge* narrate alternatives futures of Orange County on the Pacific coast of the United States.[86] While the first volume, *The Wild Shore*, set in 2047, deals with a post-apocalyptic scenario after a nuclear attack, *The Gold Coast*, set in 2027, contains a critical dystopia depicting life in a near-future California dominated entirely by militarist-consumerist interests.[87]

The final volume, *Pacific Edge*, strikes a eutopian tone and comprises Robinson's most systematic discussion of utopianism in fictional form. Orange County is here imagined as a place of civic resistance against corporate control, establishing for the first time a motif that would become dominant in Robinson's later writings: that building a better place for communal life is a process ridden with massive obstacles that no utopian author can simply push aside. Robinson thus contemplates not only in the abstract what a more sustainable future might look like, but meditates on how we may get there, focusing in particular on the political activism that would be imperative for counteracting the hegemonic order of neoliberalism.

---

[86] On the centrality of California in Robinson's early oeuvre and on the ways in which it transforms historical ideas about the Western frontier, see: Abbott, "Falling into History." Concerning Robinson's engagement with apocalyptic environmentalism for the purpose of probing various, conflicting historical possibilities, see: Evans, "The Best of Times, the Worst of Times, the End of Times?"

[87] The middle volume of the *Three Californias Tryptich* is also a key preoccupation in Tom Moylan's work on critical dystopias. See: Moylan, *Scraps of the Untainted Sky*, 203–21.

A key facet of this third volume is that it narrates, in italicized sections, the thoughts of Tom Barnard, Robinson's *alter ego* and the grandfather of the novel's protagonist, Kevin Claiborne.[88] Barnard's storyline is set in the early twenty-first century, while the main plot unfolds around fifty years later. Since these sections cover, as a meta-text, the notes that Barnard takes while setting out to write a utopian novel, the reader manages to learn more about Robinson's early understanding of utopianism. In an entry in his research diary, Barnard disavows the impulse to imagine utopias in isolation from the wider world – what he dubs "pocket utopias." These visions of an alternative future aim to delimit protected zones of equity and abundance in a world ravaged by injustice and misery. As such, they serve the purpose of exacerbating the unjust state of the current moment, by cutting the utopian project off from the deeper structures that retain the status quo firmly in place. In response to such consolatory "pocket utopias," Robinson's *alter ego* tries to recover another sense of what utopia might mean to us today. In a lengthy passage, Barnard reflects on his own motivations for writing a utopian novel:

> So the utopias in books are pocket utopias too. Ahistorical, static, why should we read them? They don't speak to us trapped in this world as we are, we look at them in the same way we look at the pretty inside of a paperweight, snow drifting down, so what? ...
>
> Must redefine utopia. It isn't the perfect end-product of our wishes, define it so and it deserves the scorn of those who sneer when they hear the word. No. Utopia is the process of making a better world, the name for one path history can take, a dynamic, tumultuous, agonizing process, with no end. Struggle forever.[89]

This interpretation of utopia as a process, rather than an ahistorical, static end state, is symptomatic of Robinson's thinking, and of a wider transformation within the genre itself. As we already observed in Chapter 2, in the late twentieth century, utopian fiction undertook a

---

[88] On the peculiar qualities of *Pacific Edge* as a utopian text see: Moylan, "Utopia Is When Our Lives Matter."

[89] Robinson, *Pacific Edge*, paras. 8.6–8.10, italics in original.

critical, self-reflective turn that provoked authors to jettison the notion of utopia as a perfect and unchangeable ideal. Robinson takes this turn one step further when he explores how the struggle for a better world might play out. In that sense, *Pacific Edge* is a text in the tradition of Ursula K. Le Guin's *The Dispossessed*: its exploration of green forms of social dreaming remains sensitive to the ambiguities and contradictions that the desire for better ways of being and living produces.[90]

For a revolution to succeed, Barnard argues, "*[w]e must imagine the way. Our imagination is stronger than theirs!*"[91] Pondering alternatives is, crucially, not the same as predicting the future. Rather, the utopian imagination serves as a heuristic tool for enabling social actors to trigger change in the face of immense resistance. As Robinson remarks in an interview later on, "[n]o one can predict the future that will really come – that's impossible. But scenarios can be outlined as a kind of modelling exercise, to help us make decisions about what to do now to get to a future we want."[92]

Characteristically, after being detained on spurious grounds, Barnard once again becomes disenchanted with his own ambition to conjure alternative futures. Although he gets close to giving up on the desire for living otherwise, declaring despondently "*[n]o more utopia for me,*"[93] he finally changes direction upon realizing that the process of creating a utopia must never be a solitary one. The last entry in Barnard's diary records his realization that imagining a better place in isolation from others is not conducive to transformation: "*Not just write a utopia, but fight for it in the real world.*"[94]

Given that these notes are inserted into the main storyline, Carol Franko's observation that *Pacific Edge* is "a utopian novel about a utopian novel that wasn't written"[95] appears highly perceptive. A paramount concern in the *Three Californias* trilogy is therefore the demolition of

---

[90] *Pacific Edge* also makes clear reference to Ernest Callenbach's *Ecotopia*. See: Lipschutz, "Eco-utopia or Eco-catastrophe?"

[91] Robinson, *Pacific Edge*, para. 10.10.

[92] Kaufman, "The King of Climate Fiction Makes the Left's Case for Geoengineering."

[93] Robinson, *Pacific Edge*, para. 14.5.

[94] Robinson, para. 15.24.

[95] Franko, "Working the 'In-Between,'" 206.

traditional tropes of utopianism, especially of the notion that utopias designate fixed end points in history. Robinson's insistence on procedural-ism, rather than perfectionism, chimes with the intuition that the means and ends of transformative politics always remain bound up with each other. It also highlights the flaws in the kind of social dreaming that Marx and Engels had lambasted: channelling our imaginative energy towards the final stage of emancipation alone makes utopianism vulnerable to the accusation of wishful thinking.[96] By contrast, if we perceive utopian projects as necessarily in flux and rife with self-doubt, we manage to factor in the massive hurdles that the desire for alternative ways of being and living needs to overcome.

Pacific Edge paved the way for Robinson's next project, which remains to this day his best-known and most celebrated: the *Mars* novels.[97] Robinson explains that the urge to write the *Mars* trilogy stemmed from his awareness that in the future histories of California he "had dodged the necessity of revolution, however broadly conceived."[98] The series continues Robinson's exploration of utopianism by transposing it from a near-future Earth to a multigenerational tale of outer space coloniza-tion. In the trilogy, Mars is depicted as an inhospitable, but ultimately malleable, planet on which the human quest for self-betterment can be reignited, while Earth edges more and more towards ecological destruc-tion at the hands of exploitative transnational corporations. The narra-tive contrast between these two lifeworlds, one on Mars, the other on Earth, is amongst Robinson's most effective trappings.[99]

Red Mars, the first volume, grapples with the pitfalls of early coloniza-tion, following conflicts between the first colonists, a group of highly skilled scientists, astronauts and politicians. Two major issues split this

---

[96] On this point see: Geuss, "The Metaphysical Need and the Utopian Impulse"; Geuss, "Realism and the Relativity of Judgement"; Geuss, "Realism, Wishful Thinking, Utopia"; Geuss.

[97] Robinson, *Red Mars*; Robinson, *Green Mars*; Robinson, *Blue Mars*. The literature on the Mars trilogy is vast. For a helpful introduction, see: Franko, "Kim Stanley Robinson." For a more comprehensive discussion of the Mars trilogy in the context of the Anthropocene debate, see: Wark, *Molecular Red*, chap. 4: Kim Stanley Robinson: The Necessity of Creation.

[98] Robinson, "Remarks on Utopia in the Age of Climate Change," 4.

[99] Mars has played a central role in the development of the utopian imagination. For a comprehensive overview of Mars as a literary trope, see: Markley, *Dying Planet*.

heterogenous group: the relationship between the new society to be formed on Mars and the acrimonious politics on Earth; and the plans for terraforming, the manipulation of the Martian atmosphere, topography and ecology to make the planet more habitable for mankind – in short, to render Mars more Earth-like.[100]

Both issues are interwoven with each other, for the creation of a life-support system in extremely adverse conditions hinges on the stability of socio-economic structures governing human life on Mars.[101] The colonists are divided over the extent to which Mars should be made to resemble Earth. On the one side, we find the Red faction, arguing for the careful conservation of the Martian ecosphere on both cultural and aesthetic grounds;[102] on the other side is the Green faction, pleading for maximum terraforming in light of humanity's dire situation back on Earth.[103] These controversies around the future of the colony occur in the context of deteriorating circumstances on our home planet. Ultimately, a revolution to overthrow the transnational corporations on Mars is sparked, yet it fails to gain sufficient traction and is quashed.[104]

---

[100] The idea of terraforming was first explored by the American science fiction writer Jack Williamson, in his short story "Collision Orbit," published in 1942. Interestingly, Lovelock has published a book on this topic as well. See: Allaby and Lovelock, *The Greening of Mars*. For an analysis of terraforming in contemporary speculative fiction, see: Pak, *Terraforming*.

[101] The process of changing humans for the new Martian society is called "areoforming." On the connection between terraforming Mars and "areoforming" humans, see: Franko, "The Density of Utopian Destiny in Robinson's Red Mars"; Pak, "'All Energy Is Borrowed' – Terraforming."

[102] As the geologist and founder of the Reds, Ann Clayborne, points out: "We are not lords of the universe. We're one small part of it. We may be its consciousness, but being the consciousness of the universe does not mean turning it all into a mirror image of us. It means rather fitting into it as it is, and worshiping it with our attention" (Robinson, *Red Mars*, para. 17.126).

[103] As one of the most outspoken advocates of terraforming and *spiritus rector* of the Greens, Sax Russell, notes: "Science is part of a larger human enterprise, and that enterprise includes going to the stars, adapting to other planets, adapting them to us. Science is creation. The lack of life here, and the lack of any finding in fifty years of the SETI program, indicates that life is rare, and intelligent life even rarer. And yet the whole meaning of the universe, its beauty, is contained in the consciousness of intelligent life. We are the consciousness of the universe, and our job is to spread that around, to go look at things, to live everywhere we can" (Robinson, para. 17.124).

[104] On the leitmotif of revolution in the *Mars* trilogy, see: Cho, "Tumults of Utopia."

In setting up the epic narrative, the first volume foregrounds a motif that will become increasingly germane throughout the entire trilogy: Robinson's incorporation of irresolvable conflict into the story, between the Reds and the Greens, but also between the Mars colonists and the authorities exerting control over Earth, demonstrates he is fully aware of the difficulties that accompany any effort to turn a utopian vision into reality.

Green Mars resumes the focus on revolution and on the terraforming project but zooms fifty years ahead. Robinson now describes in great detail the planet's sweeping manipulation: from gigantic mirrors in the orbit that capture sunlight, to "moholes," deep shafts digging under the planet's crust to release heat. These measures keep on dividing the colonists, with a large number of them advocating for the preservation of Mars' barren beauty. While the planet is more and more terraformed so as to build a viable habitat for humans, Earth is being rapidly destroyed through the sudden eruption of several volcanos. As a consequence, the Martian colonists finally manage to liberate themselves from Terran oversight. This second revolution on Mars is much more successful than the before.

Blue Mars, set in the twenty-second century, brings the trilogy to a close. Terraforming has led not only to the greening of the planet, but also to the widespread availability of water on Mars (hence the novel's title). The long-term effects of successful colonization become apparent and eventually facilitate the spreading of human civilization beyond the solar system. The political question of how a free Mars should govern itself emerges as one of the novel's central themes.

The final part also deals with the impressions of Mars settlers as they ultimately return to an Earth devastated by climatic catastrophes. A hopeful atmosphere suffuses the conclusion, with one prominent member of the Red faction solemnly stating: "Nowhere on this world were people killing each other, nowhere were they desperate for shelter or food, nowhere were they scared for their kids. There was that to be said."[105]

---

[105] Robinson, *Blue Mars*, para. 79.75. Notice that this statement appears to echo Theodor Adorno's minimal definition of utopia as "rien faire comme une bête." See: Adorno, *Minima Moralia*, 157.

As with Robinson's other novels, the *Mars* trilogy culminates without a redemptive conclusion. This embrace of open-endedness is a key component of Robinson's utopianism.[106] If struggle is an indelible feature of any utopian project, then we can never reach a moment where we might truthfully say: now our dreams have become reality. "[T]he distance between the idealized operations of a frictionless system and the wear and tear of embodied, historical existence"[107] remains fully on display in all of Robinson's utopian fiction.

In what ways does the *Mars* trilogy deepen Robinson's understanding of social dreaming, compared to the meta-textual notes interspersed throughout *Pacific Edge*? We have already observed that Robinson does not ignore vexing questions about the conflictual processes set into motion by utopian desire. The practical struggle for utopia is a dominant concern of the *Mars* trilogy. The stark disparity between life on Earth and the new settlement on Mars opens up new avenues for critiquing modes of socio-economic cooperation on our home planet. In the *Mars* trilogy, this happens primarily through the refusal of the initial colonists to view Mars solely as an external resource for a rapidly depleting and politically corrupt Earth. Instead of succumbing to the extractive pressure of transnational corporations, the organizational model on Mars is one in which environmental considerations are built into the socio-economic relations from the get-go, amounting to what Robinson dubs an "eco-economic" worldview.[108] The underlying political system is

---

[106] Note here that Lucy Sargisson, too, speaks of the open-ended nature of what she terms "transgressive utopianism." See: Sargisson, *Utopian Bodies and the Politics of Transgression*, 11.

[107] Markley, "Falling into Theory," 775.

[108] For a picture of eco-economics, see this programmatic passage: "The legislature was passing the laws of eco-economics, fleshing out the bones drawn up in the constitution. They directed co-ops that had existed before the revolution to help the newly independent metanat local subsidiaries to transform themselves into similar cooperative organizations. This process, called horizontalization, had very wide support, especially from the young natives, and so it was proceeding fairly smoothly. Every Martian business now had to be owned by its employees only. No co-op could exceed one thousand people; larger enterprises had to be made of co-op associations, working together. For their internal structures most of the firms chose variants of the Bogdanovist models, which themselves were based on the cooperative Basque community of Mondragon, Spain. In these firms all employees were co-owners, and they

akin to a radical form of democracy that breaks with the system of representative government.[109]

Robinson's commitment to proceduralism, his incorporation of conflict and his embrace of open-endedness all cohere into a systematic understanding of utopianism that is inoculated against wishful thinking. As we already observed in Chapter 2, Fredric Jameson argued that the crucial point of the utopian desire is not necessarily to make present alternative futures, but rather to bring into play new forms of imagining that undo the hegemonic power structures of the current moment. Achieving such a rupture with the status quo is the core objective of estrangement devices. Typically, this break is performed through what Jameson calls "world reduction," "a process of ontological attenuation in which the sheer teeming multiplicity of what exists, of what we call reality, is deliberately thinned and weeded out through an operation of radical abstraction and simplification."[110]

This is precisely what the *Mars* trilogy strives for, a "radical abstraction and simplification" of reality such that its constituent building blocks become visible. Hence, Robinson's novels, in all their epic grandeur, are not primarily about why and how outer space colonization might succeed or fail. Any progress made on Mars – for example, concerning the independence of Martian society from corporate control – cannot be taken as assured. For, as Jameson reminds us,

> it is an achievement that must constantly be renewed ... And it is also a structural presupposition of this utopia, since we do not ever witness its evolution as a narrative event; perhaps indeed we could not do so. Yet utopia as a form is not the representation of radical alternatives; it is rather simply the imperative to imagine them.[111]

---

bought into their positions by paying the equivalent of about a year's wages to the firm's equity fund, wages earned in apprentice programs of various kinds at the end of schooling" (Robinson, *Blue Mars*, para. 40.1).

[109] Burling, "The Theoretical Foundation of Utopian Radical Democracy in Kim Stanley Robinson's Blue Mars."

[110] Jameson, "World-Reduction in Le Guin," 223.

[111] Jameson, "If I Find One Good City I Will Spare the Man," 231.

Science and technology provide us with vital resources for the radical alternatives that Jameson advocates. This becomes clearer during the debates around terraforming in the *Mars* trilogy, but even more so in Robinson's subsequent work. In what might be the only novel set exclusively on the continent, *Antarctica*[112] contains Robinson's attempt to account for life on the "continent of science."[113] *Antarctica* seeks to project some of the chief preoccupations of the *Mars* trilogy back down to Earth: how can social relations be organized in circumstances of extreme hardship? What sort of economic system is suitable for regulating common affairs under conditions of structural scarcity? In what ways can a polity sustain itself over time, while living "lightly off the Earth"?[114]

Based on first-hand research and equipped with a grant from the National Science Foundation, Robinson set out to explore life on Antarctica. The resulting book portrays the continent as the vulnerable habitat of a utopian community of scientists and workers, governed by egalitarian principles, rather than by the profit-orientation of capitalist corporations, which remain barred from the continent to this day. As a consequence, Robinson identifies a persistent rivalry between two competing systems of valuation, capitalism and science, associating capitalism with degeneration and science with utopia.[115] In the enthusiastic elegy of one of the protagonists of *Antarctica*: "[W]hat we think of as neutral objective science is actually a utopian politics and worldview ... Things like reproducibility, or Occam's razor, or peer review – almost everything in science that makes it specifically scientific ... is utopian."[116]

Although set on a present-day Earth, *Antarctica* thus grapples with many of the themes negotiated in his earlier writings, as Robinson explains:

> As far as you can tell when you're there, the continent runs using a
> nonmonetary economic system, where food, clothing, shelter, and fuel

---

[112] Robinson, *Antarctica*, 1999.

[113] On how Antarctica came to be associated so closely with scientific endeavours, see: Howkins, "Emerging from the Shadow of Science"; Roberts, *The European Antarctic.*

[114] Pepper, "Utopianism and Environmentalism," 10.

[115] On Robinson's reassessment of the state's capacity to regulate the oppressive forces of the market, see: Moylan, "The Moment Is Here ... and It's Important."

[116] Robinson, *Antarctica*, 1999, 350.

are all provided by the community; and at the same time you get to do what you want in terms of your project. It was a limited version of utopia but interesting as a kind of laboratory experiment, a brief experience of how it might feel to live in a different social order. It was not exactly Orwell in Barcelona but exhilarating in a different way. And it was very useful in my attempt to combine utopian and wilderness thinking, as well as to bring all these things closer to home than Mars.[117]

Antarctica's description of science as utopian, as well as its setting in the near future, make the novel an important precursor to the *Science in the Capital* trilogy.[118] Robinson's decision to move the story from an extra-terrestrial setting back down to our home planet also brings with it a significant shift in the narrative's temporal horizons. *Antarctica*, as well as the *Science in the Capital* series, is located in a future much closer to the present than his prior novels. With characteristic acumen, Robinson has himself theorized these competing temporalities:

> Space operas set in the distant future use the whole Universe as a story space, sometimes to spectacular effect. Near-future science fiction is the proleptic realism ... In between these, say from about one to three centuries from now, there exists a less-populated story zone that I find interesting. You could call it future history. Stories set in this zone resemble nineteenth-century social novels: the characters interact not just with each other, but with their societies and even their planets. Possibly, confronted with the mind-boggling complexity of our present, describing events a century from now allows us to de-strand chosen elements for closer examination.[119]

Drawing on this schematic outline, it is obvious that both the *Three Californias* trilogy and the *Mars* trilogy need to be considered "future histories," located long before the advent of far-future narratives, such as Jemisin's *Broken Earth* trilogy for example. *Antarctica*, by contrast, is an example of what Robinson calls "proleptic realism," relating "the present in the way a skeet shooter targets a clay pigeon, aiming a bit ahead of the

---

[117] Robinson, "Remarks on Utopia in the Age of Climate Change," 5.
[118] Trexler, *Anthropocene Fictions*, 154.
[119] Beukes et al., "Science Fiction When the Future Is Now."

moment to reveal what is not yet present but is already having an impact."[120]

Robinson suggests that these different temporalities are all part of the wider project of science fiction, which holds in a productive tension the modelling of possible futures with the estrangement of the status quo:

> [S]cience fiction works by a kind of double action, like the glasses people wear when watching 3D movies. One lens of science fiction's aesthetic machinery portrays some future that might actually come to pass; it's a kind of proleptic realism. The other lens presents a metaphorical vision of our current moment, like a symbol in a poem. Together the two views combine and pop into a vision of History, extending magically into the future.[121]

The different timelines of science fiction – the two lenses Robinson alludes to – matter greatly to my argument around utopia's various functions. As we have seen in Jemisin's case, focusing on a far-future narrative has the virtue of radically subverting ways of seeing the world that are taken for granted. Stories set in the far future lure the reader into what I have called "planet-centred thinking." Such a de-familiarizing strategy can, however, come at the expense of concrete proposals as to how we should proceed in the real world. Urging the readers to act collectively in the face of massive obstacles is the main purpose of near-future utopias, with their "proleptic realism." The next section will explore this galvanizing effect in more detail.

4.2.2 TERRAFORMING EARTH: THE *SCIENCE IN THE CAPITAL* TRILOGY. The *Science in the Capital* trilogy, published between 2004 and 2007, tells the story of a small group of scientists, administrators, politicians and religious leaders, who all seek to address the devastating consequences of abrupt climate change. The plot is mainly set in a near-future version of Washington, DC, a city that is recognizable as

---

[120] Beukes et al. It is possible that Robinson has borrowed the term "proleptic realism" from one of his critical readers. For it was Roger Luckhurst who first employed it to interpret Robinson's recent science fiction. See: Luckhurst, "The Politics of the Network."

[121] Robinson, "Dystopias Now."

the actual capital of the United States. Through careful descriptions of Washington's topography, the reader is regularly taken on a tour of major landmarks, from the White House to the Potomac River.[122]

The trilogy's cast of characters can be divided into three broad categories: first, there is a set of scientists and administrators, collaborating at the National Science Foundation (NSF). The most important members of this group are Frank Vanderwal, a professor of mathematics, who is on a temporary secondment to the NSF; Anna Quibler, a scientist managing the evaluation of grant proposals; and Diane Chang, the powerful and cunning director of the NSF. Second, we encounter a smaller group of characters belonging to the sphere of politics. Chief amongst those is Phil Chase, a Democratic senator from California, who pursues a progressive agenda with respect to climate change and social inequality; and Charlie Quibler, Anna's spouse and Chase's long-term advisor on environmental policy. Third, a group of Tibetan Buddhist monks from the fictitious island of Khembalung,[123] recently displaced from their home due to considerable inundations, joins the crowd in Washington. This cast remains relatively stable over the almost 1,500 pages of the three novels, with only a few side characters entering and departing the main storyline.

The trilogy's first instalment, *Forty Signs of Rain*,[124] sets the scene by delving into the institutional workings of the NSF. Frank, an outsider in the science policy world, is increasingly unhappy with the shortcomings of the management delivered by the NSF, bemoaning the slowness and inefficacy of existing funding bodies. The Quiblers, by contrast, lead a family-oriented life, with Charlie occupying the role of stay-at-home dad, devoting most of his attention to raising their toddler Joe. Charlie's wife Anna is a workaholic and hyper-rationalist scientist, who by chance befriends the Khembali climate refugees. The scientists and administrators at the NSF operate within a political setting dominated by a conservative Republican president (unnamed in the book, but easily

---

[122] In fact, the city is often rendered in painstaking detail that is reminiscent of classical realist literature. See: Johns-Putra, "Ecocriticism, Genre, and Climate Change," 756.

[123] It is likely Robinson took the name for this fictitious island from one of the "secret valleys" in the Himalaya region. See: Reinhard, "Khembalung."

[124] Robinson, *Forty Signs of Rain*.

identifiable as George W. Bush), whose denialism about climate change is assailed by Phil Chase, a Democratic senator putting forth a much more environmentally ambitious plan.

The crucial events in *Forty Signs of Rain* take place over one day, during which Frank decides to quit the NSF and return to his teaching job. In a heated letter addressed to its director, Diane Chang, Frank decries the malaise in which the scientific community finds itself:

> Free market fundamentalists are dragging us back to some dismal feudal eternity and destroying everything in the process, and yet we have the technological means to feed everyone, house everyone, clothe everyone, doctor everyone, educate everyone – the ability to end suffering and want as well as ecological collapse is right here at hand, and yet NSF continues to dole out its little grants, fiddling while Rome burns!!!![125]

Immediately after posting this letter, Frank attends a lecture by a Khembali elder, Rudra Cakrin, in which the Buddhist monk makes the case for understanding science as compatible with compassion. In a surprising twist, Frank's rigorous mind proves to be susceptible to these spiritual teachings, especially as they tally with his attention to altruism as an evolutionary strategy for optimal group behaviour. During the lecture, Frank experiences an eureka moment when he hears a statement that resonates deeply with his own experience: "An excess of reason is itself a form of madness."[126] This rebuke unsettles Frank's rationalistic worldview. *Forty Signs of Rain* ends with an episode of extreme weather that brings the effects of abrupt climate change home to an American audience: a major storm reaches Washington and causes widespread flooding, leading to the inundation of the National Mall under several feet of water.[127]

The trilogy's second volume, *Fifty Degrees Below*, foregrounds the NSF's responses to climate change. Diane Chang has elected to ignore Frank Vanderwal's resignation letter and instead appoints him to chair a

---

[125] Robinson, para. 1.1463.

[126] Robinson, para. 1.1863.

[127] Note here that Robinson describes the devastation of Washington in terms that would only one year after the book's publication, in 2006, be used to capture the almost complete destruction of New Orleans by Hurricane Katrina.

committee dedicated to the development of mitigation and adaptation measures. The frantic work of this committee cuts across science funding and environmental policy, bringing together various government agencies to promote the cause of the NSF. Amongst the measures being proposed are various forms of geoengineering:

> One of the obvious places to start here was with the thermohaline circulation stall . . .
>
> So, Diane concluded, this had to be investigated. How big a sea surface was critical to downwelling? How precisely could they pinpoint potential downwelling sites? How big a volume of water were they talking about? If they needed to make it saltier in order to force it to start sinking again, how much salt were they talking about? . . .
>
> Edgardo grinned. "So – we are going to become global biosphere managers. We are going to terraform the Earth!"
>
> "We already are," Diane replied. "The problem is we don't know how."[128]

The "thermohaline circulation stall" alluded to in this passage refers to the slow breaking up of the Gulf Stream, which under normal conditions ensures that the North Atlantic and its bordering land masses stay reasonably warm. Amongst other measures, Frank Vanderwal's committee brings on the way the "first major act of planetary engineering ever attempted,"[129] a $100 billion operation to re-salinize the North Atlantic, marshalling an armada of more than 1,000 ships.

While these terraforming projects take up more and more of his time, Frank's personal life also undergoes adjustments. After getting evicted from his apartment, Frank decides to embark on a plan to "repaleolithize" his lifestyle. Informed by socio-biological research, he surmises that today's atomized self is fundamentally at odds with how our species has evolved. We have "lost touch with reality, gone mad as a collective,"[130] Frank worries.

---

[128] Robinson, *Fifty Degrees Below*, paras. 13.75–13.80.
[129] Robinson, para. 51.83.
[130] Robinson, para. 5.338.

As a remedy to this discontent, Frank sets out to completely rebuild his life in the image of a pre-modern human. Accordingly, he starts sleeping in a treehouse in the park and strikes up a friendship with a number of homeless people, many of whom are Vietnam veterans. This cultivation of a simpler lifestyle is not without its bliss: "The paleolithic pleasures, plus modern dental care; what could be nicer?"[131] Frank also connects with Caroline, an enigmatic woman, whose estranged husband, Ed Cooper, works for an undercover security agency and seems to be embroiled in a sophisticated scheme to rig the upcoming presidential elections in favour of the Republican candidate.

In the meantime, Anna and Charlie Quibler get closer to the monks from Khembalung, eventually accepting an invitation to their home in the Indian Ocean. Charlie's consultancy work for the senator takes a surprising turn when he convinces Chase to run for president. The announcement of his candidature occurs in an ominous location: on Midsummer Day, Phil Chase declares his intention to become a socially progressive, environmentally conscious president – from a boat that has crossed the ice-free sea all the way to the Arctic.

Chase's entering the race for the presidency is accompanied by a parallel experiment run by the NSF: the Vanderwal committee commissions a "Social Science Experiment in Elective Politics," whose goal is to establish a policy platform that is solely based on scientific findings about climate change and geared towards the ideal of establishing a "permaculture":

> A scientifically informed government should lead the way in the invention of a culture which is sustainable perpetually. This is the only normative bequest to the generations to come. It is not adaptive to heavily damage the biosphere when our own offspring and all the generations to follow will need it, like we do, in order to survive. If reproductive success is defined as life's goal, as it is in evolutionary theory, then stealing from descendants is maladaptive.
>
> Protection of the environment, therefore, along with restoration of landscapes and biodiversity, should become one of the principal goals of

---

[131] Robinson, para. 14.110.

the economy. Government must lead the way in investigating potential climate-altering strategies to mitigate current problems and eventually establish a balance that can be maintained in perpetuity.[132]

While global warming has led to the melting away of large swathes of the polar ice shield, winter brings with it a swing in the other direction, causing an extreme drop in temperature. This cold wave, with its attendant series of city-wide power cuts, adds to a crippling sense of urgency that everyone now feels, as Diane shrewdly remarks: "She considered that it had been a very good week for the cause. 'Everybody knows now that the problem is real. This isn't like the flood; this could happen three or four times every winter. Abrupt climate change is real, no one can deny it, and it's a big problem."[133]

After an assault on Frank in the park, he moves to the Khembali embassy, sharing a room with Rudra Cakrin, the Buddhist monk. The two become close allies, all the while Frank's fascination with the connections between science and Buddhism keeps on growing. *Fifty Degrees Below* ends with Phil Chase's election to the presidency. In the run-up, the NSF had abandoned its social science experiment and officially endorsed Chase as the closest real-world approximation of how a candidate of science might look like.

In the trilogy's final volume, *Sixty Days and Counting*,[134] the newly elected president states his policy platform during the inaugural speech:

I want us to remember how Abraham Lincoln said it: "that government of the people, by the people, and for the people shall not perish from this Earth." This is the crucial concept of American democracy – that government expresses what the majority of us would like to do as a society. It's us. We do it to us and for us. I believe this reminder is so important that I intend to add the defining phrase "of the people, by the people, and for the people" every time I use the word "government."[135]

---

[132] Robinson, paras. 27.35–27.36.
[133] Robinson, para. 36.134.
[134] Robinson, *Sixty Days and Counting.*
[135] Robinson, para. 11.8.

This radical-democratic spirit is sustained by an unwavering enthusiasm about humanity's capacity to serve as responsible steward of the ecosphere. As Chase jubilantly declares, verbalizing the idea behind the notion of a "good Anthropocene": "[W]e're making history, we are seizing the planet's history, I say, and turning it to the good."[136] Some of the trilogy's chief characters are subsequently promoted to key positions within the newly formed administration. Diane Chang becomes Chase's science tsar, overseeing the complex operation of aligning all government agencies to the task of climate change mitigation and adaptation. In this "war of the agencies"[137] her instincts as a shrewd operator are permanently tested: deftly navigating between the entrenched interests of powerful lobby groups and rival factions within the American policy apparatus, Diane turns into a pivotal figure for the new administration's ambition to launch a "New Deal"[138] pivoting around the environment.

Frank Vanderwal chooses to join Diane's team at the White House. While the attempt to restart the Gulf Stream seems to have been largely successful, an urgent challenge stems from rising sea levels, caused by the imminent break-up of the West Antarctic Ice Sheet. One of the mitigating proposals being pondered is to pump excess saltwater into largely uninhabited regions in the Sahara. Other projects pursued by Frank and his team include the installation of solar panels in space, as well as "carbon sequestration and shoreline stabilization."[139] All these terraforming missions are now perceived as matters of national security, bringing on board powerful stakeholders in the wider US government.

---

[136] Robinson, *Sixty Days and Counting*.

[137] Robinson, paras. 15.4, 15.17, 15.34, 23.14, 27.18.

[138] Robinson, para. 54.92. Note here, again, that Robinson displays considerable foresight in enlisting the language of the New Deal for the purpose of galvanizing environmental action: The current debate around a Green New Deal on the American Left does, in fact, revolve around proposals that echo what the *Science in the Capital* trilogy thematizes as well. See: Schwartzman, "Green New Deal"; Holden, "What Is the Green New Deal and Is It Technically Possible?"; Estes, "A Red Deal." For a recent book-length treatment, see: Aronoff et al., *A Planet to Win*. What this book emphasizes, however, is that socially reproductive labour (care work) would have to be at the heart of any Green New Deal – a thought that cannot be found in the *Science in the Capital* trilogy.

[139] Robinson, *Sixty Days and Counting*, para. 22.39.

The Quibler household, in the meantime, needs to learn to live under the new circumstances, too. Charlie has become a member of President Chase's inner circle, while Anna stays at the NSF, fully motivated to support Diane in her function as advisor to the president. On a hiking trip in the Californian Sierra, Charlie comes face to face with the devastating effects of climate change, crippled by ecological grief:

> Charlie fell behind the rest, stumbling from time to time in his distress, careless of his feet as his gaze wandered from one little ecodisaster to the next. He loved these high meadows with all his heart, and the fellfields between them too. Each had been so perfect, like works of art, as if hundreds of meticulous bonsai gardeners had spent centuries clipping and arranging each water-course and pad of moss. Every blade of grass deployed to best effect, every rock in its proper place. It had never occurred to Charlie that any of it could ever go away. And yet here it was, dead.
>
> Never doubt our emotions rule us, and no matter what we do, or say, or resolve, a single feeling can knock us down like a sword to the heart. A dead meadow – image of a black crisp on a bed – Charlie groaned and put his face to his knees.[140]

In the book's second half, matters speed up significantly. On the global scene, China finds itself on the brink of a "general systems crash" when its rivers suffer from substantial drought. This calamity forces the Chinese establishment to comprehensively change course and ask for assistance from the NSF. When the ecological crisis escalates, the United States cuts a pragmatic deal so as to overhaul China's energy grid.

After an attack on his life, the president strengthens the administration's efforts and highlights the ideal of a permaculture as the key objective of his progressive agenda. Guided by "eco-economics," the technological innovations of terraforming must accordingly be brought into line with principles of social justice: "We have to become the stewards of the Earth. And we have to start doing this in ignorance of the details of how to do it. We have to learn how to do it in the attempt itself. It is something we are going to have to imagine."[141]

---

[140] Robinson, paras. 33.213–33.214.
[141] Robinson, para. 58.45.

On a personal level, President Chase begins a relationship with Diane Chang. Their eventual marriage, ordained by none other than the Dalai Lama, marks the culmination of the rapprochement between the sphere of high politics and the domain of scientifically minded bureaucracy. *Sixty Days and Counting* brings the trilogy to a conclusion by allowing the chief characters to move on from their established ways of life: Frank and Caroline finally stabilize their relationship and decide to relocate to California; Charlie Quibler chooses to quit his White House job to spend more time with his youngest son; and Diane will have to adjust to her new role as first lady. Only Anna Quibler stays on as the Director of NSF's Bioinformatics Division. The book's conclusion radiates with the warmth of domestic delight, while the large-scale catastrophes of climate change are pushed to the back of the narrative.

As this synopsis of the *Science in the Capital* trilogy demonstrates, Robinson's novels take the idea of a climate-changed planet into a very different direction from Jemisin's project. One obvious way in which we can illustrate this would be by looking at the kind of future imagined by the two authors: while the Stillness embodies a barely recognizable Earth projected into the far future, Robinson's Washington is easily identifiable as almost contemporaneous with our current age. Moreover, whereas the world conjured by Jemisin is subject to magical powers that derive from the entangled relationships between humans and the more-than-human world, we, as the main agents of change in Robinson's story, deploy technologies that are, broadly speaking, already available to us in the contemporary efforts to mitigate and adapt to a climate-changed planet. These and other variations between the two narratives account for the distinct utopian visions that underpin Jemisin's and Robinson's writing respectively. The estrangement generated by a story set in the far future varies sharply from the effect produced by a practically oriented narrative that aspires to urge readers to "imagine their way out" of an ongoing crisis.

In the following section, I want to tease out three motifs that explain how Robinson interrogates the present by way of an *If-Only* inquiry that is premised on the utopian mechanism of galvanization: first, the veneration of bureaucratic modes of politics; second, the harmonizing interdependence of science and spirituality; and third, the multiple pathways out of impending catastrophe. Together, I hold, these themes cohere into another type of ecomodernism that can shed light on both the right- and left-wing perspectives discussed previously.

4.2.3 BUREAUCRATIC GOVERNANCE, WELL-TEMPERED REASON AND MULTIPLE PATHWAYS INTO THE FUTURE. A crucial feature of the *Science in the Capital* trilogy is that it envisions a challenge of planetary proportions – namely how to tackle the effects of abrupt climate change, both practically and ethically – through the prism of the outer actions and inner thoughts of a very small group of people, recruited from the science community, the political realm and the world of religion. One of the chief concerns behind the novels is hence how, in the context of the Anthropocene, the private and the public are by necessity intertwined with each other. As a consequence, Robinson demonstrates that changes on the macro level of mitigation and adaptation measures (say, the sort of geoengineering projects launched by the US government) stand in a fraught relationship with alterations on the micro level of interpersonal bonds (say, the kind of transformations Frank undergoes in his quest for a pre-modern lifestyle).[142]

We can elucidate this interplay between various levels of implication in the Anthropocene by first concentrating on the setting wherein the narrative unfolds. Surprisingly, Robinson stages the clash between the private and the public against a backdrop that appears almost uniquely unsuitable for the study of richly textured personalities: the institutionalized bureaucracy of a close-knit science community. This community, we understand from the start, is bound together by an ethos that sits uneasily with the capitalist drive for profit. Thus, the novels show us again and again to what extent the moral economy of scientific endeavours looks different from that of the firm. As Frank Vanderwal ruminates during an assessment panel for projects submitted to the NSF:

---

[142] As Ursula Heise remarks with regard to this tension between the public and the private: "While such analyses of scientific and political institutions tend to make for rather dry reading, the scientists' personal lives provide a symbolic frame for understanding global warming that emphasizes tropes of rootedness, home, and domesticity juxtaposed with those of homelessness, exile, and ferality" (Heise, *Sense of Place and Sense of Planet*, 207).

[S]cience didn't work like capitalism. That was the rub, that was one of the rubs in the general dysfunction of the world. Capitalism ruled, but money was too simplistic and inadequate a measure of the wealth that science generated. In science, one built up over the course of a career a fund of "scientific credit," by giving work to the system in a way that could seem altruistic. People remembered what you gave, and later on there were various forms of return on the gift – jobs, labs. In that sense a good investment for the individual, but in the form of a gift to the group.[143]

Robinson's reconstruction of the thoughts and actions of scientists conceives of their work as constantly in flux, as embodying the free-floating exchange of "living thought"[144] in the face of momentous challenges. But the scientific community does not amount to a self-sustaining system that could somehow operate completely in isolation from the wider world. As the trilogy asserts, the state remains integral to fostering (or smothering) a research infrastructure that is forever at risk of manipulation by profit interests.[145] Thus, it is the NSF itself – the organization keeping the science community afloat – that plays the role of the narrative's "utopian hero":[146] the meticulous and generous process of peer review, the creative anticipation of large-scale responses to climate change – all these procedures could not happen outside the framework of state-sponsored science. Adam Trexler is therefore correct to observe that the entire project can be read as extolling a "technocratic, even bureaucratic utopianism."[147]

This marks a significant shift in Robinson's appraisal of societal transformation. In contrast to his radical-democratic and anarchist leanings in the *Mars* trilogy (where technological innovations perform a crucial function as well), the *Science in the Capital* trilogy directs attention to the monumental skills of scientific, political and spiritual elites, safely

---

[143] Robinson, *Forty Signs of Rain*, para. 20.38.

[144] Prettyman, "Living Thought."

[145] In the first novel, this risk is brought to the fore by the takeover of Torrey Pines Generique, whose groundbreaking research is made inaccessible after the company is swallowed by a market competitor.

[146] Rohn, "The Day after Today."

[147] Trexler, *Anthropocene Fictions*, 155.

encumbered within the upper echelons of the state apparatus.[148] It contains a triumphant ode to what an efficient bureaucracy can accomplish – so long as it remains motivated by anti-capitalist, compassionate and environmentalist values. Robinson now seems to claim that change can, and indeed should, be instigated from above, through large-scale investments that only the state will be able to fund, coordinate and implement.

Crucially, though, the NSF is not merely depicted as a reactive distributor of research money but as a proactive vehicle for positive impact on society. This becomes evident once Frank, early on in the series, pleads for a "paradigm shift in how science interacts with society."[149] Given the enormity of the challenges, he implores his colleagues to accept the inevitability of taking an unequivocal stance in the fight against climate change. By "reinjecting rational science into the core of Washington policy making,"[150] the NSF thus tries to steer the whole system of representative politics into a more sustainable future. That is why the novels change tack once the research community acknowledges it simply cannot afford anymore to stand above the fray of partisan divisions. The exodus from the ivory tower into the public square turns out to be unavoidable once Phil Chase declares his intention to run for president. An insightful way of interpreting the trilogy is therefore as a "treatise on why politicized science is inevitable."[151]

The question remains, however, in what ways the NSF itself can become a harbinger of societal transformation. After all, the scientists behind the geoengineering projects, for example, do not possess any democratic mandate to take existential decisions that have considerable consequences for populations around the world. The NSF's involvement, then, raises not only a question of domestic accountability to the American electorate, but also one of global justice.

Does that imply that Robinson is altogether sceptical of democracy and global justice in the Anthropocene, prioritizing instead the

---

[148] On the elitist tendencies in wider ecomodernist discourse, see: Fremaux and Barry, "The 'Good Anthropocene' and Green Political Theory."

[149] Robinson, *Forty Signs of Rain*, para. 43.109.

[150] Luckhurst, "The Politics of the Network," 175.

[151] Morrell, "The Dialectic of Climate Change," 148.

technocratic capacity to forge viable pathways into the future? The answer to this question is not as straightforward as with other ecomodernists, such as Pinker, who have nothing but derision for democracy and global justice. To illuminate Robinson's ambivalent position, consider one of the emblematic schemes for alleviating rising sea levels: pumping excess sea water into dry areas, presumably somewhere in the developing world, would lead to the displacement of vast populations, as Frank and his team fully acknowledge in a conversation with an Army general, aptly named Wracke:

> Maybe, someone suggested, if that's what it takes to save the seacoasts from flooding, the global community would compensate the new lakes' host nations for whatever environmental damage was assessed. Possibly a sea water market could be established along with the carbon market; possibly they could be linked. Surely the most prosperous quarter of humanity could find ways to compensate the people, often poor, who would be negatively impacted by the creation of these reservoirs.
>
> Frank said, "We've tried some back-of-the-envelope numbers, estimating the capital worth of the major port cities and other coastal development, and got figures like five hundred trillion dollars."
>
> General Wracke, an active member of Diane's advisory group, put his hands together reverently. "A half a quadrillion dollars," he said, grinning. "That's a lot of construction funding."
>
> "Yes. On the other hand, for comparison purposes, the infrastructural value of property in the superdry basins of Africa, Asia, and the American basin and range comes to well under ten billion, unless you throw in Salt Lake City, which actually has a legal limit on the books as to how high the Great Salt Lake is allowed to rise, that isn't much higher than it is now. Anyway, in global terms, statistically, there's nothing out there in those basins. Statistically insignificant populations to displace, possibility of building new settlements by new water. Local weather deranged, but it is already. So . . ."[152]

Surely, there is something unpalatable about the nonchalance with which a group of scientists and soldiers, seated in the protected surroundings of a plush boardroom, ruminates on the enforced

---

[152] Robinson, *Sixty Days and Counting*, paras. 27.58–27.61.

displacement of "statistically insignificant populations." But the techno-cratic Earth-makers' sense of detachment from distant human suffering is fully intended by Robinson. After all, how could we even start reflecting on which way to go forward without also taking into account the immense losses that will be incurred in the course of terraforming our own planet?

To better comprehend the NSF's position at the interstices between science and politics, which is so fundamental to Robinson's view of progressive action, it might help to turn to discussions around electoral politics and to the ways in which populism and technocracy encroach on each other in the trilogy. Recall that the story gains momentum once Senator Chase becomes president, running on a progressive agenda for a Green New Deal. His ascendancy to the highest office is only successful because a ploy by a cabal of black ops agents, led by Caroline's estranged husband, is thwarted. These agents from within the "deep state" of the security establishment had tried, in vain, to sabotage the electoral pro-cess through a sophisticated computer algorithm.

Contrast their interference with the social science experiment designed by the NSF: obviously, its modelling of a "candidate for science" was also supposed to stage an intervention into the disorderliness of representative democracy, setting up a template for a scientifically grounded policy platform. Importantly, though, Diane and her team in the end abstain from undermining the electoral process and withdraw their virtual candidate before the voting starts, presumably to enhance Chase's chances of winning the presidency.

Even so, doubts about the merits of representative democracy continue to haunt the science community. As one of Frank's collaborators, the brilliant but cynical Edgardo, wonders with regard to the merits of voting:

> Maybe they [elections] don't matter. But let's say they are good, sure. Good soap opera, but also they are symbols, and symbolic action is still action. We need the illusion they give us, that we understand things and have some control. I mean, in Argentina, when elections went away, you really noticed how different things felt. As if the law had gone. Which it had. No, elections are good. It's voters who are bad.[153]

---

[153] Robinson, *Fifty Degrees Below*, para. 46.209.

One way of making voters "less bad" is, patently, to expose them to the kind of public educational material that the NSF social science experiment was meant to produce. Its stance resembles a behavioural nudge that is supposed to avoid paternalistically imposing the will of a bureaucratic elite on the wider population.

Yet, there is also another way in which Robinson attempts to grapple with the potentially undemocratic undercurrents emanating from the science community: through a powerful actor who seeks to reinterpret the meaning of representative democracy altogether, without succumbing to authoritarian fantasies.[154] Chase's presidency is fashioned after Abraham Lincoln's account of democracy as "government of the people, by the people, and for the people," first mentioned during the Gettysburg Address. His insistence on referencing Lincoln's phrase every time he uses the word "government" signals the president's favouring of a specific style of governing that appears surprisingly close to populism.

If populism can be defined as a "thin-centered ideology that considers society to be ultimately cleaved into two homogeneous and antagonistic camps, 'the pure people' versus 'the corrupt elite,' and which argues that politics should be an expression of the *volonté générale* (general will) of the people,"[155] then Chase is a populist politician of sorts, albeit one that might not be immediately recognizable as such. To be more precise, Chase's position amounts to a left-populist rejoinder to the demise of party politics when coping with global challenges such as climate change.[156] The state-sponsored science apparatus gradually turns into a powerful motor in the pursuit of a progressive agenda that is ideologically shaped by the division between "the pure people" and "the corrupt elite."

In an interview, Robinson summarizes his theory of the state through a compressed formula that arguably raises more questions than it provides answers: "The state = us. So the statement 'we need the state'

---

[154] In this regard, Lovelock's notion that the challenges of a climate-changed world cannot be dealt with by democratic means seems to be diametrically opposed to Robinson's vision. See: Hickman, "James Lovelock."

[155] Mudde and Rovira Kaltwasser, *Populism*, 6.

[156] On left-wing populism, see: Laclau, *On Populist Reason*; Mouffe, *For a Left Populism*.

reduces to 'we need us.'"[157] While the equation "the state = us" seems to be based on a conceptual shortcut that would require further unpacking to gain plausibility, the convergence of populism and technocracy within the trilogy is more persuasive. This might sound like a fanciful claim, for populism and technocracy seem to be premised on diametrically opposed forms of political mobilization. Indeed, populist leaders frequently rail against technocratic elites whose expert knowledge appeals to a higher authority that evades democratic control.[158] Does that mean that a politician, like Robinson's fictional president, cannot be both a populist and in favour of technocratic modes of governance?

The answer is more complicated than one would expect. This is the case because, upon closer examination, populism and technocracy share at least as much as separates them. Both kinds of political mobilization draw legitimacy from a deep discontent with the existing system of party democracy.[159] In such a democracy, parties are expected to fulfil a variety of interrelated functions, including the aggregation, negotiation and mediation of citizens' interests. Yet, as Peter Mair observed, "[t]he age of party democracy has passed"[160] – we now live in an era where the weakening of traditional parties is one of the key factors for why democracies have become so vulnerable to both populist and technocratic insurgencies.[161]

As expected, this erosion of the existing system of party democracy is on full display in the *Science in the Capital* trilogy. Not only are the two poles of populism and technocracy literally fused with each other, in the marriage of President Chase and his science advisor, Diane Chang, but the organized conflict rampant in a functioning party democracy becomes increasingly eclipsed as the narrative progresses.

---

[157] Canavan, Klarr, and Vu, "Science, Justice, Science Fiction," 212.

[158] Of course, nowhere does this critique of expert knowledge surface more viscerally than in current debates around climate change. This issue is also one of the key themes in Latour's *Down to Earth*.

[159] Bickerton and Accetti, "Populism and Technocracy."

[160] Mair, *Ruling the Void*, para. 7.1. See also: Mair, "Populist Democracy vs Party Democracy."

[161] Caramani, "Will vs. Reason."

After Chase is elected president, his status remains vulnerable, for he still has to surpass many hurdles in his mission to launch a New Deal, not least after an attack on his life is launched. Yet, oddly, the prior obstruction from the Republican party completely disappears from sight once the crisis hits the people on the ground.[162] The extreme weather events towards the end of the first volume, and throughout the second one, have the convenient effect of flattening the political landscape, eradicating almost all of the obstacles that had stood in the way of Chase's broad-minded platform.

My point here is that, far from being incidental, this vanishing of an organized opposition is a direct upshot of Robinson's formula "the state = us," which binds together populism and technocracy. If, from a populist viewpoint, "we" are maximally unified in "our" antipathy to a corrupt elite of climate change denialists and capitalist overlords, then the conflicting interests dividing the 99 per cent – socio-economic as well as cultural interests that are normally aggregated, negotiated and mediated through various parties – gradually wane away.

Strangely, though, Robinson appears to transpose the people's essential confrontation with a corrupt elite to a level that is thoroughly depoliticized: there are, in fact, very few signs of climate change denial or of the harmful influence of lobby groups the more the story unfolds. A state run by a populist leader can, as a consequence, represent the people's collective interests in a way that parties, with their discordant and hardly manageable constituencies, cannot. That is why bureaucratic governance performs such a dominant function in Robinson's account of progressive politics: its flexible standing vis-à-vis policymaking facilitates the fusing together of two potential futures for the Anthropocene, the democratic and the technocratic one. The NSF surfaces as a utopian figure in this climate-changed world precisely because it can gather popular support (via Robinson's reductive theory of the state) as well as enact effective solutions for the ecological crisis.

In introducing the succinct but ultimately question-begging formula "the state = us," Robinson tries to debunk an allegation that even the most competent type of bureaucratic governance at some point needs to

---

[162] Trexler, *Anthropocene Fictions*, 166.

face: that its operations, no matter how urgent and successful, must ultimately be legitimated through democratic procedures. The sidelining of party politics and the vanishing of institutional spoilers make it clear that a future for the Anthropocene that is both democratic and technocratic is only possible inasmuch as the existing system of electoral politics is thoroughly upended.

This diagnosis leaves us at a crossroad in our reading of Robinson's ecomodernism. If there is an element of wishful thinking in the trilogy, it does not surface in the context of technological innovations that are still out of our reach. Robinson seems right to reason that, to a large extent, we already possess the scientific knowledge and the engineering capacities to address many of the challenges that a climate-changed world has in store for us.[163] Unlike Jemisin's narrative, magic is therefore entirely absent from the *Science in the Capital* trilogy.

The true dilemma, however, and the origin of Robinson's tendency to sometimes think wishfully, is one that Diane Chang, the science tsar, so aptly conveys: "We know, but we can't act."[164] While Robinson's reimaging of the benign and smooth functioning of the science community is perhaps naive (as any academic working in actually existing universities would probably agree), but in the end innocuous, his implicit assumption that it would be relatively effortless to adjust democratic procedures that are currently in place, without too much pushback from a host of powerful stakeholders (parties, but also private corporations that have vested interests in upholding the status quo) reads like a Pollyannaish vision bordering on naivety.

The issue of how people can learn to move from knowledge to action is also pivotal for our second motif, concerning the relationship between reason and its others. Recall how Frank goes through a personal transformation after attending a lecture by a Buddhist monk who cautions his audience against the dangerous excesses of a purely rationalist

---

[163] In fact, as Roger Luckhurst remarks with regard to Robinson's embrace of innovative technologies, "[i]t is 'our' contemporary science and technology that has to deal with catastrophic climate change: there are no science-fictional mitigations invented in the course of the 1,500 pages; they all sit inside the horizon of current scientific research" (Luckhurst, "The Politics of the Network," 171).

[164] Robinson, *Fifty Degrees Below*, para. 19.76; 33.54.

mindset.[165] Frank takes this advice so seriously that he immediately embarks on the aforementioned endeavour to "re-palaeolithize" his entire life, forging a "link between the modern and the primitive."[166] Despite his fascination with bureaucracy, in this examination of a primitive lifestyle, Robinson's anti-statist leanings come to the fore, for the whole idea of a palaeolithic lifestyle echoes an observation shared by many anarchists, namely that a "that life outside the state – life as a 'barbarian' – may often have been materially easier, freer, and healthier than life at least for nonelites inside civilization."[167]

Beyond this anarchist element, there is a different sense in which reason's other becomes foregrounded in the novels. Adeline Johns-Putra argues that Robinson introduces the "compassionate wisdom of Buddhism"[168] as a counterbalance to the objectivity of scientific knowledge.[169] The addition of an empathetic outlook is not only essential for keeping in check fact-centred rationality, it also provides a strategy for tackling the dilemma identified by Diane: that we know what is going

---

[165] In terms of character development, it is noteworthy that Frank is the only figure in the trilogy whose personality changes in significant ways. This adds plausibility to the claim that his character is located at the centre of the narrative, even though he is not leading the revolution of mitigation and adaptation measures – that would be Diane's achievement. On this point, see: Trexler, *Anthropocene Fictions*, 158. For an argument to the effect that the trilogy actually has no central character, see: Johns-Putra, *Climate Change and the Contemporary Novel*, 149–50. Be this as it may, Frank is certainly a farcical hero, whose pronouncements cannot be taken at face value. In an interview, Robinson jokingly proposes that in his many novels "all of my liars are called Frank" (Larsen, "In the Interests of Frankness").

[166] Heer, "The New Utopians."

[167] Scott, *Against the Grain*, xii. Robinson has also written a novel set in the Ice Age, centred around a young boy's struggle to survive under immensely harsh conditions. See: Robinson, *Aurora*. Although primitivism remains a preoccupation for some anarchist thinkers, perhaps most notably John Zerzan, there are also opposing voices emphasizing the centrality of science and technology for anarchism. See: Thorpe and Welsh, "Beyond Primitivism."

[168] Johns-Putra, *Climate Change and the Contemporary Novel*, 146.

[169] While empathy figures prominently in the *Science and the Capital* trilogy, another aspect of Buddhism receives comparatively less attention: the interconnectedness that unites all beings with one another. In line with Robinson's interest in science, he downplays the religious teachings of Buddhism, while highlighting its philosophical dimensions. For a short survey of Buddhist views on the environment, see: Sponsel and Natadecha-Sponsel, "Buddhist Views of Nature and the Environment."

wrong, but simply cannot act appropriately. In marrying insights from evolutionary biology and Buddhist spirituality, compassion and altruism are introduced as potential rejoinders to the challenge of climate change.[170] As one of the monks, Drepung, explains:

> Does true altruism exist, and is it a good adaptation? Does compassion work, in other words? You have done studies that suggest altruism is the best adaptive strategy, if seen from the group context. This then becomes a kind of ... admonishment. To practice compassion in order to successfully evolve – this, coming from your science, which claims to be descriptive only! Only describing what has worked to make us what we are. But in Buddhism we have always said, if you want to help others, practice compassion; if you want to help yourself, practice compassion. Now science adds, if you want to help your species, practice compassion.[171]

Frank's embrace of empathy does not only turn his personal life upside down, it also reveals another trajectory for humanity: a science community caring for the world – in other words, a bureaucratic organization like the NSF that does not shirk from its responsibility to take controversial stances in defence of planet Earth – manages to overcome precisely those obstacles that the existing system of representative democracy cannot adequately address. On this view, "the union of politics and science ... is the intergenerational solution that humans have evolved to make."[172]

What is important about Robinson's insistence on compassion as a personal as well as collective strategy for survival in the Anthropocene is that it does not negate science. Robinson cites scientific evidence to demonstrate that compassion and altruism amount to more than

---

[170] Robinson seems to be especially drawn to non-monotheistic religions: "Although I don't like any of the big patriarchal religions with their hierarchies and faked traditions and fundamentalisms. In that sense, I'm a secular person. But I want that old Earth religion and I feel it in myself. These feelings of significance and meaning need to be religious (from the Latin for binding together), and they're already spiritual or mystical. There's a big part of our brain that lights up on the scans when we're feeling these feelings, and devotion is surely one of the most beautiful feelings" (Hamner, "Odd Couples, Carbon Coins, and Narrative Scopes").

[171] Robinson, *Forty Signs of Rain*, para. 38.54.

[172] Johns-Putra, *Climate Change and the Contemporary Novel*, 147.

spiritual beliefs that rein in unfettered self-interest; they may in fact be the outcomes of evolutionary processes that made us into the peculiar species we are. While driving on a busy highway, Frank is reminded of the game-theoretical "prisoners' dilemma" and meditates on whether it can teach us something about how we should act in the wider world:

> It was like a giant game of prisoners' dilemma, the classic game in which two prisoners are separated and asked to tell tales on the other one, with release offered to them if they do. The standard computer model scoring system had it that if the prisoners cooperate with each other by staying silent, they each get three points; if both defect against the other, they each get one point; and if one defects and the other doesn't, the defector gets five points and the sap gets zero points. Using this scoring system to play the game time after time, there is a first iteration which says, it is best always to defect. That's the strategy that will gain the most points over the long haul, the computer simulations said – if you are only playing strangers once, and never seeing them again. And of course traffic looked as if it were that situation.
>
> But the shadow of the future made all the difference. Day in and day out you drove into the same traffic jam, with the same basic population of players. If you therefore played the game as if playing with the same opponent every time, which in a sense you were, with you learning them and them learning you, then more elaborate strategies would gain more points than always defect ...
>
> In traffic, at work, in relationships of every kind – social life was nothing but a series of prisoners' dilemmas. Compete or cooperate? Be selfish or generous? It would be best if you could always trust other players to cooperate, and safely practice always generous; but in real life people did not turn out to earn that trust.[173]

So, the practice of empathy, initially advocated by the Buddhist monks, ends up establishing an affective link between the realm of science and the world of politics. It tempers both the aimless hunger for ever-more knowledge and the endless thirst for ever-more power. Importantly, the stress on the excesses of a purely rationalist mindset also implies a

---

[173] Robinson, *Forty Signs of Rain*, paras. 20.4–20.6.

critique of techno-fixes that purport to handle the consequences of climate change.

Despite his obvious passion for terraforming Earth, Robinson distances himself from "a technological determinism that could drive us toward desirable outcomes willy-nilly; rather, he offers the vision of a transcendent, science-based politics that is a projection of the people who practice it."[174] The type of ecomodernism emerging from this narrative is one that openly acknowledges the necessity of imposing limits on self-interested rationality, even (or especially) in the service of scientific discovery. In contrast with Jemisin's communitarian outlook, however, the starting point for Robinson's investigation is the individual's quest for spiritual fulfilment.

This brings us to our final motif, the multiple pathways leading into the future. As we have already observed, through its proleptic realism, the *Science in the Capital* trilogy dramatizes the present crisis by conjuring scenarios that could soon happen in the near future. Indeed, some of the events described in the novels, such as the flooding of Washington, have already happened in many parts of the world, and even in the United States, during the devastation wreaked by Hurricane Katrina in 2006. The sense of impending catastrophe, Robinson surmises in an interview, can thus have a restorative impact on the public's disposition to act:

> It has occurred to me more than once that the imminent possibility of an environmental disaster – indeed the sheer fact that we are already entering one, either abrupt or not – might force us to change our ways sooner rather than later, and that this would be a very good thing for our children and our children's children, and all the generations to come. Thus, depending on how we react to it, the possibility of abrupt climate change could be a good thing.[175]

Note how the apocalypse is here figured as an occasion for a future-orientated renewal of gigantic proportions, focusing our minds and

---

[174] Kilgore, "Making Huckleberries," 93. Kilgore goes on to argue that the racialized, mostly White, identity of the main characters is integral to understanding the restricted scope of the trilogy's radical appeal.

[175] Robinson, *Imagining Abrupt Climate Change.*

hastening the willingness to embark on transformative action.[176] The contrast with Jemisin's account of repeating cycles of catastrophic collapse and reconstruction, some of which have already happened in the distant past, others are still going on, could not be starker: in the *Science in the Capital* trilogy, the environmental breakdown is portrayed in such a manner as to keep the planetary ecosphere susceptible to mitigation and adaptation efforts. The destructive deluge and the extreme cold wave in Washington, even the inundation of the island of Khembalung, represent nothing but "contingent or partial apocalypses," facilitating "a way of thinking about climate change that acknowledges apocalyptic present realities and future possibilities while still actively inviting systemic action against it."[177]

Another way of expressing the same thought would be to assert that the trilogy construes a "'fortunate crisis,'" which

> liberates people from their ordinary habits and modes of thought; it reminds people of the ecological big picture; it shows the ultimate contingency and vulnerability of the present order of things; it causes people to reassess their true needs and their relationship to 'business as usual'; it frees people to be altruistic; it serves as a catalyst for experiment and for adoption of new habits."[178]

What Robinson wants to avoid at all cost is exacerbating feelings of fatalistic resignation about climate change that have already taken root in many corners of society.[179] The optimism undergirding this *If-Only* plot line, its attempt to affectively galvanize people into transformative

---

[176] For a more sceptical take on the mobilizing force of instances of abrupt climate change, which draws on the notion of "shifting baselines," see: Roberts, "The Scariest Thing about Global Warming (and Covid-19)."

[177] Evans, "The Best of Times, the Worst of Times, the End of Times?," 517. Evans uses the term "*open-ended* environmental apocalypse" to capture a number of critical utopias/ dystopias from the 1980s onwards, but the main focus of her paper is Robinson's *Mars* trilogy. The term nicely captures what is specific about the *Science in the Capital* series.

[178] Prettyman, "Living Thought," 192.

[179] Naturally, Robinson is not the only author who remains deeply suspicious of fatalistic narratives, but he is perhaps the most outspoken defender of eutopian fiction as a remedy to the paralyzing effect of some types of apocalyptic stories. On the issue of fatalism, see: Canavan et al., "Symposium on Science Fiction and the Climate Crisis."

action, is spurred by Robinson's rejoinder to those who are all too willing to give up:

> Use the optimism as a club, to beat the crap out of people who are saying that we are doomed, who are saying let's give up now ... My story is: the optimism that I'm trying to express is that there won't be an apocalypse, there will be a disaster. But after the disaster comes the next world on.[180]

With the proper alignment of science, politics and spirituality, we can successfully move from merely possessing the right kind of knowledge about the Anthropocene to putting into practice plans for building more sustainable futures – the next world to come, after this one has finally perished. The open-ended engagement with catastrophic scenarios, whose horizon has not yet closed down, allows the trilogy's protagonists to experiment with different ways of inhabiting a climate-changed world. While Frank fashions his lifestyle according to pre-modern standards before relocating back to California with his long-lost love Caroline, Anna and her family even toy with the idea of moving in with the Buddhist monks. Hence, the narrative does not prescribe one set of providential choices at the expense of others, but rather lays out a panoply of valuable options for the main characters (and the readers) to try out.

This flexibility is also mirrored in the policy proposals developed by the NSF. Recall how its task force comes up with an array of geoengineering projects, ranging from the sinking of huge amounts of salt into the Atlantic to once again kick-start the Gulf Stream, to the emergency provision of nuclear power to disaster-struck communities. Crucially, none of these technological interventions is embraced as a silver bullet that would halt or reverse anthropogenic climate change once and for all. Despite frequent invocations of environmental steward-ship, the trilogy does not present terraforming Earth as a welcome opportunity for hubristically asserting the human dominion over nature.[181] Rather, caring for the planet becomes the prerogative of a

---

[180] Vicente, "Angry Optimism in a Drowned World." On this point, see also: Hamner, "Angry Optimism."
[181] Rose, "The Unknowable Now," 266.

scientifically enlightened and spiritually informed species that is willing to break with the capitalist status quo, as Robinson speculates in an interview:

> So we have to stop burning carbon, because none of the geo-engineering ideas are any good even as imaginary solutions, meaning on their own terms. In essence, stopping burning carbon IS the geo-engineering required; any replacement for that plan is even huger in impacts and difficulties. The most powerful geoengineering technology for reducing our carbon burn would be a rapid shift to social justice and an end to capitalism.[182]

Even though an end to capitalism might be Robinson's preferred pathway into the future, we have already noted that the novels survey various directions that humanity could be taking. This approach resonates with President Chase's policy platform, which states explicitly that "[w]e have to become the stewards of the Earth. And we have to start doing this in ignorance of the details of how to do it. We have to learn how to do it in the attempt itself. It is something we are going to have to imagine."[183]

Summing up my interpretation of the *Science in the Capital* trilogy, I want to return to the specific nature of Robinson's utopianism, which I have discussed under the triple heading of proceduralism, conflictuality and open-endedness. Utilizing the lens of a proleptic realism, which minimizes the use of estrangement devices, the trilogy examines various ways of caring for the world, rising from the personal level of self-improvement to the comprehensive structures of society at large. Technology does play a key role in this process, but it is by itself not capable of manufacturing blueprints for a more sustainable future. Rather, Robinson gestures towards the need to unravel the bonds between science and capitalism: only a scientific community that is unshackled from profit-driven corporations can truly reform a corrupt political system that exacerbates the ecological crisis.

---

[182] Canavan, Klarr, and Vu, "Science, Justice, Science Fiction," 214. For a restatement of the same sentiment about the importance of relinquishing capitalism, see a recent interview: Billings, "Q&A."

[183] Robinson, *Sixty Days and Counting*, para. 58.45.

The story's eutopian dimension manifests itself in the fortuitous alignment of parallel vectors of progressive action. While the members of the NSF's technocratic elite openly take responsibility by becoming political actors in the fight against climate change, they are also supported by an audacious president who firmly stands on a green policy platform. In the background, spiritual leaders such as Drepung operate, wielding their influence to moderate the excesses of Western rationalism. A reimagined landscape wherein science, politics and spirituality join forces to negotiate our species' place in the Anthropocene anew enables Robinson to send the ecomodernist dream on a course that deviates from the theorists and commentators discussed before.

4.3 ORIENTATION BEYOND BLUEPRINTS?

In what ways, then, do ecomodernists provide orientation around the hyperobject of a climate-changed world? As champions of a utopian constellation that is framed by an *If-Only* plot line, both right- and left-wing commentators are driven by the ardent wish to prove doomsayers wrong. Their key contention is seemingly straightforward: nobody can presume to know what the future will actually look like. But we do know, with a high level of certainty, what enormous steps forward science and technology have already taken. This awareness of our species' accomplishments in stewarding planet Earth supplies humanity with a stable ledge to bootstrap itself out of the current predicament. Through this consciousness-raising, ecomodernism's inflationary mode of critiquing the status quo becomes operative.

Yet, upon closer inspection, the way ecomodernists conceive of humanity's prowess varies significantly. Given this utopian constellation's concern with uncovering viable routes towards a "good Anthropocene," proponents of the *If-Only* plot line will be tempted to adopt a blueprint mentality, advertising techno-fixes as promissory notes for a beautiful world to come. And indeed, a lot of passages in the ecomodernist manifesto and in Pinker's work smack of "solutionism" – the flawed assumption that multilayered phenomena can always be neatly broken down into manageable sub-problems. Some also display perfectionist tendencies, painting the future in bright colours that leave scant room for scepticism and doubt.

The issue with this mode of picturing a climate-changed world is that it tends to mistake the Anthropocene for an ordinary object that can be surveyed with the support of conventional maps. The ecomodernists' propensity to underrate the scale of the current emergency manifests itself in the frequently heard statement that humanity already possesses all the practical and moral knowledge to move around a climate-changed world. Ecomodernists typically decry that we simply get the basics wrong – from formulating efficient and just responses to collective action problems to developing a sustainable and affordable infrastructure for our energy grids – because we have become paralyzed by irrational fear and anxiety about the future.

There is something obviously alluring about this framework, for it revels in the unique ingenuity of our species. Nevertheless, as a utopian vision, it ultimately runs up against major obstacles. Once we grasp that the Anthropocene is a hyperobject, to again draw on Timothy Morton's terminology, it becomes clear that our climate-changed world cannot be surveyed using conventional maps, neatly organized around established systems of knowledge and practice.

As we saw in Chapter 1, the Anthropocene's ramifications are so varied that radically new techniques of mapping need to be honed. So, past scientific and technological success does not automatically warrant optimism about the future. In the present moment, it is imperative to push the boundaries of our imagination to match the staggering scale of the problem. This is precisely why the education of our desire for better ways of being and living is such a central task for ecomodernism.

Some champions of a "good Anthropocene" are entirely aware of this obligation to eschew the facile logic of solutionism. Their utopias aim to galvanize an audience into action by modelling alternative ways of being and living, often without settling on a single best pathway forward. When these utopias provide orientation around the hyperobject of the Anthropocene, they do so in the absence of blueprints, jettisoning static images of perfect worlds that are supposed to guide real-world action. Science and technology continue to play vital roles in this constellation, but they constitute only a single piece of a complicated puzzle.

Although it might require a fundamental rethink of traditional frame-works, acknowledging the inaccessibility of blueprints is crucial for any project that endeavours to rehabilitate utopianism for our times. Many of the positions rehearsed in this chapter have accordingly incorporated the interdiction of perfectionism into their flexible designs. The majority of left-wing ecomodernists shy away from techno-fixes, just as Kim Stanley Robinson insists on experimenting with various intersecting strategies for coping with life on a climate-changed planet. This shows that the education of desire can proceed without static images of an alluring future.

That said, the unsettling question remains: how exactly can social dreaming become directional, if conjuring perfect worlds is not suitable for the task at hand? One promising answer is to search for modes of desiring and hoping that openly embrace utopianism's intrinsic flaws and contradictions. To conclude this chapter, let us hence attempt to tease out the sensibilities shared between the social and political theorists advocating for ecomodernism and Robinson's project.

The most significant strand that connects both Pinker, the members of the *Jacobin* collective and the author of the *Science in the Capital* trilogy is their consistent aversion to the debilitating impact of fatalism on the public's aptitude to imagine a way out of the current crisis. It is typical of *If-Only* narratives that they try to persuade their audience that another world lies just on the horizon. Ecomodernists keep on contending that it would still be feasible to avert the impending catastrophe. Without downplaying the severity of climate change, they therefore search for glimmers of hope within and beyond the existing order. In that sense, their social dreaming is, despite its grand plans for the future, also sustained by an archaeological method, to use Levitas' taxonomy: a concerted effort to excavate promising initiatives that are buried within the status quo.

What exactly the incubators of real-world change are remains one of the dividing lines within the ecomodernist camp. Pinker as well as the authors of the ecomodernist manifesto seem to believe that it is our lack of confidence in the Enlightenment project that is holding us back. If only we were able to absorb the key insights the Enlightenment has in store for us (trust in reason, science and humanism) we would be in a good position to free ourselves from the constraints holding us back. On this view, the socio-economic structures of capitalism pose no major hindrance to the inauguration of a "good Anthropocene." Quite to the contrary, it is the conviction that we have to alter global politics altogether – an opinion Pinker derisively attributes to the "climate justice movement" – that hampers plans to tackle climate change.

As I have argued, the main worry about this eutopian vision is that it underestimates the practical challenges awaiting us. Although Pinker and the authors of the ecomodernist manifesto are wont to assert that we are on track to a much better future, as testified by demographic trends and groundbreaking inventions, they invest too much hope in the Promethean function of technology.

The left-wing response seeks to assuage this concern by focusing on the wider repercussions that a socialist appropriation of the "good Anthropocene" might have. While some members in this camp continue to subscribe to an understanding of our species as unapologetic Earth-makers, others caution against hubristic self-elevation and espouse degrowth as the only option from a socialist standpoint. This is where the main crack within the left-wing case for ecomodernism becomes visible. The question of whether the power of science and technology can be harnessed in a context where economic growth under conditions of global capitalism persists remains hugely divisive.

The crux of fictional engagements with ecomodernism, such as Kim Stanley Robinson's, is that they trace the interconnections between science and politics at great length, but decline to prescribe a single best way forward. The *Science in the Capital* trilogy directs attention to the many ways in which public institutions (the NSF, the presidency, organized religion, etc.) are shaped by unique individuals. It lays out concrete scenarios, rather than ready-made certainties.

This is how some forms of ecomodernism manage to circumvent the indeterminacy of the *What-If* plot line. Robinson's reconstruction of the chief characters' affective states puts the reader in a position to gauge different, even conflicting possibilities of living a meaningful life in the Anthropocene: from the loner who experiments with a "barbarian" lifestyle, to the idealistic official willing to ponder difficult compromises for her worthwhile goals.

The proleptic realism with which the *Science in the Capital* trilogy approaches the future still has a decisively eutopian bent: Robinson underlines, again and again, that a revolution in our imaginative repertoire will be necessary for humanity to grapple with a climate-changed world. His narrative is meant to serve as a spark for igniting such a revolution, without resorting to estrangement devices, such as the ones encountered in Jemisin's work. Robinson gestures towards the need for system-wide transformation, while simultaneously praising virtuous scientific and political elites who take action when faced with imminent disaster. Note also that the positive appraisal of spirituality adds depth to the exploration of radical change.

My criticism of Robinson's project has not so much focused on his Promethean view of technology or his relative neglect of the degrowth paradigm, but rather on his naive account of representative democracy. Even though the *Science in the Capital* trilogy condemns misguided faith in science and calls into question the sustainability of unfettered capitalism, it remains tethered to a picture of politics that clashes with at least some worthwhile aspects of democracy as we know it. Given Robinson's plea for an alliance between a creative, caring technocratic elite and a populist, daring political class it is not surprising that the reader acquires only to a limited degree a sense of how the coming climate catastrophe affects the lives of those who do not belong to the Washington upper class. Remedial action from below is clearly not a concern for Robinson, because the ordinary people inhabiting this near-future world are not part of the scientific, political or spiritual leadership that alone can steer humanity into a brighter future.[184]

In this utopian constellation, the relationship between theory building and storytelling looks different compared to our first case. This is so because of the timescales involved. Whereas Jemisin's fantasy land is set in a future that is historically very remote from the Gaia hypothesis,

---

[184] In his most recent book, Robinson appears to have addressed this lacuna. In *The Ministry for the Future*, a diverse raft of actors struggles to respond to climate change. In this novel, subaltern populations are represented in a way that deviates sharply from the spiritual leadership of the Khembalis. For example, Indian eco-terrorists aim to disrupt global capitalism, while a new UN institution is set up to coordinate global efforts at sustainable development. See: Robinson, *The Ministry for the Future*.

ecomodernism's temporal range corresponds to Kim Stanley Robinson's proleptic realism, disclosing what is still concealed from public purview but already exerting influence on our existence.

Like Robinson's metaphor of the skeet shooters, who must aim slightly ahead of their target to hit it, the social and political theorists we encountered in this chapter operate on basically the same timescale as the author of the *Science in the Capital* trilogy. This is why it is not astonishing to find so many of the key phrases in ecomodernist discourse picked up verbatim in Robinson's narrative.

Still, the *Science in the Capital* trilogy does much more than fictionalize abstract thought; it also probes the inherent contradictions and ambiguities that plague any attempt at inducing a complete break with the status quo. Recall that, as Jameson reasons, the material and ideological conditions of the present cannot but mould our imagination, undercutting the ambition to come up with a radically different vision of the future that bears no trace whatsoever of the world as we know it. In a situation where we have to imagine our way out of the ecological crisis, Robinson's storytelling examines, amongst other things, why and how social dreaming can frequently go awry.

In concluding this chapter, we might want to return to an iconic image of utopia – that of a distant, superior world that is hard to reach. In More's *Utopia*, the island's geography is characterized by its utter seclusion. Spatial enclosure of this kind is frequently associated with utopianism altogether, even though, as I remarked in Chapter 2, the literary genre took a decidedly temporal turn in the eighteenth century.[185] Against this backdrop, champions of ecomodernism unfold a distinctively optimistic perspective insofar as they seek to build bridges across the trenches that separate the real world from the desired alternative. All the ideas we engaged with in this chapter aim to go beyond pronouncing an ideal end state towards which we should be striving.

With Robinson, we might hence say that the galvanizing appeal of ecomodernist stories and theories needs to be understood as a "dynamic, tumultuous, agonizing process, with no end." Yet, the challenge remains:

---

[185] Jameson, "Of Islands and Trenches."

envisioning a better future as well as reflecting on how we may construct it amounts to a paradoxical operation, for

> [t]he problem, however, with this and all other utopian alternatives, is that we can't imagine how we might get there. We can't imagine the bridge over the Great Trench, given the world we're in and the massively entrenched power of the institutions that shape our lives – and the guns that are still there under the table, indeed right on the table.[186]

This passage demonstrates that Robinson, just like other ecomodernists, recognizes the many respects in which the utopian imagination gets conditioned by the material and ideological circumstances that shape our sense of reality. Educating the desire for being otherwise is akin to a kind of double vision that simultaneously pays attention to the solid frames structuring our existence and to the open doors that enable us to change our life.

New Jerusalem and *Arcadia* are two eutopian visions for a climate-changed world that are premised on the assumption that the future is not yet foreclosed. As I have claimed in this chapter, theories and stories that incentivize our willingness to act in the face of climate change spring from a eutopian wish: to conjure scenarios that reveal better ways of being and living, urging us to envision various paths out of the current conundrum. The orientating function that these narratives perform exceeds the defamiliarization of the status quo. Transforming our lived experience, here and now, is a professed goal of ecomodernist social dreaming. While Chapter 2's speculative *What-If* plot line sets into motion estrangement devices, at the expense of concrete proposals for how transformative action might take place, the *If-Only* frame investigates a variety of concrete alternatives, from individual self-transformation, to the adoption of a palaeolithic lifestyle and the terraforming of Earth via grand geoengineering projects.

The potential weakness of the ecomodernist wager is, however, that its proleptic realism glosses over the risks and dangers inherent in the status quo, either by exaggerating the influence of science and technology or

---

[186] Robinson, "Remarks on Utopia in the Age of Climate Change," 8.

by downplaying the political hurdles that any transformative movement would have to overcome. The postulated openness of the future can hence be both stimulating and seductive – which is why eutopian theory building and storytelling frequently approximate wishful thinking. Our next utopian constellation tries to step back from this precipice by painting a much bleaker picture of our climate-changed world.

CHAPTER 5

If This Goes On

Hope Lost, Hope Regained

I N THIS CHAPTER, the tone changes dramatically. Whereas ecomo-dernists of various stripes underline the importance of optimistic visions of the future, the writers discussed here paint a much more fearful picture, one in which the impending catastrophe is not only on the horizon, but already here with us. Through a focus on the imminent or ongoing apocalypse, they operate with a speculative register that is shaped by an *If-This-Goes-On* sensibility.

If we look a bit more closely, we grasp, however, that these messengers of doom typically waver between two contradictory impulses: either they posit that, unless we comprehensively and swiftly change course, our species is headed for extinction; or they admonish us that our efforts already come too late, for there is nothing we can do to avert the impending breakdown. Where one stands on these two positions is generally a good indicator for what utopian commitments one is willing to entertain and what guidance for navigating the Anthropocene one is offering.

All the dystopian visions we will revisit in this chapter are grounded in a diagnosis of climate change that affords only a limited degree of hope. What exactly the hope that remains looks like is one of the recurring questions in this literature. Returning to a theme introduced in Chapter 2, we are now entering the territory of critical dystopianism – a discourse that seeks to warn its audience of what is to come, by highlighting a view of the future that renders it considerably worse than the present moment, while avoiding as much as possible a fatalistic attitude that would stymy campaigns for resistant action.

In critical dystopias, cataclysmic collapse is figured in ways that are different from *What-If* or *If-Only* narratives. To better comprehend this, recall that catastrophes and breakdowns are hardly absent from the works of Lovelock, Latour, the members of the *Breakthrough Institute* or the writers of *Jacobin*. They are also operative in both Jemisin's and Robinson's speculative fiction. In the *Broken Earth* trilogy, the violent outbursts of Father Earth represent not one-off events but rolling waves of destruction against which the main protagonists must learn to guard themselves. In the *Science in the Capital* trilogy, the crises triggered by abrupt climate change are depicted in an open-ended manner, eliciting transformative interventions that are – at least partially – successful in forestalling the wholesale collapse of human civilization.

Neither of these two plot lines strongly foregrounds dystopian motifs, however. As we have observed in regard to Jemisin, her writing meshes together dystopian and eutopian motifs, permitting solidary bonds between the oppressed to thrive when the situation seems most dire. In Robinson's case, utter despair is kept at bay through a veneration of our species' ingenuity. Anguish about environmental degradation is typically portrayed in terms of private sensations of loss and melancholy, such as when Charlie Quibler bemoans the despicable state of the Californian Sierra during a long hike with his friends.

By contrast, in the contributions I engage with in this chapter, the dystopian perspective, with its bleak outlook on the past, present and future, takes centre stage. Indeed, it has a tendency to eclipse anything else. The opening sentence of a recent book on the Anthropocene aptly condenses the sentiment on which this constellation feeds into a memorable motto: "It is worse, much worse, than you think."[1] Such a statement is itself premised on the assumption that the reader will already have formed an awareness of current threats; it will not manage to rally those who straightforwardly deny that our climate-changed world might produce devastating outcomes, for our species and for the planetary ecosphere more broadly.

What is clear, then, is that such a mode of reflecting on the Anthropocene presupposes a deflationary kind of critique. A central

---

[1] Wallace-Wells, *The Uninhabitable Earth*, para. 6.1.

insight of this utopian constellation is hence that confidence in our species to inaugurate a good Anthropocene must be shown to be groundless, delusional and perilous. At the same time, it is left open to further inquiry whether knowledge of the actual extent of the ecological crisis will have a "mobilizing, cathartic or disempowering"[2] impact on its readers.

All hope may be gone at the moment, but it could well be recaptured in the future. Some commentators reason that a head-on confrontation with the coming apocalypse, in all its terrifying details, will inspire people to take action – this is clearly Robinson's view of abrupt climate change, when he pictures the flooding of Washington as an agonizing, but ultimately opportune, catalyst for collective empowerment.[3] A similar intuition inspires much of the ecomodernist discourse, which marshals the shock of looming breakdown to make people see the true merit of science and technology.

Others suggest, more modestly, that even the dreariest facets of the ecological crisis will not succeed in rallying people to change their lives, but they might at least enable us to more thoughtfully face up to our fate as a species on the brink of extinction: "We are not going to 'save the planet,'" the poet Paul Kingsnorth sombrely announces, because "the planet is not ours to save. The planet is not dying; but our civilisation might be, and neither green technology nor ethical shopping is going to prevent a serious crash."[4] Others, yet again, voice profound concerns about the potentially paralyzing consequences that relentless talk of catastrophe might have: "Fear," one commentator remarks, "can hinder, rather than help ... attempts to halt the disaster."[5] Catastrophism, in other words, may actually have debilitating, rather than liberatory, effects.[6]

---

[2] Bettini, "Environmental Catastrophe," 41.

[3] On this view, see: Veldman, "Narrating the Environmental Apocalypse."

[4] Kingsnorth, "Why I Stopped Believing in Environmentalism and Started the Dark Mountain Project."

[5] Lilley, "Introduction," 2.

[6] On the radical openness of apocalyptic imaginaries in contemporary environmental discourse, see: Garforth, "Environmental Futures, Now and Then."

These conflicting stances vis-à-vis both the form and the content of apocalyptic imaginaries will interest us here. As in prior chapters, I try to instigate a conversation between two faces of the utopian imagination: theory building and storytelling. The crux of my argument is that, far from eliminating all traces of hope, today's heralds of cataclysmic collapse engage in social dreaming that strives to become inoculated against wishful thinking. Theorists attempt to do this by assembling a variety of conceptual frameworks, from future histories to advocating the withdrawal from public affairs. The novelist I am grappling with in this chapter brings her own set of anxieties to bear on this debate: Margaret Atwood's *MaddAddam* trilogy portrays a post-apocalyptic world wherein hope gets radically reconfigured. While humanity's dominance of our planet might be on the verge of disintegrating, there is still a future for *Homo sapiens* in a post-Anthropocene world – as an equal member in a multispecies community of Earth dwellers.

5.1 OUR HOME IS ON FIRE: LIFE AND DEATH ON AN UNINHABITABLE PLANET

In *The Death of Environmentalism*, Michael Shellenberger and Ted Nordhaus remind us, for example, that Martin Luther King, Jr., did not proclaim, "I have a nightmare." My reply to them was that he did not need to say it – his people were living a nightmare. They needed a dream. But we, I fear, are living a dream. We need to be reminded of the nightmare ahead. Here is the truth as I see it: we will never do the things that are needed unless we know the full extent of our predicament.[7]

Climate change and the Anthropocene are the triumph of an undead species, a mindless shuffle toward extinction, but this is only a lopsided imitation of what we really are. This is why political depression is important: zombies don't feel sad, and they certainly don't feel helpless; they just are. Political depression is, at root, the experience of a creature that is being prevented from being itself; for all its crushingness, for all its feebleness, it's a cry of protest. Yes, political depressives feel as if they don't know how to be

---

[7] Speth, *The Bridge at the Edge of the World*, 233–34.

human; buried in the despair and self-doubt is an important realization. If humanity is the capacity to act meaningfully within our surroundings, then we are not really, or not yet, human.[8]

Adults keep saying: "We owe it to the young people to give them hope." But I don't want your hope. I don't want you to be hopeful. I want you to panic. I want you to feel the fear I feel every day. And then I want you to act. I want you to act as you would in a crisis. I want you to act as if our house is on fire. Because it is.[9]

What does the recent rise of apocalyptic visions of climate change tell us about ourselves? How, exactly, do these visions construct the future and how do they affect our ability to act in the present? Can dystopian imaginaries serve as guides for alternative ways of living? Is the suspicion of these narratives as defeatist warranted?

These are difficult questions that circulate in both the public debate and the scholarly conversation between philosophers, historians and social scientists. In the theoretical part of this chapter, I will approach them via three steps: first, I unravel the discussion around dystopian visions by giving an overview of the uses of apocalyptic themes in recent environmental discourse. This will be followed, second, by an analysis of a number of archetypal positions around catastrophism, concentrating on scholars such as Naomi Oreskes, Erik Conway, Roy Scranton and the authors of the Dark Mountain project's manifesto. In the final step, I aim to outline what remains of hope – before, during and after the apocalypse.

5.1.1 From Future Cataclysm to the Normalization of Ongoing Crisis.

It is no exaggeration to claim that modern environmentalism was borne out of an apocalyptic sensibility.[10] To grasp this, consider the very first chapter of *Silent Spring* entitled "A Fable for Tomorrow," originally published in 1962. After describing the bucolic countryside surrounding a town in the heart of rural America, Rachel

---

[8] Kriss and O'Hagan, "Tropical Depressions."

[9] Thunberg, "Our House Is on Fire."

[10] For an overview of the wider context, see: Garrard, *Ecocriticism*, chap. 5: Apocalypse.

Carson paints a bleak picture of environmental degradation that evokes the setting of a horror film:

Then a strange blight crept over the area and everything began to change. Some evil spell had settled on the community: mysterious maladies swept the flocks of chickens; the cattle and sheep sickened and died. Everywhere was a shadow of death. The farmers spoke of much illness among their families. In the town the doctors had become more and more puzzled by new kinds of sickness appearing among their patients. There had been several sudden and unexplained deaths, not only among adults but even among children, who would be stricken suddenly while at play and die within a few hours. There was a strange stillness. The birds, for example – where had they gone? Many people spoke of them, puzzled and disturbed. The feeding stations in the backyards were deserted. The few birds seen anywhere were moribund; they trembled violently and could not fly. It was a spring without voices. On the mornings that had once throbbed with the dawn chorus of robins, catbirds, doves, jays, wrens, and scores of other bird voices there was now no sound; only silence lay over the fields and woods and marsh ... No witchcraft, no enemy action had silenced the rebirth of new life in this stricken world. The people had done it themselves.[11]

Carson's narrative is anchored in a dystopian imaginary. It contains a cautionary tale about the lethal consequences of chemical pollution.[12] With the help of evidence gathered by groundbreaking devices, such as Lovelock's *Electron Capture Detector*, Carson shows that our bodies are already drenched in a "sea of carcinogens,"[13] due to now-banned pesticides like DDT, the main target of her anger and scorn.

Just like other contributions to the debate around environmental damage in the 1960s and 1970s, *Silent Spring* aimed to "question progress and challenge modern humanity to develop a new story."[14] Seminal texts

---

[11] Carson, *Silent Spring*, paras. 14.4–14.9. For an analysis of the wider ramifications of *Silent Spring*'s opening scene, see: Soles, "And No Birds Sing."

[12] On Carson's engagement with scientific uncertainty and dystopian rhetoric, see: Walsh, *Scientists as Prophets*, 128–30.

[13] Carson, *Silent Spring*, para. 27.74.

[14] Lewis, "Telling Stories about the Future," 46.

such as Paul Ehrlich's *The Population Bomb*[15] and Barry Commoner's *The Closing Circle*[16] also made strategic use of catastrophist tropes to bring about transformations both in the scientific community and society at large.[17] What is unique about the decade during which Carson, Ehrlich and Commoner published their groundbreaking works is that their critiques envisaged humanity on a path to certain self-destruction. As Frederick Buell has claimed, these commentators promoted a radical agenda, driven by the sense that the world was about to end:

> For writers in the 1960s and 1970s, these rhetorics were all equally logics and revelations. Deployed against the era's fundamental attitudes, they overturned them: they revealed. Depicting humans as having trapped themselves in a terrible rush towards world-end, they expressed a terrible logic. Together, they distinctively and creatively gave force to the feeling that the environmental problems of the day amounted to apocalypse – to rupture, world-end and a last judgment on humanity.[18]

It is illuminating to contemplate what exactly happened in the period immediately after these authors had condemned chemical toxicity and escalating population growth. In the 1980s, a culture of denial quickly gained traction. Aspersion was cast on the integrity and motivation of environmental "doomsayers." During the reign of Margaret Thatcher and Ronald Reagan, the public debate successively turned away from framing environmental problems in catastrophist terms.[19] This shift was stimulated by what Naomi Oreskes and Erik Conway identified as "merchants of doubts." To undermine the environmentalist campaign against

---

[15] Ehrlich, *The Population Bomb*.

[16] Commoner, *The Closing Circle*.

[17] On the underlying connection between environmental discourse and neo-Malthusian concerns about population growth, see: Robertson, *The Malthusian Moment.*

[18] Buell, "A Short History of Environmental Apocalypse," 18.

[19] On this development, see: Buell, *The Future of Environmental Criticism*, 2–33. The situation in the United Kingdom was, however, rather different from the United States in that Thatcher expressed far greater concern for the environment than Reagan. That said, the free-market ideology underpinning British neoliberalism by default clashed with the fundamental principles of an environmentally conscious politics. For a useful work comparing different types of environmentalism, see: Dryzek et al., *Green States and Social Movements.*

acid rain, for example, the Reagan administration commissioned a scientific review of all the existing evidence, which was ultimately deemed so contradictory that governmental reticence with respect to emission controls seemed judicious.[20] The panel undertaking the review, however, was stacked with affiliates of well-funded conservative think tanks, who conspired to sabotage federal regulation by exaggerating the statistical unreliability of research results. This in turn fuelled a generalized suspicion of scientific findings around the ecological crisis.

But the denunciation of apocalyptic imaginaries as baseless fearmongering in the 1980s marks only the beginning of the story. From the 1990s onwards, the mood in the public shifted once again. Rather than interpreting the effects of climate change as signs of a world-ending cataclysm, people began to experience the ecological crisis differently, as "global warming makes people realize that they dwell in a steadily increasing condition of risk, uncertainty, and unpredictability."[21] Knowledge of the apocalypse, in other words, has turned into a way of life, prompting everyone to assess the various risks associated with the destruction of nature. As Frank Kermode put it, "no longer imminent, the End is immanent."[22]

This historical sketch suggests that a newly formed understanding of planetary breakdown has gone hand in hand with the normalization of ecological crisis. The exception has become the new normal. This points to a dilemma that contemporary environmentalism needs to confront. For, on the one hand, it appears evident that too much talk of doom and gloom may cause "crisis fatigue," rendering people less, rather than more, susceptible to pleas for resistant action. On the other hand, dwelling in crisis can also become a symptom of "passivity and quiet desperation."[23] If the apocalypse cannot be arrested anymore, what reasons do we have to do anything at all?

In sum, the two horns of the dilemma – lazy inaction and nervous fatalism – expose that the apocalyptic imaginary has manoeuvred itself

---

[20] Oreskes and Conway, *Merchants of Doubt*, chap. 3: Sowing the Seeds of Doubt: Acid Rain.

[21] Buell, *From Apocalypse to Way of Life*, 95.

[22] Kermode, *The Sense of an Ending*, 25.

[23] Buell, "A Short History of Environmental Apocalypse," 30.

into a dead end. Ursula Heise attempts to investigate this development by distinguishing apocalyptic from risk perspectives: "In the apocalyptic perspective, utter destruction lies ahead but can be averted and replaced by an alternative future society; in the risk perspective, crises are already underway all around, and while their consequences can be mitigated, a future without their impact has become impossible to envision."[24] Heise asserts that, starting in the 1990s, a profound shift occurred, from a frame whereby the apocalypse is imagined as a rupture with a more or less bucolic present, to a situation where the future comes to resemble the present in that we will continue to "dwell in crisis," aspiring to reduce risks as much as possible, without ever managing to successfully eradicate them.[25]

A good illustration of this second, risk-centred perspective can be found in David Wallace-Wells' recent bestseller *The Uninhabitable Earth.* Wallace-Wells seeks to study the "existential crisis" global warming has brought about, leaving us "between two hellish poles, in which our best-case outcome is death and suffering at the scale of twenty-five Holocausts, and the worst-case outcome puts us on the brink of extinction."[26] The book's overall objective is to shake readers out of their complacency about climate change, with the help of huge amounts of data proving the lethal effects that hotter weather and extreme flooding, for example, will have on humans around the world.[27]

Despite this bleak outlook, Wallace-Wells appears to believe that the fate of *Homo sapiens* is not yet sealed – our species will only become

---

[24] Heise, *Sense of Place and Sense of Planet,* 142.

[25] It should be noted that Heise's approach is heavily influenced by Ulrich Beck's work. See especially: Beck, *World Risk Society.*

[26] Wallace-Wells, *The Uninhabitable Earth,* para. 6.52.

[27] In an annotated version of the article on which the book is based, Wallace-Wells reflects on the ethical implications of painting such bleak pictures of the future: "Is it helpful, or journalistically ethical, to explore the worst-case scenarios of climate change, however unlikely they are? How much should a writer contextualize scary possibilities with information about how probable those outcomes are, however speculative those probabilities may be? What are the risks of terrifying or depressing readers so much they disengage from the issue, and what should a journalist make of those risks?" (Wallace-Wells, "When Will the Planet Be Too Hot for Humans?"). One of the poignant criticisms of Wallace-Wells' book suggests that he ignores the effects of climate change on the non-human world. See: Gibbons, "The Uninhabitable Earth Review."

extinguished if it fails to turn things around. The mechanics of remedial and transformative action are deceptively simple, bordering on what I have glossed as "solutionism": "If humans are responsible for the problem, they must be capable of undoing it."[28] This is also the gist of Greta Thunberg's message to the world, which has been positively received and elaborated on by a number of social and political theorists.[29]

In what follows, I build on Buell's and Heise's thinking insofar as I start from the conjecture that ideas about environmental degradation, and our ability to counteract it, have significantly changed over the past decades. While Rachel Carson remains one of the icons of the environmental justice movement, her portrayal of toxic pollution has lost at least some of its shocking appeal, for we have generally come to accept a basic measure of risk as part of our ordinary lives. Another way of describing the motion from an earlier focus on apocalyptic imaginaries to the routinization of risk today would be to stress that we currently inhabit a "post-apocalyptic" age in which "loss [is] experienced as already having occurred, as ongoing or as impossible to prevent, rather than as a future risk or threat."[30]

Although this analysis seems largely correct, it also strikes me as overdrawn, for apocalyptic visions still circulate in the current debate, as any reader of climate fiction will be able to confirm. But these narratives usually do not presuppose idyllic images of harmonious nature, set in opposition to the imminent devastation of the planet in the near future. As the journalist and activist Bill McKibben observes, we should reconcile ourselves to the fact that "the old planet – the one with an Arctic ice cap, the one where hurricanes didn't strike Spain and Brazil, the one where jellyfish didn't bloom in great slimy clouds across the oceans"[31] has simply vanished. According to this view, our new home ought to be called "Eaarth," a planet where social dreaming might still be

---

[28] Wallace-Wells, *The Uninhabitable Earth*, para. 28.4. This rather sketchy picture of human ingenuity is the reason why Roy Scranton seems deeply sceptical of Wallace-Wells' approach. See: Scranton, "No Happy Ending."

[29] For a representative example see: Read and Alexander, *This Civilisation Is Finished.*

[30] Cassegård and Thörn, "Toward a Postapocalyptic Environmentalism?," 563.

[31] McKibben, *Eaarth*, para. 8.69.

possible, but only against the backdrop of a sober acknowledgement that humanity has already fundamentally altered its habitat.[32]

The question remains, though, whether the inclusion of crisis and breakdown into quotidian routines – the swerve from apocalyptic to post-apocalyptic scenarios – leaves sufficient space for what is, after all, the paramount task of all dystopian thinking, namely to provide an "extrapolation from the present that involve[s] a warning."[33] How can such a warning be given if the environmental crisis becomes absorbed into our everyday ways of life? And, perhaps even more unsettling, what remains of dystopian thinking if the very idea of a warning becomes obsolete, for we have already moved past the beginning of the apocalypse?

5.1.2 THREE WAYS OF SAYING: APOCALYPSE NOW!. In the following two sections, my goal is to address these questions by providing a survey of contemporary expressions of (post-)apocalyptic thinking. To achieve this goal, I will distinguish between three registers in which the (post-) apocalyptic imaginary can be couched: first, through a future history of present disasters that leaves space for resistant action; second, through the cultivation of an art of perishing in the Anthropocene that foregrounds the commemorative function of cultural artefacts; and third, through a complete renunciation of hope that still attempts to keep nihilism at bay.

A crucial difference between these three imaginaries concerns the question of when the apocalypse is supposed to be happening: in the present or rather in the near future. It matters, politically speaking and in terms of which alternatives are being pondered, whether we believe "ecological Armageddon is already a reality"[34] or whether we hope the

---

[32] This thought also resonates with the observation of Indigenous scholars who insist that apocalyptic visions of a climate-changed world are not to be directed at a near future, but rather at a not-so-distant past ravaged by settler colonialism. On this point, see: Whyte, "Indigenous Science (Fiction) for the Anthropocene."

[33] Sargent, "The Three Faces of Utopianism Revisited," 8. See also: Baccolini and Moylan, "Introduction: Dystopia and Histories."

[34] Swyngedouw, "Apocalypse Now! Fear and Doomsday Pleasures," 11. For a critique of the discourse around environmental apocalypse, see also: Swyngedouw, "Apocalypse Forever?"

final reckoning can still be forestalled. Some of the visions discussed shortly are more successful than others in holding firm to the key objective of utopianism: to enable us to imagine better ways of being and living and to provide orientation around hyperobjects, such as a climate-changed world. The cautionary pedagogy that dystopias necessarily advance is always imperilled by defeatism – the feeling that it is already too late to do anything meaningful about what is to come.

My first example unpacks an argument we have already come across in Robinson's writings. Apart from condemning the army of denialists who lent credence to industries such as tobacco and energy, Naomi Oreskes and Erik Conway have also written a short book on a near-future scenario where the environmental breakdown has already taken place.[35] In *The Collapse of Western Civilization*, the two historians adopt the standpoint of a scholar from the Second People's Republic of China, living in 2393 and looking back at the upheavals of the twenty-first century. These commotions, our future historian informs us, ultimately triggered the Great Collapse and Mass Migration (2073–2093), which brought Western civilization to a close.

Oreskes and Conway focus specifically on the short period in the immediate run-up to the apocalypse, which they dub the "Penumbral Age." The puzzle that the narrator tries to solve is one that Diane Chang has faced in the *Science in the Capital* trilogy – only this time it is approached from the other side of the cataclysm: why was humanity fully aware of the catastrophic consequences of climate change, and yet did so little?

> To the historian studying this tragic period of human history, the most astounding fact is that the victims *knew what was happening and why*. Indeed, they chronicled it in detail precisely *because* they knew that fossil fuel combustion was to blame. Historical analysis also shows that Western civilization had the technological know-how and capability to effect an orderly transition to renewable energy, yet the available technologies were not implemented in time. As with all great historical events, there is no

---

[35] That book has itself grown out of an essay: Oreskes and Conway, "The Collapse of Western Civilization," January 1, 2013.

easy answer to the question of why this catastrophe occurred, but key factors stand out. The thesis of this analysis is that Western civilization became trapped in the grip of two inhibiting ideologies: *positivism* and *market fundamentalism.*[36]

The root causes of the Great Collapse and Mass Migration can thus be traced back to problems in the scientific community and the economic sector. The chronicler then goes on to examine what exactly was going wrong during the Penumbral Age, underscoring that knowledge about climate change had proven toothless in the face of the "carbon-combustion complex." The almost religious belief in the power of the market to sort things out added yet another factor that explains the system-wide failure of mitigation and adaptation efforts.

Just as in *Merchants of Doubt,* Oreskes and Conway home in on the nexus between knowledge and power to explain why collective action did not gain momentum in due time.[37] Much of the blame is accordingly placed on the shoulders of scientists, who are accused of clinging to disciplinary norms that undercut humanity's ability to tackle climate change. Tractability, for example, is supposed to ensure that problems that appear to be too big to be solved are treated on a lower level of complexity. While central to the functioning of normal science, this reductionist mantra has the disadvantage of removing seemingly "intractable" problems, such as climate change, from the purview of scientific inquiry. "Even scientists who had a broad view of climate change often felt it would be inappropriate for them to articulate it, because that would require them to speak beyond their expertise, and seem to be taking credit for other people's work."[38]

While scientists are excoriated for their narrow-mindedness, the narrator also points to various paths not taken, which might have forestalled the catastrophe. One of those is forged by writers dealing with climate change. Referring to the author of the *Science in the Capital* trilogy himself, our fictional Chinese historian laments "that [artists] were

---

[36] Oreskes and Conway, *The Collapse of Western Civilization,* 2014, 35, italics in original.

[37] This is why Ursula Heise considers *The Collapse of Western Civilization* a "companion piece" to *Merchants of Doubt.* See: Heise, *Imagining Extinction,* 217.

[38] Oreskes and Conway, *The Collapse of Western Civilization,* 2014, 14–15.

among the first to truly grasp the significance of the changes that were occurring,"[39] but their harrowing jeremiads were not taken seriously enough.

As the book's title evinces, the Great Collapse and Mass Migration had global repercussions, but they primarily precipitated the demise of the West. In terms of a viable counter-model, the book praises the home country of the chronicler, the Second People's Republic of China, whose centralized government made responding to climate change much easier. Political systems upheld by market fundamentalism, however, distrust the state too much to conduct meaningful mitigation and adaptation.

Oreskes and Conway's blending together of science fiction and history strives for something other than merely the frisson of contemplating our own fall: it clearly delivers "moral instruction,"[40] as one reviewer has remarked. In that regard, the book differs from rival attempts to look back at humanity's extermination, which foreground the rock record of our species and ask what conclusions an alien explorer might draw about *Homo sapiens*, purely based on our future fossil traces.[41]

In terms of genre, Oreskes and Conway's text can hence be best described as "science faction," or a "fiction of science fact."[42] *The Collapse of Western Civilization* contains, accordingly, a typical *If-this-goes-on* story: through a meticulous account of past failures, which we are in fact witnessing at the present moment, it offers a macro view of why the world falls short of adequately responding to climate change. The book depicts a scenario that starts from a future apocalypse, but by implication sketches how resistant action could still be taken.[43] Its warning signal is based on a procedure of temporal extrapolation, whose function is both

---

[39] Oreskes and Conway, 13. As Oreskes and Conway confess in an interview accompanying their book, Kim Stanley Robinson has indeed been a major inspiration for writing *The Collapse of Western Civilization*. See: Oreskes and Conway, 65–6.

[40] Hulme, "Review of the Collapse of Western Civilization."

[41] Zalasiewicz, *The Earth after Us*. For yet another account, see: Farrier, *Footprints*.

[42] Bellamy and Szeman, "Life after People," 195.

[43] On the galvanizing effect of such apocalyptic discourse on activism, see: Veldman, "Narrating the Environmental Apocalypse."

critical and transformative – to shake up the readers' perception of a precarious status quo.

Our second interlocutor, Roy Scranton, thinks that this is the wrong way to tell the story of our climate-changed world. Scranton is amongst those who believe that we urgently need to change tack so as to come to terms with the Anthropocene, by completely reorienting our affective and cognitive frameworks. In *Learning to Die in the Anthropocene*, he posits that the basic premise of ecomodernist discourse is flawed, for, given the depth of the ecological crisis we are going through, the very notion of redemption and resolution is a non-starter:

> The greatest challenge the Anthropocene poses isn't how the Department of Defense should plan for resource wars, whether we should put up sea walls to protect Manhattan, or when we should abandon Miami. It won't be addressed by buying a Prius, turning off the air conditioning, or signing a treaty. The greatest challenge we face is a philosophical one: understanding that this civilization is already dead. The sooner we confront our situation and realize that there is nothing we can do to save ourselves, the sooner we can get down to the difficult task of adapting, with mortal humility, to our new reality.[44]

Scranton thus maintains that a look at the available data – such as the one assembled and analyzed in detail by Wallace-Wells – makes a mockery of any optimism about the future. The gist of his argument is that we simply do not possess the knowledge to "solve" the problems generated by climate change. This makes it imperative for humanity to reinvent itself in and for the Anthropocene, via original stories and tantalizing myths that thematize our own extinction.

Switching from a eutopian stance that emphasizes technological efficiency to a dystopian position anchored in our civilizational demise, Scranton argues that carbon-based capitalism has already passed its expiration date. We would be naive to invest faith into the human ability to escape from the current predicament unscathed. The thought that we could somehow harness our species' ingenuity to "decouple" resource systems from the ecosphere is nothing but a self-aggrandizing illusion.

---

[44] Scranton, *Learning to Die in the Anthropocene*, para. 7.28.

Scranton speaks disparagingly of the search for "techno-utopian solutions," which aim to retain the capitalist order in place, while tweaking energy processes on the system's margins.

Does that mean that all that is left for our species is to opt for collective suicide, perhaps even by accelerating the damage we have already inflicted on the planet – to go out with a loud bang, since no way out of this disaster seems viable?[45] Despite issuing a death certificate to our way of life, Scranton rejects nihilism of any kind, for "humanity can survive and adapt to the new world of the Anthropocene if we accept human limits and transience as fundamental truths, and work to nurture the variety and richness of our collective cultural heritage."[46] The "acceptance of human limits and transience" is a lesson that every individual should learn. Referring to his personal experience as a soldier in Iraq, Scranton draws solace from Stoic philosophy, which teaches that a fulfilled life is one unhampered by fear and attachment.

If we forego all certainties about permanence and stability, what is left for us to keep going? Scranton claims that the cultural practice of memory-making can "save those who are already dead."[47] This includes the creation and curation of an archive of human experiences that connects our momentary being on an uninhabitable planet to past and future generations. Scranton's vision for life after our extinction in the Anthropocene is therefore geared towards the building of shelter zones where the memory of the already dead can be preserved:

> As biological and cultural diversity is threatened across the world by capitalist monoculture and mass extinction, we must build arks: not just biological arks, to carry forward endangered genetic data, but also cultural arks, to carry forward endangered wisdom. The library of human cultural technologies that is our archive, the concrete record of human thought in all languages that comprises the entirety of our existence as historical

---

[45] As Eric Hobsbawm is supposed to have said in response to a question about how his famously lush lifestyle could be squared with his Communist commitments: "If you are on a ship that's going down, you might as well travel first class" (Evans, *Eric Hobsbawm*, 488).

[46] Scranton, *Learning to Die in the Anthropocene*, para. 7.30.

[47] Scranton, para. 12.20.

beings, is not only the seed stock of our future intellectual growth, but its soil, its source, its womb. The fate of the humanities, as we confront the end of modern civilization, is the fate of humanity itself.[48]

This stance is difficult to evaluate because Scranton openly embraces the paradox at the heart of his argument. On the one hand, he dismisses optimism, by gesturing towards evidence that the ecomodernist dream, with its yearning for redemption and resolution through scientific and technological progress, is naive and dangerous. In that sense, and in contradistinction with our first dystopian vision, Scranton insists that the apocalypse is already under way. There is nothing we can do to put a break on it. In reality, we now live, Scranton admonishes, in a post-apocalyptic world, so warning about the consequences of our actions is a futile enterprise – it is, quite literally, too late to do anything about the future.

On the other hand, however, Scranton wishes to rebuff nihilism, by claiming that "[a]ccepting the fatality of our situation isn't nihilism, but rather the necessary first step in forging a new way of life."[49] So, the lesson of letting go is not supposed to aggravate individual or collective despair. Rather, it is meant to carve out a space for restructuring our affective and cognitive frameworks, through the establishment of a repository for the meanings and recollections of our climate-changed world.

In sum, Scranton's dystopian analysis points out that there is nothing we can do to avert the catastrophe. As a consequence, there is also no need to zoom ahead into the near future to look for signs of the impending downfall of our species – it is already in the past. This reckoning notwithstanding, we can still receive considerable consolation from the fact that cultural artefacts may yet survive our own extinction. This is where our outstanding energy should be channelled: making memories for ourselves and for whomever comes after us. The contrast to neoliberal discourses around resilience for the sake of endurance could not be starker.

---

[48] Scranton, para. 12.56.
[49] Scranton, "We're Doomed. Now What?"

Scranton's eulogy to culture can be contrasted with a third perspective that is even bleaker. The Dark Mountain project is the name of a loose group of artists and activists, founded in 2009 by the writers Paul Kingsnorth and Dougald Hine. Since its foundation, the collective appears to have grown significantly in size, bringing together poets, philosophers, economists and scientists. The Dark Mountain project also organizes a number of events ranging from an annual festival to creative writing classes and wilderness expeditions abroad.[50]

Their manifesto from 2009, *Uncivilisation*, reads like an echo of the Breakthrough Institute's techno-utopian fantasies. It was followed up by fifteen volumes of "essays, fiction, poetry and artwork" produced by an international community of "mountaineers." The manifesto contains not so much a declaration of clearly defined goals and strategies, but rather a statement of intent that outlines possible paths forward. Written during the onset of the financial crisis and the subsequent Great Recession, Kingsnorth and Hine set out to dismantle the notion of progress undergirding contemporary life. In complete opposition to ecomodernist pronouncements about the necessity of "decoupling" humanity, the Dark Mountain project's manifesto is founded on deep ecology:

> We are the first generations to grow up surrounded by evidence that our attempt to separate ourselves from "nature" has been a grim failure, proof not of our genius but our hubris. The attempt to sever the hand from the body has endangered the "progress" we hold so dear, and it has endangered much of "nature" too. The resulting upheaval underlies the crisis we now face.[51]

Like Wallace-Wells, Kingsnorth and Hine suggest that the relentless optimism of those who assure us that everything will be fine is entirely misplaced.[52] Business-as-usual is not an option anymore, and

---

[50] The collective's website contains a useful overview of these activities: "Home." For a portrait of Kingsnorth and a reportage on the operations of the Dark Mountain project, see: Smith, "It's the End of the World as We Know It . . . and He Feels Fine." For a French equivalent to the Dark Mountain project, see the recent rise of so-called *collapsologues*: Stetler, "Collapsologie."

[51] Kingsnorth and Hine, "Uncivilization."

[52] But note that Wallace-Wells is, in other respects, deeply critical of the Dark Mountain project. See: Wallace-Wells, *The Uninhabitable Earth*, paras. 26.23–26.28.

technological fixes will not resolve the material and ideological contradictions from which the ecological crisis emerges.

This critique also extends to what they see as the neoliberal hegemony within contemporary environmentalism, which the "mountaineers" object to on the grounds that it has been co-opted by capitalism. Kingsnorth in particular is adamant about his decision to withdraw from lifelong activism: the focus of much of today's green movement, he laments, lies exclusively on boosting the sustainability credentials of profit-oriented corporations, without shaking up the foundations of our whole way of life. This blunting of environmentalism's edge means that a retreat from public engagement becomes the only responsible option.[53]

At the same time, however, the members of the Dark Mountain project also attempt to hold fatalism and nihilism at bay. In denying that "the future will give us either unbroken progress or apocalypse, and there are no spaces between,"[54] they seek to pry open a gap through which a new form of hope may yet arise. The only way this can succeed is through a rebuttal of the notion that our civilization is worth saving at all. As the manifesto draws to a close, the authors therefore stipulate eight principles of "uncivilization" that are neither under the spell of historical progressivism nor overshadowed by fatalism and nihilism. These principles revolve around the requirement for a sober reckoning with the present moment, the centrality of storytelling, an aversion to abstract theorizing and the investment in a novel kind of hope: "The end of the world as we know it is not the end of the world full stop. Together, we will find the hope beyond hope, the paths which lead to the unknown world ahead of us."[55]

The utopian desire for alternative ways of being and living is apprehended here through a clash with wishful thinking. As Kingsnorth remarks in an interview, the Dark Mountain project activates the potential of accepting our civilization's moribundity. This also implies disenchanting other illusions:

[53] Kingsnorth, *Confessions of a Recovering Environmentalist*, 61–82.
[54] Kingsnorth and Hine, "Editorial," 3.
[55] Kingsnorth and Hine, "Uncivilization."

Whenever I hear the word "hope" these days, I reach for my whisky bottle. It seems to me to be such a futile thing. What does it mean? What are we hoping for? And why are we reduced to something so desperate? Surely we only hope when we are powerless? This may sound a strange thing to say, but one of the great achievements for me of the Dark Mountain project has been to give people permission to give up hope. What I mean by that is that we help people get beyond the desperate desire to do something as impossible as "save the Earth", or themselves, and start talking about where we actually are, what is actually possible and where we are actually coming from. I don't think we need hope. I think we need imagination. We need to imagine a future which can't be planned for and can't be controlled.[56]

By drawing on various kinds of artistic practice – from poetry to painting – the Dark Mountain project wants to both rehabilitate forgotten narratives and foster new ones, all in the spirit of shattering the myth of progress.[57] Just like Scranton, the members of the collective are interested in spinning "post-cautionary tales" – stories that start with the realization that there is nothing we can do to stop the crisis from escalating further.[58]

Their admonitions are, strictly speaking, not jeremiads, but funeral orations: the mountaineers' gaze seems to be directed backwards, into the past, with only furtive glances towards an undefined and frightening future. Both Scranton and the members of the Dark Mountain project hence operate within a horizon of expectations that is radically different from Oreskes and Conway's project: their pedagogy is premised on a procedure of temporal interpolation, whose purpose is simultaneously critical and consolatory – to remind the audience about how little time we have left on this planet.

---

[56] Stephenson, "I Withdraw."

[57] Adams, "Inaction and Environmental Crisis."

[58] Hine et al., "Editorial." In a later iteration of the principles behind the movement, Kingsnorth first praises the beauty of the scythe with which he cultivates the land he is living on, expresses his (qualified) admiration for Theodore Kaczynski's (aka the Unabomber) unflinching critique of industrial society and then ruminates on the importance of withdrawing completely from engagement. Inaction, he argues, can be much more revolutionary than action. See: Kingsnorth, "Dark Ecology."

5.1.3 WHAT REMAINS OF HOPE: BEFORE AND AFTER THE APOCALYPSE. What should we make of these different appropriations of the (post-)apocalypse? Are they genuinely helpful in terms of articulating bleak accounts of the future that still keep ablaze the fire of social dreaming? Or do they ultimately collapse into fatalism, stifling the utopian desire once and for all? My goal in this section is not to issue a conclusive judgement on these expressions of the dystopian imaginary, but rather to identify where rifts within them can be located.

As evidenced by the previous section, the contemporary landscape remains divided between those who imagine the collapse of our way of life to occur in the near future and those who insist that we are already living through a systemic breakdown. The chasm between apocalyptic and post-apocalyptic perspectives is therefore on full display in the current debate. My first example, Oreskes and Conway's depiction of how disaster will have occurred, essentially mirrors Robinson's account, albeit by turning the frame on its head, pivoting from a eutopian to a dystopian perspective. Just like the *Science in the Capital* trilogy, *The Collapse of Western Civilization* identifies the nexus between science and politics, or between knowledge and power, as the central linkage that will decide our species' fate.

The message here is easy to decipher: unless science and politics can be happily married (as they literally are in Robinson's trilogy), capitalism's destructive tendencies will hasten humanity's extinction. Only if scientists adjust their standards of validation and politicians stop worshipping the market, will the environmental apocalypse be thwarted. The similarities with Robinson's position are unmistakable, because, although the story is told from the vantage point of 2393, the imagined future remains fundamentally open. There is nothing inevitable about the way in which Western civilization eventually collapses. Since the Anthropocene is riddled with human-made problems, it must also be feasible to devise human-made solutions to avert the impending calamity. *The Collapse of Western Civilization* thus contains an admonition as to what will happen if those solutions are not pursued with utmost determination.

One possible challenge to this type of dystopianism is that it does not go far enough in interrogating the status quo – that its deflationary critique is not sufficiently thoroughgoing. We can tease this point out by revisiting the *Science in the Capital* trilogy. Despite a shared interest in the intersections between science and politics, as a cautionary tale, Oreskes and Conway's "science faction" is much less nuanced than Robinson's positive vision, with its probing of manifold, intersecting pathways into the future. This should perhaps not surprise us, given that the authors of *The Collapse of Western Civilization* are professional historians, who deploy the genre of a future history to communicate their insights into climate change.

Yet, their book still seems to suffer from a shortcoming that equally affects the *Science in the Capital* trilogy: the social landscape of potential actors for change is curiously flat and almost exclusively composed of elites.[59] What is absent from their dystopia is an awareness of the multiplicity of actors that could effectively step up to salvage the present moment. As the activism of Indigenous environmental groups, for example, testifies, pressure often builds up from popular movements that are unwilling to fall in line with elite-driven agendas.[60] Concentrating exclusively on high-flying scientists and power-wielding politicians makes this dystopian vision a rather restricted affair.

Lack of critical depth is not something that Scranton or the members of the Dark Mountain project can be accused of. In stark contrast to Oreskes and Conway, they take issue with the very notion of our future still remaining wide open. On Scranton's reading, a complete reorientation of prevailing affective and cognitive frameworks will be necessary to cope with the effects of climate change. His rejoinder to the relentless optimism of ecomodernists is that they display a level of exuberant self-delusion that impedes a sober reckoning with our current predicament.

What is required, then, is an acknowledgement of our shortcomings as a species: letting go of the longing for mastery of the world will free up resources for responsibly dealing the ecological crisis.[61] On a personal

---

[59] On this point, see: Cohn, "A Tragic Scenario."

[60] Schlosberg and Carruthers, "Indigenous Struggles, Environmental Justice, and Community Capabilities." For a sustained argument about the need for popular pressure (including the sabotage of physical infrastructure) to cease fossil fuel extraction, see: Malm, *How to Blow Up a Pipeline.*

[61] This view also resonates with Timothy Morton's diagnosis that the world has come to an end in the Anthropocene. See: "Clearly, planet Earth has not exploded. But the concept

level, this means that Stoical virtues of accepting one's mortality and of doubting one's sovereign agency ought to be cultivated. On a collective level, calling for an archive of cultural artefacts that safely stores the multifaceted memory of humanity appears to be Scranton's favoured strategy for defusing the suspicion that the focus on perishing in the Anthropocene will frustrate his audience.

Jedediah Purdy has put his finger on the main tension in Scranton's approach. The posture of enlightened resignation may end up looking like "the sort of suggestive but, upon scrutiny, meaningless gesture that makes talk of 'responsibility' feel self-important and ineffective."[62] The objection holds that building cultural arks is insufficient, so long as it remains unclear what the preservation of cultural heritage would eventually be for. Scranton's endorsement of memory-making diminishes the range of options available to those yearning for better ways of being and living.

In response to Purdy's suggestion that we should try to inaugurate a democratic Anthropocene, Scranton's position is an avowedly morbid one: "[W]e don't need more politics. We need more hospice."[63] As the rejoinder shows, in this post-apocalyptic world, there is absolutely no room for inspiring encouragement to save our species from itself. Nobody talks politics in a hospice.

We have already observed that Scranton struggles with the tendency of his dystopian perspective to collapse into fatalism. The Dark Mountain project faces a similar obstacle. George Monbiot, Britain's most vocal environmentalist and erstwhile colleague of Kingsnorth's, charges the proponents of the Dark Mountain project with adopting an attitude of *faux* detachment from untold suffering. The real upshot of their decision

---

world is no longer operational, and hyperobjects are what brought about its demise. The idea of the end of the world is very active in environmentalism. Yet I argue that this idea is not effective, since, to all intents and purposes, the being that we are supposed to feel anxiety about and care for is gone. This does not mean that there is no hope for ecological politics and ethics. Far from it. Indeed, as I shall argue, the strongly held belief that the world is about to end 'unless we act now' is paradoxically one of the most powerful factors that inhibit a full engagement with our ecological coexistence here on Earth" (Morton, *Hyperobjects*, 6–7).

[62] Purdy, *After Nature*, para. 6.11.

[63] Scranton, "Response to the New Nature."

to withdraw from activism is to "sit back and watch billions die."[64] Similarly, the psychoanalyst Paul Hoggett has accused Kingsnorth, Hine and the other members of the collective of assuming a view of the impending catastrophe that is

> contemptuous of what it sees as the myopia of those (in peace or environ-
> mental movements) who believe that it is never too late to act. Such beliefs
> are seen as consolatory illusions, the resort of the weak. Tough mind-
> edness (as we have seen from the Dark Mountain project) means being
> able to think the unthinkable, have the foresight to prepare for the worst
> and the moral fibre to prevail. The conceit and superiority in this stance is
> not hard to spot.[65]

But not everybody concurs with these assessments. While some aspects of the Dark Mountain project undoubtedly smack of New Age primitivism,[66] the proposition to hold on to some kind of hope even after the apocalypse deserves further attention. Carl Cassegård and Hakån Thörn describe this suggestion as the "paradox of hope," "the fact that hope is sometimes gained not by promoting explicitly hopeful messages, but by ostensibly denying hope."[67] The retreat from activism, despite its potentially debilitating consequences, is different from a complete depoliticization of the Anthropocene.[68] If Cassegård and Thörn's interpretation is correct, then it would be misguided to charge the champions of post-apocalyptic thinking with embracing "antisocial dreaming since they reject the possibility of human action to perfect or save the ecosphere."[69]

Given that Kingsnorth, Hine and the other members of the collective openly advocate inaction, the question remains, though, how this

---

[64] Kingsnorth and Monbiot, "Is There Any Point in Fighting to Stave Off Industrial Apocalypse?" See also: Monbiot, "I Share Their Despair, but I'm Not Quite Ready to Climb the Dark Mountain."

[65] Hoggett, "Climate Change and the Apocalyptic Imagination," 268.

[66] Miller, "What Kind of Novel Do You Write When You Believe Civilization Is Doomed?"

[67] Cassegård and Thörn, "Toward a Postapocalyptic Environmentalism?," 571.

[68] The Dark Mountain project could also be rehabilitated through a philosophical defence of the virtues of fatalism. As will become evident, I am not convinced by the prospects of such a project, but believe that it would be capable of buttressing the more inchoate statements of Kingsnorth and Hine. See: Ruda, *Abolishing Freedom.*

[69] Jendrysik, "Back to the Garden," 36.

different type of hope, this hope inoculated against wishful thinking, would look in practice. The crux of their dystopian vision seems to be that its negativity raises the bar of distrust to such an extent that any hint of a potentially constructive engagement with climate change immediately falls prey to a hermeneutics of suspicion.[70] Once all forms of activism have been discredited as futile, any prospect of real-world change must appear delusional.

The exit that these writers advocate can be seen as an expressive, rather than resistant, one: by extolling the virtues of quitting, the Dark Mountain project seeks to communicate something essential about the state of the world. But this expressive function does not prepare the ground for any kind of organized opposition against dominant power structures – instead it severs all ties to the societal mainstream.[71] Since the dystopian critique is deflationary to such an extent that all mobilizing energy gets exhausted, there is little left for hope to latch on.[72] If the future appears to be foreordained, locked into a trajectory towards certain breakdown, why should we care about what we leave behind? Whom are Scranton's cultural arks for? What is the point of conjuring "a future which can't be planned for and can't be controlled," as Kingsnorth wants us to, if humanity will not be at home on Earth anymore?

To answer these questions, it is helpful to return to an issue I touched upon in Chapter 2. Recall how, in my reading of the utopian desire for other ways of being and living, I tried to complicate Ruth Levitas'

---

[70] I borrow the idea of a "hermeneutics of suspicion" from Paul Ricœur's study of Marx, Nietzsche and Freud. See: Ricœur, *Freud and Philosophy*.

[71] On the distinction between expressive and resistant exit see: Kirkpatrick, *The Virtues of Exit*.

[72] One might be reminded here of a conversation between Franz Kafka and Max Brod, as referenced by Walter Benjamin: "'I remember,' Brod writes, 'a conversation with Kafka which began with present-day Europe and the decline of the human race. "We are nihilistic thoughts, suicidal thoughts that come into God's head," Kafka said. This reminded me at first of the Gnostic view of life: God as the evil demiurge, the world as his Fall. "Oh no," said Kafka, "our world is only a bad mood of God, a bad day of his." "Then there is hope outside this manifestation of the world that we know." He smiled. "Oh, plenty of hope, an infinite amount of hope – but not for us"'" (Benjamin, "Franz Kafka," 116).

separation of (wilful) hope and (wishful) desire, by claiming that we can gesture towards a hope that is unfettered by concerns about feasibility: what Jonathan Lear calls "radical hope." While its object remains indeterminate – Plenty Coups could not picture what would become of his tribe's memory – radical hope conveys not only a basic yearning for survival, but also a diffuse faith in the prospect of an open future.

So, given that both Scranton and the members of the Dark Mountain collective clearly do not want to embrace a fatalistic attitude, it seems plausible to suppose that it is radical hope, in Lear's sense, that they keep being attached to.[73] This is not a form of hoping that lends itself to individual activism, of course. Neither can it galvanize people into launching resistance movements. But Scranton and the members of the Dark Mountain collective keep being animated by the belief, however deeply buried it might be within their bleak stories, that "*something good will emerge.*"[74] Without that belief dystopia's cautionary pedagogy would lose its functional purpose.

We can further flesh out this intuition by focusing on what constitutes the opposite of radical hope – false hope, or what one may call "cruel optimism." One way of investigating the differences between Oreskes and Conway's "science faction" of and the much bleaker stories told by Scranton and the Dark Mountain project would be to concentrate on the degree to which they think that false hope is itself part of the problem. *The Collapse of Western Civilization* essentially claims that trust in capitalism's capacity to respond to climate change amounts to an irrational and toxic form of market fundamentalism. Yet, Oreskes and Conway simultaneously posit that state-sponsored coordination measures, promoted by the Second People's Republic of China (and reminiscent of Robinson's elegy to the well-oiled machinery of state bureaucracy), may yet give rise to a form of hoping that is not marred by wishful thinking. So, hope is not altogether compromised – under conditions of capitalism it is simply directed at the wrong kind of ideals and prescriptions.

---

[73] For a critical application of Lear's concept to debates around the Anthropocene, see: Flores and Rousse, "Ecological Finitude as Ontological Finitude."

[74] Lear, *Radical Hope*, 94, italics in original.

Scranton and the Dark Mountain project amplify this criticism. In disputing positive development (Scranton) and in encouraging apathy (Dark Mountain project), their respective viewpoints rest on a rebuttal of what Lauren Berlant has glossed as "cruel optimism." "Cruel optimism" describes a relation whereby "something you desire is actually an obstacle to your flourishing."[75] A paradigmatic example of cruel optimism would be the continued prevalence of the American Dream's totemic attachment to meritocracy. The myth of upward social mobility for deserving, hard-working people is in fact upheld by the fantastical notion of economic uplift and constant growth. Due to the impenetrability of the class structure in the United States, however, the wish for individual betterment actually becomes an impediment to leading a good life.

In a similar vein, *Learning How to Die in the Anthropocene* as well as the various texts produced by the Dark Mountain project claim that working towards a more democratic Anthropocene is far from benign – it actually blocks the path to a sober reckoning with our current predicament. An implication of this diagnosis is that some types of hope can by themselves stand in the way of addressing the roots of the ongoing ecological crisis.[76]

Investing hope in a solution that comprises within it the very causes of the problem is ultimately a form of self-harming cruelty. That is why Berlant's analysis appears so useful for illuminating the specific character of this dystopian position – it conceives of remedial and transformative action in an interesting way that dovetails with what the aforementioned authors discussed: as "the action of not being worn out by politics."[77] This phrase communicates precisely the perspective that both Scranton and the members of the Dark Mountain project subscribe to. Since they want to renounce defeatism, they must affirm at the very least the possibility that some form of hope – radical hope – is still available to those living through the end of times. But their reflections do not allow for the belief that "something good will emerge" to be reinscribed into social struggles that are already under way today. Consequently, all that remains is a faint motion towards decidedly apolitical memory-making.

---

[75] Berlant, *Cruel Optimism*, 1.
[76] Lynch, "Why Hope Is Dangerous When It Comes to Climate Change."
[77] Berlant, *Cruel Optimism*, 262.

As we shall see in the following section, one of the exceptional advantages of dystopian fiction is that it adds experiential texture and depth to this (post-)apocalyptic constellation. This way, the social as well as psychological ramifications of inhabiting a climate-changed world are drawn out in substantial detail. Through the depiction of life continuing after the breakdown, Margaret Atwood's narratives manage to inspect how hope needs to be reconfigured when the end is near, summoning the readers to experience the paradox of radical hope in a more visceral manner.

5.2 "WHEN ANY CIVILIZATION IS DUST AND ASHES, ART IS ALL THAT'S LEFT": MARGARET ATWOOD'S CAUTIONARY TALES

Ustopia is a world I made up by combining utopia and dystopia – the imagined perfect society and its opposite – because, in my view, each contains a latent version of the other. In addition to being, almost always, a mapped location, Ustopia is also a state of mind, as is every place in literature of whatever kind.[78]

Is it real? No, it is not real. What is this not real? Not real can tell us about real.[79]

The Adams and the Eves used to say, We are what we eat, but I prefer to say, We are what we wish. Because if you can't wish, why bother?[80]

Margaret Atwood is one of the most revered and acclaimed authors today. Her rise to global fame can probably be best explained by the enormous success of the recent TV adaptation of her dystopian novel *The Handmaid's Tale*.[81] Atwood herself seems to think that the presidency of Donald Trump significantly boosted the TV show's ratings, allowing the book to reach new audiences as well.[82] Atwood is an extraordinarily prolific writer, having published sixteen novels, several collections of

---

[78] Atwood, "Margaret Atwood."

[79] Atwood, *Oryx and Crake*, vol. 1: MaddAddam Trilogy, para. 16.25.

[80] Atwood, *The Year of the Flood*, vol. 2: MaddAddam Trilogy, para. 112.61.

[81] Atwood, *The Handmaid's Tale*. The HBO series, which started in 2017, is more than an adaptation: now in its fourth season, it extends the story of *The Handmaid's Tale* and pushes it in a different direction than Atwood's recent sequel, *The Testaments*.

[82] Setoodeh, "Margaret Atwood on How Donald Trump Helped 'The Handmaid's Tale.'"

short stories, more than ten books of poetry as well as numerous works of non-fiction.[83] Given that humanity's relationship with the environment is one of her persistent preoccupations, starting with ecofeminist themes in her early novel *Surfacing*,[84] Atwood can moreover be considered a major voice in the field of climate fiction. Just like Jemisin's and Robinson's, Atwood's oeuvre thus lends itself to an analysis that connects her peculiar interpretation of utopianism to a critical engagement with the natural world.

My interest in the following is in Atwood's *MaddAddam* trilogy, which grapples with life after the Anthropocene, after the age of the "human planet." The trilogy raises a question we already touched upon in the survey of theoretical positions: what hope and desire, if any, can be cultivated when the world as we know it has ceased to exist? Against the lure of defeatism, Atwood foregrounds the need for social dreaming to outlast the apocalypse.

I hold that this amounts to the trilogy's greatest achievement – its ambition to vindicate a form of hoping and desiring that becomes immune to cruel optimism. As such, Atwood helps us in examining the cautionary pedagogy behind all dystopian projects. Her work thus complements and complicates the theoretical contributions from the prior section.

In order to sustain this claim, I begin with a reconstruction of Atwood's understanding of utopianism. It is one of Atwood's convictions that eutopias and dystopias are always entwined with each other. What she calls "ustopia" hence represents a creative blending of eutopian and dystopian motifs. Another organizing idea throughout her writing pertains to the distinction between "speculative fiction" and "science fiction," which has caused some controversy.

Based on an analysis of Atwood's oeuvre, I then claim that the *MaddAddam* trilogy can be described as an "ustopia" set in a post-apocalyptic world. Its structure is, more specifically, resonant with my third plot line, the *If-This-Goes-On*, as Atwood herself explains: "*What if we continue down the road we're already on? How slippery is the slope? What are our*

---

[83] For a list of her published work see: "Full Bibliography."
[84] Atwood, *Surfacing.*

saving graces? Who's got the will to stop us?"[85] In the final section, I shall try to tease out three key motifs that run through the trilogy: first, the desire for a post-human future; second, the commemorative power of narrative; and third, the emerging sense of a multispecies community. My argument is that these ideas coalesce into an original statement of what should remain of hope when the apocalypse is coming.

5.2.1 USTOPIAS AND THE "ATWOOD PRINCIPLE". Just like Kim Stanley Robinson, Margaret Atwood not only writes utopian fiction, she also expands on her understanding of social dreaming and situates her novels within the literary canon. Atwood's grasp of utopianism might perhaps not be as inventive as Robinson's, but it still contains valuable insights into the specific nature of dystopian narratives especially. Through her rendering of post-apocalyptic scenarios, Atwood seeks to construct visions of the future that combine eutopian and dystopian images, while grounding her cautionary tales in a historically informed analysis of the status quo.

In order to better comprehend Atwood's approach, it will be conducive to first concentrate on what is undoubtedly her most celebrated novel, *The Handmaid's Tale*. It is this story, as well as Atwood's reflections on the ideas that influenced it, that will assist us in hashing out the general characteristics of Atwood's views. Another reason for commencing with Atwood's bestseller from the 1980s is that it can, in some ways, be seen as a precursor to the trilogy I am interested in: environmental degradation is the spark of catastrophic, world-changing events in both texts.[86] Together with her consistent interest in dystopian imaginaries, Atwood's keen attention to humanity's stance vis-à-vis nature serves as a thread running through almost all her novels.[87]

The Handmaid's Tale is set in a near-future version of the United States, in a country now named the Republic of Gilead. Gilead is governed by a

---

[85] Atwood, "Writing 'Oryx and Crake,'" italics in original.

[86] On the links between *The Handmaid's Tale* and the *MaddAddam* trilogy, see: Howells, "Margaret Atwood's Dystopian Visions."

[87] Hengen, "Margaret Atwood and Environmentalism." Notice that in the eighteen years between the publication of the *Handmaid's Tale* and *Oryx and Crake* Atwood did not publish any dystopian fiction.

militaristic and theocratic regime with Christian-fundamentalist features. While all individual rights have been curtailed in what is effectively a fascistic caste society, women's roles are specifically circumscribed by their national duty to bear children. Since pollution has led to rapidly decreasing birth rates, some women with healthy reproductive organs, so-called handmaids, are even forced to join the households of the political leadership, where their "job" is to be raped and impregnated by the regime's elite.

The plot pivots around the fate of one such handmaid, Offred, who lives together with a Commander, Frederick Waterford, and his wife, Serena. Apart from reconstructing in fine-grained detail the oppressive and violent life in the Waterford household, Atwood also shows how pockets of resistance against the militaristic and theocratic regime have formed, under the guidance of the "Mayday" movement. Secretly, Offred enjoys an illicit dalliance with the Commander's chauffeur, Nick. The novel concludes, like many of Atwood's writings, in an ambiguous manner: the reader does not learn whether Offred is ultimately saved or sent away to be executed when a van picks her up from the Waterford residence.

Yet, the book does not end with Offred absconding from the Commander's household. Interestingly, in a move that foreshadows Oreskes and Conway's *The Collapse of Western Civilization*, Atwood inserts a report from a scientific conference dating from the future, in the year 2195, where participants debate research around the so-called Gilead Period. The reader is thus invited to infer that the Republic of Gilead has indeed fallen and that Offred's story of resistance has somehow been passed on to future generations. Notably, though, the reader does not reach any kind of closure when it comes to grasping how exactly the regime has been defeated, or whether Offred has managed to safely escape from Gilead at all. Through concerted action or sheer luck – Atwood leaves us in the dark about the detailed mechanics of the transition to a more optimistic future.[88]

---

[88] This ambiguity in Atwood's understanding of utopianism is reflected in Tom Moylan's appraisal of the novel: "Overall, therefore, in what might ultimately be seen as the stance of an engaged liberal who faces the evils of social reality and yet takes one considered

Despite the novel's dystopian character, an element of hope is clearly present in the text. We know with certainty that Gilead's oppression and violence have somehow been overcome.[89] In fact, we even glimpse, to a small degree, what the rejuvenated society after Gilead's collapse looks like: the "Symposium on Gileadean Studies" is attended by a multiracial bunch of researchers, such as the Indigenous scholar "Professor Maryann Crescent Moon," whose expertise, in a reversal of the orientalist gaze, is in "Caucasian Anthropology."[90]

The addition of this appendix, indicating the fall of Gilead's terror regime, is a nod to George Orwell's genre-defining *1984*, which also contains a section after the end of the main story: "Principles of Newspeak."[91] That chapter, written in past tense, signals to the readers that there might still be other ways of being and living than the ones practiced in Oceania.[92]

Two preoccupations emerge from this compressed summary of *The Handmaid's Tale*. Atwood's insistence on the intermingling of eutopian and dystopian ideas as well as her espousal of the literary principle of realism. Regarding the first issue, Atwood does not believe that there is such a thing as a "pure dystopia," or a "pure eutopia" for that matter. While Gilead is characterized as a regime bent on total domination, the look back to its eventual demise is supposed to provide us with assurances that another society is already on the horizon. What is more, as a geographically bounded place, Gilead is part of a global structure where rival political systems compete with its theocratic constitution. As such,

---

step back from a radical political praxis, Atwood stretches the creative range of the classical dystopian form, working it in one direction toward anti-utopian closure, then turning it toward a utopian horizon, and then again leaving a space in between for her unresolved questions as they grow out of the accounts of the society's internal flaws, the opposition's vulnerability, and the clearly imperfect and perhaps always compromised 'utopian' reality revealed in the symposium narrative" (Moylan, *Scraps of the Untainted Sky*, 166).

[89] On this point, see: Ketterer, "Margaret Atwood's 'The Handmaid's Tale.'"

[90] Atwood, *The Handmaid's Tale*, para. 19.3.

[91] Orwell, *Nineteen Eighty-Four*.

[92] Atwood explicitly acknowledges Orwell as one of her inspirations for writing *The Handmaid's Tale*. See: Atwood, "The Handmaid's Tale and Oryx and Crake in Context," 516–17. On the impact of *1984* on Atwood's thinking, see also: Ingersoll, "Margaret Atwood's 'The Handmaid's Tale'"; Caldwell, "Wells, Orwell, and Atwood."

wriggling out of the grip of the authoritarian regime always remains an option. The border to Canada can in principle still be crossed, even though escaping might come at an extremely high cost.[93]

On Atwood's account, we therefore need a new concept to capture what is distinctive about *The Handmaid's Tale*: "ustopia." The argument for "ustopia" derives from a critique of perfectionism that is not too dissimilar from the one we encountered in Chapter 2. Recall how Lucy Sargisson reasons that the identification of utopias with perfect societies impedes a nuanced appreciation of how utopias actually work. Atwood seems to concur: since all attempts at imagining a better way of being and living harbour within themselves imperfections, it would be more productive to conceive of utopias as intrinsically hybrid creations that interlace hopeful and fearful perspectives.

Importantly, this observation does not imply that utopias are undifferentiated, made up in equal measure of eutopian and dystopian visions of the future. *The Handmaid's Tale* is, without a doubt, a story with a dystopian bent, just as the *Science in the Capital* series clearly advances a eutopian outlook. Jemisin's work is more difficult to classify, as I claimed in Chapter 3: its focus on the cyclical recurrence of violence, for example, makes it much harder to determine whether the overall tone and the atmospheric mood of her *Broken Earth* trilogy is a hopeful or fearful one.[94]

Concerning the second theme emerging from my reading of *The Handmaid's Tale* (her espousal of literary realism), we need to steer attention to Atwood's interpretation of science fiction as a genre. In a number of essays, Atwood tried to expound why she refutes the label "science fiction" for her novels. In a collection from the early 2000s, she first defined science fiction as writing "in which things happen that are

---

[93] This point about Gilead being just one isolated country amongst others reveals a vital difference to the climate crisis we all find ourselves in: due to the globality of that crisis, there can be no hope of relinquishing our Earthbound existence.

[94] This is an upshot of the kind of speculation favoured by Jemisin. Proponents of a *What-If* frame are by default sceptical of both eutopian and dystopian perspectives, declining to position their proposals within this binary grid. As we have seen, their main goal is the generation of estrangement – the sense that what is habitually taken for granted is, in fact, not natural at all.

not possible today – that depend, for instance, on advanced space travel, time travel, the discovery of green monsters on other planets or galaxies, or that contain various technologies we have not yet developed."[95]

Following this line of reasoning, *The Handmaid's Tale* as well as the novels discussed next, ought not be considered works of science fiction, for the worlds described therein are the result of – more or less exalted – extrapolations from developments already under way in our times. In the case of *The Handmaid's Tale*, for example, Atwood draws a long arc into the past, reaching back to the history of American Puritanism as one of the dormant milieus from which a theocratic regime could spring even today.[96]

Instead of science fiction, she prefers the label "speculative fiction" for her oeuvre. Although diverging from my definition of speculative fiction, she foregrounds a facet that Kim Stanley Robinson has conveyed in his work as well – that her novels remain committed to principles of literary realism. Recall how for Robinson "proleptic realism," with its stress on near-future scenarios, is only one amongst several modes of science fiction proper, which also includes "future histories," such as Oreskes and Conway's *The Collapse of Western Civilization*, and "space operas" set in a far more distant future. What Atwood suggests, by contrast, is to split near-future utopias off from the broader category of science fiction, by excising all traces of a *novum*, in Suvin's terminology: "no interstellar travel, no Martians."[97]

In his treatise on the history of dystopian thinking, Gregory Claeys elevates this genre-defining remark about the character of speculative fiction to the status of a distinguishing criterion for *If-This-Goes-On* narratives: what he calls the "Atwood principle" captures a mechanism whereby the dystopian imagination discharges of its cautionary function:

> However fanciful such scenarios appear, all are plausible. They are not predictions, and not science fiction, but projections, on the Atwood principle, of some worst-case scenarios. But neither are they inevitable: many factors might forestall or divert their development ... The task of

---

[95] Atwood, "Writing Utopia," 92.
[96] Atwood, 96–7.
[97] Mancuso, "Speculative or Science Fiction?"

the literary dystopia, then, is to warn us against and educate us about real-life dystopias. It need not furnish a happy ending to do so: pessimism has its place. But it may envision rational and collective solutions where irrationality and panic loom. Entertainment plays a role in this process. But the task at hand is serious.[98]

Claeys' contention is that, if enlightening an audience about dangers that lie on society's horizon is the essential purpose of any dystopian project, then the envisioned future must appear credible to the readers addressed in the text. Simply put, the readers of a dystopia must be able to deduce from what they are prompted to imagine that this other world could be theirs, too. If "things happen that are not possible today" – as per Atwood's definition of science fiction – such inference is stymied by the appearance of fantastical entities, such as "green monsters on other planets or galaxies." As a consequence, the narrative will fail in its goal of warning the audience about threats lurking in their real life, for they will not be able to establish the requisite association between the other world and theirs.[99]

One problem with this formulation of the "Atwood principle" is that it erects far too stringent a dichotomy between scenarios that are plausible and those that are not. Raymond Geuss makes this point when he objects to an unreflective acceptance of what is presented as possible or impossible at any given moment:

> The distinction between what is possible and what is impossible is itself in most political contexts to some extent a social construct. A realist who understands this will refuse to take this distinction as it is socially defined at any given moment to be the final and unquestioned framework for thought or action ... After all, in the human world, much of what we might desire is not antecedently given as possible or impossible. Many options are not available until someone has made a play for them, perhaps

---

[98] Claeys, *Dystopia*, 501.

[99] Using Levitas' distinction between utopia's consolatory, critical and transformative purposes, we could therefore maintain that both critique and transformation are premised on a basic level of realism. Without a grounding of utopias in an assessment of what is "possible today," the potential for critique and transformation is eclipsed by a yearning for consolation, or so the argument goes.

an unconditioned and cognitively thinly grounded play. Wishing does not make things so, but there are things that can become possible only if enough people want them (and pursue them) in the right way, and which otherwise are "impossible". This set of facts about the human situation is the continuing soil in which utopianism rightly flourishes.[100]

This passage demonstrates that educating readers about perils that are concealed in the status quo is but one task that "ustopias" pursue. Another one is keeping the hope alive that a regime like Gilead's will not be around forever. Offred's desire for her world to be otherwise thus always runs up against the recalcitrant solidity of the status quo.

In a review of the second novel in the *MaddAddam* trilogy, the *Year of the Flood*, Ursula K. Le Guin took Atwood's aversion to the science fiction label to task. Le Guin's conclusion is that the only way to make sense of Atwood's insistence on speculative fiction being a genre apart is to read it as a symptom of intellectual snobbery: "This arbitrarily restrictive definition seems designed to protect her novels from being relegated to a genre still shunned by hidebound readers, reviewers and prize-awarders. She doesn't want the literary bigots to shove her into the literary ghetto."[101]

In the autumn of 2010, the two literary giants met to discuss their differences. What emerged from this debate is that Le Guin, too, has a name reserved for a genre of writing that deals with things that could not happen right now – "fantasy." So, on one level, the main difference between Atwood's and Le Guin's standpoints is around where they wish to draw the line between science fiction and its neighbouring genres: realism on one side and fantasy on the other. Both authors agree, however, that such a line needs to be drawn somewhere.[102]

---

[100] Geuss, "Realism and the Relativity of Judgement," 15–16.

[101] Le Guin, "The Year of the Flood."

[102] In later essays, Atwood appears to have reconciled herself to the disagreement with Le Guin, while accepting the porosity of all genre boundaries: "When it comes to genres, the borders are increasingly undefended, and things slip back and forth across them with insouciance" (Atwood, "Introduction," 7). In a somewhat confusing further reversal of her prior views, Atwood now appears to apply the science fiction label for her own writing: "I'm not a prophet ... Let's get rid of that idea right now. Prophecies are really about now. In science fiction it's always about now. What else could it be about?

As we saw in Chapter 2, where I turned to Suvin's and his followers' attempt to demarcate the limits of science fiction, such efforts in ring-fencing an author's proper domain are endemic in controversies around utopian writing. While one may endlessly quarrel over the precise content of specific labels, it is hard to avoid the impression that disputes over the realm of science fiction are about more than just terminology. Atwood seems to miss one crucial aspect in her defence of "speculative fiction" (narrowly conceived), namely that such designations are bound up with the longing to locate an author within what Pierre Bourdieu calls a stratified "field": a socially constructed network of meaning wherein science fiction, put bluntly, yields less cultural capital than realistic writing, but slightly more than fantasy.[103] This observation has also been at the root of China Miéville's worry about the "uncomfortably patrician and antidemocratic class politics"[104] behind the policing of science fiction.

Despite these concerns with Atwood's constricted rendering of her own oeuvre, there is still something to learn from her (and Claeys') claim that dystopia's cautionary pedagogy is predicated on an inference between the imagined scenario of an *If-This-Goes-On* story and the real world. It is surely right to assert that, the stronger the readers' feeling of estrangement gets, the more difficult it will be for them to draw the conclusion that this other world could be theirs, too. In other words: if utopianism is to have an impact that exceeds wishful thinking, we must be able to read the "new maps of hell"[105] drafted by writers of dystopian fiction as reliable guides to a future that could await us sooner rather than later. Realism in that sense is indeed a precondition for utopianism.

Where Atwood and Claeys go wrong is in the suggestion that we could identify a steadfast benchmark of plausibility that would cleave possible

---

There is no future. There are many possibilities, but we do not know which one we are going to have" (Allardice, "Margaret Atwood").

[103] On Bourdieu's notion of a field of cultural production with regard to literature, see: Bourdieu, *The Field of Cultural Production*. For Bourdieusian analyses of science fiction as a field, see: Milner, "Science Fiction and the Literary Field"; Wright, "Cultural Capital and the Literary Field."

[104] Miéville, "Cognition as Ideology," 240.

[105] Amis, *New Maps of Hell*.

from impossible scenarios. Because utopias strive to subvert the impression that the status quo is fixed and unchangeable – that Gilead will rule forever – they must by necessity make claims and envision futures that appear implausible, perhaps even inconceivable, to some. It is therefore from within the tension between a credible warning about the future and an imaginative break with the present that dystopian narratives gain their action-guiding power.

5.2.2 LIFE AFTER THE ANTHROPOCENE: THE *MADDADDAM* TRILOGY.

In order to appreciate how the intermingling of eutopian and dystopian motifs as well as Atwood's endorsement of realism are instantiated in a specific text, I now turn to the *MaddAddam* trilogy. This trilogy represents Atwood's most systematic foray into the genre of utopian fiction. The novels also probe, through the deployment of both horror and satirical tropes, what life on Earth after the Anthropocene might look like, no matter whether humans will still be present on the planet or not. As in prior chapters, I shall begin with a summary of the plot, followed by an attempt at reading the trilogy as a paradigmatic *If-This-Goes-On* narrative.[106]

The first volume, *Oryx and Crake,* traces two storylines in parallel: one that sets off against a post-apocalyptic scenario, revolving around a lone survivor called Snowman; and another one that tells of the developments that led to the cataclysm, centred around the friendship between two kids, Jimmy, who would later become known as Snowman, and Glenn, a highly gifted, if emotionally stunted, boy genius.

The book starts with a lengthy section following Jimmy/Snowman in his quest to orient himself in a barren and depressing landscape devastated by a global extinction event. Apart from a host of strange animals, the only other survivors appear to be a group of genetically modified humans, the "Crakers," who treat Jimmy/Snowman with veneration and respect. The Crakers, we will later learn, are the product of Glenn's

---

[106] For more comprehensive analyses, which guide the reader deeper into Atwood's universe, see: Bouson, "It's Game Over Forever"; Bouson, "We're Using Up the Earth. It's Almost Gone"; Bouson, "A 'Joke-Filled Romp' through End Times."

ingenious plan to engineer a post-human race that would not be as destructive to the planet and to itself as our own species.

The world before the cataclysm in which Jimmy/Snowman and Glenn have grown up is shown to the reader through flashbacks. This world is a near-future version of our current order, wherein multinational corporations have taken complete control over all aspects of society. The United States is a heavily segregated country, divided between rich gated communities, in which privileged kids like Jimmy/Snowman and Glenn thrive, and the impoverished and dangerous "pleeblands," where the left-behind are doing their best to eke out a living.[107] Resistance to this oppressive system is seemingly very feeble: a few terrorist cells appear to operate, alongside a pacifist ecological movement called the "God's Gardeners," but their impact on the overall situation is negligible.

Outside school, Jimmy/Snowman and Glenn spend their time at the *HelthWyzer* compound watching porn, cheering on live beheadings online and playing computer games. During one of their sessions, they come across a website with child pornography featuring an Asian girl who both of the boys feel attracted to. This unnamed child would later perform an important role in the education of the Crakers. Jimmy/Snowman and Glenn enjoy playing a computer game, *Extincthaton*, for which Glenn uses the pseudonym "Crake."[108]

After graduating from high school, Jimmy/Snowman and Glenn/Crake part ways. The supremely talented Glenn/Crake is admitted to the elite Watson-Crick Institute, where he enrols in a course on bioengineering, while Jimmy/Snowman, due to his poor educational record, only gets into the Martha Graham Academy, a liberal arts college with no prestige at all. His academic training consists in nothing but propaganda writing, so he is extremely pleased when his old friend Glenn/Crake, who has in the meantime risen to the top of big pharma, contacts him with an invitation to join his research team.

---

[107] Michael Spiegel borrows the term "neomedievalism" from International Relations theory to describe the basic set-up of the world before the Fall. See: Spiegel, "Character in a Post-National World."

[108] Both "oryx" (an antelope) and "crake" (a bird) are already extinct in the world inhabited by Jimmy/Snowman and his friend. On our planet they still exist.

Glenn/Crake's unit is working on a pill that both enhances the libido and protects against all types of sexually transmitted diseases. This *BlyssPluss* drug has another undisclosed side effect, though: it sterilizes all those who ingest it. Jimmy/Snowman is hired to advertise the pill as vigorously and quickly as possible. When he remarks that *BlyssPluss* seems like an altruistic medication, advancing "population reduction" via the enjoyment of erotic pleasures, Glenn/Crake responds with a neo-Malthusian commonplace:

> "It's not altruism exactly," said Crake. "More like sink or swim. I've seen the latest confidential Corps demographic reports. As a species we're in deep trouble, worse than anyone's saying. They're afraid to release the stats because people might just give up, but take it from me, we're running out of space-time. Demand for resources has exceeded supply for decades in marginal geopolitical areas, hence the famines and droughts; but very soon, demand is going to exceed supply for everyone. With the BlyssPluss Pill the human race will have a better chance of swimming."[109]

Apart from this sterilization programme, Glenn/Crake also pursues another project that is even more heavily guarded: in a top-secret location, he designs genetically modified humans – latterly known as Crakers – with characteristics that prepare them better for life on a climate-changed planet. Through his connections within the network of multinationals, Glenn/Crake also manages to bring on board the abused girl who, as adolescents, he and Jimmy/Snowman had been watching on the porn channel. Glenn/Crake christens her "Oryx" and gives her a key mission in the bioengineering project: to teach the Crakers basic knowledge of the world, which should enable them to live by themselves.

As the two storylines converge, the reader comes to understand why and how Glenn/Crake triggers the pandemic that would wipe humanity from planet Earth. The *BlyssPluss* drug, which has in the meantime been widely distributed, was engineered not only to sterilize all humans, but to kill them. As a consequence, the great extinction kicks off, and only

---

[109] Atwood, *Oryx and Crake*. MaddAddam Trilogy 1, para. 43.50.

those who have been completely isolated from their fellow humans manage to survive.

Back in the post-apocalyptic scenario, Jimmy/Snowman is injured on one of his scavenging expeditions. Upon returning to the Crakers' camp, he grasps that other humans appear to have outlived the apocalypse. The novel ends with a cliffhanger, for we do not learn whether Jimmy/Snowman approaches the survivors and how the encounter goes.

The trilogy's second instalment, *The Year of the Flood*, fills in some of the gaps in the narrative that *Oryx and Crake* left unanswered. While the first novel is centred around the difficult friendship between two men, *The Year of the Flood* concentrates on the viewpoints of two women. Even though the novel covers much of the same events as *Oryx and Crake*, it thus changes perspective, from the safe zones of the upper-class compounds to the dingy territories of the "pleeblands." Just like in the first volume of the trilogy, the book is split between a pre- and a post-apocalyptic storyline.

The main protagonists of *The Year of the Flood* are two women from different generations, middle-aged Toby and young adult Ren. The plot commences after the catastrophe has already taken place: Toby is trying to defend herself against marauding animals, while Ren attempts to get out of a locked isolation cell that saved her life when the global pandemic began. Toby's existence previous to the cataclysm takes a turn for the worse when her parents die, as a consequence of the exploitative practices of big pharma. As a precarious employee in a burger joint, she is sexually harassed by her sadistic boss. One day, she manages to escape, with the help of a group of ecological activists called the "God's Gardeners." The God's Gardeners have secretly built a commune of like-minded outsiders and non-conformists, wishing to live outside of the societal mainstream. At their helm are the Adams and the Eves, a vanguard of spiritual leaders who inspire the community by spiritual example. A chief goal of this collective involves preparing all its members for the coming "Waterless Flood," a decisive moment of reckoning during which the whole system of capitalist overconsumption and military subjugation will come to a final close:

> A massive die-off of the human race was impending, due to overpopula-
> tion and wickedness, but the Gardeners exempted themselves: they

intended to float above the Waterless Flood, with the aid of the food they were stashing away in the hidden storeplaces they called Ararats. As for the flotation devices in which they would ride out this flood, they themselves would be their own Arks, stored with their own collections of inner animals, or at least the names of those animals. Thus they would survive to replenish the Earth.[110]

The leader of the Adams and Eves is an enigmatic figure, Adam One, whose teachings bring together science and religion in creative ways. Not too dissimilar from Frank Vanderwal's yearning for a resolution between the findings of sociobiology and the wisdom of Buddhism in the *Science in the Capital* series, the God's Gardeners want to marry Darwinian theory with a radically pacifist version of Christianity.[111] They do not abandon the building blocks of natural selection and evolution, but rather reject rampant fantasies of human dominion over the biosphere.

The novel's other protagonist, Ren, also joins the God's Gardeners and quickly becomes best friends with Amanda, a desolate "pleebrat" who is allowed to stay in the commune as well. Ren ends up going to the same high school with Jimmy/Snowman and Glenn/Crake, starting a short fling with the former. The reader slowly understands how the underworld of the "pleeblands" and the God's Gardeners is in fact deeply enmeshed with the upper-class society of the compounds. Both Toby and Ren survive the global pandemic out of sheer luck. After a while, they realize that, due to their meticulous preparation, a significant number of God's Gardeners endured the "Waterless Flood." The book ends at exactly the same moment as *Oryx and Crake*, for it is Amanda and her captors that Jimmy/Snowman encounters.

The trilogy's final volume, *MaddAddam*, propels the story further into the future. Jimmy/Snowman, Toby, Ren, as well as a small cast of God's Gardeners and members of the MaddAddam collective, with the mysterious Zeb at their helm, are now united. The central theme of this novel – apart from Zeb's coming-of-age story – concerns the ways in which humans and Crakers should live together.

---

[110] Atwood, *The Year of the Flood*: MaddAddam Trilogy 2, para. 19.14.
[111] The saints that they revere are, amongst others, primatologists like Dian Fossey, oceanographers like Jacques Cousteau and palaeontologists like Stephen Jay Gould.

The plot takes off where *The Year of the Flood* stopped. While Jimmy/ Snowman slowly recovers from an injury, Toby begins a love affair with Zeb. Since the Crakers have a seemingly insatiable hunger for stories, they ask Toby for more and more tales about the world before they were created. Zeb in particular attracts the Crakers' attention, which is why Toby starts detailing his life before the apocalypse, from Zeb's upbringing as the son of a wealthy and powerful reverend at a megachurch, to his loving relationship with his half-brother Adam, who would later become Adam One, the leader of the God's Gardeners. Their father runs the church of PetrOleum, which is part of the wider Petrobaptist movement.

In her depiction of the Petrobaptists, Atwood underlines once again that humanity's thirst for natural resources has profoundly adverse effects on the environment. Consumer capitalism and religious fervour are in this dystopian setting entangled with each other. Ultimately, both Zeb and Adam flee from their parents' home and rebel against the system of privileges into which they were born, kickstarting the environmentalist commune that is at the heart of the resistance movement.

In the world after the pandemic, the surviving humans start to understand the Crakers better. Speculating about the motives of Glenn/Oryx in creating the genetically modified humans, one of the God's Gardeners muses that he must have seen the "Crakers as indigenous people, no doubt," and "*Homo sapiens sapiens* as the greedy, rapacious Conquistadors."[112] The Crakers are, thus, radically different from humans, but their emotional set-up – their serene and cooperative character – points to a possible future for life on Earth after the cataclysm.

Slowly the notion that humans are in every respect superior to the Crakers shifts to a more subtle assessment of the situation. Initially, the Crakers are disparaged as "Frankenpeople," as soulless automata with no agency of their own, beautiful to look at, but ultimately empty. Yet, over time this perception changes, especially once a major menace presents itself: the Painballers, who had abducted Amanda, managed to flee once again and are now threatening to assail the settlement. The Crakers serve as a communicative link between the human realm and the inhabitants

---

[112] Atwood, *MaddAddam*. MaddAddam Trilogy 3, para. 40.12.

of the "brave new world" after the apocalypse. Together, this multispecies coalition succeeds in opening up the prospect of a future where humans accept their place amongst equally important kin.

The process of rapprochement between the humans and the Crakers is most vividly exemplified by two further developments: first, through the close bonds between Toby and a Craker boy called Blackbeard, who becomes her storytelling amanuensis. Towards the conclusion of the trilogy, Blackbeard has taken over from Toby, narrating both Zeb's and Toby's passing away. Second, some of the young women have been impregnated by Craker men, thereby initiating a radical process of hybridization: while the Crakers become more like humans, through their desire for more and more stories, the newly born human-Craker babies signal the inception of a new era.

5.2.3 HOPE FOR A POST-HUMAN FUTURE, THE POWER OF NARRATIVES AND A SENSE OF MULTISPECIES COMMUNITY.

In interpreting these three books, I want to highlight a number of themes that strike me as crucial for understanding dystopian narratives about climate change more broadly: first, the potential of the apocalypse to disclose routes towards a new beginning; second, the centrality of polyphonic storytelling; and third, an emerging form of sociality that is non-anthropocentric.

My engagement with Atwood's oeuvre builds on the abundant secondary literature, which has already illuminated a great variety of topics, from her representation of gender[113] to the critique of instrumental reason[114] and her examination of ecological grief as an antidote to the excesses of capitalism.[115] However, my approach to the *MaddAddam* trilogy deviates from the existing commentary in that it stresses Atwood's frequently overlooked commitment to utopianism. I will thus demonstrate that her novels should be understood as admonitory "ustopias," to use Atwood's own terminology. Seen this way, the *MaddAddam* trilogy can assist us in adding experiential and affective texture to the

---

[113] For a discussion of this motif through the lens of the trilogy's "zero hour," see: Mohr, "Anthropocene Fiction."

[114] DiMarco, "Paradice Lost, Paradice Regained."

[115] Harland, "Ecological Grief and Therapeutic Storytelling in Margaret Atwood's Maddaddam Trilogy."

reflections about the (post-)apocalyptic imaginary we have reconstructed in prior sections.

Beginning with our first motif, let us inquire into the multiple purposes that the apocalypse serves in the *MaddAddam* trilogy. All three books move back and forth between episodes that occur before and after the pandemic. When Jimmy/Snowman enters the plot for the first time, his appearance conjures notable figures from the Western canon, such as Daniel Defoe's *Robinson Crusoe* or Mary Shelley's *The Last Man*.[116] But once we learn more about what life before the apocalypse looked like, it becomes increasingly evident that nostalgia vis-à-vis the lost past would be an entirely inappropriate feeling. A lot gets broken in the cataclysm caused by the *BlyssPluss* drug; the question remains, however, whether any of it would have been worth preserving at all.[117]

As per the "Atwood principle," the world that the pandemic devastates results from a near-future projection of socio-economic divisions and scientific discoveries that are already under way today.[118] Atwood articulates the material and ideological analysis upon which the *MaddAddam* trilogy builds in the non-fiction essay *Payback*, which reimagines Ebenezer Scrooge being confronted with two potential futures for mankind, a eutopian one in which degrowth has gone hand in hand with the proliferation of sustainable energy systems; and a dystopian one that closely mirrors the universe of the *MaddAddam* trilogy:

> Mankind made a Faustian bargain as soon as he invented his first technologies, including the bow and arrow. It was then that human beings, instead of limiting their birth rate to keep their population in step with natural resources, decided instead to multiply unchecked. Then they increased the food supply to support this growth by manipulating those resources, inventing ever newer and more complex technologies to do so.

---

[116] On the importance of *Robinson Crusoe* for contemporary post-apocalyptic fiction, see: Hicks, *Post-Apocalyptic Novel in the Twenty-First Century*.

[117] On this point, see: Ferwerda, "Narrating the Anthropocene," 77.

[118] As Atwood notes in the afterword to *MaddAddam*: "Although MaddAddam is a work of fiction, it does not include any technologies or biobeings that do not already exist, are not under construction, or are not possible in theory" (Atwood, *MaddAddam: MaddAddam Trilogy 3*, para. 89.1).

Now we have the most intricate system of gizmos the world has ever known. Our technological system is the mill that grinds out anything you wish to order up, but no one knows how to turn it off. The end result of a totally efficient technological exploitation of Nature would be a lifeless desert: all natural capital would be exhausted, having been devoured by the mills of production, and the resulting debt to Nature would be infinite. But long before then, payback time will come for Mankind.[119]

If this stark choice provides the backdrop to the *MaddAddam* trilogy, what should we make of Glenn/Crake's murderous plan to wipe out humanity and repopulate Earth with a fitter species? In an interview, Atwood clarifies her own view when she intimates that Glenn/Crake might in fact be "the most altruistic person around,"[120] for he appears to be drawing the only compelling conclusion from the ruin that humanity has already wreaked upon the planet. Although Glenn/Crake is clearly modelled on the figure of a mad, immoral scientist, his misanthropic attitude towards all of mankind appears to resonate with Atwood's account of the one-way road that we are on once we acquire basic technologies.[121] In line with thoughts that we have already detected in both Scranton's writings and the Dark Mountain project, humanity's extinction can therefore be viewed as a paradoxical act of care for a planet that has already suffered too much in the Anthropocene. The mass murder unleashed by the *BlyssPluss* drug would, on this reading, administer a solution to the intractable problems of human overpopulation and capitalist expansionism. All that the pandemic does is effectively accelerate a process that could not be halted anyhow, which is precisely why we should refrain from branding Glenn/Crake as an unequivocal

---

[119] Atwood, *Payback*, 201. The pointer to read *Payback* as a meta-text to the *MaddAddam* trilogy can be found in: Mohr, "Eco-dystopia and Biotechnology," 290.

[120] Bethune, "Book Review."

[121] Interestingly, this diagnosis appears quite close to Robinson's endorsement of a Palaeolithic lifestyle. But recall that the entire *Science in the Capital* series is premised on the idea that primitivism must be reconciled with scientific progress to offer a truly transformative alternative to the status quo. For Atwood, scientific discoveries today are already paving the way for catastrophe – their capacity to bring a "good Anthropocene" on its way seems rather limited.

villain; he simply took things in his hands to speed up a slow, inevitable decline.

Against Atwood's proposal to conceive of Glenn/Crake as an altruistic figure, Gerry Canavan asserts we should not endorse such an interpretation of the *MaddAddam* trilogy, for it makes our own species' extinction appear preordained and erase the morally salient difference between genocide and humanitarianism. Indeed, it is Glenn/Crake's plan for who should take humanity's place that betrays Atwood's true (if unacknowledged) intentions, Canavan surmises:

> The Crakers, in this context, should be understood as a hyperbolic version of the fantasy that we might turn back the clock and begin history anew, this time avoiding the mistake of so-called "civilization" that has brought down so much pain, misery, and death upon nearly everyone it touches through its awful past, miserable present, and terrible future alike. The Crakers are manifestly not an actual plan to save the world – Crake's plan employs unethical methods and impossible genomics towards a plainly ridiculous purpose. Rather, the Crakers allegorize the radical transformation of both society and subjectivity that will be necessary in order to save the planet – showing us how very difficult the project will be, and giving us a sideways, funhouse-mirror, only-kidding glimpse at the kinds of revolutionary changes that will be required to make the future better than the present.[122]

The satirical depiction of the Crakers' peculiar features, which runs through the pages of the *MaddAddam* trilogy, highlights the absurd difficulty of orienting ourselves around the hyperobject of a climate-changed world. A profound contradiction suffuses these novels, because Atwood's warning signals are directed at both the near-future present and the world after the cataclysm. Going back to her analysis in *Payback*, it therefore seems plausible to suggest that the choice between a euto-pian and a dystopian future is ultimately not as straightforward as eco-modernists, for example, would want us to believe. The *MaddAddam* trilogy reveals that, even if preserving the status quo is completely

---

[122] Canavan, "Hope, But Not for Us," 152.

indefensible, taking the next step, beyond the current conundrum, might be equally risky.

This is the case because, despite her mentioning of Glenn/Crake's altruism, Atwood indisputably disapproves of the fantasy of bioengineering a post-human race. Glenn/Crake's thoughts on how better ways of being and living might be brought about are symptomatic of the violence that social dreaming can unleash.[123] In this respect, it is evident that Atwood opposes utopianism of a particular kind: just like Gilead, so is the world after the "Waterless Flood" the product of a yearning for destroying, once and for all, a corrupt, rotten order. This longing is, on Atwood's view, problematic so long as it gets expressed in forceful terms – which it frequently does, as the anti-totalitarian critics of utopianism lament.

Yet Atwood also reasons, through her harrowing account of a dystopian near-present ravaged by global capitalism, that business as usual is not an option. At first sight, the God's Gardeners present themselves as candidates for nurturing a hope that would survive the breakdown of civilization. Their egalitarian and peaceful organization offers an alluring alternative to the status quo.

But even a superficial glance at these ecological separatists confirms that they do not have a viable plan for dealing with the ecological crisis. This is so because they deliberately withdraw from the public sphere and channel all their energy into planning for the coming apocalypse. These hippie preppers are principally concerned with ensuring that they will outlast the "Waterless Flood" by themselves, without paying heed to the plight of other inhabitants of the wretched "pleeblands."[124]

The God's Gardeners' *raison d'être* is premised on the expectation of a radical break with the present. Their hymns and prayers would be meaningless if the pandemic could still be averted. As a consequence, Atwood's utopianism lies "not in prediction or in program, but in this reopening of possibility: the assertion of the radical break, the strident

---

[123] On this issue, see: Dunlap, "Eco-dystopia."

[124] The God's Gardeners reference to the "hidden storeplaces they called Ararats" resonates with Scranton's call to build "cultural arks" for the sake of preserving humanity's patrimony.

insistence that things might yet be otherwise – however that might happen, and whatever else we might become along the way."[125] The apocalypse, then, enables the readers to envision a future unfettered by the iron cage of global capitalism, with its inherent tendency to generate overpopulation and inflict environmental damage, while simultaneously stressing the devastating consequences that a radical break with the status quo will produce. Our species is, in essence, caught between the two horns of this dilemma.[126]

In this situation, hope is both foregone and recovered. It is foregone insofar as it becomes clear that the world of the compounds and of *CorpSeCorps*, the world where socio-economic inequality becomes enmeshed with the utter degradation of nature, has nothing to offer. This civilization is already dead, as both Scranton and the members of the Dark Mountain project remind us.

But hope is also recovered inasmuch as the break triggered by the pandemic facilitates a reflection on what will come after the final reckoning. Humanity may yet somehow survive, so long as its sociality will be completely reconstituted. How exactly that might happen, remains characteristically unanswered in the trilogy. Just as with Lear's notion of radical hope, the reader cannot hold on to anything other than the hazy, yet stubborn belief that "*something good will emerge.*"

This point brings us to my second motif: what is the role of storytelling in the process of moving beyond the impasse of the two dystopian moments, one in the near-present and the other in the future? When Glenn/Crake designs his post-human race, he deliberately edits out any appetite for art, because he gathers it serves no evolutionary purpose. Jimmy/Snowman disagrees with this assertion, not least because he studies at a liberal arts college: "When any civilization is dust and ashes ... art is all that's left over. Images, words, music. Imaginative structures."[127] Over the course of the *MaddAddam* trilogy, it emerges that, on this occasion, Jimmy/Snowman has the upper hand: art is,

---

[125] Canavan, "Hope, But Not for Us," 156.

[126] For an account of the God's Gardeners and Crakers as exemplars of Atwood's "negative utopianism," see: Jergenson, "Negative Utopianism and Catastrophe in Margaret Atwood's MaddAddam Trilogy."

[127] Atwood, *Oryx and Crake.* MaddAddam Trilogy 1, para. 24.27.

astonishingly, one of the few things that even the Crakers cannot do without. They crave stories and are grateful to both Jimmy/Snowman and Toby for constantly supplying them.

This becomes evident in *Oryx and Crake*, when Jimmy/Snowman begins to spin a tale that satisfies the Crakers' hunger for an origin myth. Even though Glenn/Crake believes that symbolic thinking is dangerous – "*Watch out for art*, Crake used to say. *As soon as they start doing art, we're in trouble.*"[128] – his own creatures do not manage to exist without stories about where they come from and where they might be going. In the trilogy's second volume, the precarious status of writing takes centre stage even more. The God's Gardeners are forever afraid of being infiltrated by *CorpSeCorps* and hence refrain from putting anything into writing. By contrast, Amanda, one of the protagonists of *The Year of the Flood*, at some point engages in land art "spelling words out in giant letters, using bioforms to make the words appear and then disappear, just like the words she used to do with ants and syrup."[129] Writing as a form of resistance is perceived as a real threat to the continued existence of the compounds, for it allows the forging of solidary bonds between the oppressed.

Compared to the first two volumes, in *MaddAddam* the role of storytelling is really pivotal, because the main narrator – Toby – relates three connected narratives: one about the budding relationships between the surviving humans and their Craker kin; one about her love for Zeb, the macho God's Gardener who inadvertently assisted Glenn/Crake in building his weapon of mass destruction; and one that the Crakers request, about their ancestries as well as the heroes they cannot but worship.[130]

It is through these interwoven stories that the humans manage to cultivate closer rapports with the Crakers. The decisive development occurs when Toby's apprentice – the precociously talented Blackbeard – commences to hone the craft of spinning a tale himself.

---

[128] Atwood, *Oryx and Crake*: MaddAddam Trilogy 1, para. 52.34, italics in original.

[129] Atwood, *The Year of the Flood*: MaddAddam Trilogy 2, para. 84.8.

[130] The following reflections are shaped by my reading of: Mohr, "Eco-dystopia and Biotechnology," 296–97.

After Toby's death, he even takes over as the main narrator, recounting her heartbreak at Zeb's disappearance. This transfer of the power to deliver an authoritative account marks a final shift in the ordering of this post-apocalyptic world: the age of human supremacy is once and for all over. We are being narratively introduced into the epoch after the Anthropocene.

Apart from forging collective identities and facilitating contact across different species, storytelling plays one further role that is crucial for unlocking Atwood's trilogy: it keeps the memory of the past alive.[131] Once again resonating with a thought that is shared by both Scranton and the Dark Mountain project, Atwood seems to concur that this commemorative function is key to inhabiting a climate-changed world. What art does is preserve forgotten or destroyed gestures that demand constant reinterpretation. Toby's life, for example, might be over once Blackbeard becomes the book's narrator, but the memory of her deeds lives on in the proliferating myths of the human-Craker hybrids. The ultimate ark is thus language itself, a living vessel for preserving that which needs safeguarding in a dystopian future. If there is an unapologetically eutopian strand in the *MaddAddam* trilogy, it must be this, Atwood's unwavering faith in the artistic voice to supply both solace and reassurance.

This idea can be further unpacked by pointing to the novels' polyphonic structure. We have already remarked how the narrator's viewpoint migrates between the three volumes, from a male-centred monologue in *Oryx and Crake*, to a female-centred dialogue in *The Year of the Flood*, to a multispecies polylogue in *MaddAddam*. This array of voices also reflects palpable shifts in textual mood and atmosphere: while the first volume's tone is perceptibly "masculine, pessimistic and tragic" the later novels are more "feminist, comic and optimistic."[132] This rhetorical strategy tallies with Atwood's conviction that eutopian and dystopian themes can never be fully disentangled: the protagonists' grief over

---

[131] Atwood's celebration of the power of narrative dovetails with feminist attempts to reclaim storytelling for the purpose of marginalized people. See: Stone-Mediatore, *Reading across Borders*; Stone-Mediatore, "Storytelling/Narrative."

[132] Northover, "Ecological Apocalypse in Margaret Atwood's MaddAddam Trilogy," 93. I also take the idea of a polyphonic structure in Atwood's work from this text.

a world devastated by both global capitalism (before the apocalypse) and by a deadly virus (after the apocalypse) is always balanced by the fleeting joys of solidarity and love and by the long-term prospects of peaceful cooperation between various species.

This brings us to my third point, regarding the emergence of a multi-species community towards the end of the trilogy. One thing that becomes surer as the final volume progresses is that human supremacy has completely run its course. Power is now more equitably shared between the few human survivors and other non-human species, encompassing the Crakers as well as, notably, the pigoons, who forge an alliance with the humans to protect themselves against the Painballers.

An instructive way to understand this new sense of belonging would be to read it as an instantiation of Donna Haraway's thoughts on multi-species community.[133] Recall from Chapter 1 how Haraway refutes – what she considers – the arrogant undercurrents of the Anthropocene idea, expressing instead a preference for an ethics of entanglement in which humanity becomes profoundly decentred:

> We are at stake to each other. Unlike the dominant dramas of Anthropocene and Capitalocene discourse, human beings are not the only important actors in the Chthulucene, with all other beings able simply to react. The order is reknitted: human beings are with and of the earth, and the biotic and abiotic powers of this earth are the main story.[134]

The *MaddAddam* trilogy is full of examples of kin-making à la Haraway, from Zeb's fierce encounter with a bear in the wilderness to Toby's tender care for a beehive, which she maintains over a long period. Through these episodes of multispecies "becoming-with," Atwood explores a diverse range of interactions between the human and the more-than-human world. This brings yet another eutopian desire in the

---

[133] For an attempt to read Haraway and Atwood together, on which I draw in the following, see: Nugent, "Odd Apocalyptic Panics."

[134] Haraway, *Staying with the Trouble*, 55.

text to the fore: that our species does not have to live under the oppressive conditions dictated by anthropocentrism.[135]

Other ways of being and living are already available to us, but they can only be excavated (as per Levitas' account of utopianism-as-archaeology) if a momentous shift in social relations takes place, away from a self-centred conception of belonging to a novel mode of multispecies sociality. This sociality, which cannot be found in the theoretical positions reviewed before, offers a critical counterpoint to the bioengineering projects that cleared the ground for the viral wipe-out: new ways of being and living cannot be commandeered from above, they need to arise organically, through slow and tentative encounters between potential antagonists.

While Atwood's sympathy for this alternative form of community shines through the trilogy, her focus on the alliance between humans, Crakers and pigoons presupposes a prior rupture, instigated by the deranged altruist Glenn/Crake. Only after the vast majority of humanity has been wiped out, can the encounters across various species emerge. One concern with this temporal sequence – first comes the genocide, then the reconstruction – is that Atwood fails to think through how the current capitalist order might be overcome without a drastic decimation of populations across the globe. Ursula Heise makes this point when she states that

> [s]omewhat surprisingly, Atwood here repeats one of the most troubling aspects of a good deal of postapocalyptic science fiction, including environmentalist science fiction: the tendency to do away with complicated mechanisms of democracy and justice until most of those who might disagree have exited the stage, and then symbolically to inaugurate a new society whose promise of freedom and peace almost inevitably appears like sleight-of-hand.[136]

---

[135] On the emerging debate around multispecies justice, see: Celermajer et al., "Multispecies Justice"; Thaler, "What If"; Tschakert, "More-than-Human Solidarity and Multispecies Justice in the Climate Crisis"; Tschakert et al., "Multispecies Justice."

[136] Heise, *Imagining Extinction*, 228.

Tellingly, a similar objection has also been raised against Haraway's plea to "make kin, not babies."[137] Sophie Lewis argues that the desire to imagine a drastically depopulated planet originates in a deep-seated misanthropy, for the "vision of trans-species Gemeinschaft that emerges is not so much post- as antihuman."[138] The worry here is that Atwood's exploration of a multispecies sociality, just like Haraway's call to make kin with other species rather than reproduce biologically, is motivated by an unacknowledged wish to get rid of human plurality. Otherwise, it would be hard to understand why Atwood intimates that Glenn/Oryx was pursuing an altruistic agenda when he orchestrated the viral wipeout of almost all humans.[139]

Summing up, we can now grasp in what ways the *MaddAddam* trilogy affects the debate around the (post-)apocalyptic imaginary. In examining how life after the Anthropocene might continue, Atwood goes farther than the theorists we encountered in the previous sections. Through a rupture with the oppressive structures governing the near future, the *MaddAddam* trilogy issues a warning about the present moment: given that the basic technologies put to use in the compounds already exist today, Atwood cautions her readers about the effects that scientific discoveries driven by greed and exploitation can have. In this context, only a cataclysmic disaster is capable of loosening the steely grip of global capitalism.

So, the object of Atwood's dystopian anxiety is clearly defined and easy to decipher. But as my reading of these books has suggested, it is significantly harder to ascertain what positive visions for the future might be encapsulated in the *MaddAddam* trilogy. While hope for an emerging type of sociality is sustained throughout the novels, the open ending

---

[137] Haraway, *Staying with the Trouble*, 103.

[138] Lewis, "Cthulhu Plays No Role for Me."

[139] This anti-human tendency also manifests itself in the survivors' decision, by a simple voting procedure, to execute the arrested Painballers, who had been posing a constant threat to the alliance between humans, Crakers and pigoons. Rather than following the principle of rehabilitating deviant outsiders into the newly formed community, the trilogy takes a more conventional route: excising them from the frail body politic. This decision tarnishes the promise of a different sense of belonging that is supposed to mark the positive future.

precludes the drawing of clear-cut lessons. Will the human-Craker hybrids be a viable species? Are the dreadful Painballers gone for good or are there further outcasts lurking in the wild? How will the bonds between the humans, the Crakers and the bioengineered species, such as the pigoons, evolve over time?

Atwood leaves all these questions unanswered. The utopian desire for living otherwise is therefore most visible in her ambition to think through the apocalypse itself. The insight that only a radical break from the status quo can truly change global capitalism is one that Atwood shares with the theorists discussed previously. Yet, the probing of what comes after the cataclysm pushes her speculative fiction beyond the ideas that either Conway and Oreskes, Scranton or the members of the Dark Mountain project propose. Both satire and horror tropes are central to this endeavour: without humour, Atwood's tale would become unbearably bleak; without dread, it would turn out to be merely light entertainment.

5.3 HOW NOT TO GET SHELL-SHOCKED

In the final section of the chapter, I want to conclude my discussion of the *If-This-Goes-On* plot line by examining how the two poles of the dystopian imagination (theory building and storytelling) inform each other. Given that dystopia's main purpose involves warning an audience about imminent, yet often concealed, dangers, a challenge that all proponents of such imaginaries confront relates to the way in which an extrapolation from the present is attempted. Atwood highlights this in especially stark terms when she insists on keeping the label of "speculative fiction" reserved for those kinds of strange, yet plausible, stories that stay closely connected to the real world.

Two general questions surface in this context: what kinds of risk are surveyed in a dystopian narrative? And second: how are those risks represented through theories and stories, to maximize the thrust of a narrative's cautionary pedagogy? Regarding the first question, if the risks that dystopias alert us to are considered trivial or exaggerated, then their creators will be accused of alarmism – seeking to raise awareness about a threat that is, in the end, not all that pressing. Up until the 1990s, this was the main strategy for delegitimizing ecological activism. Rachel Carson's *Silent Spring*, to give just one prominent example, was upon publication immediately censured as the product of a hysterical mind, unable to process complex scientific data.[140]

In today's scholarly and public debate around the Anthropocene, the accusation of baseless fearmongering clearly does not hold anymore.[141] While anxiety about climate change has become deeply entrenched in the societal mainstream, with outright denialism more and more on the wane, there is another charge frequently levelled against dystopias: that their bleak visions project a negative vision of the future that cannot be changed at all anymore. The suspicion here is that despairing, perhaps even panicking, about what is to come might be an entirely reasonable reaction to such a scenario. We find ourselves in the midst of an escalating crisis, as a consequence of which the apocalypse has somehow become incorporated into our normal ways of life.

The worry with these approaches, then, is not so much that concern about the planet is misguided or overstated, but rather that there might be an excess of it: too much knowledge about a truly climate-changed world might in the end feed nothing but incapacitating emotions, such as resignation, depression and mourning. If we indeed ride on a one-way track towards the breakdown of human civilization, with no opportunity for a reversal of the planetary fate, all hope must be lost.

On the opposite side of alarmism hence lies the other trap into which dystopian theories and stories are prone to step. When their cautionary pedagogy foregrounds a threat that ostensibly cannot be averted, the target audience will draw the conclusion that no escape from an ill-fated outcome is feasible. Defeatism seems unavoidable when the future is

---

[140] Lear, *Rachel Carson*, chap. 18: Rumblings of an Avalanche; Lear, "Rachel Carson's 'Silent Spring.'"

[141] That does not mean, of course, that the charge of exaggerated alarmism has completely gone away. Prominent critics of the environmental movement, such as the ecomodernists we encountered in Chapter 4, continue to attack emotive and – what they consider – misguided tendencies within the current debate. All I am suggesting here is that the societal mainstream has significantly shifted away from where it was in the 1970s. For two prominent exemplars of the contemporary case against "eco-miserabilism," see: Lomborg, *False Alarm*; Shellenberger, *Apocalypse Never*.

perceived as foreordained. In such a situation, dystopia's warning function is disabled by the inaccessibility of resistant action. If the very possibility of positive transformation is denied, the counsel to urgently change direction will sound vacuous and go unheard.

Or, worse still, it might be taken to mean that the only way forward is "prepping" for the apocalypse, just as the God's Gardeners in Atwood's trilogy do. Such an attitude can have profoundly damaging impacts. Contemporary eco-fascism appears to have roots not so much in climate change denial, but in a peculiar kind of isolationist chauvinism. As Naomi Klein observes,

> "[t]he climate science will no longer be denied; what *will* be denied is the idea that the nations that are the largest historical emitters of carbon owe anything to the black and brown people impacted by that pollution. This will be denied based on the only rationale possible: that those non-white and non-Christian people are lesser than, are the other, are dangerous invaders".[142]

Hence, navigating between alarmism and defeatism amounts to the greatest difficulty for all dystopian theories and stories.

This brings us to the second question, regarding the portrayal of those risks that dystopias of a climate-changed world want to warn about. If both alarmism and defeatism tend to endanger dystopia's cautionary pedagogy, then special care has to be taken, in the face of existential threats, to allow for the persistent cultivation of some form of residual, stubborn hope. All the authors we have discussed in this chapter acknowledge the importance of holding on to the desire for other ways of being and living. The chief hurdle that theorists like Scranton and the members of the Dark Mountain project face stems from their assumption that our civilization is somehow, despite appearances to the contrary, beyond repair. Unlike Conway and Oreskes' future history, which construes the present as fundamentally malleable, for Scranton and the members of the Dark Mountain project the coming apocalypse is irreversible. Since they recognize the debilitating implications that such an

---

[142] Klein, *On Fire*, para. 6.164.

analysis might have, they struggle with the requirement to keep the flame of hope alive.

This struggle manifests itself in their twisted commitment to a desire for living otherwise, even after all hope has been lost. Scranton and the members of the Dark Mountain project are therefore bound to conceive of our inevitable social death as an occasion for collective renewal – against all odds, the hospice turns out to be a site for the education of utopian desires. Their paradoxical rehabilitation of hope remains a fragile operation, though: since the crux of their proposals is that we find ourselves on a straight path towards the cataclysm, it is difficult to see how we may get beyond a state of incapacitating anxiety.

The *MaddAddam* trilogy puts forth an alternative vision that resolves, or at least weakens, some of these tensions. Since Atwood's tale moves back and forth between a time before and after the breakdown, the reader acquires an awareness of the obstacles that all survivors of the Anthropocene would have to overcome. Given her conviction that eutopian and dystopian ideas are always entangled with each other, it is unsurprising that the *MaddAddam* trilogy contains both hopeful and fearful scenarios: not only places of death and decay, but also vistas for communal renewal.

So, how do these messengers of doom and gloom provide orientation for us, the inhabitants of the Anthropocene? On a first approach, the answer to this question seems straightforward: insofar as all *If-This-Goes-On* stories aim to issue a warning about imminent dangers, their central purpose is to stop the readers from continuing on a path that will end in certain destruction. This dystopian didactic is most obviously at work in Oreskes and Conway's text, whose aspiration to morally instruct is transparent to anyone. It also seems operative in Atwood's analysis of what comes before the cataclysm. This is the logic behind the inscription on the Hunt-Lenox globe, *here be dragons.*

The increasing prevalence of post-cautionary tales complicates matters significantly, however. As we have observed in the writings of Scranton and the members of the Dark Mountain project, the very purpose of dystopias gets called into question once the reader is interpellated to realize that the apocalypse cannot be averted anymore. In that moment, the character of the utopian desire morphs: from what we can reasonably expect to achieve in the near future to a steadfast belief that something good (yet undefinable) will eventually happen, referring once again to Lear's notion of radical hope.

Atwood's fiction testifies to the fact that cautionary and post-cautionary tales are not mutually exclusive, that dystopias can serve important functions, even though their pedagogy has allegedly run its course. In urging the readers to look both back from, and ahead to, the rupture, the *MaddAddam* trilogy foregrounds the utter precariousness of radical hope. Its orientating function exceeds the mere highlighting of roads to be dodged under all circumstances; it also points to modes of being and living that might become alternative models for our species' sense of belonging.

This facet reveals that the relationship between theory building and storytelling in this third constellation differs from our first two cases. Once we focus again on the timescales involved in this plot line, it becomes possible to identify what is rather distinctive about the various engagements with apocalyptic imaginaries. Due to their professed goal of sending warning signals, dystopian visions are by default geared towards "reducing the distance between fictive and empirical world[s]."[143] This explains their proximity to near- or indeed no-future narratives, as our discussion of Oreskes and Conway, Scranton and the members of the Dark Mountain collective has shown.

So, if warning an audience about imminent dangers will be only partially successful in these greatly deranged times, perhaps the ultimate aim of *If-This-Goes-On* narratives is to prepare the readers for, or ideally shield them from, getting shell-shocked: thinking through the cataclysm as a preventative exercise in cognitive and affective resilience. On an unhabitable planet, we will likely need it.

---

[143] Murphy, "Reducing the Dystopian Distance."

CHAPTER 6

Sober Realism and Radical Imagination

I N GERMAN, a *Sollbruchstelle* marks the location in any given structure where a breaking point is to be foreseen.[1] To properly function, many industrial tools and machines rely on such predetermined fault lines (which is how I would translate *Sollbruchstellen*); otherwise, they may break down in unpredictable ways, thereby causing further, uncontrolled and ultimately more severe damage. Importantly, when a predetermined fault line is created within a tool or machine, the intended purpose is not to render them dysfunctional before their normal expiration date. Inserting a *Sollbruchstelle* is decidedly not the same as planned obsolescence, one of the engines behind today's unsustainable levels of wasteful consumerism. Rather, the motivation is to render the tool or machine safer for use. If you know the location at which a given structure is likely to fail, you can prepare its operators for the worst case.

I want to suggest that we can learn something important about utopianism from the notion of a *Sollbruchstelle*. Applied to our topic, my argument in this chapter is hence that familiarity with its breaking points is a crucial precondition for defending utopianism today. Only an account of social dreaming that becomes self-reflectively attentive to its weaknesses will be capable of offering orientation in these greatly deranged times. The question, then, becomes how we should think about these failures and flaws – do we understand them as serious indictments against social dreaming or can we envisage another way of dealing with them?

---

[1] Chocolate bars typically have *Sollbruchstellen* – presumably not only to consume them with more ease, but also to accurately measure and fairly distribute the goods.

This is the issue I plan to investigate in this conclusion, by taking three interrelated steps: First, I review the predetermined fault lines that materialize from my three utopian constellations. Then, in a second step, I try to cash out some of the key lessons that this view of utopianism holds for the disciplinary pillars on which this book stands: political theory, utopian studies and the environmental humanities. The third and last section of the chapter raises the most basic question imaginable: where to now? My answer will be that walking the tightrope between defeatism and self-aggrandizement is our only option if we wish to attend to both the solid frames that structure our existence and to the open doors that enable us to change our life. A final look at Musil's anti-hero, Ulrich, can help us explore how this may be done.

6.1 THE PREDETERMINED FAULT LINES OF UTOPIANISM

Throughout this book, I have highlighted the Janus-faced nature of all utopias: their much-needed promise to remodel the solid frames of our planetary existence into open doors for collective renewal is constantly accompanied by the shadow of failure, their inability to properly devise alternatives to the current state of affairs. This effect is already fore-shadowed in Jameson's assertion that utopianism forces us to imaginatively explore how a rupture with the status quo might be achieved, without ever managing to anticipate what the world after the break will look like. While some deduce from this tension a fatal shortcoming, it contains a positive aspect as well: acknowledging the structurally ambivalent character of utopianism allows for a valorization of anti-perfectionist forms of social dreaming. On a very basic level, failure is thus an inevitable, and to some degree welcome, element of all maps of an uncertain and risky future.

But this seems to be still too sketchy a picture of the difficulties that utopian projects typically run into. We require a more granular analysis of what can go wrong with utopias set in the Anthropocene, if the goal is to vindicate contemporary forms of social dreaming against the charge of being useless or dangerous. In order to deliver such an analysis, I want to parse two kinds of questions: substantively, we may, first, ask what the specific pitfalls of utopian projects are. Second, the matter of failure more broadly comes into view, prompting us to investigate what exactly it means to fail in educating our desire for alternative ways of being and living.

To commence with the first issue, let us quickly return to the three constellations and review the conditions under which estranging, galvanizing and cautioning go awry. Recall the fault line I identified within the idea of planet Earth as a living agent. While both the Gaia figure, reinvigorated by Bruno Latour, and N. K. Jemisin's fantastical depiction of the Stillness serve the objective of unsettling an anthropocentric common sense, their defamiliarization strategy may have the unintended consequence of leaving the reader in the dark about what should concretely be done about our climate-changed world, here and now.

This indeterminacy cannot be effortlessly removed without also troubling the utopian vision's fundamental outlook. Adding concreteness to Gaia and the Stillness remains, of course, an option, but such a move would also affect the overall purpose of their narrative devices. It is, in other words, both an advantage and a downside of our first constellation that it seeks to subvert established manners of viewing Earth and our place on it. The strain between world-negating and world-disclosing estrangement is a persistent component of all utopian visions framed by a *What-If* plot line.

With regard to ecomodernism, the fault line runs through another concern – that of wishful thinking. In contradistinction to the first constellation, modelling a desirable world wherein science and technology inaugurate a "good Anthropocene" is premised on an optimistic view of humanity's inclinations and abilities. In this account, we are not only able to imagine our way out of the ecological crisis, but even know what needs practical doing to avert the most devastating impacts of a climate-changed world.

As Chapter 4 demonstrated, there is considerable disagreement within the ecomodernist camp about the actors and instruments driving positive change. However, all adherents of this *If-Only* plot line embrace a belief in the future as fluid and amenable to transformative intervention on the part of humanity. The clarity of their inflationary critique has the benefit of restoring the audience's sense of self-empowerment. It does, after all, feel good to learn how humans can become confident and competent Earth-makers.

Yet, this mobilizing energy also gives rise to a predisposition for making the challenges confronting us appear smaller and more manageable than they actually are. A modicum of wishful thinking can therefore be detected in all expressions of this type of social dreaming: from Pinker's skewed rendition of Enlightenment progressivism to Robinson's exuberant ode to techno-populism, defenders of ecomodernism must on balance assert that the opportunities in our climate-changed world outweigh the obstacles lying ahead. The challenge for this utopian constellation is therefore to find the right balance between the galvanizing appeal of self-empowerment and the peril of delusional hubris.

Finally, proponents of an *If-This-Goes-On* plot line diagnose the optimistic attitude of those who invest in a "good Anthropocene" as symptomatic of our species' obliviousness to the severity of the ecological crisis. Their bleak stories contain an admonition about the dire state of the world. Such a warning to take the likelihood of our own extinction seriously is based on a procedure of extrapolation, commencing with an assessment of the present moment and culminating in an appeal to change direction. Dystopia's gloomy view of the future is supposed to throw today's climate-changed world into sharper relief, bidding the readers to come to terms with the existentially threatening hurdles they are facing.

In Chapter 5, I contemplated why the experience of fear and despair, on which this kind of dystopianism feeds, cannot be easily controlled: too much of it might actually end up paralyzing the audience, generating fatalism, a debilitating feeling that the game is already lost. The worry with this mode of social dreaming is that its cautionary pedagogy ultimately collapses into helplessness and hopelessness. Its fault line inversely mirrors the one we uncovered in the *If-Only* plot line. Commentators like Roy Scranton and writers like Margaret Atwood hence attempt to keep the desire for other ways of being and living ablaze – albeit in ways that are completely at odds with the ecomodernists' bright image of the future.

From this summary of the pitfalls that contemporary types of utopianism are prone to succumb to, one can derive an understanding of how a productive education of the desire for better ways of being and living may unfold. Once we become cognizant of the multiple respects in which social dreaming will go wrong, we are in a better position to factor these expected failures into our appraisal of contemporary utopianism.

So, competing utopian maps for navigating a climate-changed world can be compared by the degree to which they are alert to, and manufactured around, the predetermined fault lines along which they will break down. Accordingly, a self-reflective benchmark for judging various utopias is revealed: the capacity to avow the problems that utopias run into serves as an indicator for their suitability in the ecological crisis.

What does this underscoring of utopianism's failures and flaws entail more specifically? Concentrating on whether a given type of social dreaming meets the criterion of acknowledging its fault lines permits one to inquire how well various utopian visions cope with the problems of indeterminacy, wishful thinking and defeatism. It is at this stage that the strengths of speculative fiction come to the surface. Via character-driven plot lines that intensify experiential texture and depth, storytelling in the Anthropocene enables the reader to navigate a perplexing future, which in turn sheds light on the present moment. All the authors we have encountered in this book expose through their narratives the uncertainty, contingency and complexity of human action. As such, they complement and complicate the theoretical insights produced by the likes of Latour, the contributors to *Jacobin* magazine and the members of the Dark Mountain collective.

This becomes evident in the *Broken Earth* trilogy's nuanced portrayal of resistance against oppression, for example. Jemisin does not rejoice in human efforts to push back against Father Earth's vengeful attacks. On the contrary, by demonstrating that any form of responding to the violence of a climate-changed world will bring with it unforeseen costs, she drives home the point that there is no getting away from the disorderliness of inhabiting the Anthropocene.

To contend with Gaia – via diplomatic or more belligerent channels – is literally to "stay with the trouble," in Haraway's phrasing. The fictional thought experiment of an interconnected planet, which undergirds this utopian constellation, is meant to impress on us the truth that, for our species, Earth is all we will ever have. The outcome of the ensuing conflict between humanity and the planetary ecosphere must by default remain undecided; a painful proposition to ponder, but one that needs contemplation in these greatly deranged times.

The *Science in the Capital* trilogy deals with the predetermined fault line of wishful thinking differently. Without sacrificing an overall sanguine mood and atmosphere, Robinson takes account of the immense risks that social dreaming inevitably carries. In tracing multiple pathways into a positive future, he simulates competing alternatives to the status quo, from the micro level of personal spiritual awakening to the macro level of global power structures. Some of those clearly veer into wishful thinking, such as when Robinson considers the political opposition to a Green New Deal to be negligible, demoting the backers of the conservative class to passive and docile bystanders in the fight for a better future. Other pathways strike a more realistic note, such as when Robinson points to the mobilizing impact that climate disruptions may exert on both science and technology.

Finally, the *MaddAddam* trilogy grapples with the issue of defeatism by moving back and forth between the build-up to the apocalypse and the thorny reconstruction thereafter. In illustrating both how our species engineered its demise and how it might yet be reborn (albeit under entirely different circumstances), Atwood enlists a cautionary pedagogy that is targeting destructive tendencies already at work today, most notably due to the rapacious appetite of some privileged members of our species for exploitative profit. Her thinking through of the manner in which the "age of the humans" might come to a close illuminates the paradoxical nature of social dreaming: even if there is nothing that could be done to forestall the collapse of civilization, it is still incumbent upon us to cling to the radical hope that in the aftermath of the global breakdown something good will come about.

The flaws that this book has unearthed within contemporary utopianism can thus be self-reflectively accommodated, if not eradicated, through theories and stories that equip their readers with new perspectives for envisaging the world. In evaluating these fault lines more closely, we might then ask ourselves what the status of failure is here. On one view, the frequently patent, sometimes latent shortcomings of utopias supply extra ammunition to the anti-totalitarian objections to social dreaming. Consistent with these sceptical voices, the fact that utopian visions can go awry is seen as corroborating their generally problematic tenets.

I want to suggest that there is another, more auspicious route for capturing the flaws of social dreaming, namely in terms of permanent features that keep a check on the utopian desire for other ways of being and living. Samuel Beckett's dictum "Fail again. Fail Better"[2] affords a powerful motto for the rationale behind this alternative reading. Espousing the maxim of "failing again better" involves that we perceive both the successes and failures of utopian projects as temporary stations on a continuous, yet rocky journey. Trying to draw maps of our climate-changed world is an experimental endeavour, full of promises and disappointments. An anti-perfectionist conceptualization of social dreaming lets us judge this process in a subtle fashion, which is not only sensitive to its shortcomings, but also attentive to its accomplishments.

Viewing utopias through this lens facilitates an appreciation of the criticism that they deploy. Once the fact is conceded that utopias will fail one way or another, a certain mode of critiquing the status quo becomes inaccessible, or at least much less attractive than previously assumed. We can clarify this thought by returning to the issue of how utopian visions became temporalized during the Enlightenment period. While the classical utopian setting was on an isolated island or a remote continent, in the eighteenth century the education of desire was gradually projected into the near or distant future. This led to a chronic dynamization of social dreaming, for now the utopian project constituted not so much a static (if hard-to-reach) ideal that could be admired and emulated from afar, but rather turned into a site for indirectly critiquing the status quo, by affectively and cognitively positioning the audience on a hypothetical trajectory leading from their point in time to the envisaged society to come.

Structurally, the deliberative force of such future-oriented visions hinges on their anchoring in the cultural repertoire of the current moment, either by inflating or by deflating the assurances of the status

---

[2] "All of old. Nothing else ever. Ever tried. Ever failed. No matter. Try again. Fail again. Fail better" (Beckett, *Nohow On*, 101).

quo. It must be conceivable, in other words, for the readers to establish a connection, however tenuous, between the conjured alternative society and their own lifeworlds, here and now. This is the lesson that the "Atwood principle" (in spite of its inadequacies) holds for us.

Why does this shift in perspective matter to the problem of critique? What happens to the process of criticizing something when the benchmark of a perfect ideal is forsaken? To answer these questions, it will help to swiftly refer to a recent attempt at recuperating utopianism for political theory. According to the established terminology, ideal theory, with its predilection for formulating doctrines of justice that are shielded from contact with the real world, can be described as utopian, in the sense of reifying a static (if hard-to-reach) end goal: it aims at formulating arguments that reveal the truth of certain abstract principles.[3] In so doing, ideal theory bears striking similarities with the classical utopian setting and its blueprint approach. The critique that ideal theory exercises is thus predicated on an account of perfect justice. This account then makes it possible to correct injustices in the real world, via the application of so-called non-ideal theory.[4] On the basis of this quasi-Platonic architecture, the philosophical exploration of justice always comes first and the pursuit of politics second.[5] Only by knowing for certain what the principles of justice demand are we capable of fighting against violations of freedom and equality in the real world.[6]

This picture does not adequately capture how the education of desire operates, though. Non-perfectionist utopias are intrinsically dynamic insofar as they seek to model various alternatives to the status quo and build into their scenarios predetermined fault lines. The *What-If, If-Only*

---

[3] For a paradigmatic example of this kind of approach, see: Cohen, *Rescuing Justice and Equality*. On Cohen's utopianism, see: Sypnowich, "G. A. Cohen's Socialism."

[4] This is one of the most vibrant debates in contemporary political theory, so I will evidently not have sufficient space to do it full justice. The main reason why I turn to it in the conclusion is to demonstrate the wider implications that my view of utopianism has for political theory. For an overview see: Valentini, "Ideal vs. Non-Ideal Theory."

[5] Raymond Geuss calls this view of political theory the "ethics-first" one. See: Geuss, *Philosophy and Real Politics*, chap.: introduction.

[6] Needless to say, this model of theorizing has received a great deal of criticism, which I cannot engage with here. For an illuminating discussion, see: Mills, "'Ideal Theory' as Ideology"; Mills, "White Time."

and *If-This-Goes-On* narratives analyzed here do not engage in prediction. Neither do they indulge the impulse for managerial solutionism. Rather, their various mechanisms – estranging, galvanizing and cautioning – reach for a deeper understanding of our present moment by illuminating the uncertainty, contingency and complexity of human action.

The orientation that these utopian visions provide relies on "dissolving" and "neutralizing" the status quo (in Jameson's terminology), but their immanent mode of critique is markedly dissimilar from the one advocated by ideal theory. To illustrate this, consider Iris Marion Young's project, in which the pretension of perfect blueprints for society is resolutely discarded.[7] In its stead, Young proposes a type of social inquiry that

> rejects as illusory the effort to construct a universal normative system insulated from a particular society. Normative reflection must begin from historically specific circumstances because there is nothing but what is, the given, the situated interest in justice, from which to start. Reflecting from within a particular social context, good normative theorizing cannot avoid social and political description and explanation.[8]

This framework, which reverberates with a wider set of conceptual developments in Critical Theory,[9] can be linked to the distinct forms of social

---

[7] It should be added, though, that Young herself seemed rather hostile to the idea of utopia, presumably because she identified it exclusively with the quest for perennial truth of certain abstract principles. Throughout her work, indications of this aversion can be found at several points. When Young wants to disparage an idea, she calls it either "wildly utopian," "laughably utopian" or "hopelessly utopian" (Young, *Justice and the Politics of Difference*, 233, 237, 241). I would like to think that, had she been aware of alternative conceptions of utopianism, Young would not have referred to this idea in such pejorative terms.

[8] Young, 5.

[9] Most prominent amongst these is Rahel Jaeggi's defence of "immanent critique," which builds on both Jürgen Habermas' and Axel Honneth's understandings of social criticism. In fact, the longer trajectory of this notion of critique reaches back to Hegel and Marx. On Jaeggi's account, immanent critique is characterized by the refutation of an Archimedean standpoint from which to judge specific social formations, while combining the "idea that the standard of criticism resides in the thing itself with the claim to provide a context-transcending critique" (*Critique of Forms of Life*, para. 15.3). See also: Jaeggi, "Was ist Ideologiekritik?" On the concept of "immanent critique," see: Stahl,

dreaming in the Anthropocene that we have studied in this book. In contrast to the critique endorsed by ideal theory, utopias are, due to their dynamism and open-endedness, always engaged in a dual movement, trafficking between what Musil calls the "sense of reality" and the "sense of possibility." Diagnosing the status quo and anticipating transformative potentials amount to separate activities, but they are both germane to social dreaming. It is in the interplay between theory building and speculative fiction that this movement can be best observed.

6.2 INTERDISCIPLINARY LESSONS

Such a view of utopianism's critical motivation leads to a related issue: what are the implications of our findings for the three disciplinary pillars on which this book rests? Which concrete benefits can political theory, utopian studies and the environmental humanities accrue from the approach taken in this book?

In regard to political theory, we have already remarked that the status of normativity is profoundly affected by the notion of utopias as anti-perfectionist, dynamic and open-ended. Once we adopt the concept of socially embedded utopia as a process, it becomes possible to conceive of the critical function that political theory exercises in an analogous fashion – as fusing together a sober realism with the radical imagination.[10] The debate around "how to do" political theory thereby shifts, pivoting away from a simplistic binary between ideal and nonideal theory that still holds sway over so much of the contemporary discussion.[11] Utopianism may thus become a vital heuristics in the arsenal of political theory to enhance understanding, evaluation and orientation.[12]

"Immanent Critique and Particular Moral Experience"; Pensky, "In Search of the Negative in Rahel Jaeggi's Kritik von Lebensformen."

[10] Vázquez-Arroyo, *Political Responsibility*, 251–56.

[11] On this point, see: Thaler, "Hope Abjuring Hope."

[12] Another heuristics of equal importance to political theory is genealogy. For three recent appropriations of this approach, which develop the Nietzschean and Foucauldian project in interestingly varied directions, see: Geuss, "Genealogy as Critique"; Skinner, "A Genealogy of the Modern State"; Williams, *Truth and Truthfulness*.

Opening up political theory to conversations with other genres of writing has a further ramification: it prompts us to reconsider where theorizing usually takes place. In Chapter 1, I mentioned that literature may contribute to theory building by entering into a fruitful dialogue with more scholarly forms of knowledge production. Throughout this book, this intuition has been supported at various junctures: from Jemisin's engagement with the cruel impacts of "weathering," continuing with Robinson's account of spiritual transformation on the individual and the collective level, all the way to Atwood's experiment with a multi-species community, literary texts clearly hold resources that social and political theorists would be well advised to engage with.

At the same time, it is the distinct approaches of social and political theorists that enable a creative interpretation of speculative fiction, producing novel and illuminating insights. In this book, I have sought to stage encounters between the two poles of each constellation, theory building and storytelling. Such dialogues enrich the usual techniques of reading speculative fiction by scholars in utopian studies.

In decoding the novels of Jemisin, Robinson and Atwood as, amongst other things, repositories of theoretical insight, a broader reflection around the Anthropocene is set into motion. This is consequential insofar as there still seems to be a chasm separating students of utopianism's three faces: theory building, storytelling and practical forms of social dreaming. While commentators, such as Sargisson and Levitas, have begun to look into the multiple interfaces between these three dimensions, this book has insisted on the importance of envisaging different expressions of the desire for being and living otherwise as contributing to the same overarching conversation.

Benjamin's notion of a constellation assisted me in conjoining under one umbrella utopian visions that would ordinarily not be seen as contiguous. The linking together of the works of theorists and writers has brought to the fore that their forms of social dreaming can become mutually illuminating – a fact that might extend the horizon of utopian studies.

Finally, with regard to the environmental humanities, the book's focus on orientation highlights the normative aspect of all utopian maps of our climate-changed world. This has hitherto not been fully accounted for in the existing literature. Working with a conception of utopianism that pays attention to both its accomplishments and its shortcomings makes it imperative to judge specific expressions of social dreaming in light of their suitability to a specific moment in time. Accordingly, my goal has not only been to sketch the contours of rival utopian constellations, but also to subject them to evaluative scrutiny. Foregrounding normativity in this manner adds an original contribution to the state of the art in the environmental humanities.

6.3 REALITY: SOMETHING YET TO BE INVENTED

A key assumption behind this book has been that, in spite of its significance for our greatly deranged times, utopianism remains pervaded by a fundamental tension: the education of our desire for better ways of being and living is torn between the push to negate and dissolve reality and the magnetic pull of the world as we know it. This strain reveals itself, for example, in debates around the appropriate distance between an instance of social dreaming and the real world, with its material and ideological constraints from which we can never fully liberate ourselves. The fault lines running through our *What-If*, *If-Only* and *If-This-Goes-On* plot lines have their origins in this very tension. Indeterminacy, wishful thinking and defeatism are not incidental byproducts of the utopian desire; they are intrinsic to conjuring anti-perfectionist scenarios of the future that critically interrogate the present.

Standards of intellectual hygiene appear to demand that we should want to at least ease or perhaps even remove this strain altogether. Ideally, this could be done via two opposing routes – either by resolving it towards the pole of negation and dissolution of reality, or by evermore closely approximating utopian visions to the world as we know it. Accordingly, on the one hand, we might ponder how much more attractive utopian visions would be if we were absolutely free to conjure alternative models of our climate-changed world, if we were not always dragged back into the forcefield of the status quo. On the other hand, we might think how much more appealing utopian visions would look if we were able to draw clear-cut and unequivocal lessons from them, if we could straightforwardly apply their ideas and practices to improve our brittle lifeworlds.

The impulse to tread one of these paths unites many of the theorists and writers discussed in this book. But my conclusion suggests that we should resist it. Navigating our climate-changed world, looking for orientation around the hyperobject that is the Anthropocene cannot be achieved with the help of either escapist fantasizing or status quo–affirming realism; both lead to a dead end that the education of desire must avoid. It follows that, only if we devote ourselves to keeping the tension between these two poles alive, will we be prepared to properly face up to the enormity of the challenges awaiting us.

To shed light on the entanglement of the sense of reality and the sense of the possibility, let us finally revisit the author I began this book with. In *The Man without Qualities*, Musil dramatizes the contrast between these modes of guiding our existence on this planet into a Manichean difference of character.[13] Realists (*Wirklichkeitsmenschen*) tend to make the best of the existing circumstances so as to settle down in the world and, more prosaically, climb the social ladder. People of such a disposition are not overly bothered by the contradictions and ambiguities of the status quo, channelling all their energy on smoothly trudging along.[14]

Possibilists (*Möglichkeitsmenschen*), by contrast, are driven by a "conscious utopianism that does not shrink from reality but sees it as a project, something yet to be invented."[15] Ulrich himself, the story's anti-hero, represents a prime exemplar of a possibilist. What is distinctive about his personality is that he is in equal measure wedded to the sense of reality and to the sense of possibility. This becomes clearer in the

---

[13] On the centrality of such dualisms in the novel, see: Blok, "Robert Musil's Literary Ethics."

[14] The professional success of Ulrich's father, for example, ascending from the lowly status of house tutor to the prestigious position of law professor and legal advisor to the Austrian aristocracy, can be explained by his utter dedication to upholding the staid decorum of the status quo. See: Musil, *The Man without Qualities*, chap. 3: Even a Man without Qualities Has a Father with Qualities.

[15] Musil, para. 8.5.

exploration of the protagonist's ethics, which is explicitly couched in terms of utopianism.[16]

Ulrich's strategy for organizing the world around him follows, initially, the image of a "utopia of precision"[17] whereby the natural sciences afford a blueprint for the good life. This model is later juxtaposed to the competing framework of a "utopia of essayism," which shapes "the unique and unalterable form assumed by a man's inner life in a decisive thought."[18] The essay exemplifies a life form that departs from a rationalistic worldview, bringing into a closer union the powers of reason and sentiment.[19]

Key to grasping Musil's point here is an insight that has also been instrumental for our inquiry into the Anthropocene's imaginary maps: conceiving of the sense of reality and the sense of possibility as inextricably woven together discloses that the quest for perfection is misguided. In its stead, Musil's proposal is to keep "continually on the lookout for new possibilities, trans-valuations of values, and new perspectives on material 'reality' that are bound to overturn any outworn status quos."[20] The "utopia of essayism" proves particularly promising in this regard, for it bears a striking resemblance to the notion of failing again.

Reality – something yet to be invented: this is a disquieting proposition that underscores our epochal responsibility, vacillating between hubris and humility, as inhabitants of Earth. Inasmuch as utopias demonstrate that, despite the illusory facade of quasi-natural and transhistorical solidity, what has been constructed can also be undone and remade,

---

[16] On the role of utopianism in Musil's oeuvre, see: Shin, *Der "bewusste Utopismus" im Mann ohne Eigenschaften von Robert Musil*; McBride, *The Void of Ethics*, chap. 5: Staging the Failure of an Aesthetic Utopia: The Man without Qualities; Leucht, "Utopie"; Voßkamp, "Wenn es Wirklichkeitssinn gibt, muß es auch Möglichkeitssinn geben."

[17] Musil, *The Man without Qualities*, para. 66.7.

[18] Musil, para. 67.13.

[19] On the intersection between moral and cognitive norms in Musil's writings, see: Mulligan, "Foolishness, Stupidity, and Cognitive Values." A third sense in which Ulrich's character is drawn to a utopian way of living is through the prospect of what Musil enigmatically calls the "other condition," a poetic rejoinder to the perplexingly fractured nature of our modern existence.

[20] Grill, *The World as Metaphor in Robert Musil's The Man without Qualities*, 111.

their concrete, hopeful and cautious implications for our precarious life in the Anthropocene are forthright. In reinventing reality, it is we humans, not the planet, who need to be undone and remade. Only then will our species be able to actualize a potential that is still within its grasp, but only just so: to thrive, together with all other beings, on this planet that is like no other.

Bibliography

Abbott, Carl. "Falling into History: The Imagined Wests of Kim Stanley Robinson in the 'Three Californias' and Mars Trilogies." *Western Historical Quarterly* 34, no. 1 (February 1, 2003): 27–47. https://doi.org/10.2307/25047207.

Abensour, Miguel. "Persistent Utopia." *Constellations* 15, no. 3 (September 1, 2008): 406–21. https://doi.org/10.1111/j.1467-8675.2008.00501.x.

"William Morris: The Politics of Romance." In *Revolutionary Romanticism: A Drunken Boat Anthology*, edited by Max Blechman, 126–61. San Francisco: City Lights Books, 1999.

Adams, Matthew. "Inaction and Environmental Crisis: Narrative, Defence Mechanisms and the Social Organisation of Denial." *Psychoanalysis, Culture & Society* 19, no. 1 (April 1, 2014): 52–71. https://doi.org/10.1057/pcs.2013.21.

Adorno, Theodor W. *Minima Moralia: Reflections on a Damaged Life*. New York: Verso, 2005.

Negative Dialectics. London: Routledge & Kegan Paul, 1973.

Ahmed, Sara. *The Cultural Politics of Emotion*. Edinburgh: Edinburgh University Press, 2014.

Queer Phenomenology: Orientations, Objects, Others. Durham, NC: Duke University Press, 2006.

Willful Subjects. Durham, NC: Duke University Press, 2014.

Aitkenhead, Decca. "James Lovelock: 'Enjoy Life While You Can: In 20 Years Global Warming Will Hit the Fan.'" *The Guardian*, March 1, 2008. www.theguardian.com/theguardian/2008/mar/01/scienceofclimatechange.climatechange.

Alexander, Bryan N. "Jameson's Adorno and the Problem of Utopia." *Utopian Studies* 9, no. 2 (1998): 51–7.

Alkon, Paul K. *Origins of Futuristic Fiction*. Athens: University of Georgia Press, 2010.

Allaby, Michael, and James Lovelock. *The Greening of Mars*. New York: St. Martin's Press, 1984.

Allardice, Lisa. "Margaret Atwood: 'I Am Not a Prophet. Science Fiction Is Really about Now.'" *The Guardian*, January 20, 2018. www.theguardian.com/books/2018/jan/20/margaret-atwood-i-am-not-a-prophet-science-fiction-is-about-now.

Allen, Amy. "Emancipation without Utopia: Subjection, Modernity, and the Normative Claims of Feminist Critical Theory." *Hypatia* 30, no. 3 (August 1, 2015): 513–29. https://doi.org/10.1111/hypa.12160.

Amis, Kingsley. *New Maps of Hell: A Survey of Science Fiction*. London: Penguin Classics, 2012.

Anthony, Andrew. "Steven Pinker: 'The Way to Deal with Pollution Is Not to Rail against Consumption.'" *The Observer*, February 11, 2018. www.theguardian.com/science/2018/feb/11/steven-pinker-enlightenment-now-interview-inequality-consumption-environment.

Arendt, Hannah. *The Human Condition*. Chicago: University of Chicago Press, 1998.

Arias-Maldonado, Manuel. "The 'Anthropocene' in Philosophy: The Neo-material Turn and the Question of Nature." In *Anthropocene Encounters: New Directions in Green Political Thinking*, edited by Frank Biermann and Eva Lövbrand, 50–66. Cambridge: Cambridge University Press, 2019. https://doi.org/10.1017/9781108646673.003.

Arjomand, Minou. *Staged: Show Trials, Political Theater, and the Aesthetics of Judgment*. New York: Columbia University Press, 2018.

Aronoff, Kate. "The Eco-right's One Simple Trick." *Jacobin*, 2017. www.jacobinmag.com/2017/08/the-eco-rights-one-simple-trick.

Aronoff, Kate, Alyssa Battistoni, Daniel Aldana Cohen, and Thea N. Riofrancos. *A Planet to Win: Why We Need a Green New Deal*. London: Verso, 2019.

Asafu-Adjaye, John, Linus Blomqvist, Stewart Brand et al. "An Ecomodernist Manifesto," 2015. www.ecomodernism.org.

Asayama, Shinichiro. "Catastrophism toward 'Opening up' or 'Closing down'? Going beyond the Apocalyptic Future and Geoengineering." *Current Sociology* 63, no. 1 (January 1, 2015): 89–93. https://doi.org/10.1177/0011392114559849.

Ashenden, Samantha, and Andreas Hess, eds. *Between Utopia and Realism: The Political Thought of Judith N. Shklar*. Philadelphia: University of Pennsylvania Press, 2019.

Atchison, Amy L., and Shauna L. Shames. *Survive and Resist: The Definitive Guide to Dystopian Politics*. New York: Columbia University Press, 2019.

Attebery, Brian. "Introduction: Epic Fantasy." *Journal of the Fantastic in the Arts* 29, no. 1 (2018): 1.

——— *Strategies of Fantasy*. Bloomington: Indiana University Press, 1992.

Atwood, Margaret. *The Handmaid's Tale*. E-Book. Boston: Houghton Mifflin Company, 1986

"The Handmaid's Tale and Oryx and Crake in Context." *PMLA* 119, no. 3 (May 2004): 513–17. https://doi.org/10.1632/003081204X20578.

"Introduction." In *In Other Worlds: SF and the Human Imagination*, 1–13. London: Virago, 2011.

MaddAddam. E-Book. MaddAddam Trilogy 3. New York: Nan A. Talese, 2013.

Oryx and Crake. E-Book. MaddAddam Trilogy 1. New York: Nan A. Talese, 2003.

Payback: Debt and the Shadow Side of Wealth. New York: House of Anansi Press, 2011.

"The Road to Ustopia." *The Guardian*, October 14, 2011. www.theguardian .com/books/2011/oct/14/margaret-atwood-road-to-ustopia.

Surfacing. Toronto: McClelland and Stewart, 1972.

The Testaments. New York: Nan A. Talese, 2019.

"Writing 'Oryx and Crake.'" In *Curious Pursuits: Occasional Writing 1970–2005*, 321–23. London: Virago, 2005.

"Writing Utopia." In *Writing with Intent: Essays, Reviews, Personal Prose, 1983–2005*, 92–100. New York: Carroll & Graf Publishers, 2005.

The Year of the Flood. E-Book. MaddAddam Trilogy 2. New York: Nan A. Talese, 2009.

Auerbach, Erich. *Mimesis: The Representation of Reality in Western Literature*. Princeton, NJ: Princeton University Press, 2003.

Baccolini, Raffaella, and Tom Moylan. "Introduction: Dystopia and Histories." In *Dark Horizons: Science Fiction and the Dystopian Imagination*, edited by Raffaella Baccolini and Tom Moylan, 1–12. New York: Routledge, 2003.

Bai, Ronnie. "Dances with Mei Lanfang: Brecht and the Alienation Effect." *Comparative Drama* 32, no. 3 (1998): 389–433. https://doi.org/10.1353/cdr .1998.0040.

Barca, Stefania. "Labour and the Ecological Crisis: The Eco-modernist Dilemma in Western Marxism(s) (1970s–2000s)." *Geoforum* 98 (January 1, 2019): 226–35. https://doi.org/10.1016/j.geoforum.2017.07.011.

Barnett, David. "Hugo Awards: Women Clean Up as N. K. Jemisin Wins Best Novel Again." *The Guardian*, August 20, 2018. www.theguardian.com/books/ 2018/aug/20/hugo-awards-women-nk-jemisin-wins-best-novel.

Bastani, Aaron. *Fully Automated Luxury Communism: A Manifesto*. London: Verso, 2019.

Bastiaansen, Fenne. "*The Entanglement of Climate Change, Capitalism and Oppression in the Broken Earth Trilogy by N. K. Jemisin*." MA thesis, Utrecht University, 2020. https://dspace.library.uu.nl/handle/1874/399139.

Battistoni, Alyssa. "Living, Not Just Surviving." *Jacobin*, August 15, 2017. https://jacobinmag.com/2017/08/living-not-just-surviving.

"Within and against Capitalism." *Jacobin*, 2017. https://jacobinmag.com/2017/08/within-and-against-capitalism.

Beck, Ulrich. *World Risk Society.* Cambridge: Polity Press, 1999.

Beckett, Samuel. *Nohow on: Three Novels.* London: John Calder, 1989.

Bell, David A. "Waiting for Steven Pinker's Enlightenment." *The Nation*, March 7, 2018. www.thenation.com/article/waiting-for-steven-pinkers-enlightenment.

Bell, Duncan. *Dreamworlds of Race: Empire and the Utopian Destiny of Anglo-America.* Princeton, NJ: Princeton University Press, 2020.

"Pragmatism and Prophecy: H. G. Wells and the Metaphysics of Socialism." *American Political Science Review*, December 2017, 1–14. https://doi.org/10.1017/S0003055417000508.

Bellamy, Brent, and Imre Szeman. "Life after People: Science Faction and Ecological Futures." In *Green Planets: Ecology and Science Fiction*, edited by Gerry Canavan and Kim Stanley Robinson, 192–205. Middletown, CT: Wesleyan University Press, 2014.

Benhabib, Seyla. "Judith Shklar's Dystopic Liberalism." *Social Research* 61, no. 2 (1994): 477–88.

Benjamin, Walter. "Franz Kafka: On the Tenth Anniversary of His Death." In *Illuminations*, edited by Hannah Arendt, 111–40. New York: Schocken Books, 1986.

The Origin of German Tragic Drama. Translated by John Osborne. New York: Verso, 1998.

Bennett, Jane. *Vibrant Matter: A Political Ecology of Things.* Durham, NC: Duke University Press, 2010.

Bereola, Abigail. "A True Utopia: An Interview with N. K. Jemisin." *The Paris Review*, December 3, 2018. www.theparisreview.org/blog/2018/12/03/a-true-utopia-an-interview-with-n-k-jemisin.

Bergman, Jay. "The Idea of Individual Liberation in Bolshevik Visions of the New Soviet Man." *European History Quarterly* 27, no. 1 (January 1, 1997): 57–92. https://doi.org/10/cbv8cs.

Berlant, Lauren. *Cruel Optimism.* Durham, NC: Duke University Press, 2011.

Berlin, Isaiah. "The Pursuit of the Ideal." In *The Proper Study of Mankind: An Anthology of Essays*, edited by Henry Hardy and Roger Hausheer, 1–16. London: Chatto & Windus, 1997.

Bethune, Brian. "Book Review: Atwood's Oryx and Crake." *Maclean's*, May 27, 2003. www.thecanadianencyclopedia.ca/article/book-review-atwoods-book oryx-and-crakebook.

Bettini, Giovanni. "Environmental Catastrophe." In *Companion to Environmental Studies*, edited by Noel Castree, Mike Hulme and James D. Proctor, 39–42. New York: Routledge, 2018.

Beukes, Lauren, Kim Stanley Robinson, Ken Liu, Hannu Rajaniemi, Alastair Reynolds, and Aliette de Bodard. "Science Fiction When the Future Is Now." December 20, 2017. https://doi.org/10.1038/d41586-017-08674-8.

Bhatt, Chetan. "Book Review Symposium: Steven Pinker, *The Better Angels of Our Nature: A History of Violence and Humanity.*" *Sociology* 47, no. 6 (December 1, 2013): 1229–32. https://doi.org/10.1177/0038038513513853.

Bickerton, Christopher, and Carlo Invernizzi Accetti. "Populism and Technocracy: Opposites or Complements?" *Critical Review of International Social and Political Philosophy* 20, no. 2 (March 4, 2017): 186–206. https://doi.org/10.1080/13698230.2014.995504.

Biermann, Frank. "The Anthropocene: A Governance Perspective." *The Anthropocene Review* 1, no. 1 (April 1, 2014): 57–61. https://doi.org/10.1177/2053019613516289.

Earth System Governance: World Politics in the Anthropocene. London: The MIT Press, 2014.

Biermann, Frank, K. Abbott, S. Andresen et al. "Navigating the Anthropocene: Improving Earth System Governance." *Science* 335, no. 6074 (March 16, 2012): 1306–7. https://doi.org/10.1126/science.1217255.

Biermann, Frank, and Eva Lövbrand. "Encountering the 'Anthropocene': Setting the Scene." In *Anthropocene Encounters: New Directions in Green Political Thinking*, edited by Frank Biermann and Eva Lövbrand, 1–22. Cambridge: Cambridge University Press, 2019. https://doi.org/10.1017/9781108646673.001.

Biermann, Frank, and Rakhyun Kim, eds. *Architectures of Earth System Governance: Institutional Complexity and Structural Transformation.* Earth System Governance Series. New York: Cambridge University Press, 2020.

Billet, Alexander. "Bono Kills the Planet." *Jacobin*, 2017. www.jacobinmag.com/2017/08/bono-kills-the-planet.

Billings, Lee "Black Lives Matter Inspired This Chilling Fantasy Novel." Geek's Guide to the Galaxy. Accessed April 17, 2019. www.wired.com/2015/08/geeks-guide-nk-jemisin.

"Q&A: Kim Stanley Robinson Explains How He Flooded Manhattan." *Scientific American*, March 13, 2017. www.scientificamerican.com/article/q-a-kim-stanley-robinson-explains-how-he-flooded-manhattan.

Bloch, Ernst. *The Principle of Hope: Volume 1.* Translated by Neville Plaice, Stephen Plaice, and Paul Knight. 3 vols. Studies in Contemporary German Social Thought. Cambridge: MIT Press, 1995.

"Something's Missing: A Discussion between Ernst Bloch and Theodor W. Adorno on the Contradictions of Utopian Longing." In *The Utopian Function of Art and Literature: Selected Essays*, 1–17. Studies in Contemporary German Social Thought. Cambridge, MA: MIT Press, 1988.

Blok, Mette. "Robert Musil's Literary Ethics: The Man without Qualities Reconsidered." *New German Review: A Journal of Germanic Studies* 26, no. 1 (2014): 1–16.

Boeckmann, Staci L von. "Marxism, Morality, and the Politics of Desire: Utopianism in Fredric Jameson's The Political Unconscious." *Utopian Studies* 9, no. 2 (1998): 31–50.

Bould, Mark, and China Miéville, eds. *Red Planets: Marxism and Science Fiction*. Middletown, CT: Wesleyan University Press, 2009.

Bould, Mark, and Sherryl Vint. "Political Readings." In *The Cambridge Companion to Fantasy Literature*, edited by Edward James and Farah Mendlesohn, 102–12. Cambridge: Cambridge University Press, 2014.

Boulding, Elise. "Utopianism: Problems and Issues in Planning for a Peaceful Society." *Alternatives* 11, no. 3 (July 1, 1986): 345–66. https://doi.org/10.1177/030437548601100302.

Boulton, Elizabeth. "Climate Change as a 'Hyperobject': A Critical Review of Timothy Morton's Reframing Narrative." *Wiley Interdisciplinary Reviews: Climate Change* 7, no. 5 (2016): 772–85. https://doi.org/10/f84jzr.

Bourdieu, Pierre. *The Field of Cultural Production: Essays on Art and Literature*. New York: Columbia University Press, 1993.

Bouson, J. Brooks. "'It's Game Over Forever': Atwood's Satiric Vision of a Bioengineered Posthuman Future in Oryx and Crake." *The Journal of Commonwealth Literature* 39, no. 3 (September 1, 2004): 139–56. https://doi.org/10.1177/0021989404047051.

———. "A 'Joke-Filled Romp' through End Times: Radical Environmentalism, Deep Ecology, and Human Extinction in Margaret Atwood's Eco-apocalyptic MaddAddam Trilogy." *The Journal of Commonwealth Literature* 51, no. 3 (September 1, 2016): 341–57. https://doi.org/10.1177/0021989415573558.

———. "'We're Using Up the Earth. It's Almost Gone': A Return to the Post-apocalyptic Future in Margaret Atwood's *The Year of the Flood*." *The Journal of Commonwealth Literature* 46, no. 1 (March 1, 2011): 9–26. https://doi.org/10.1177/0021989410395430.

Boym, Svetlana. "Poetics and Politics of Estrangement: Victor Shklovsky and Hannah Arendt." *Poetics Today* 26, no. 4 (2005): 581–611. https://doi.org/10.1215/03335372-26-4-581.

Brannen, Peter. "The Anthropocene Is a Joke." *The Atlantic*, August 13, 2019. www.theatlantic.com/science/archive/2019/08/arrogance-anthropocene/595795.

———. "The Breakthrough Institute." Accessed May 6, 2019. https://thebreakthrough.org/about.

Brecht, Bertolt. "On Chinese Acting." *The Tulane Drama Review* 6, no. 1 (1961): 130–36. https://doi.org/10.2307/1125011.

"A Short Organum for the Theatre." In *Brecht on Theatre: The Development of an Aesthetic*, by Bertolt Brecht, *179–205*, edited by John Willett. London: Eyre Methuen, 1974.

Brodie, Renee. "The Aryan New Era: Apocalyptic Realizations in *The Turner Diaries*." *Journal of American Culture* 21, no. 3 (September 1, 1998): 13–22. https://doi.org/10.1111/j.1542-734X.1998.00013.x.

Brown, Susan Love, ed. *Intentional Community: An Anthropological Perspective*. Albany: State University of New York Press, 2002.

Brown, Valerie A., John A. Harris and Jacqueline Y. Russell, eds. *Tackling Wicked Problems through the Transdisciplinary Imagination*. London: Earthscan, 2010.

Buchanan, Ian. "Metacommentary on Utopia, or Jameson's Dialectic of Hope." *Utopian Studies* 9, no. 2 (1998): 18–30.

Buck, Holly Jean. *After Geoengineering: Climate Tragedy, Repair, and Restoration*. New York: Verso, 2019.

Buell, Frederick. *From Apocalypse to Way of Life: Environmental Crisis in the American Century*. London: Routledge, 2004.

"A Short History of Environmental Apocalypse." In *Future Ethics: Climate Change and Apocalyptic Imagination*, edited by Stefan Skrimshire, 13–36. New York: Continuum, 2010.

Buell, Lawrence. *The Environmental Imagination: Thoreau, Nature Writing, and the Formation of American Culture*. Cambridge, MA: Belknap Press of Harvard University Press, 1996.

The Future of Environmental Criticism: Environmental Crisis and Literary Imagination. Malden, MA: Blackwell, 2005.

Burling, William J. "The Theoretical Foundation of Utopian Radical Democracy in Kim Stanley Robinson's Blue Mars." *Utopian Studies* 16, no. 1 (2005): 75–96.

Burns, Tony. *Political Theory, Science Fiction, and Utopian Literature: Ursula K. Le Guin and the Dispossessed*. Lanham, MD: Lexington Books, 2008.

Burrow, Colin. "It's Not Jung's, It's Mine." *London Review of Books*, January 21, 2021. www.lrb.co.uk/the-paper/v43/n02/colin-burrow/it-s-not-jung-s-it-s-mine.

Butler, Judith. *Notes toward a Performative Theory of Assembly*. Cambridge, MA: Harvard University Press, 2015.

Butler, Octavia. "'Devil Girl From Mars': Why I Write Science Fiction." Lecture, MIT, February 19, 1998. http://web.mit.edu/m-i-t/articles/butler_talk_index.html.

Caldwell, Larry W. "Wells, Orwell, and Atwood: (EPI)Logic and Eu/Utopia." *Extrapolation* 33, no. 4 (January 1992): 333–45. https://doi.org/10.3828/extr.1992.33.4.333.

Canavan, Gerry. "Hope, but Not for Us: Ecological Science Fiction and the End of the World in Margaret Atwood's *Oryx and Crake* and *The Year of the Flood*." *Lit: Literature Interpretation Theory* 23, no. 2 (April 1, 2012): 138–59. https://doi.org/10.1080/10436928.2012.676914.

"Introduction: If This Goes On." In *Green Planets: Ecology and Science Fiction*, edited by Gerry Canavan and Kim Stanley Robinson, 1–21. Middletown, CT: Wesleyan University Press, 2014.

"Unless Someone Like You Cares a Whole Awful Lot: Apocalypse as Children's Entertainment." *Science Fiction Film & Television* 10, no. 1 (2017): 81–104. https://doi.org/10/gjmxfq.

Canavan, Gerry, Chan Kit-Sze Amy, Moritz Ingerwersen et al. "Symposium on Science Fiction and the Climate Crisis." *Science Fiction Studies* 45, no. 3 (2018): 420–32.

Canavan, Gerry, Lisa Klarr and Ryan Vu. "Science, Justice, Science Fiction: A Conversation with Kim Stanley Robinson." *Polygraph*, no. 22 (2010): 201–17.

Canavan, Gerry, and Kim Stanley Robinson, eds. *Green Planets: Ecology and Science Fiction*. Middletown, CT: Wesleyan University Press, 2014.

Caramani, Daniele. "Will vs. Reason: The Populist and Technocratic Forms of Political Representation and Their Critique to Party Government." *American Political Science Review* 111, no. 1 (February 2017): 54–67. https://doi.org/10.1017/S0003055416000538.

Carrington, André M. *Speculative Blackness: The Future of Race in Science Fiction*. Minneapolis: University of Minnesota Press, 2016.

Carson, Rachel. *Silent Spring*. Boston: Houghton Mifflin, 2002.

Cassegård, Carl, and Håkan Thörn. "Toward a Postapocalyptic Environmentalism? Responses to Loss and Visions of the Future in Climate Activism." *Environment and Planning E: Nature and Space* 1, no. 4 (December 1, 2018): 561–78. https://doi.org/10.1177/2514848618793331.

Celermajer, Danielle, David Schlosberg, Lauren Rickards et al. "Multispecies Justice: Theories, Challenges, and a Research Agenda for Environmental Politics." *Environmental Politics* 30, no. 1–2 (2021): 119–40. https://doi.org/10/ghd4fd.

Chakrabarty, Dipesh. "Anthropocene Time." *History and Theory* 57, no. 1 (2018): 5–32. https://doi.org/10/ggpmb6.

"The Climate of History: Four Theses." *Critical Inquiry* 35, no. 2 (2009): 197–222. https://doi.org/10.1086/596640.

"Postcolonial Studies and the Challenge of Climate Change." *New Literary History* 43, no. 1 (May 25, 2012): 1–18. https://doi.org/10.1353/nlh.2012.0007.

Chiro, Giovanna Di. "Environmental Justice and the Anthropocene Meme." In *The Oxford Handbook of Environmental Political Theory*, edited by Teena Gabrielson, Cheryl Hall, John M. Meyer and David Schlosberg, 362–83. Oxford: Oxford University Press, 2016. https://doi.org/10.1093/oxfordhb/9780199685271.001.0001.

———. "Welcome to the White (M)Anthropocene? A Feminist-Environmentalist Critique." In *Routledge Handbook of Gender and Environment*, edited by Sherilyn MacGregor, 487–505. Routledge International Handbooks. London: Routledge, 2017.

Cho, K. Daniel. "Tumults of Utopia: Repetition and Revolution in Kim Stanley Robinson's Mars Trilogy." *Cultural Critique* no. 75 (2010): 65–81.

Christoyannopoulos, Alexandre. "The Subversive Potential of Leo Tolstoy's 'Defamiliarisation': A Case Study in Drawing on the Imagination to Denounce Violence." *Critical Review of International Social and Political Philosophy* 22, no. 5 (July 29, 2019): 562–80. https://doi.org/10.1080/13698230.2019.1565700.

Claeys, Gregory. *Dystopia: A Natural History: A Study of Modern Despotism, Its Antecedents, and Its Literary Diffractions*. Oxford: Oxford University Press, 2017.

———. "News from Somewhere: Enhanced Sociability and the Composite Definition of Utopia and Dystopia." *History* 98, no. 330 (April 1, 2013): 145–73. https://doi.org/10.1111/1468-229X.12005.

———. "The Origins of Dystopia: Wells, Huxley and Orwell." In *The Cambridge Companion to Utopian Literature*, edited by Gregory Claeys, 107–32. Cambridge: Cambridge University Press, 2010.

———. "Three Variants on the Concept of Dystopia." In *Dystopia(n) Matters: On the Page, on Screen, on Stage*, edited by Fátima Vieira, 14–18. Newcastle upon Tyne: Cambridge Scholars Publishing, 2013.

Clark, John P. *Between Earth and Empire: From the Necrocene to the Beloved Community*. Oakland, CA: PM Press, 2019.

Clute, John, and John Grant, eds. "Fantasy." In *The Encyclopedia of Fantasy*, 337–39. London: Orbit, 1999.

———. "Fantasyland." In *The Encyclopedia of Fantasy*, 341. London: Orbit, 1999.

Cochrane, Alasdair. *An Introduction to Animals and Political Theory*. New York: Palgrave Macmillan, 2014.

———. *Sentientist Politics: A Theory of Global Inter-species Justice*. Oxford: Oxford University Press, 2018.

Cohen, G. A. *Rescuing Justice and Equality*. Cambridge, MA: Harvard University Press, 2008.

Cohn, Jonathan. "A Tragic Scenario: Narrowly Cast." *Great Transition Initiative*, August 2015. www.greattransition.org/publication/a-tragic-scenario-narrowly-cast.

Cole, Matthew Benjamin. "'At the Heart of Human Politics': Agency and Responsibility in the Contemporary Climate Novel." *Environmental Politics* 31, no. 1 (January 2, 2022): 132–51. https://doi.org/10.1080/09644016 .2021.1902699.

Collier, Simon. "Mercier's Enlightenment Utopia: Progress and Social Ideals." In *The Enlightenment and Its Shadows*, edited by Peter Hulme and Ludmilla Jordanova, 84–100. New York: Routledge, 1990.

Commoner, Barry. *The Closing Circle: Nature, Man, and Technology*. New York: Alfred A. Knopf, 1971.

Conroy, Gemma. "'Ecological Grief' Grips Scientists Witnessing Great Barrier Reef's Decline." *Nature* 573, no. 7774 (September 13, 2019): 318–19. https://doi.org/10/ggrd68.

Cooper, Davina. *Everyday Utopias: The Conceptual Life of Promising Spaces*. Durham, NC: Duke University Press, 2014.

Crist, Eileen. "The Reaches of Freedom: A Response to An Ecomodernist Manifesto." *Environmental Humanities* 7, no. 1 (May 1, 2016): 245–54. https://doi.org/10.1215/22011919-3616452.

Cronon, William. "The Trouble with Wilderness; or, Getting Back to the Wrong Nature." In *Uncommon Ground: Toward Reinventing Nature*, 1st ed., edited by William Cronon, 69–90. New York: W.W. Norton & Co, 1995.

Crutzen, Paul J., and Eugene F. Stoermer. "The 'Anthropocene.'" *Global Change Newsletter* no. 41 (2000): 17–18.

Csicsery-Ronay, Istvan. "Marxist Theory and Science Fiction." In *The Cambridge Companion to Science Fiction*, edited by Edward James and Farah Mendlesohn, 113–24. Cambridge: Cambridge University Press, 2003.

Cuddon, J. A. "Defamiliarization." In *A Dictionary of Literary Terms and Literary Theory*, edited by Matthew Birchwood, Vedrana Velickovic, Martin Dines and Shanyn Fiske, 192–93. Oxford: John Wiley & Sons, 2013.

Czech, Brian. "The Steady State Economy." In *Routledge Handbook of Ecological Economics: Nature and Society*, edited by Clive L. Spash, 467–76. New York: Routledge, 2017.

Dalby, Simon. "Framing the Anthropocene: The Good, the Bad and the Ugly." *The Anthropocene Review* 3, no. 1 (April 1, 2016): 33–51. https://doi.org/10/ggftd8.

D'Alisa, Giacomo, Federico Demaria and Giorgos Kallis, eds. *Degrowth: A Vocabulary for a New Era*. New York: Routledge, 2015.

Danaher, John. *Automation and Utopia: Human Flourishing in a World without Work*. Cambridge, MA: Harvard University Press, 2019.

Danowski, Déborah, and Eduardo Batalha *Viveiros de Castro. The Ends of the World*. Malden, MA: Polity, 2017.

Davies, Jeremy. *The Birth of the Anthropocene*. Oakland: University of California Press, 2016.

Davis, Heather, and Bruno Latour. "Diplomacy in the Face of Gaia: Bruno Latour in conversation with Heather Davis." In *Art in the Anthropocene: Encounters among Aesthetics, Politics, Environments and Epistemologies*, edited by Heather Davis and Etienne Turpin, 43–55. London: Open Humanities Press, 2015.

Davis, Heather, and Zoe Todd. "On the Importance of a Date, or, Decolonizing the Anthropocene." *ACME: An International Journal for Critical Geographies* 16, no. 4 (December 20, 2017): 761–80.

Davis, J. C. *Utopia and the Ideal Society: A Study of English Utopian Writing, 1516–1700*. Cambridge: Cambridge University Press, 1983.

Davis, Janae, Alex A. Moulton, Levi Van Sant and Brian Williams. "Anthropocene, Capitalocene … Plantationocene? A Manifesto for Ecological Justice in an Age of Global Crises." *Geography Compass* 13, no. 5 (2019): e12438. https://doi.org/10.1111/gec3.12438.

Davis, Laurence. "History, Politics, and Utopia: Toward a Synthesis of Social Theory and Practice." In *Existential Utopia: New Perspectives on Utopian Thought*, edited by Patricia I. Vieira and Michael Marder, 127–39. New York: Continuum, 2012.

Davis, Laurence, and Peter Stillman, eds. *The New Utopian Politics of Ursula K. Le Guin's The Dispossessed*. Lanham, MD: Lexington Books, 2005.

Dawkins, Richard. *The Extended Phenotype: The Long Reach of the Gene*. New York: Oxford University Press, 1999.

Delany, Samuel R. "Critical Methods/Speculative Fiction." In *The Jewel-Hinged Jaw: Notes on the Language of Science Fiction*, 17–28. Middletown, CT: Wesleyan University Press, 2009.

    and RMP. "On 'Triton' and Other Matters: An Interview with Samuel R. Delany." *Science Fiction Studies* 17, no. 3 (1990): 295–324.

Delbourgo, James. "No More EasyJet: On Bruno Latour's 'Où Atterrir?'" *Los Angeles Review of Books*, September 6, 2018. https://lareviewofbooks.org/article/no-more-easyjet-on-bruno-latours-ou-atterrir.

Delingpole, James. "James Lovelock on Voting Brexit, 'Wicked' Renewables and Why He Changed His Mind on Climate Change." *The Spectator*, September 9, 2017. www.spectator.co.uk/2017/09/james-lovelock-on-voting-brexit-wicked-renewables-and-why-he-changed-his-mind-on-climate-change.

Dibley, Ben. "'The Shape of Things to Come': Seven Theses on the Anthropocene and Attachment." *Australian Humanities Review* no. 52 (2012): 139–53.

DiMarco, Danette. "Paradise Lost, Paradise Regained: Homo Faber and the Makings of a New Beginning in Oryx and Crake." *Papers on Language and Literature* 41, no. 2 (2005): 170–95.

Doherty, Thomas J., and Susan Clayton. "The Psychological Impacts of Global Climate Change." *American Psychologist* 66, no. 4 (2011): 265–76. https://doi.org/10/bgrths.

Donaldson, Sue, and Will Kymlicka. *Zoopolis: A Political Theory of Animal Rights.* New York: Oxford University Press, 2011.

Donskis, Leonidas. "The End of Utopia?" *Soundings: An Interdisciplinary Journal* 79, no. 1/2 (1996): 197–219.

Downing, Keith, and Peter Zvirinsky. "The Simulated Evolution of Biochemical Guilds: Reconciling Gaia Theory and Natural Selection." *Artificial Life* 5, no. 4 (October 1, 1999): 291–318. https://doi.org/10.1162/106454699568791.

Dryzek, John S., David Downes, Christian Hunold, David Schlosberg and Christian Hunold. *Green States and Social Movements: Environmentalism in the United States, United Kingdom, Germany, and Norway.* New York: Oxford University Press, 2003.

Dryzek, John S., and Jonathan Pickering. *The Politics of the Anthropocene.* New York: Oxford University Press, 2019.

Dunlap, Allison. "Eco-dystopia: Reproduction and Destruction in Margaret Atwood's Oryx and Crake." *Journal of Ecocriticism* 5, no. 1 (December 29, 2012): 1–15.

Durón, Maximilíano. "Taipei Biennial Names Bruno Latour and Martin Guinard-Terrin Curators for 2020 Edition." *ARTnews* (blog), March 7, 2019. www.artnews.com/2019/03/07/taipei-biennial-2020-bruno-latour-martin-guinard-terrin.

Dutreuil, Sébastien. "What Good Are Abstract and What-If Models? Lessons from the Gaïa Hypothesis." *History and Philosophy of the Life Sciences* 36, no. 1 (2014): 16–41.

Duzer, Chet Van. "Hic Sunt Dracones: The Geography and Cartography of Monsters." In *The Ashgate Research Companion to Monsters and the Monstrous,* edited by Asa Simon Mittman and Peter Dendle, 387–435. Burlington: Ashgate, 2012.

Eco, Umberto. *On the Shoulders of Giants.* Translated by Alastair McEwen. Cambridge, MA: Belknap Press of Harvard University Press, 2019.

The Economist. "A Man-Made World." *The Economist,* May 26, 2011. www.economist.com/briefing/2011/05/26/a-man-made-world.

Ehrlich, Paul R. *The Population Bomb.* 1968. New York: Ballantine Books, 1989.

Elahi, Shirin. "Here Be Dragons ... Exploring the 'Unknown Unknowns.'" *Futures,* Special Issue: Postnormal Times, 43, no. 2 (March 1, 2011): 196–201. https://doi.org/10/c6nxfb.

Ellis, Erle C. *Anthropocene: A Very Short Introduction.* New York: Oxford University Press, 2018.

"Neither Good Nor Bad." *New York Times*, May 23, 2011. www.nytimes.com/roomfordebate/2011/05/19/the-age-of-anthropocene-should-we-worry/neither-good-nor-bad.

Engels, Friedrich. *Socialism, Utopian and Scientific.* Translated by Edward B. Aveling. *Chicago: Charles H. Kerr & Company*, 1908.

Estes, Nick. "A Red Deal." *Jacobin*, June 8, 2019. https://jacobinmag.com/2019/08/red-deal-green-new-deal-ecosocialism-decolonization-indigenous-resistance-environment.

Estlund, David M. "Utopophobia." *Philosophy & Public Affairs* 42, no. 2 (2014): 113–34. https://doi.org/10.1111/papa.12031.

——. *Utopophobia: On the Limits (If Any) of Political Philosophy.* Princeton, NJ: Princeton University Press, 2020.

Evans, Rebecca M. "The Best of Times, the Worst of Times, the End of Times? The Uses and Abuses of Environmental Apocalypse." *ASAP/Journal* 3, no. 3 (December 21, 2018): 501–22. https://doi.org/10.1353/asa.2018.0037.

Evans, Richard J. *Eric Hobsbawm: A Life in History.* New York: Oxford University Press, 2019.

Falcon-Lang, Howard. "Anthropocene: Have Humans Created a New Geological Age?," May 11, 2011. www.bbc.com/news/science-environment-13335683.

Farrier, David. *Footprints: In Search of Future Fossils.* London: Fourth Estate, 2020.

Feder, Helena, and Kim Stanley Robinson. "The Realism of Our Time: Interview with Kim Stanley Robinson." *Radical Philosophy*, February 2018. www.radicalphilosophy.com/interview/the-realism-of-our-time.

Ferwerda, Susanne. *"Narrating the Anthropocene: Threading Contemporary Feminist Theory and Fiction in a Human-Dominated World."* MA thesis, Utrecht University, 2016. https://dspace.library.uu.nl/handle/1874/330543.

Fischbach, Franck. "Marx and Utopia." In *Political Uses of Utopia: New Marxist, Anarchist, and Radical Democratic Perspectives*, edited by S. D. Chrostowska and James D. Ingram, 117–25. New York: Columbia University Press, 2016. www.jstor.org/stable/10.7312/chro17958.7.

Fisher, Mark. *Capitalist Realism: Is There No Alternative?* Winchester: Zero Books, 2009.

Fiskio, Janet. "Apocalypse and Ecotopia: Narratives in Global Climate Change Discourse." *Race, Gender & Class* 19, no. 1/2 (2012): 12–36.

Fitting, Peter. "The Concept of Utopia in the Work of Fredric Jameson." *Utopian Studies* 9, no. 2 (1998): 8–17.

——. "Utopias beyond Our Ideals: The Dilemma of the Right-Wing Utopia." *Utopian Studies* 2, no. 1/2 (1991): 95–109.

Flikschuh, Katrin, and Lea Ypi, eds. *Kant and Colonialism: Historical and Critical Perspectives.* Oxford: Oxford University Press, 2014.

Flood, Alison. "Hugo Award Nominees Withdraw amid 'Puppygate' Storm." *The Guardian*, April 17, 2015. www.theguardian.com/books/2015/apr/17/hugo-award-nominees-withdraw-amid-puppygate-storm.

"N. K. Jemisin: 'It's Easier to Get a Book Set in Black Africa Published If You're White.'" *The Guardian*, May 2, 2020. www.theguardian.com/books/2020/may/02/nk-jemisin-its-easier-to-get-a-book-set-in-black-africa-published-if-youre-white.

"N. K. Jemisin Leads 2020 Round of MacArthur 'Genius Grants.'" *The Guardian*, October 7, 2020. www.theguardian.com/books/2020/oct/07/nk-jemisin-leads-2020-round-of-macarthur-genius-grants.

Flores, Fernando, and B. Scot Rousse. "Ecological Finitude as Ontological Finitude: Radical Hope in the Anthropocene." *Telos* 2016, no. 177 (December 21, 2016): 127–43. https://doi.org/10/gh2d44.

Forrester, Katrina. "Hope and Memory in the Thought of Judith Shklar." *Modern Intellectual History* 8, no. 3 (November 2011): 591–620. https://doi.org/10.1017/S1479244311000369.

Foster, John Bellamy. "The Long Ecological Revolution." *Monthly Review*, November 1, 2017. https://monthlyreview.org/2017/11/01/the-long-ecological-revolution.

Franko, Carol. "The Density of Utopian Destiny in Robinson's Red Mars." *Extrapolation* 38, no. 1 (1997): 57–65. https://doi.org/10.3828/extr.1997.38.1.57.

"Kim Stanley Robinson: Mars Trilogy." In *A Companion to Science Fiction*, edited by David Seed, 544–55. Oxford: Blackwell, 2008.

"Working the 'In-Between': Kim Stanley Robinson's Utopian Fiction." *Science Fiction Studies* 21, no. 2 (1994): 191–211.

Frase, Peter. "By Any Means Necessary." *Jacobin*, 2017. www.jacobinmag.com/2017/08/by-any-means-necessary.

Four Futures: Visions of the World after Capitalism. London: Verso, 2016.

Freedman, Carl. *Critical Theory and Science Fiction*. Middletown, CT: Wesleyan University Press, 2000.

"Marxism, Cinema and Some Dialectics of Science Fiction and Film Noir." In *Red Planets: Marxism and Science Fiction*, edited by Mark Bould and China Miéville, 66–82. Middletown, CT: Wesleyan University Press, 2009.

Fremaux, Anne, and John Barry. "The 'Good Anthropocene' and Green Political Theory: Rethinking Environmentalism, Resisting Eco-modernism." In *Anthropocene Encounters: New Directions in Green Political Thinking*, edited by Frank Biermann and Eva Lövbrand, 171–90. Cambridge: Cambridge University Press, 2019. https://doi.org/10.1017/9781108646673.009.

Fukuyama, Francis. *The End of History and the Last Man*. New York: Free Press, 2006.

Margaret Atwood. "Full Bibliography." Accessed November 5, 2019. http://margaretatwood.ca/full-bibliography-2.

Fung, Archon, and Erik Olin Wright. *Deepening Democracy: Institutional Innovations in Empowered Participatory Governance*. The Real Utopias Project 4. London: Verso, 2003.

Gaard, Greta. "Ecofeminism Revisited: Rejecting Essentialism and Re-placing Species in a Material Feminist Environmentalism." *Feminist Formations* 23, no. 2 (August 20, 2011): 26–53. https://doi.org/10/ggjr63.

Galaz, Victor. "Time and Politics in the Anthropocene: Too Fast, Too Slow?" In *Anthropocene Encounters: New Directions in Green Political Thinking*, edited by Frank Biermann and Eva Lövbrand, 109–27. Cambridge: Cambridge University Press, 2019. https://doi.org/10.1017/9781108646673.006.

Gardiner, Stephen M. "Is 'Arming the Future' with Geoengineering Really the Lesser Evil? Some Doubts about the Ethics of Intentionally Manipulating the Climate System." In *Climate Ethics: Essential Readings*, edited by Stephen M. Gardiner, Simon Caney, Dale Jamieson and Henry Shue, 284–312. Oxford: Oxford University Press, 2010.

Garforth, Lisa. "Book Review Symposium: An Inquiry into Modes of Existence: An Anthropology of the Moderns, by Bruno Latour." *Global Discourse* 6, no. 1–2 (January 2, 2016): 140–43. https://doi.org/10.1080/23269995.2014.933055.

"Environmental Futures, Now and Then: Crisis, Systems Modeling, and Speculative Fiction." *Osiris* 34, no. 1 (June 2019): 238–57. https://doi.org/10/gh24tm.

Green Utopias: Environmental Hope before and after Nature. Cambridge: Polity, 2018.

Garrard, Greg. *Ecocriticism*. New York: Routledge, 2012.

Gemes, Ken. "Life's Perspectives." In *The Oxford Handbook of Nietzsche*, edited by Ken Gemes and John Richardson, 553–75. New York: Oxford University Press, 2013.

Geoghegan, Vincent. *Utopianism and Marxism*. New York: Peter Lang, 2008.

The Geological Society of America. "GSA Geologic Time Scale (v. 5.0)," 2018. www.geosociety.org/GSA/Education_Careers/Geologic_Time_Scale/GSA/timescale/home.aspx.

Geronimus, Arline T., Margaret Hicken, Danya Keene and John Bound. "'Weathering' and Age Patterns of Allostatic Load Scores among Blacks and Whites in the United States." *American Journal of Public Health* 96, no. 5 (2006): 826–33. https://doi.org/10/dr55vz.

Gertenbach, Lars, and Henning Laux. *Zur Aktualität von Bruno Latour: Einführung in sein Werk*. Wiesbaden: Springer VS, 2019.

Geus, Marius de. *Ecological Utopias: Envisioning the Sustainable Society.* Utrecht: International Books, 1999.

Geuss, Raymond. "Genealogy as Critique." *European Journal of Philosophy* 10, no. 2 (2002): 209–15. https://doi.org/10.1111/1468-0378.00157.

"*The Metaphysical Need and the Utopian Impulse.*" In *Actions, Reasons and Reason,* edited by Marco Iorio and Ralf Stoecker, 141–60. Berlin: De Gruyter, 2015.

Philosophy and Real Politics. Princeton, NJ: Princeton University Press, 2008.

"Realism and the Relativity of Judgement." *International Relations* 29, no. 1 (March 1, 2015): 3–22. https://doi.org/10.1177/0047117815569517.

"Realism, Wishful Thinking, Utopia." In *Political Uses of Utopia: New Marxist, Anarchist, and Radical Democratic Perspectives,* edited by S. D. Chrostowska and James D. Ingram, 233–47. New York: Columbia University Press, 2017.

Ghosh, Amitav. *The Great Derangement: Climate Change and the Unthinkable.* E-Book. London: Penguin, 2016.

Gibbons, John. "The Uninhabitable Earth Review: Astonishingly Reductive View of Impending Disaster." *The Irish Times,* February 23, 2019. www.irishtimes .com/culture/books/the-uninhabitable-earth-review-astonishingly-reduc tive-view-of-impending-disaster-1.3791418.

Ginzburg, Carlo. "Making Things Strange: The Prehistory of a Literary Device." *Representations* no. 56 (1996): 8–28. https://doi.org/10.2307/2928705.

Goodwin, Barbara. "Utopia Defended against the Liberals." *Political Studies* 28, no. 3 (1980): 384–400. https://doi.org/10.1111/j.1467-9248.1980.tb00476.x.

Gordon, Lewis R., Annie Menzel, George Shulman and Jasmine Syedullah. "Afro Pessimism." *Contemporary Political Theory* 17, no. 1 (2018): 105–37.

Graeber, David. *The Democracy Project: A History, a Crisis, a Movement.* New York: Spiegel & Grau, 2013.

Grandin, Greg. *The End of the Myth: From the Frontier to the Wall in the Mind of America.* New York: Metropolitan Books, 2019.

Gray, John. *Black Mass: Apocalyptic Religion and the Death of Utopia.* New York: Farrar Straus and Giroux, 2007.

"Unenlightened Thinking: Steven Pinker's Embarrassing New Book Is a Feeble Sermon for Rattled Liberals." *New Statesman,* February 22, 2018. www .newstatesman.com/culture/books/2018/02/unenlightened-thinking-steven-pinker-s-embarrassing-new-book-feeble-sermon.

Gribbin, John, and Mary Gribbin. *He Knew He Was Right: The Irrepressible Life of James Lovelock.* London: Penguin, 2009.

Grill, Genese. *The World as Metaphor in Robert Musil's The Man without Qualities: Possibility as Reality.* Rochester, NY: Camden House, 2012.

Grusin, Richard A., ed. *After Extinction.* Minneapolis: University of Minnesota Press, 2018.

Gunnell, John G. "Leaving Everything as It Is: Political Inquiry after Wittgenstein." *Contemporary Political Theory* 12, no. 2 (2013): 80–101. https://doi.org/10.1057/cpt.2012.17.

Hämäläinen, Nora. "Sophie, Antigone, Elizabeth – Rethinking Ethics by Reading Literature." In *Fictional Characters, Real Problems: The Search for Ethical Content in Literature*, edited by Garry L. Hagberg, 15–30. New York: Oxford University Press, 2016.

Hamilton, Clive. "The Theodicy of the 'Good Anthropocene.'" *Environmental Humanities* 7, no. 1 (2016): 233–38. https://doi.org/10.1215/22011919-3616434.

Hammond, Marit. "Imagination and Critique in Environmental Politics." *Environmental Politics* 30, no. 1–2 (February 23, 2022): 285–305. https://doi.org/10.1080/09644016.2021.1880062.

Hamner, Everett. "Angry Optimism: Climate Disaster and Restoration in Kim Stanley Robinson's Alternate Futures." In *The Palgrave Handbook of Twentieth and Twenty-First Century Literature and Science*, edited by Neel Ahuja, Monique Allewaert, Lindsey Andrews et al., 449–67. Palgrave Handbooks of Literature and Science. Cham: Springer International Publishing, 2020. https://doi.org/10.1007/978-3-030-48244-2_25.

"Odd Couples, Carbon Coins, and Narrative Scopes: An Interview with Kim Stanley Robinson." *Los Angeles Review of Books.* Accessed December 9, 2020. www.lareviewofbooks.org/article/odd-couples-carbon-coins-and-narrative-scopes-an-interview-with-kim-stanley-robinson.

Haran, Joan. "Instantiating Imaginactivism: Le Guin's *The Dispossessed as Inspiration.*" *Ada: A Journal of Gender, New Media, and Technology* no. 12 (October 6, 2017). https://adanewmedia.org/2017/10/issue12-haran.

"Redefining Hope as Praxis." *Journal for Cultural Research* 14, no. 4 (October 1, 2010): 393–408. https://doi.org/10/cmmp4q.

"Re-visioning Feminist Futures: Literature as Social Theory." PhD thesis, University of Warwick, 2003. http://wrap.warwick.ac.uk/1239/1/WRAP_THESIS_Haran_2003.pdf.

Haraway, Donna J. *Staying with the Trouble: Making Kin in the Chthulucene.* Durham, NC: Duke University Press, 2016.

When Species Meet. Minneapolis: University of Minnesota Press, 2008.

Hard, Robin. *The Routledge Handbook of Greek Mythology.* New York: Routledge, 2004.

Harland, Paul W. "Ecological Grief and Therapeutic Storytelling in Margaret Atwood's Maddaddam Trilogy." *ISLE: Interdisciplinary Studies in Literature and Environment* 23, no. 3 (November 1, 2016): 583–602. https://doi.org/10.1093/isle/isw001.

Harman, Graham. *Bruno Latour: Reassembling the Political.* Modern European Thinkers. London: Pluto Press, 2014.

Harrabin, Roger. "Gaia Creator Rows Back on Climate," May 8, 2012. www.bbc .com/news/science-environment-17988492.

Hart, Heidi. *Music and the Environment in Dystopian Narrative: Sounding the Disaster.* Cham: Springer International Publishing, 2018.

Hartman, Saidiya. *Lose Your Mother: A Journey along the Atlantic Slave Route.* New York: Farrar, Straus and Giroux, 2013.

Hausknost, Daniel. "Degrowth and Democracy." In *Routledge Handbook of Ecological Economics: Nature and Society,* edited by Clive L. Spash, 457–66. New York: Routledge, 2017.

He, Qiang, and Brian R. Silliman. "Climate Change, Human Impacts, and Coastal Ecosystems in the Anthropocene." *Current Biology* 29, no. 19 (October 7, 2019): R1021–35. https://doi.org/10/ggtkh8.

Heath, Joseph, and Andrew Potter. *The Rebel Sell: How the Counterculture Became Consumer Culture.* Chichester: Capstone, 2006.

Heathcote, Edwin. "Rem Koolhaas's Countryside at the Guggenheim Remakes Rural Life." *Financial Times,* February 21, 2020. www.ft.com/content/ fc136dba-530b-11ea-90ad-25e377c0ee1f.

Heer, Jeet. "The New Utopians." *The New Republic,* November 10, 2015. https:// newrepublic.com/article/123217/new-utopians.

Heinlein, Robert A. *Farnham's Freehold.* New York: Baen, 2011.

Heise, Ursula. "Climate Stories: Review of Amitav Ghosh's 'The Great Derangement.'" *Boundary 2* (blog), February 19, 2018. www.boundary2 .org/2018/02/ursula-k-heise-climate-stories-review-of-amitav-ghoshs-the- great-derangement.

Imagining Extinction: The Cultural Meanings of Endangered Species. Chicago: University of Chicago Press, 2018.

Sense of Place and Sense of Planet: The Environmental Imagination of the Global. Oxford: Oxford University Press, 2010.

Helmling, Steven. *The Success and Failure of Fredric Jameson: Writing, the Sublime, and the Dialectic of Critique.* Albany: State University of New York Press, 2001.

Hengen, Shannon. "Margaret Atwood and Environmentalism." In *The Cambridge Companion to Margaret Atwood,* edited by Coral Ann Howells, 72–85. New York: Cambridge University Press, 2006.

Hepplewhite, Jim. "The Stone Sky by N. K. Jemisin." Matador Review. Accessed April 9, 2019. www.matadorreview.com/the-stone-sky.

Heringman, Noah. "Deep Time at the Dawn of the Anthropocene." *Representations* 129, no. 1 (February 1, 2015): 56–85. https://doi.org/10/ ggffs3.

Hesiod. *Theogony and Works and Days.* Translated by Catherine Schlegel and Henry Weinfield. Ann Arbor: University of Michigan Press, 2006.

Hettinger, Ned. "Naturalness, Wild-Animal Suffering, and Palmer on Laissez-Faire." *Les Ateliers de l'éthique* 13, no. 1 (2018): 65–84. https://doi.org/10/gj8jmj.

Hickman, Leo. "James Lovelock: Humans Are Too Stupid to Prevent Climate Change." *The Guardian*, March 29, 2010. www.theguardian.com/science/ 2010/mar/29/james-lovelock-climate-change.

Hicks, Heather J. *Post-apocalyptic Novel in the Twenty-First Century: Modernity beyond Salvage.* Houndmills: Palgrave MacMillan, 2017.

Hill Collins, Patricia. *Black Feminist Thought: Knowledge, Consciousness, and the Politics of Empowerment.* New York: Routledge, 2000.

Hine, Dougald, Nick Hunt, Paul Kingsnorth and Adrienne Odasso. "Editorial: Post-cautionary Tales." *Dark Mountain*, 2013.

Hoggett, Paul. "Climate Change and the Apocalyptic Imagination." *Psychoanalysis, Culture & Society* 16, no. 3 (September 1, 2011): 261–75. https://doi.org/10.1057/pcs.2011.1.

Holden, Emily "Home." Accessed September 24, 2019. https://dark-mountain.net.

"What Is the Green New Deal and Is It Technically Possible?" *The Guardian*, December 29, 2018. www.theguardian.com/environment/2018/dec/29/ green-new-deal-plans-proposal-ocasio-cortez-sunrise-movement.

Horkheimer, Max, and Theodor W. Adorno. *Dialectic of Enlightenment: Philosophical Fragments*, edited by Gunzelin Schmid Noerr. Translated by Edmund Jephcott. Stanford, CA: Stanford University Press, 2002.

Howells, Coral Ann. "Margaret Atwood's Dystopian Visions: *The Handmaid's Tale* and *Oryx and Crake*." In *The Cambridge Companion to Margaret Atwood*, edited by Coral Ann Howells, 161–75. New York: Cambridge University Press, 2006.

Howkins, Adrian. "Emerging from the Shadow of Science: Challenges and Opportunities for Antarctic History." In *Antarctica and the Humanities*, edited by Peder Roberts, Lize-Marié Van der Watt and Adrian Howkins, 251–72. Palgrave Studies in the History of Science and Technology. London: Palgrave Macmillan, 2016.

Huebner, Stefan. "Tackling Climate Change, Air Pollution, and Ecosystem Destruction: How US-Japanese Ocean Industrialization and the Metabolist Movement's Global Legacy Shaped Environmental Thought (circa 1950s– Present)." *Environmental History* 25, no. 1 (January 1, 2020): 35–61. https:// doi.org/10/ggk976.

Hulme, Mike. *Can Science Fix Climate Change? A Case against Climate Engineering.* E-Book. New Human Frontiers Series. Cambridge: Polity Press, 2014.

"Reducing the Future to Climate: A Story of Climate Determinism and Reductionism." *Osiris* 26, no. 1 (January 1, 2011): 245–66. https://doi.org/ 10/bxc7rc.

Review of *Review of The Collapse of Western Civilization: A View from the Future.* New York: Columbia University Press, 2014, by Naomi Oreskes and Erik M. Conway. *H-HistGeog*, November 2014. https://networks.h-net.org/node/5280/reviews/51812/hulme-oreskes-and-conway-collapse-western-civilization-view-future.

Hurley, Jessica, and N. K. Jemisin. "An Apocalypse Is a Relative Thing: An Interview with N. K. Jemisin." *ASAP/Journal* 3, no. 3 (December 21, 2018): 467–77. https://doi.org/10.1353/asa.2018.0035.

Huxley, Aldous. *Brave New World.* New York: Penguin Books, 2010.

———. *Island.* New York: Harper & Row, 1993.

Iles, Alastair. "Repairing the Broken Earth: N. K. Jemisin on Race and Environment in Transitions." *Elementa: Science of the Anthropocene* 7, no. 1 (July 11, 2019): 26. https://doi.org/10/ghf4k5.

Ingersoll, Earl. "Margaret Atwood's 'The Handmaid's Tale': Echoes of Orwell." *Journal of the Fantastic in the Arts* 5, no. 4 (1993): 64–72.

Ingwersen, Moritz. "Geological Insurrections: Politics of Planetary Weirding from China Miéville to N. K. Jemisin." In *Spaces and Fictions of the Weird and the Fantastic: Ecologies, Geographies, Oddities,* edited by Julius Greve and Florian Zappe, 73–92. Geocriticism and Spatial Literary Studies. Cham: Springer International Publishing, 20319. https://doi.org/10.1007/978-3-030-28116-8_6.

Isenhour, Cindy. "Unearthing Human Progress? Ecomodernism and Contrasting Definitions of Technological Progress in the Anthropocene." *Economic Anthropology* 3, no. 2 (2016): 315–28. https://doi.org/10/ggk977.

Jackson, Rosemary. *Fantasy: The Literature of Subversion.* London: Routledge, 1998.

Jacobs, Struan, and Ian Tregenza. "Rationalism and Tradition: The Popper–Oakeshott Conversation." *European Journal of Political Theory* 13, no. 1 (January 1, 2014): 3–24. https://doi.org/10/gjg45x.

Jacoby, Russell. *Picture Imperfect: Utopian Thought for an Anti-utopian Age.* New York: Columbia University Press, 2005.

Jaeggi, Rahel. *Critique of Forms of Life.* E-Book. Cambridge, MA: The Belknap Press of Harvard University Press, 2018.

———. "Was ist Ideologiekritik?" In *Was ist Kritik?,* edited by Rahel Jaeggi and Tilo Wesche, 266–95. Frankfurt am Main: Suhrkamp, 2019.

James, Edward. "Tolkien, Lewis and the Explosion of Genre Fantasy." In *The Cambridge Companion to Fantasy Literature,* edited by Edward James and Farah Mendlesohn, 62–78. Cambridge: Cambridge University Press, 2014. https://doi.org/10.1017/CCOL9780521429597.007.

———. "Yellow, Black, Metal, and Tentacled: The Race Question in American Science Fiction." In *Black and Brown Planets: The Politics of Race in Science Fiction,* edited by Isiah Lavender III, 199–222. Jackson: University Press of Mississippi, 2014.

Jameson, Fredric. *Archaeologies of the Future: The Desire Called Utopia and Other Science Brecht and Method.* New York: Verso, 2000.

———. "'If I Find One Good City I Will Spare the Man': Realism and Utopia in Kim Stanley Robinson's Mars Trilogy." In *Learning from Other Worlds: Estrangement, Cognition and the Politics of Science Fiction and Utopia,* edited by Patrick Parrinder, 208–32. Liverpool Science Fiction Texts and Studies 17. Liverpool: Liverpool University Press, 2000.

———. *Late Marxism: Adorno, or, The Persistence of the Dialectic.* Radical Thinkers 18. London: Verso, 2007.

———. *Marxism and Form: Twentieth-Century Dialectical Theories of Literature.* Princeton, NJ: Princeton University Press, 1972.

———. "A New Reading of Capital." *Mediations: Journal of the Marxist Literary Group* 25, no. 1 (2010): 5–14.

———. "Of Islands and Trenches: Neutralization and the Production of Utopian Discourse." *Diacritics* 7, no. 2 (Summer 1977): 2–21.

———. "Progress versus Utopia; Or, Can We Imagine the Future?" *Science Fiction Studies* 9, no. 2 (1982): 147–58.

———. "Utopia and Failure." *Politics and Culture* no. 2 (2000). https://politicsandculture.org/2010/08/10/utopia-and-failure-by-fredric-jameson-2.

———. "World-Reduction in Le Guin: The Emergence of Utopian Narrative." *Science Fiction Studies* 2, no. 3 (1975): 221–30.

Jasanoff, Sheila. "Genealogies of STS." *Social Studies of Science* 42, no. 3 (June 2012): 435–41. https://doi.org/10.1177/0306312712440174.

Jeauneau, Edouard. "'Nani gigantum humeris insidentes': Essai d'interprétation de Bernard de Chartres." *Vivarium* 5 (1967): 79–99. https://doi.org/10/bsphz4.

Jemisin, N. K. *The Broken Kingdoms.* Inheritance Trilogy 2. New York: Orbit, 2010.

———. "The Effluent Machine." In *Steam Powered: Lesbian Steampunk Stories,* edited by JoSelle Vanderhooft, 8–45. Round Rock: Torquere Press, 2011.

———. *The Fifth Season.* E-Book. Broken Earth Trilogy 1. New York: Orbit, 2015.

———. *How Long' til Black Future Month?* New York: Orbit, 2018.

———. *The Hundred Thousand Kingdoms.* Inheritance Trilogy 1. New York: Orbit, 2010.

———. *The Kingdom of Gods.* Inheritance Trilogy 3. New York: Orbit, 2012.

———. *The Stone Sky.* E-Book. Broken Earth Trilogy 3. New York: Orbit, 2017.

———. "Why I Talk So Damn Much about Non-writing Stuff." *Epiphany 2.0* (blog), October 13, 2014. https://nkjemisin.com/2014/10/why-i-talk-so-damn-much-about-non-writing-stuff.

Jendrysik, Mark S. "Back to the Garden: New Visions of Posthuman Futures." *Utopian Studies* 22, no. 1 (2011): 34–51. https://doi.org/10.5325/utopianstudies.22.1.0034.

Jensen, Tim. *Ecologies of Guilt in Environmental Rhetorics.* Cham: Palgrave, 2019.

Jergenson, Casey. "Negative Utopianism and Catastrophe in Margaret Atwood's MaddAddam Trilogy." *Utopian Studies* 30, no. 3 (2019): 486–504. https://doi.org/10/ggfs93.

Jestrovic, Silvija. *Theatre of Estrangement: Theory, Practice, Ideology.* German and European Studies. Toronto: University of Toronto Press, 2006.

Johns-Putra, Adeline. *Climate Change and the Contemporary Novel.* Cambridge: Cambridge University Press, 2019. https://doi.org/10.1017/9781108610162.

——— "Ecocriticism, Genre, and Climate Change: Reading the Utopian Vision of Kim Stanley Robinson's Science in the Capital Trilogy." *English Studies* 91, no. 7 (November 1, 2010): 744–60. https://doi.org/10.1080/0013838X.2010.518043.

Jørgensen, Dolly. "Rethinking Rewilding." *Geoforum* 65 (October 1, 2015): 482–88. https://doi.org/10.1016/j.geoforum.2014.11.016.

Kant, Immanuel. "Idea for a Universal History from a Cosmopolitan Perspective." In *Toward Perpetual Peace and Other Writings on Politics, Peace, and History,* edited by Pauline Kleingeld. Translated by David L. Colclasure, 3–16. New Haven, CT: Yale University Press, 2006.

Katti, Christian S. G. "Mediating Political 'Things,' and the Forked Tongue of Modern Culture: A Conversation with Bruno Latour." *Art Journal* 65, no. 1 (March 1, 2006): 94–115. https://doi.org/10/ghndz4.

Kaufman, Alexander C. "The King of Climate Fiction Makes the Left's Case for Geoengineering." *Huffington Post,* July 28, 2018. www.huffpost.com/entry/climate-geoengineering-kim-stanley-robinson_n_5b4e54bde4b0de86f487b0b9.

Kearse, Stephen. "The Worldmaking of N. K. Jemisin," January 25, 2021. www.thenation.com/article/culture/nk-jemisin-city-we-become-review.

Kellner, Douglas, and Sean Homer, eds. *Fredric Jameson: A Critical Reader.* Houndmills: Palgrave Macmillan, 2004.

Kelly, Duncan. *Politics and the Anthropocene.* Cambridge: Polity, 2019.

Kermode, Frank. *The Sense of an Ending: Studies in the Theory of Fiction: With a New Epilogue.* Oxford: Oxford University Press, 2000.

Ketterer, David. "Margaret Atwood's 'The Handmaid's Tale': A Contextual Dystopia." *Science Fiction Studies* 16, no. 2 (1989): 209–17.

Kilgore, De Witt Douglas. "Making Huckleberries: Reforming Science and Whiteness in Science in the Capital." *Configurations* 20, no. 1 (2012): 89–108. https://doi.org/10.1353/con.2012.0010.

King, Darryn. "Steven Pinker on the Past, Present, and Future of Optimism." *Medium,* January 14, 2019. https://medium.com/s/2069/steven-pinker-on-the-past-present-and-future-of-optimism-f362398c604b.

Kingsnorth, Paul. *Confessions of a Recovering Environmentalist.* London: Faber & Faber, 2017.

———. "Dark Ecology." *Orion Magazine,* 2013. https://orionmagazine.org/article/dark-ecology.

———. "Why I Stopped Believing in Environmentalism and Started the Dark Mountain Project." *The Guardian,* April 29, 2010. www.theguardian.com/environment/2010/apr/29/environmentalism-dark-mountain-project.

Kingsnorth, Paul, and Dougald Hine. "Editorial: It's the End of the World as We Know It (and We Feel Fine)." *Dark Mountain,* 2010.

———. "Uncivilisation: Dark Mountain Manifesto," 2009. https://dark-mountain.net/about/manifesto.

Kingsnorth, Paul, and George Monbiot. "Is There Any Point in Fighting to Stave off Industrial Apocalypse?" *The Guardian,* August 17, 2009. www.theguardian.com/commentisfree/cif-green/2009/aug/17/environment-climate-change.

Kinna, Ruth. "Utopianism and Prefiguration." In *Political Uses of Utopia: New Marxist, Anarchist, and Radical Democratic Perspectives,* edited by S. D. Chrostowska and James D. Ingram, 198–215. New York: Columbia University Press, 2017.

Kirkpatrick, Jennet. *The Virtues of Exit: On Resistance and Quitting Politics.* Chapel Hill: University of North Carolina Press, 2017.

Klein, Naomi. *On Fire: The Burning Case for a Green New Deal.* E-Book. Toronto: Knopf Canada, 2019.

Knapp, Liza. "The Development of Style and Theme in Tolstoy." In *The Cambridge Companion to Tolstoy,* edited by Donna Tussing Orwin, 161–75. New York: Cambridge University Press, 2002.

Kołakowski, Leszek. "The Death of Utopia Reconsidered." In *Modernity on Endless Trial,* 131–45. Chicago: University of Chicago Press, 1990.

Kolbert, Elizabeth. *The Sixth Extinction: An Unnatural History.* New York: Henry Holt, 2014.

Kolinjivadi, Vijay. "The Enlightenment of Steven Pinker: Eco-modernism as Rationalizing the Arrogance (and Violence) of Empire." *ENTITLE Blog: A Collaborative Writing Project on Political Ecology* (blog), May 31, 2018. https://entitleblog.org/2018/05/31/the-enlightenment-of-steven-pinker-eco-modernism-as-rationalizing-the-arrogance-and-violence-of-empire.

Koselleck, Reinhart. "The Temporalization of Utopia." In *The Practice of Conceptual History: Timing History, Spacing Concepts,* 84–99. Cultural Memory in the Present. Stanford, CA: Stanford University Press, 2002.

Kozakavich, Stacy C., and Michael S. Nassaney. *The Archaeology of Utopian and Intentional Communities.* Gainesville: University Press of Florida, 2018.

Kreider, Tim. "Our Greatest Political Novelist?" *New Yorker,* December 12, 2013. www.newyorker.com/books/page-turner/our-greatest-political-novelist.

Kriss, Sam, and Ellie Mae O'Hagan. "Tropical Depressions: On Climate Change and Human Futilitarianism." *The Baffler,* September 2017. https://thebaffler .com/salvos/tropical-depressions-kriss-ohagan.

Kumar, Krishan. *Utopia and Anti-utopia in Modern Times.* Oxford: Basil Blackwell, 1991.

Utopianism. Buckingham: Open University Press, 1991.

Kunkel, Benjamin. *Utopia or Bust: A Guide to the Present Crisis.* New York: Verso, 2014.

Laclau, Ernesto. *On Populist Reason.* New York: Verso, 2005.

Lal, Rattan. "Carbon Sequestration." *Philosophical Transactions of the Royal Society B: Biological Sciences* 363, no. 1492 (February 27, 2008): 815–30. https://doi .org/10.1098/rstb.2007.2185.

Lampitt R. S., Achterberg E. P., Anderson T. R., Hughes et al. "Ocean Fertilization: A Potential Means of Geoengineering?" *Philosophical Transactions of the Royal Society A: Mathematical, Physical and Engineering Sciences* 366, no. 1882 (November 13, 2008): 3919–45. https://doi.org/10 .1098/rsta.2008.0139.

Lang, Anthony F. *International Political Theory: An Introduction.* New York: Palgrave MacMillan, 2015.

Lara, María Pía. "Reflective Judgment as World Disclosure." *Philosophy & Social Criticism* 34, no. 1–2 (January 1, 2008): 83–100. https://doi.org/10.1177/ 0191453707084275.

Larsen, David. "In the Interests of Frankness: An Interview with Kim Stanley Robinson." *Leaflemming* (blog), March 9, 2016. https://leaflemming .wordpress.com/2016/03/09/in-the-interests-of-frankness-an-interview-with-kim-stanley-robinson.

Latour, Bruno. "Agency at the Time of the Anthropocene." *New Literary History* 45, no. 1 (April 23, 2014): 1–18. https://doi.org/10.1353/nlh.2014.0003.

"Bruno Latour Tracks Down Gaia." *Los Angeles Review of Books,* July 3, 2018. https://lareviewofbooks.org/article/bruno-latour-tracks-down-gaia.

Down to Earth: Politics in the New Climatic Regime. E-Book. Cambridge: Polity Press, 2018.

Facing Gaia: Eight Lectures on the New Climatic Regime. E-Book. Cambridge: Polity, 2017.

An Inquiry into Modes of Existence: An Anthropology of the Moderns. Cambridge, MA: Harvard University Press, 2013.

"Is Re-modernization Occurring – And If So, How to Prove It? A Commentary on Ulrich Beck." *Theory, Culture & Society* 20, no. 2 (April 1, 2003): 35–48. https://doi.org/10.1177/0263276403020002002.

"On Actor-Network Theory: A Few Clarifications." *Soziale Welt* 47, no. 4 (1996): 369–81.

Politics of Nature: How to Bring the Sciences into Democracy. Cambridge, MA: Harvard University Press, 2004.

Reassembling the Social: An Introduction to Actor-Network-Theory. New York: Oxford University Press, 2005.

"Telling Friends from Foes in the Time of the Anthropocene." In *The Anthropocene and the Global Environmental Crisis: Rethinking Modernity in a New Epoch*, edited by Clive Hamilton, Christophe Bonneuil and François Gemenne, 145–55. New York: Routledge, 2015.

We Have Never Been Modern. Cambridge, MA: Harvard University Press, 1993.

"Why Gaia Is Not a God of Totality." *Theory, Culture & Society* 34, no. 2–3 (May 1, 2017): 61–81. https://doi.org/10.1177/0263276416652700.

"Why Has Critique Run out of Steam? From Matters of Fact to Matters of Concern." *Critical Inquiry* 30, no. 2 (2004): 225–48. https://doi.org/10.1086/421123.

Latour, Bruno, and Christophe Leclercq, eds. *Reset Modernity!* Cambridge, MA: MIT Press, 2016.

Latour, Bruno, and Peter Weibel, eds. *Iconoclash.* Cambridge, MA: MIT Press, 2002.

Making Things Public: Atmospheres of Democracy. Cambridge, MA: MIT Press, 2005.

Latour, Bruno, and Steve Woolgar. *Laboratory Life: The Construction of Scientific Facts.* Princeton, NJ: Princeton University Press, 1986.

Latour, Bruno, and Timothy M. Lenton. "Extending the Domain of Freedom, or Why Gaia Is So Hard to Understand." *Critical Inquiry* 45, no. 3 (2019): 659–80. https://doi.org/10/gf7nxw.

Law, John. "STS as Method." In *The Handbook of Science and Technology Studies*, edited by Ulrike Felt, Rayvon Fouché, Clark A. Miller and Laurel Smith-Doerr, 31–57. Cambridge, MA: The MIT Press, 2017.

Le Guin, Ursula K. "Author's Note." In *The Left Hand of Darkness.* E-Book. New York: Ace Books, 2019.

The Dispossessed: A Novel. E-Book. New York: HarperCollins, 2009.

"*The Gift of Place.*" In *Ursula K. Le Guin: The Last Interview and Other Conversations*, edited by David Streitfeld. E-Book. The Last Interview Series. Brooklyn, NY: Melville House, 2019.

Review of *The Year of the Flood*, by Margaret Atwood. *The Guardian*, August 29, 2009. www.theguardian.com/books/2009/aug/29/margaret-atwood-year-of-flood.

Lea, John. "Book Review Symposium: Steven Pinker, *The Better Angels of Our Nature: A History of Violence and Humanity.*" *Sociology* 47, no. 6 (December 1, 2013): 1226–27. https://doi.org/10.1177/0038038513513856.

Lear, Jonathan. *Radical Hope: Ethics in the Face of Cultural Devastation.* Cambridge, MA: Harvard University Press, 2006.

Lear, Linda J. *Rachel Carson: Witness for Nature.* Boston: Mariner Books, 2009.

"Rachel Carson's 'Silent Spring.'" *Environmental History Review* 17, no. 2 (1993): 23–48. https://doi.org/10/dhz6q5.

Lenton, Timothy M., and James Lovelock. "Daisyworld Is Darwinian: Constraints on Adaptation Are Important for Planetary Self-Regulation." *Journal of Theoretical Biology* 206, no. 1 (2000): 109–14. https://doi.org/10.1006/jtbi.2000.2105.

"Daisyworld Revisited: Quantifying Biological Effects on Planetary Self-Regulation." *Tellus B* 53, no. 3 (2001): 288–305. https://doi.org/10.1034/j.1600-0889.2001.01191.x.

Leonard, Elisabeth Anne. "Race and Ethnicity in Science Fiction." In *The Cambridge Companion to Science Fiction*, edited by Edward James and Farah Mendlesohn, 253–63. Cambridge: Cambridge University Press, 2003.

Leonardi, Emanuele. "Reframing the Left Eco-modernism vs. Orthodox Eco-socialism Debate, Or: Assessing the Transformation of the Value-Nature Nexus." *ENTITLE Blog: A Collaborative Writing Project on Political Ecology* (blog), February 22, 2018. https://entitleblog.org/2018/02/22/reframing-the-left-eco-modernism-vs-orthodox-eco-socialism-debate-or-assessing-the-transformation-of-the-value-nature-nexus.

Leopold, David. "On Marxian Utopophobia." *Journal of the History of Philosophy* 54, no. 1 (January 4, 2016): 111–34. https://doi.org/10/gg33qp.

Lepore, Jill. "A Golden Age for Dystopian Fiction." *The New Yorker*, May 29, 2017. www.newyorker.com/magazine/2017/06/05/a-golden-age-for-dystopian-fiction.

Leucht, Robert. "Utopie." In *Robert-Musil-Handbuch*, edited by Birgit Nübel and Norbert Christian Wolf, 725–30. New York: De Gruyter, 2016.

Levene, Mark. "Climate Blues: Or How Awareness of the Human End Might Re-instil Ethical Purpose to the Writing of History." *Environmental Humanities* 2, no. 1 (May 1, 2013): 147–67. https://doi.org/10.1215/22011919-3610387.

Levitas, Ruth. *The Concept of Utopia.* Oxford: Peter Lang, 2011.

"Educated Hope: Ernst Bloch on Abstract and Concrete Utopia." *Utopian Studies* 1, no. 2 (1990): 13–26.

Utopia as Method: The Imaginary Reconstruction of Society. New York: Palgrave Macmillan, 2013.

Lewis, Chris H. "Telling Stories about the Future: Environmental History and Apocalyptic Science." *Environmental History Review* 17, no. 3 (1993): 43–60. https://doi.org/10.2307/3984604.

Lewis, Simon L., *The Human Planet: How We Created the Anthropocene.* London: Penguin Books, 2018.

"A Transparent Framework for Defining the Anthropocene Epoch." *The Anthropocene Review* 2, no. 2 (August 1, 2015): 128–46. https://doi.org/10 .1177/2053019615588792.

Lewis, Simon L., and Mark A. Maslin. "Defining the Anthropocene." *Nature* 519, no. 7542 (March 12, 2015): 171–80. https://doi.org/10.1038/ nature14258.

Lewis, Sophie. "Cthulhu Plays No Role for Me." *Viewpoint Magazine*, May 8, 2017. www.viewpointmag.com/2017/05/08/cthulhu-plays-no-role-for-me.

"Dreams of Gilead." *Blind Field: A Journal of Cultural Inquiry*, June 14, 2017. https://blindfieldjournal.com/2017/06/14/dreams-of-gilead.

Liegey, Vincent, and Anitra Nelson. *Exploring Degrowth: A Critical Guide.* London: Pluto Press, 2020.

Lilley, Sasha. "Introduction: The Apocalyptic Politics of Collapse and Rebirth." In *Catastrophism: The Apocalyptic Politics of Collapse and Rebirth*, edited by Sasha Lilley, David McNally, Eddie Yuen and James Davis, 1–14. Oakland, CA: PM Press, 2012.

Lin, Cynthia S., Alisa A. Pykett, Constance Flanagan and Karma R. Chávez. "Engendering the Prefigurative: Feminist Praxes That Bridge a Politics of Prefigurement and Survival." *Journal of Social and Political Psychology* 4, no. 1 (May 24, 2016): 302–17. https://doi.org/10/ggp26k.

Lipschutz, Ronnie D. "Eco-utopia or Eco-catastrophe? Imagining California as an Ecological Utopia." *Elementa: Science of the Anthropocene* 6, no. 1 (October 17, 2018). https://doi.org/10.1525/elementa.320.

Lomborg, Bjørn. *Cool It: The Skeptical Environmentalist's Guide to Global Warming.* New York: Vintage Books, 2010.

False Alarm: How Climate Change Panic Costs Us Trillions, Hurts the Poor, and Fails to Fix the ... Planet. New York: Basic Books, 2020.

The Skeptical Environmentalist: Measuring the Real State of the World. New York: Cambridge University Press, 2001.

Lorimer, Jamie, Chris Sandom, Paul Jepson, Chris Doughty, Maan Barua and Keith J. Kirby. "Rewilding: Science, Practice, and Politics." *Annual Review of Environment and Resources* 40, no. 1 (2015): 39–62. https://doi.org/10.1146/ annurev-environ-102014-021406.

Lovelock, James. "The Electron-Capture Detector – A Personal Odyssey." *Journal of Chromatography Library* 20 (1981): 1–11. https://doi.org/10.1016/S0301–4770(08)60125-6.

——— *Gaia: A New Look at Life on Earth.* New York: Oxford University Press, 2000.

——— *Homage to Gaia: The Life of an Independent Scientist.* New York: Oxford University Press, 2001.

——— "A Physical Basis for Life Detection Experiments." *Nature* 207, no. 4997 (August 1965): 568. https://doi.org/10.1038/207568a0.

——— *The Revenge of Gaia.* London: Penguin, 2007.

——— "A Sensitive Detector for Gas Chromatography." *Journal of Chromatography A* 1 (January 1, 1958): 35–46. https://doi.org/10.1016/S0021–9673(00)93398-3.

——— *The Vanishing Face of Gaia: A Final Warning.* New York: Basic Books, 2009.

——— "We Need Nuclear Power, Says the Man Who Inspired the Greens," August 15, 2001. www.telegraph.co.uk/news/science/science-news/4765409/We-need-nuclear-power-says-the-man-who-inspired-the-Greens.html.

Lovelock, James, and Lynn Margulis. "Atmospheric Homeostasis by and for the Biosphere: The Gaia Hypothesis." *Tellus* 26, no. 1–2 (1974): 2–10. https://doi.org/10.1111/j.2153-3490.1974.tb01946.x.

Luckhurst, Roger. "The Politics of the Network: The Science in the Capital Trilogy." In *Kim Stanley Robinson Maps the Unimaginable: Critical Essays*, edited by William Burling, 170–80. Jefferson, NC: McFarland Books, 2009.

Lukes, Steven. "Marxism and Utopianism." In *Utopias*, edited by Peter Alexander and Roger Gill, 153–67. London: Duckworth, 1984.

Lydon, Christopher, and Kim Stanley Robinson. "Kim Stanley Robinson: We Have Come to a Bad Moment, and We Must Change." Literary Hub, November 17, 2017. https://lithub.com/kim-stanley-robinson-we-have-come-to-a-bad-moment-and-we-must-change.

Lynch, Tommy. "Why Hope Is Dangerous When It Comes to Climate Change." *Slate Magazine*, July 25, 2017. https://slate.com/technology/2017/07/why-climate-change-discussions-need-apocalyptic-thinking.html.

Maeckelbergh, Marianne. "Doing Is Believing: Prefiguration as Strategic Practice in the Alterglobalization Movement." *Social Movement Studies* 10, no. 1 (January 1, 2011): 1–20. https://doi.org/10/cp4q89.

Mair, Peter. "Populist Democracy vs Party Democracy." In *Democracies and the Populist Challenge*, edited by Yves Mény and Yves Surel, 81–98. Basingstoke: Palgrave, 2002.

——— *Ruling the Void: The Hollowing of Western Democracy.* E-Book. London: Verso, 2013.

Majeed, Haris, and Jonathan Lee. "The Impact of Climate Change on Youth Depression and Mental Health." *The Lancet Planetary Health* 1, no. 3 (June 1, 2017): e94–95. https://doi.org/10/ggzt3k.

Malhi, Yadvinder, Toby A. Gardner, Gregory R. Goldsmith, Miles R. Silman and Przemyslaw Zelazowski. "Tropical Forests in the Anthropocene." *Annual Review of Environment and Resources* 39, no. 1 (2014): 125–59. https://doi.org/10/f25nxx.

Malm, Andreas. *Corona, Climate, Chronic Emergency: War Communism in the Twenty-First Century.* London: Verso Books, 2020.

——. *How to Blow Up a Pipeline: Learning to Fight in a World on Fire.* London: Verso Books, 2021.

Malm, Andreas, and Alf Hornborg. "The Geology of Mankind? A Critique of the Anthropocene Narrative." *The Anthropocene Review* 1, no. 1 (April 1, 2014): 62–69. https://doi.org/10/gftcsm.

Mancuso, Cecilia. "Speculative or Science Fiction? As Margaret Atwood Shows, There Isn't Much Distinction." *The Guardian*, August 10, 2016. www.theguardian.com/books/2016/aug/10/speculative-or-science-fiction-as-margaret-atwood-shows-there-isnt-much-distinction.

Marcetic, Branko. "People Make the World Go Round." *Jacobin*, 2017. www.jacobinmag.com/2017/08/people-make-the-world-go-round.

Margulis, Lynn. *The Symbiotic Planet: A New Look at Evolution.* London: Phoenix, 2001.

Maris, Virginie. *La part sauvage du monde: Penser la nature dans l'Anthropocène.* Anthropocène Seuil. Paris: Éditions du Seuil, 2018.

Markley, Robert. *Dying Planet: Mars in Science and the Imagination.* Durham, NC: Duke University Press, 2005.

——. "Falling into Theory: Simulation, Terraformation, and Eco-economics in Kim Stanley Robinson's Martian Trilogy." *Modern Fiction Studies* 43, no. 3 (1997): 773–99.

Marshall, Nadine, William Neil Adger, Claudia Benham et al. "Reef Grief: Investigating the Relationship between Place Meanings and Place Change on the Great Barrier Reef, Australia." *Sustainability Science* 14, no. 3 (May 1, 2019): 579–87. https://doi.org/10/ggrd67.

Martin, Adrienne M. *How We Hope: A Moral Psychology.* Princeton, NJ: Princeton University Press, 2014.

Marx, Karl, and Friedrich Engels. "The Communist Manifesto." In *Selected Writings* by Karl Marx, 245–71, edited by David McLellan. New York: Oxford University Press, 2000.

Maslin, Mark A., "Anthropocene vs Meghalayan: Why Geologists Are Fighting over Whether Humans Are a Force of Nature." The Conversation. Accessed January 21, 2019. http://theconversation.com/anthropocene-vs-meghala yan-why-geologists-are-fighting-over-whether-humans-are-a-force-of-nature-101057.

Maslin, Mark A., and Simon L. Lewis. "Anthropocene: Earth System, Geological, Philosophical and Political Paradigm Shifts." *The Anthropocene Review* 2, no. 2 (August 1, 2015): 108–16. https://doi.org/10.1177/2053019615588791.

Mason, Paul. *Clear Bright Future: A Radical Defence of the Human Being.* London: Allen Lane, 2019.

Mazzocchi, Paul. "Excavating Abensour: The Dialectics of Democracy and Utopia at a Standstill." *Constellations* 22, no. 2 (2015): 290–301. https://doi.org/10.1111/1467-8675.12162.

McBride, Patrizia C. *The Void of Ethics: Robert Musil and the Experience of Modernity.* Evanston, IL: Northwestern University Press, 2006.

McBrien, Justin. "Accumulating Extinction: Planetary Catastrophism in the Necrocene." In *Anthropocene or Capitalocene? Nature, History, and the Crisis of Capitalism,* edited by Jason W. Moore, 116–37. Oakland, CA: PM Press, 2016.

McGee, Kyle. *Bruno Latour: The Normativity of Networks.* Abingdon: Routledge, 2014.

McKean, Benjamin Laing. *Disorienting Neoliberalism: Global Justice and the Outer Limit of Freedom.* New York: Oxford University Press, 2020.

McKibben, Bill. *Eaarth: Making a Life on a Tough New Planet.* E-Book. New York: Time Books, 2010.

The End of Nature. New York: Random House, 2006.

"How Does Bill Gates Plan to Solve the Climate Crisis?" *The New York Times,* February 15, 2021. www.nytimes.com/2021/02/15/books/review/bill-gates-how-to-avoid-a-climate-disaster.html.

Mehnert, Antonia. *Climate Change Fictions: Representations of Global Warming in American Literature.* New York: Palgrave Macmillan, 2016.

Merteuil, Morgane, and Sophie Lewis. "Gestational Decrim: Sophie Lewis Interviewed by Morgane Merteuil." *Salvage,* November 8, 2019. https://salvage.zone/articles/gestational-decrim.

Merton, Robert K. *On the Shoulders of Giants: A Shandean Postscript.* New York: Free Press, 1965.

Meyer, John M. "Politics in – but Not of – the Anthropocene." *RCC Perspectives,* no. 2 (2016): 47–52.

Meyer, Robinson. "Geology's Timekeepers Are Feuding." *The Atlantic,* July 20, 2018. www.theatlantic.com/science/archive/2018/07/anthropocene-holocene-geology-drama/565628.

Miéville, China. *The City and the City.* New York: Ballantine Books, 2009.

"Cognition as Ideology: A Dialectic of SF Theory." In *Red Planets: Marxism and Science Fiction,* edited by Mark Bould and China Miéville, 231–48. Middletown, CT: Wesleyan University Press, 2009.

Embassytown. New York: Del Ray, 2011.

Iron Council. New York: Del Ray, 2004.

King Rat. London: Pan Books, 1998.

Perdido Street Station. Random House, Inc., 2003.

"Weird Fiction." In *The Routledge Companion to Science Fiction,* edited by Mark Bould, Andrew M. Butler, Adam Roberts and Sherryl Vint, 510–15. London: Routledge, 2010.

Mihai, Mihaela. "Epistemic Marginalisation and the Seductive Power of Art." *Contemporary Political Theory* 17, no. 4 (2018): 395–416. https://doi.org/10.1057/s41296-017-0186-z

Milkoreit, Manjana. "Imaginary Politics: Climate Change and Making the Future" edited by Anne R. Kapuscinski, Kim Locke and Alastair Iles. *Elementa: Science of the Anthropocene* 5, no. 62 (November 6, 2017). https://doi.org/10/gf35df.

Miller, Laura. "What Kind of Novel Do You Write When You Believe Civilization Is Doomed?" *Slate Magazine,* July 26, 2017. https://slate.com/culture/2017/07/the-world-without-us.html.

Mills, Charles W. "'Ideal Theory' as Ideology." *Hypatia* 20, no. 3 (2005): 165–83. https://doi.org/10.1111/j.1527-2001.2005.tb00493.x.

"White Time: The Chronic Injustice of Ideal Theory." *Du Bois Review: Social Science Research on Race* 11, no. 1 (2014): 27–42. https://doi.org/10.1017/S1742058X14000022.

Mills, Tom. "What Has Become of Critique? Reassembling Sociology after Latour." *The British Journal of Sociology* 69, no. 2 (2018): 286–305. https://doi.org/10/gdq8cx.

Milner, Andrew. "Science Fiction and the Literary Field." *Science Fiction Studies* 38, no. 3 (2011): 393–411. https://doi.org/10.5621/sciefictstud.38.3.0393.

Mirowski, Philip. *Never Let a Serious Crisis Go to Waste: How Neoliberalism Survived the Financial Meltdown.* New York: Verso, 2014.

Mitchell, Stanley. "From Shklovsky to Brecht: Some Preliminary Remarks towards a History of the Politicisation of Russian Formalism." *Screen* 15, no. 2 (1974): 74–81.

Mitman, Gregg. "Hubris or Humility? Genealogies of the Anthropocene." In *Future Remains: A Cabinet of Curiosities for the Anthropocene,* edited by Gregg Mitman, Marco Armiero and Robert S. Emmett, 59–68. London: University of Chicago Press, 2018.

Mitzen, Jennifer. "The Irony of Pinkerism." *Perspectives on Politics* 11, no. 2 (June 2013): 525–28. https://doi.org/10.1017/S1537592713001114.

Mohr, Dunja M. "Anthropocene Fiction: Narrating the 'Zero Hour' in Margaret Atwood's MaddAddam Trilogy." In *Writing beyond the End Times? The Literatures of Canada and Quebec,* edited by Ursula Mathis-Moser and Marie J. Carrière, 25–46. Innsbruck: Innsbruck University Press, 2017.

"Eco-dystopia and Biotechnology: Margaret Atwood, *Oryx and Crake* (2003), *The Year of The Flood* (2009) and *MaddAddam* (2013)." In *Dystopia, Science Fiction, Post-apocalypse: Classic, New Tendencies and Model Interpretation*, edited by Eckhard Voigts and Alessandra Boller, 283–302. Trier: WVT Wissenschaftlicher Verlag, 2015.

Moir, Cat. "Ernst Bloch: The Principle of Hope." In *The SAGE Handbook of Frankfurt School Critical Theory*, edited by Beverly Best, Werner Bonefeld and Chris O'Kane, 199–215. Thousand Oaks, CA: SAGE, 2018.

Monbiot, George. "I Share Their Despair, but I'm Not Quite Ready to Climb the Dark Mountain." *The Guardian*, May 10, 2010. www.theguardian.com/com mentisfree/cif-green/2010/may/10/deepwater-horizon-greens-collapse-civilisation.

"Interstellar: Magnificent Film, Insane Fantasy." *The Guardian*, November 11, 2014. www.theguardian.com/commentisfree/2014/nov/11/interstellar-insane-fantasy-abandoning-earth-political-defeatism.

"Meet the Ecomodernists: Ignorant of History and Paradoxically Old-Fashioned." *The Guardian*, September 24, 2015. www.theguardian.com/envir onment/georgemonbiot/2015/sep/24/meet-the-ecomodernists-ignorant-of-history-and-paradoxically-old-fashioned.

Moore, Jason W., ed. *Anthropocene or Capitalocene? Nature, History, and the Crisis of Capitalism*. Oakland, CA: PM Press, 2016.

"The Capitalocene, Part I: On the Nature and Origins of Our Ecological Crisis." *The Journal of Peasant Studies* 44, no. 3 (May 4, 2017): 594–630. https://doi.org/10.1080/03066150.2016.1235036.

"The Capitalocene, Part II: Accumulation by Appropriation and the Centrality of Unpaid Work/Energy." *The Journal of Peasant Studies* 45, no. 2 (February 23, 2018): 237–79. https://doi.org/10.1080/03066150.2016.1272587.

More, Thomas. *Utopia*, edited by George M. Logan and Robert Merrihew Adams. New York: Cambridge University Press, 2002.

Morozov, Evgeny. *To Save Everything, Click Here: The Folly of Technological Solutionism*. New York: PublicAffairs, 2013.

"The Tech 'Solutions' for Coronavirus Take the Surveillance State to the Next Level." *The Guardian*, April 15, 2020. www.theguardian.com/commentis free/2020/apr/15/tech-coronavirus-surveilance-state-digital-disrupt.

Morrell, John J. "The Dialectic of Climate Change: Apocalypse, Utopia and the Environmental Imagination." PhD, Vanderbilt University, 2012. https://etd .library.vanderbilt.edu/available/etd-03212012-142522/unrestricted/ MorrellDissertation.pdf.

Morton, Oliver. *The Planet Remade: How Geoengineering Could Change the World*. E-Book. Princeton, NJ: Princeton University Press, 2016.

Morton, Timothy. *Hyperobjects: Philosophy and Ecology after the End of the World.* Minneapolis: University of Minnesota Press, 2013.

Mouffe, Chantal. *For a Left Populism.* London: Verso, 2018.

Moylan, Tom. *Demand the Impossible: Science Fiction and the Utopian Imagination,* edited by Raffaella Baccolini. Oxford: Peter Lang, 2014.

———. *Scraps of the Untainted Sky: Science Fiction, Utopia, Dystopia.* Boulder, CO: Westview Press, 2000.

———. "'The Moment Is Here . . . and It's Important': State, Agency, and Dystopia in Kim Stanley Robinson's *Antarctica* and Ursula K. Le Guin's *The Telling.*" In *Dark Horizons: Science Fiction and the Dystopian Imagination,* edited by Raffaella Baccolini and Tom Moylan, 135–54. New York: Routledge, 2003.

———. "'Utopia Is When Our Lives Matter': Reading Kim Stanley Robinson's Pacific Edge." *Utopian Studies* 6, no. 2 (1995): 1–24.

Moyn, Samuel. "Hype for the Best." *The New Republic,* March 19, 2018. https://newrepublic.com/article/147391/hype-best.

Mudde, Cas, and Cristóbal Rovira Kaltwasser. *Populism: A Very Short Introduction.* New York: Oxford University Press, 2017.

Müller, Jan-Werner. "Fear and Freedom: On 'Cold War Liberalism.'" *European Journal of Political Theory* 7, no. 1 (2008): 45–64. https://doi.org/10.1177/1474885107083403.

Mulligan, Kevin. "Foolishness, Stupidity, and Cognitive Values:" *Monist* 97, no. 1 (2014): 66–85. https://doi.org/10/f2n9bp.

Muñoz, José Esteban. *Cruising Utopia: The Then and There of Queer Futurity.* New York: New York University Press, 2009.

Murphy, Patrick D. "Reducing the Dystopian Distance: Pseudo-Documentary Framing in Near-Future Fiction (La Réduction de La Distance Dystopique: L'encadrement Pseudo-Documentaire Dans Les Romans Du Proche-Futur)." *Science Fiction Studies* 17, no. 1 (1990): 25–40.

Musil, Robert. *The Man without Qualities.* E-Book. London: Picador, 2017.

Nadir, Christine. "Utopian Studies, Environmental Literature, and the Legacy of an Idea: Educating Desire in Miguel Abensour and Ursula K. Le Guin." *Utopian Studies* 21, no. 1 (June 9, 2010): 24–56. https://doi.org/10.1353/utp.0.0014.

Nehamas, Alexander. *Nietzsche, Life as Literature.* Cambridge, MA: Harvard University Press, 1985.

New Scientist. "Climate Change and Nature Loss Must Be Tackled Together, Says Report." Accessed June 17, 2021. www.newscientist.com/article/2280587-climate-change-and-nature-loss-must-be-tackled-together-says-report.

Nietzsche, Friedrich Wilhelm. *On the Genealogy of Morality,* edited by Keith Ansell-Pearson. Translated by Carol Diethe. New York: Cambridge University Press, 2007.

Nikoleris, Alexandra, Johannes Stripple and Paul Tenngart. "The 'Anthropocene' in Popular Culture: Narrating Human Agency, Force, and Our Place on Earth." In *Anthropocene Encounters: New Directions in Green Political Thinking*, edited by Frank Biermann and Eva Lövbrand, 67–84. Cambridge: Cambridge University Press, 2019. https://doi.org/10.1017/9781108646673.004.

"Narrating Climate Futures: Shared Socioeconomic Pathways and Literary Fiction." *Climatic Change* 143, no. 3 (August 1, 2017): 307–19. https://doi.org/10/gbn5hp.

Nixon, Rob. "The Anthropocene: The Promise and Pitfalls of an Epochal Idea." In *Future Remains: A Cabinet of Curiosities for the Anthropocene*, edited by Gregg Mitman, Marco Armiero and Robert S. Emmett, 1–18. Chicago: University of Chicago Press, 2018.

"The Great Acceleration and the Great Divergence: Vulnerability in the Anthropocene – Profession." Accessed March 31, 2021. https://profession.mla.org/the-great-acceleration-and-the-great-divergence-vulnerability-in-the-anthropocene.

Nogués-Bravo, David, Daniel Simberloff, Carsten Rahbek and Nathan James Sanders. "Rewilding Is the New Pandora's Box in Conservation." *Current Biology* 26, no. 3 (February 8, 2016): R87–91. https://doi.org/10.1016/j.cub.2015.12.044.

Northover, Richard Alan. "Ecological Apocalypse in Margaret Atwood's MaddAddam Trilogy." *Studia Neophilologica* 88, no. sup1 (March 31, 2016): 81–95. https://doi.org/10.1080/00393274.2015.1096044.

Noys, Benjamin. "The Discreet Charm of Bruno Latour." In *(Mis)Readings of Marx in Continental Philosophy*, edited by Jernej Habjan and Jessica Whyte, 195–210. New York: Palgrave Macmillan, 2014.

Nugent, Ashley Frances. "'Odd Apocalyptic Panics': Chthonic Storytelling in Margaret Atwood's Maddaddam." MA thesis, Florida Atlantic University, 2018. https://fau.digital.flvc.org/islandora/object/fau%3A40746.

Oakeshott, Michael. "On Being Conservative." In *Rationalism in Politics: And Other Essays*, 168–96. London: Methuen, 1962.

Oldfield, Frank. "When and How Did the Anthropocene Begin?" *The Anthropocene Review* 2, no. 2 (August 1, 2015): 101–101. https://doi.org/10.1177/2053019615590922.

Ollman, Bertell. "Marx's Vision of Communism: A Reconstruction." *Critique: Journal of Socialist Theory* 8, no. 1 (1977). https://doi.org/10/chmrvj.

Opperman, Romy. "We Need Histories of Radical Black Ecology Now." Blog of the African American Intellectual History Society. *Black Perspectives* (blog),

August 3, 2020. www.aaihs.org/we-need-histories-of-radical-black-ecology-now.

Oreskes, Naomi, and Erik M. Conway. *The Collapse of Western Civilization*. New York: Columbia University Press, 2014.

"The Collapse of Western Civilization: A View from the Future." *Daedalus* 142, no. 1 (January 1, 2013): 40–58. https://doi.org/10.1162/DAED_a_00184.

Merchants of Doubt: How a Handful of Scientists Obscured the Truth on Issues from Tobacco Smoke to Global Warming. E-Book. New York: Bloomsbury Press, 2011.

Orwell, George. *Nineteen Eighty-Four*. London: Penguin, 2003.

Out of the Woods. "The Uses of Disaster." *Commune* (blog), October 22, 2018. https://communemag.com/the-uses-of-disaster.

Oziewicz, Marek. "Speculative Fiction." In *Oxford Research Encyclopedia of Literature*, March 29, 2017. http://oxfordre.com/view/10.1093/acrefore/9780190201098.001.0001/acrefore-9780190201098-e-78.

Paden, Roger. "Marx's Critique of the Utopian Socialists." *Utopian Studies* 13, no. 2 (2002): 67–91.

Paik, Peter Yoonsuk. *From Utopia to Apocalypse: Science Fiction and the Politics of Catastrophe*. Minneapolis: University of Minnesota Press, 2010.

Pak, Chris. "'All Energy Is Borrowed' – Terraforming: A Master Motif for Physical and Cultural Re(up)Cycling in Kim Stanley Robinson's Mars Trilogy." *Green Letters* 18, no. 1 (January 2, 2014): 91–103. https://doi.org/10.1080/14688417.2014.890527.

Terraforming: Ecopolitical Transformations and Environmentalism in Science Fiction. Liverpool: Liverpool University Press, 2016.

Parenti, Christian. "If We Fail." *Jacobin*, 2017. https://jacobinmag.com/2017/08/if-we-fail.

Tropic of Chaos: Climate Change and the New Geography of Violence. New York: Nation Books, 2011.

Parrinder, Patrick. "Revisiting Suvin's Poetics of Science Fiction." In *Learning from Other Worlds: Estrangement, Cognition and the Politics of Science Fiction and Utopia*, edited by Patrick Parrinder, 36–50. Liverpool: Liverpool University Press, 2000.

Parrinder, Patrick, and John S. Partington, eds. *The Reception of H. G. Wells in Europe*. New York: Thoemmes Continuum, 2005.

Partington, John S. *Building Cosmopolis: The Political Thought of H. G. Wells*. Aldershot: Ashgate, 2003.

Patterson, Orlando. *Slavery and Social Death: A Comparative Study*. Cambridge, MA: Harvard University Press, 1982.

Pensky, Max. "In Search of the Negative in Rahel Jaeggi's *Kritik von Lebensformen.*" In *From Alienation to Forms of Life: The Critical Theory of Rahel Jaeggi*, edited by Amy Allen and Eduardo Mendieta. University Park: The Pennsylvania State University Press, 2018.

"Method and Time: Benjamin's Dialectical Images." In *The Cambridge Companion to Walter Benjamin*, edited by David S. Ferris, 177–98. Cambridge: Cambridge University Press, 2004.

Pepper, David. "Utopianism and Environmentalism." *Environmental Politics* 14, no. 1 (February 1, 2005): 3–22. https://doi.org/10.1080/0964401042000310150.

Phelan, Jo C., and Bruce G. Link. "Is Racism a Fundamental Cause of Inequalities in Health?" *Annual Review of Sociology* 41, no. 1 (2015): 311–30. https://doi.org/10/gfpn9n.

Phillips, Leigh. *Austerity Ecology and the Collapse-Porn Addicts: A Defence of Growth, Progress, Industry and Stuff.* Winchester: Zero Books, 2015.

Phillips, Leigh, and Michal Rozworski. "Planning the Good Anthropocene." *Jacobin*, 2017. www.jacobinmag.com/2017/08/planning-the-good-anthropocene.

Pierce, John J. "The Literary Experience of Hard Science Fiction." *Science Fiction Studies* 20, no. 2 (1993): 176–83.

Pinker, Steven. *The Better Angels of Our Nature: The Decline of Violence in History and Its Causes.* London: Allen Lane, 2011.

The Blank Slate: The Modern Denial of Human Nature. New York: Viking, 2002.

Enlightenment Now: The Case for Reason, Science, Humanism, and Progress. E-Book. New York: Penguin, 2018.

The Language Instinct. New York: Harper Perennial, 1995.

Language Learnability and Language Development. Cambridge, MA: Harvard University Press, 1996.

Planinc, Emma. "Catching up with Wells: The Political Theory of H. G. Wells's Science Fiction." *Political Theory* 45, no. 5 (October 1, 2017): 637–58. https://doi.org/10.1177/0090591716642496.

Pleij, Herman. *Dreaming of Cockaigne: Medieval Fantasies of the Perfect Life.* New York: Columbia University Press, 2003.

Pope Francis. "Laudato Si'." Vatican City Press, May 24, 2015. http://w2.vatican.va/content/dam/francesco/pdf/encyclicals/documents/papa-francesco_20150524_enciclica-laudato-si_en.pdf.

Popper, Karl R. "Utopia and Violence." *World Affairs* 149, no. 1 (1986): 3–9.

The Open Society and Its Enemies. Princeton, NJ: Princeton University Press, 2013.

Post, W. M., and K. C. Kwon. "Soil Carbon Sequestration and Land-Use Change: Processes and Potential." *Global Change Biology* 6, no. 3 (2000): 317–27. https://doi.org/10.1046/j.1365-2486.2000.00308.x.

Prettyman, Gib. "Living Thought: Genes, Genres and Utopia in the Science in the Capital Trilogy." In *Kim Stanley Robinson Maps the Unimaginable: Critical Essays*, edited by William J. Burling, 181–203. Jefferson, NC: McFarland Books, 2009.

Purdy, Jedediah. *After Nature: A Politics for the Anthropocene*. E-Book. Cambridge, MA: Harvard University Press, 2015.

"Anthropocene Fever." Aeon, March 31, 2015. https://aeon.co/essays/should-we-be-suspicious-of-the-anthropocene-idea.

Raekstad, Paul, and Sofa Saio Gradin. *Prefigurative Politics: Building Tomorrow Today*. Cambridge: Polity, 2020.

Ray, Larry. "Book Review Symposium: Steven Pinker, *The Better Angels of Our Nature: A History of Violence and Humanity*." *Sociology* 47, no. 6 (December 1, 2013): 1224–25. https://doi.org/10.1177/0038038513513855.

Read, Rupert J., and Samuel Alexander. *This Civilisation Is Finished: Conversations on the End of Empire – and What Lies Beyond*. Coburg: Simplicity Institute Publishing, 2019.

Reinhard, Johan. "Khembalung: The Hidden Valley." *Kailash: A Journal of Himalayan Studies* 6, no. 1 (1978): 5–28.

Renault, Gregory. "Science Fiction as Cognitive Estrangement: Darko Suvin and the Marxist Critique of Mass Culture." *Discourse* 2 (1980): 113–41.

Rengger, Nicholas. "Realism Tamed or Liberalism Betrayed? Dystopic Liberalism and the International Order." In *After Liberalism?*, edited by Rebekka Friedman, Kevork Oskanian and Ramon Pacheco Pardo, 51–66. London: Palgrave Macmillan, 2013.

Revkin, Andrew C. "Building a 'Good' Anthropocene from the Bottom Up." *Dot Earth Blog* (blog), October 6, 2016. https://dotearth.blogs.nytimes.com/2016/10/06/building-a-good-anthropocene-from-the-bottom-up.

"A Darker View of the Age of Us – the Anthropocene." *Dot Earth Blog* (blog), June 18, 2014. https://dotearth.blogs.nytimes.com/2014/06/18/a-darker-view-of-the-age-of-us-the-anthropocene.

"Natural Resources and the Environment." *Dot Earth Blog* (blog), December 5, 2016. https://dotearth.blogs.nytimes.com.

Rich, Adrienne. "When We Dead Awaken: Writing as Re-vision." *College English* 34, no. 1 (1972): 18–30. https://doi.org/10/cvf9qw.

Ricœur, Paul. *Freud and Philosophy*. New Haven, CT: Yale University Press, 1970.

Lectures on Ideology and Utopia. Translated by George H. Taylor. New York: Columbia University Press, 1986.

Riofrancos, Thea. "Digging Free of Poverty." *Jacobin*, 2017. www.jacobinmag.com/2017/08/digging-free-of-poverty.

Riskin, Jessica. "Pinker's Pollyannish Philosophy and Its Perfidious Politics." *Los Angeles Review of Books*, December 15, 2019. www.lareviewofbooks.org/art icle/pinkers-pollyannish-philosophy-and-its-perfidious-politics.

Rivera, Joshua. "N. K. Jemisin Is Trying to Keep the World From Ending." *GQ*, November 28, 2018. www.gq.com/story/nk-jemisin-is-trying-to-keep-the-world-from-ending.

Rivkin, Julie, and Michael Ryan, eds. *Literary Theory: An Anthology*. Malden, MA: Blackwell Publishing, 2004.

Roberts, Adam. *Fredric Jameson*. Routledge Critical Thinkers. New York: Routledge, 2000.

Roberts, David. "The Scariest Thing about Global Warming (and Covid-19)." Vox, July 7, 2020. www.vox.com/energy-and-environment/2020/7/7/ 21311027/covid-19-climate-change-global-warming-shifting-baselines.

Roberts, Peder. *The European Antarctic: Science and Strategy in Scandinavia and the British Empire*. Palgrave Studies in Cultural and Intellectual History. New York: Palgrave Macmillan, 2011.

Robertson, Thomas. *The Malthusian Moment: Global Population Growth and the Birth of American Environmentalism*. Studies in Modern Science, Technology, and the Environment. New Brunswick, NJ: Rutgers University Press, 2012.

Robinson, Douglas. *Estrangement and the Somatics of Literature: Tolstoy, Shklovsky, Brecht*. Baltimore: Johns Hopkins University Press, 2008.

Robinson, Kim Stanley. *Antarctica.*, 1998.

Aurora. New York: Orbit, 2015.

Blue Mars. E-Book. Mars Trilogy 3. New York: Bantam Spectra, 1997.

"Dystopias Now." *Commune*, Spring 2019. https://communemag.com/dysto pias-now.

"Empty Half the Earth of Its Humans. It's the Only Way to Save the Planet." *The Guardian*, March 20, 2018. www.theguardian.com/cities/2018/mar/20/ save-the-planet-half-earth-kim-stanley-robinson.

Fifty Degrees Below. E-Book. Science in the Capital Trilogy 2. New York: Bantham, 2005.

Forty Signs of Rain. E-Book. Science in the Capital Trilogy 1. New York: Bantham, 2004.

"Geoengineering Makes Everyone Uneasy, but It Shouldn't." *Slate Magazine*, December 4, 2012. https://slate.com/technology/2012/12/geoengineer ing-science-fiction-and-fact-kim-stanley-robinson-on-how-we-are-already-terra forming-earth.html.

Green Mars. E-Book. Mars Trilogy 2. Bantam Spectra, 1995.

Imagining Abrupt Climate Change: Terraforming Earth. Seattle: Amazon Shorts, 2005.

The Ministry for the Future. New York: Orbit, 2020.

New York 2140. London: Orbit, 2018.

Pacific Edge. Three Californias Triptych 3. New York: Orb, 1995.

Red Mars. E-Book. Mars Trilogy 1. New York: Bantam Spectra, 1993.

"Remarks on Utopia in the Age of Climate Change." *Utopian Studies* 27, no. 1 (March 11, 2016): 2–15.

Sixty Days and Counting. E-Book. Science in the Capital Trilogy 3. New York: Bantham, 2007.

Rockström, Johan, Will Steffen, Kevin Noone et al. "A Safe Operating Space for Humanity." *Nature* 461 (September 23, 2009): 472–75. https://doi.org/10.1038/461472a.

Rohn, Jennifer. "The Day after Today: Interview with Novelist Kim Stanley Robinson." LabLit.com, February 4, 2007. www.lablit.com/article/208.

Romano, Aja. "The Hugo Awards Just Made History – and Defied Alt-Right Extremists in the Process." Vox, August 21, 2018. www.vox.com/2018/8/21/17763260/n-k-jemisin-hugo-awards-broken-earth-sad-puppies.

Rose, Andrew. "The Unknowable Now: Passionate Science and Transformative Politics in Kim Stanley Robinson's Science in the Capital Trilogy." *Science Fiction Studies* 43, no. 2 (July 2016): 260–86. https://doi.org/10.5621/sciefictstud.43.2.0260.

Rose, Deborah Bird, Thom Van Dooren and Matthew Chrulew, eds. *Extinction Studies: Stories of Time, Death, and Generations.* New York: Columbia University Press, 2017.

Rose, Deborah Bird, Thom van Dooren, Matthew Chrulew, Stuart Cooke, Matthew Kearnes and Emily O'Gorman. "Thinking through the Environment, Unsettling the Humanities." *Environmental Humanities* 1, no. 1 (May 1, 2012): 1–5. https://doi.org/10.1215/22011919-3609940.

Rose, Hilary. "Book Review Symposium: Steven Pinker, *The Better Angels of Our Nature: A History of Violence and Humanity.*" *Sociology* 47, no. 6 (December 1, 2013): 1227–29. https://doi.org/10.1177/0038038513513854.

Rossi, Enzo. "Being Realistic and Demanding the Impossible." *Constellations* 26, no. 4 (2019): 638–52. https://doi.org/10/gg3mqv.

The Royal Society. "*Geoengineering the Climate: Science, Governance and Uncertainty.*" London: The Royal Society, 2009. https://royalsociety.org/~/media/royal_society_content/policy/publications/2009/8693.pdf.

Ruda, Frank. *Abolishing Freedom: A Plea for a Contemporary Use of Fatalism.* Lincoln: University of Nebraska Press, 2016.

Ruse, Michael. "Earth's Holy Fool?" Aeon. Accessed March 14, 2019. https://aeon.co/essays/gaia-why-some-scientists-think-it-s-a-nonsensical-fantasy.

The Gaia Hypothesis: Science on a Pagan Planet. Chicago: University of Chicago Press, 2013.

Sahraoui, Nassima, and Caroline Sauter. "Introduction." In *Thinking in Constellations: Walter Benjamin in the Humanities,* edited by Nassima Sahraoui and Caroline Sauter, ix–xviii. Newcastle upon Tyne: Cambridge Scholars Publishing, 2018.

Samuelson, David N. "Modes of Extrapolation: The Formulas of Hard SF." *Science Fiction Studies* 20, no. 2 (1993): 191–232.

Sande, Mathijs van de. "Fighting with Tools: Prefiguration and Radical Politics in the Twenty-First Century." *Rethinking Marxism* 27, no. 2 (April 3, 2015): 177–94. https://doi.org/10.1080/08935696.2015.1007791.

Santos, Boaventura de Sousa. *The Rise of the Global Left: The World Social Forum and Beyond.* London: Zed Books, 2006.

Sargent, Lyman Tower. "Authority and Utopia: Utopianism in Political Thought." *Polity* 14, no. 4 (1982): 565–84. https://doi.org/10.2307/3234464.

——. "The Three Faces of Utopianism Revisited." *Utopian Studies* 5, no. 1 (1994): 1–37.

——. "Utopia—The Problem of Definition." *Extrapolation* 16, no. 2 (May 1, 1975): 137–48. https://doi.org/10.3828/extr.1975.16.2.137.

——. *Utopianism: A Very Short Introduction.* Oxford: Oxford University Press, 2010.

Sargisson, Lucy. *Fool's Gold? Utopianism in the Twenty-First Century.* New York: Palgrave Macmillan, 2014.

——. "Strange Places: Estrangement, Utopianism, and Intentional Communities." *Utopian Studies* 18, no. 3 (2007): 393–424.

——. *Utopian Bodies and the Politics of Transgression.* New York: Routledge, 2000.

Sargisson, Lucy, and Lyman Tower Sargent. *Living in Utopia: New Zealand's Intentional Communities.* Aldershot: Ashgate Publishing Company, 2004.

Sattler, Barbara. "Contingency and Necessity: Human Agency in Musil's 'The Man without Qualities.'" *The Monist* 97, no. 1 (2014): 86–103. https://doi.org/10/f2n9bq.

Sawyer, Stephen W., and Iain Stewart, eds. *In Search of the Liberal Moment: Democracy, Anti-totalitarianism, and Intellectual Politics in France since 1950.* New York: Palgrave Macmillan, 2016.

Schaub, Michael. "N. K. Jemisin Makes History at the Hugo Awards with Third Win in a Row for Best Novel." *LA Times,* August 21, 2018. www.latimes.com/books/la-et-jc-nk-jemisin-hugo-awards-20180821-story.html.

Schlosberg, David, and David Carruthers. "Indigenous Struggles, Environmental Justice, and Community Capabilities." *Global Environmental Politics* 10, no. 4 (October 25, 2010): 12–35. https://doi.org/10.1162/GLEP_a_00029.

Schneider-Mayerson, Matthew. "The Influence of Climate Fiction: An Empirical Survey of Readers." *Environmental Humanities* 10, no. 2 (November 1, 2018): 473–500. https://doi.org/10/gjbv8d.

———. "'Just as in the Book'? The Influence of Literature on Readers' Awareness of Climate Injustice and Perception of Climate Migrants." *ISLE: Interdisciplinary Studies in Literature and Environment* 27, no. 2 (May 1, 2020): 337–64. https://doi.org/10/gjkp98.

Schwartzman, David. "Green New Deal: An Ecosocialist Perspective." *Capitalism Nature Socialism* 22, no. 3 (September 1, 2011): 49–56. https://doi.org/10.1080/10455752.2011.593886.

Science Museum. "Unlocking Lovelock: Scientist, Inventor, Maverick." Accessed March 15, 2019. www.sciencemuseum.org.uk/what-was-on/unlocking-lovelock-scientist-inventor-maverick.

Scott, James C. *Against the Grain: A Deep History of the Earliest States*. New Haven, CT: Yale University Press, 2017.

Scranton, Roy. *Learning to Die in the Anthropocene: Reflections on the End of a Civilization*. E-Book. San Francisco: City Lights Books, 2015.

———. "No Happy Ending: On Bill McKibben's 'Falter' and David Wallace-Wells's 'The Uninhabitable Earth.'" *Los Angeles Review of Books*, June 3, 2019. https://lareviewofbooks.org/article/no-happy-ending-on-bill-mckibbens-falter-and-david-wallace-wellss-the-uninhabitable-earth.

———. "Response to The New Nature." *Boston Review*, January 4, 2016. http://bostonreview.net/forum/new-nature/roy-scranton-roy-scranton-response-new-nature.

———. "We're Doomed. Now What?" *Opinionator* (blog), December 21, 2015. https://opinionator.blogs.nytimes.com/2015/12/21/were-doomed-now-what.

Searle, Rick. "Three Anthopocenes." *Utopia or Dystopia* (blog), October 9, 2017. https://utopiaordystopia.com/tag/ecomodernism.

Seeds of Good Anthropocenes. "Planting Seeds of the Future." Accessed September 11, 2019. https://goodanthropocenes.net.

Sella, Andrea. "Lovelock's Detector." Chemistry World, November 27, 2015. www.chemistryworld.com/opinion/lovelocks-detector/9181.article.

Sepkoski, David. *Catastrophic Thinking: Extinction and the Value of Diversity*. Science Culture. Chicago: University of Chicago Press, 2020.

Setoodeh, Ramin. "Margaret Atwood on How Donald Trump Helped 'The Handmaid's Tale.'" *Variety*, April 10, 2018. https://variety.com/2018/tv/news/margaret-atwood-handmaids-tale-trump-feminism-1202748535.

Sexton, Jared. "Afro-Pessimism: The Unclear Word." *Rhizomes: Cultural Studies in Emerging Knowledge*, no. 29 (2016). https://doi.org/10.20415/rhiz/029.e02.

Sharpe, Christina Elizabeth. *In the Wake: On Blackness and Being.* E-Book. Durham, NC: Duke University Press, 2016.

Shellenberger, Michael. *Apocalypse Never: Why Environmental Alarmism Hurts Us All.* New York: Harper, 2020.

Shin, Jiyoung. *Der "bewusste Utopismus" im Mann ohne Eigenschaften von Robert Musil.* Würzburg: Königshausen & Neumann, 2008.

Shklar, Judith. *After Utopia: The Decline of Political Faith.* Princeton, NJ: Princeton University Press, 1957.

"Liberalism of Fear." In *Liberalism and the Moral Life,* edited by Nancy L. Rosenblum, 21–38. Cambridge, MA: Harvard University Press, 1989.

"Nineteen Eighty-Four: Should Political Theory Care?" *Political Theory* 13, no. 1 (February 1985): 5–18.

"Obligation, Loyalty, Exile." *Political Theory* 21, no. 2 (May 1993): 181–97.

"The Political Theory of Utopia: From Melancholy to Nostalgia." *Daedalus* 94, no. 2 (Spring 1965): 367–81.

Shklovsky, Viktor. "Art, as Device." Translated by Alexandra Berlina. *Poetics Today* 36, no. 3 (2015): 151–74. https://doi.org/10.1215/03335372-3160709.

Theory of Prose. Elmwood Park, IL: Dalkey Archive Press, 1991.

Viktor Shklovsky: A Reader, edited by Alexandra Berlina. New York: Bloomsbury Academic, 2016.

Shorten, Richard. *Modernism and Totalitarianism: Rethinking the Intellectual Sources of Nazism and Stalinism, 1945 to the Present.* Houndmills: Palgrave Macmillan, 2012.

Simons, Massimiliano. "The Parliament of Things and the Anthropocene: How to Listen to 'Quasi-Objects.'" *Techné: Research in Philosophy and Technology* 21, no. 2–3 (2017): 1–25. https://doi.org/10.5840/techne201752464.

Sium, Aman, and Eric Ritskes. "Speaking Truth to Power: Indigenous Storytelling as an Act of Living Resistance." *Decolonization: Indigeneity, Education & Society* 2, no. 1 (May 9, 2013). https://jps.library.utoronto.ca/index.php/des/art icle/view/19626.

Skinner, Quentin. "A Genealogy of the Modern State." *Proceedings of the British Academy* 162 (2009): 325–70.

Skrimshire, Stefan. "What Is Anti-utopianism? Gray, Jacoby, Jameson." *Cultural Politics* 4, no. 2 (July 2008): 231–48. https://doi.org/10/cg2p3s.

Slezkine, Yuri. *The House of Government: A Saga of the Russian Revolution.* Oxford: Princeton University Press, 2017.

Smith, Daniel. "It's the End of the World as We Know It … and He Feels Fine." *The New York Times,* April 17, 2014. www.nytimes.com/2014/04/20/maga zine/its-the-end-of-the-world-as-we-know-it-and-he-feels-fine.html.

Smith, Paul B. "Reflections on Aspects of Marxist Anti-Utopianism." *Critique* 37, no. 1 (February 1, 2009): 99–120. https://doi.org/10.1080/03017600802598260.

Soles, Carter. "'And No Birds Sing': Discourses of Environmental Apocalypse in 'The Birds' and 'Night of the Living Dead.'" *ISLE: Interdisciplinary Studies in Literature and Environment* 21, no. 3 (2014): 526–37. https://doi.org/10/ghmp9v.

Solnit, Rebecca. *A Paradise Built in Hell: The Extraordinary Communities That Arise in Disaster.* E-Book. New York: Viking, 2009.

———. "'The Way We Get through This Is Together': Mutual Aid under Coronavirus." *The Guardian,* May 14, 2020. www.theguardian.com/world/2020/may/14/mutual-aid-coronavirus-pandemic-rebecca-solnit.

Speth, James Gustave. *The Bridge at the Edge of the World: Capitalism, the Environment, and Crossing from Crisis to Sustainability.* New Haven, CT: Yale University Press, 2008.

Spiegel, Michael. "Character in a Post-national World: Neomedievalism in Atwood's 'Oryx and Crake.'" *Mosaic: An Interdisciplinary Critical Journal* 43, no. 3 (2010): 119–34.

Spiegel, Simon. "Things Made Strange: On the Concept of 'Estrangement' in Science Fiction Theory." *Science Fiction Studies* 35, no. 3 (2008): 369–85.

Sponsel, Leslie, and Poranee Natadecha-Sponsel. "Buddhist Views of Nature and the Environment." In *Nature across Cultures: Views of Nature and the Environment in Non-Western Cultures,* edited by Helaine Selin, 351–71. Boston: Kluwer Academic Publishers, 2010.

Stahl, Titus. "Immanent Critique and Particular Moral Experience." *Critical Horizons,* October 11, 2017, 1–21. https://doi.org/10/ggb5b4.

Stedman Jones, Gareth. "Utopian Socialism." In *A Dictionary of Marxist Thought,* edited by Tom Bottomore, 561–63. Oxford: Blackwell Reference, 2001.

Steffen, Will, Katherine Richardson, Johan Rockström et al. "Planetary Boundaries: Guiding Human Development on a Changing Planet." *Science* 347, no. 6223 (February 13, 2015): 1259855. https://doi.org/10.1126/science.1259855.

Steffen, Will, Wendy Broadgate, Lisa Deutsch, Owen Gaffney and Cornelia Ludwig. "The Trajectory of the Anthropocene: The Great Acceleration." *The Anthropocene Review* 2, no. 1 (April 1, 2015): 81–98. https://doi.org/10/gdm38t.

Steiner, Peter. *Russian Formalism: A Metapoetics.* Ithaca, NY: Cornell University Press, 1984.

Stephenson, Wen. "'I Withdraw': A Talk with Climate Defeatist Paul Kingsnorth." *Grist* (blog), April 11, 2012. https://grist.org/climate-energy/i-withdraw-a-talk-with-climate-defeatist-paul-kingsnorth.

Stetler, Harrison. "'Collapsologie': Constructing an Idea of How Things Fall Apart." *The New York Review of Books* (blog), January 21, 2020. www.nybooks .com/daily/2020/01/21/collapsologie-constructing-an-idea-of-how-things-fall-apart.

Stone-Mediatore, Shari. *Reading across Borders: Storytelling and Knowledges of Resistance.* New York: Palgrave Macmillan, 2003.

———. "Storytelling/Narrative." In *The Oxford Handbook of Feminist Theory,* edited by Lisa Disch and Mary Hawkesworth, 934–54. New York: Oxford University Press, 2016.

Storey, John. "The Happy Place That Exists Nowhere." *Critical Survey* 32, no. 3 (2020): 33–44. https://doi.org/10/gjn6tj.

Stow, Simon. *Republic of Readers? The Literary Turn in Political Thought and Analysis.* Albany: State University of New York Press, 2007.

Streeby, Shelley. *Imagining the Future of Climate Change: World-Making through Science Fiction and Activism.* Oakland: University of California Press, 2018.

Strong, Aaron, Sallie Chisholm, Charles Miller and John Cullen. "Ocean Fertilization: Time to Move On." *Nature* 461 (September 16, 2009): 347–48. https://doi.org/10.1038/461347a.

Suvin, Darko. "Considering the Sense of 'Fantasy' or 'Fantastic Fiction': An Effusion." *Extrapolation* 41, no. 3 (2000): 209–47. https://doi.org/10.3828/ extr.2000.41.3.209.

———. *Metamorphoses of Science Fiction: Studies in the Poetics and History of Cognitive Estrangement in Fiction.* New Haven, CT: Yale University Press, 1978.

———. *Positions and Presuppositions in Science Fiction.* Houndmills: Macmillan Press, 1988.

———. "Wells as the Turning Point of the SF Tradition." *Minnesota Review* 4 (1975): 106–15.

Swanson, Heather Anne, Nils Bubandt and Anna Tsing. "Less Than One but More Than Many: Anthropocene as Science Fiction and Scholarship-in-the-Making." *Environment and Society* 6, no. 1 (September 1, 2015): 149–66. https://doi.org/10/ghjs7z.

Swanson, Lori J. "A Feminist Ethic That Binds Us to Mother Earth." *Ethics and the Environment* 20, no. 2 (2015): 83–103. https://doi.org/10/ghmvpk.

Swyngedouw, Erik. "Apocalypse Forever?" *Theory, Culture & Society* 27, no. 2–3 (March 2010): 213–32. https://doi.org/10.1177/0263276409358728.

———. "Apocalypse Now! Fear and Doomsday Pleasures." *Capitalism Nature Socialism* 24, no. 1 (March 1, 2013): 9–18. https://doi.org/10.1080/10455752.2012 .759252.

Symons, Jonathan. *Ecomodernism: Technology, Politics and the Climate Crisis.* Cambridge: Polity Press, 2019.

Sypnowich, Christine. "G. A. Cohen's Socialism: Scientific but Also Utopian." *Socialist Studies/Études Socialistes*, December 11, 2012. https://doi.org/10/ghj6xs.

Szerszynski, Bronislaw. "The Anthropocene Monument: On Relating Geological and Human Time." *European Journal of Social Theory* 20, no. 1 (2017): 111–31. https://doi.org/10.1177/1368431016666087.

——— . "Getting Hitched and Unhitched with the Ecomodernists." *Environmental Humanities* 7, no. 1 (May 1, 2016): 239–44. https://doi.org/10.1215/22011919-3616443.

——— . "Reading and Writing the Weather." *Theory, Culture & Society* 27, no. 2–3 (March 2010): 9–30. https://doi.org/10.1177/0263276409361915.

Szerszynski, Bronislaw, Matthew Kearnes, Phil Macnaghten, Richard Owen and Jack Stilgoe. "Why Solar Radiation Management Geoengineering and Democracy Won't Mix." *Environment and Planning A: Economy and Space* 45, no. 12 (December 1, 2013): 2809–16. https://doi.org/10.1068/a45649.

Tally, Robert T. *Fredric Jameson: The Project of Dialectical Criticism*. London: Pluto Press, 2014.

——— . *Utopia in the Age of Globalization: Space, Representation, and the World-System*. Houndmills: Palgrave MacMillan, 2013.

Tănăsescu, Mihnea. *Environment, Political Representation, and the Challenge of Rights: Speaking for Nature*. New York: Palgrave MacMillan, 2016.

Tarnoff, Ben. "Bill Gates Won't Save Us." *Jacobin*, 2017. www.jacobinmag.com/2017/08/bill-gates-wont-save-us.

Taylor, Bron. "Earth and Nature-Based Spirituality (Part I): From Deep Ecology to Radical Environmentalism." *Religion* 31, no. 2 (2001): 175–93. https://doi.org/10.1006/reli.2000.0256.

——— . "Earth and Nature-Based Spirituality (Part II): From Earth First! And Bioregionalism to Scientific Paganism and the New Age." *Religion* 31, no. 3 (2001): 225–45. https://doi.org/10.1006/reli.2000.0257.

Thaler, Mathias. "Bleak Dreams, Not Nightmares: Critical Dystopias and the Necessity of Melancholic Hope." *Constellations* 26, no. 4 (2019): 607–22. https://doi.org/10/gft37p.

——— . "Hope Abjuring Hope: On the Place of Utopia in Realist Political Theory." *Political Theory* 46, no. 5 (2018): 671–97. https://doi.org/10/gfck5k.

——— . *Naming Violence: A Critical Theory of Genocide, Torture, and Terrorism. New Directions in Critical Theory*. New York: Columbia University Press, 2018.

——— . "Peace as a Minor, Grounded Utopia: On Prefigurative and Testimonial Pacifism." *Perspectives on Politics* 17, no. 4 (2019): 1003–18. https://doi.org/10/ggdxfj.

——— . "Political Imagination and the Crime of Crimes: Coming to Terms with 'Genocide' and 'Genocide Blindness.'" *Contemporary Political Theory* 13, no. 4 (2014): 358–79. https://doi.org/10/f6kwkc.

"Reconciliation through Estrangement." *The Review of Politics* 80, no. 4 (2018): 649–73. https://doi.org/10/ggdxff.

"Unhinged Frames: Assessing Thought Experiments in Normative Political Theory." *British Journal of Political Science* 48, no. 4 (2018): 1119–41. https://doi.org/10/gd9cqf.

"What If: Multispecies Justice as the Expression of Utopian Desire." *Environmental Politics* 31, no. 2 (February 23, 2022): 258–76. https://doi.org/10.1080/09644016.2021.1899683.

Thompson, Edward. "Romanticism, Utopianism and Moralism: The Case of William Morris." *New Left Review*, I, no. 99 (1976): 83–111.

Thorpe, Charles, and Ian Welsh. "Beyond Primitivism: Towards a Twenty-First Century Anarchist Theory and Praxis for Science and Technology." *Anarchist Studies* 16, no. 1 (March 22, 2008): 48–76.

Thunberg, Greta. "'Our House Is on Fire': Greta Thunberg, 16, Urges Leaders to Act on Climate." *The Guardian*, January 25, 2019. www.theguardian.com/environment/2019/jan/25/our-house-is-on-fire-greta-thunberg16-urges-leaders-to-act-on-climate.

Tomalin, Emma. *Biodivinity and Biodiversity: The Limits to Religious Environmentalism.* Burlington, VT: Ashgate, 2009.

Traverso, Enzo. *Left-Wing Melancholia: Marxism, History, and Memory.* New York: Columbia University Press, 2016.

Trexler, Adam. *Anthropocene Fictions: The Novel in a Time of Climate Change.* Charlottesville: University of Virginia Press, 2015.

Trexler, Adam, and Adeline Johns-Putra. "Climate Change in Literature and Literary Criticism." *Wiley Interdisciplinary Reviews: Climate Change* 2, no. 2 (March 1, 2011): 185–200. https://doi.org/10.1002/wcc.105.

Trott, Carlie D. "Constructing Alternatives: Envisioning a Critical Psychology of Prefigurative Politics." *Journal of Social and Political Psychology* 4, no. 1 (May 24, 2016): 266–85. https://doi.org/10/ggp26m.

Trotta, Joe, Petra Platen and Houman Sadri, eds. *Broken Mirrors: Representations of Apocalypses and Dystopias in Popular Culture.* New York: Routledge, 2019.

Tschakert, Petra. "More-than-Human Solidarity and Multispecies Justice in the Climate Crisis." *Environmental Politics* 31, no. 2 (February 23, 2022): 277–96. https://doi.org/10.1080/09644016.2020.1853448.

Tschakert, Petra, David Schlosberg, Danielle Celermajer et al. "Multispecies Justice: Climate-Just Futures with, for and beyond Humans." *Wiley Interdisciplinary Reviews: Climate Change* 12, no. 2 (2021): e699. https://doi.org/10/ghq9vw.

Tuhus-Dubrow, Rebecca. "Cli-Fi: Birth of a Genre." *Dissent* 60, no. 3 (July 3, 2013): 58–61. https://doi.org/10.1353/dss.2013.0069.

Tully, James. "Public Philosophy as a Critical Activity." In *Public Philosophy in a New Key*, I: Democracy and Civic Freedom: 15–38. Cambridge: Cambridge University Press, 2008.

Tyrrell, Toby. *On Gaia: A Critical Investigation of the Relationship between Life and Earth*. Princeton, NJ: Princeton University Press, 2013.

Tyszczuk, Renata, and Joe Smith. "Culture and Climate Change Scenarios: The Role and Potential of the Arts and Humanities in Responding to the '1.5 Degrees Target.'" *Current Opinion in Environmental Sustainability*, 31 (April 1, 2018): 56–64. https://doi.org/10/gcp3h6.

Uhrqvist, Ola, and Björn-Ola Linnér. "Narratives of the Past for Future Earth: The Historiography of Global Environmental Change Research." *The Anthropocene Review* 2, no. 2 (August 1, 2015): 159–73. https://doi.org/10.1177/2053019614567543.

Valentini, Laura. "Ideal vs. Non-ideal Theory: A Conceptual Map." *Philosophy Compass* 7, no. 9 (2012): 654–64. https://doi.org/10.1111/j.1747-9991.2012.00500.x.

Vansintjan, Aaron. "Decolonizing Nature, the Academy, and Europe: An Interview with Métis Writer Zoe Todd." *Uneven Earth: Finding Common Ground in an Unequal World* (blog), September 21, 2015. http://unevenearth.org/2015/09/decolonizing-nature-the-academy-and-europe.

Vaughan, Adam. "James Lovelock: Environmentalism Has Become a Religion." *The Guardian*, March 30, 2014. www.theguardian.com/environment/2014/mar/30/james-lovelock-environmentalism-religion.

Vázquez-Arroyo, Antonio Y. *Political Responsibility: Responding to Predicaments of Power*. New York: Columbia University Press, 2016.

Veldman, Robin Globus. "Narrating the Environmental Apocalypse: How Imagining the End Facilitates Moral Reasoning Among Environmental Activists." *Ethics and the Environment* 17, no. 1 (2012): 1–23. https://doi.org/10.2979/ethicsenviro.17.1.1.

Vicente, José Luis de. "Angry Optimism in a Drowned World: A Conversation with Kim Stanley Robinson." *CCCB LAB* (blog), October 31, 2017. http://lab.cccb.org/en/angry-optimism-in-a-drowned-world-a-conversation-with-kim-stanley-robinson.

Vieira, Fátima. "The Concept of Utopia." In *The Cambridge Companion to Utopian Literature*, edited by Gregory Claeys, 3–27. Cambridge: Cambridge University Press, 2010.

Voßkamp, Wilhelm. "'Wenn es Wirklichkeitssinn gibt, muß es auch Möglichkeitssinn geben.' Traditionen des utopischen Denkens bei Robert Musil." In *Was ist der Mensch, was Geschichte?*, edited by Friedrich Jaeger and

Jürgen Straub, 447–362. Bielefeld: transcript-Verlag, 2015. www.degruyter
.com/document/doi/10.14361/9783839402665-toc/html.

Vries, Gerard de. *Bruno Latour.* Cambridge: Polity Press, 2016.

Wallace-Wells, David. "The Uninhabitable Earth, Annotated Edition."
Intelligencer, July 9, 2017. http://nymag.com/intelligencer/2017/07/cli
mate-change-earth-too-hot-for-humans.html.

   The Uninhabitable Earth: Life after Warming. E-Book. New York: Tim Duggan
   Books, 2019.

Wallin-Ruschman, Jennifer, and Mazna Patka. "Learning From Critical Collective
Spaces: Reflections on the Community-Diversity Dialectic in Safe Spaces."
Journal of Social and Political Psychology 4, no. 1 (May 24, 2016): 318–31.
https://doi.org/10/ggp26n.

Walsh, Lynda. *Scientists as Prophets: A Rhetorical Genealogy.* New York: Oxford
University Press, 2013.

Walsh, Stephen, Felix Gradstein, and Jim Ogg. "History, Philosophy, and
Application of the Global Stratotype Section and Point (GSSP)." *Lethaia*
37, no. 2 (2004): 201–18. https://doi.org/10/bm5f4g.

Wark, McKenzie. *Molecular Red: Theory for the Anthropocene.* London: Verso, 2015.

Waters, Colin N., James P. M. Syvitski, Agnieszka Gałuszka et al. "Can Nuclear
Weapons Fallout Mark the Beginning of the Anthropocene Epoch?" *Bulletin
of the Atomic Scientists* 71, no. 3 (January 1, 2015): 46–57. https://doi.org/10
.1177/0096340215581357.

Watson, Andrew J., and James Lovelock. "Biological Homeostasis of the Global
Environment: The Parable of Daisyworld." *Tellus B: Chemical and Physical
Meteorology* 35, no. 4 (July 1, 1983): 284–89. https://doi.org/10.3402/
tellusb.v35i4.14616.

Watts, Jonathan. "Bruno Latour: 'This Is a Global Catastrophe That Has Come
from Within.'" *The Observer,* June 6, 2020. www.theguardian.com/world/
2020/jun/06/bruno-latour-coronavirus-gaia-hypothesis-climate-crisis.

Watts, Vanessa. "Indigenous Place-Thought and Agency amongst Humans and
Non-humans (First Woman and Sky Woman Go on a European World
Tour!)." *Decolonization: Indigeneity, Education & Society* 2, no. 1 (2013): 20–34.

Weber, Max. "The Profession and Vocation of Politics." In *Weber: Political Writings,*
edited by Peter Lassman and Ronald Speirs, 309–69. *Cambridge Texts in the
History of Political Thought.* New York: Cambridge University Press, 1994.

Wegner, Phillip E. "Horizons, Figures, and Machines: The Dialectic of Utopia in
the Work of Fredric Jameson." *Utopian Studies* 9, no. 2 (1998): 58–77.

Weissberg, Liliane. "Versuch einer Sprache des Möglichen: Zum Problem des
Erzählens bei Robert Musil." *Deutsche Vierteljahresschrift für Literaturwissenschaft*

und Geistesgeschichte 54, no. 3 (September 1, 1980): 464–84. https://doi.org/10/gjkrb3.

Wells, H. G. *The Island of Dr. Moreau*, edited by Nita A. Farahany and John L. Flynn. 1896. Reprint, New York: Signet Classics, 2014.

——. *A Modern Utopia.* Mineola, NY: Dover Publications, 2016.

——. "Preface to The Scientific Romances." In *Science Fiction Criticism: An Anthology of Essential Writings*, edited by Rob Latham, 13–16. London: Bloomsbury, 2017.

Westfahl, Gary. "'The Closely Reasoned Technological Story': The Critical History of Hard Science Fiction." *Science Fiction Studies* 20, no. 2 (1993): 157–75.

White, Hayden. *Metahistory: The Historical Imagination in Nineteenth-Century Europe.* Baltimore: Johns Hopkins University Press, 1973.

Whiteduck, Mallory. "'But It's Our Story. Read It.': Stories My Grandfather Told Me and Writing for Continuance." *Decolonization: Indigeneity, Education & Society* 2, no. 1 (May 4, 2013). https://jps.library.utoronto.ca/index.php/des/article/view/19119.

Whyte, Kyle. "Indigenous Climate Change Studies: Indigenizing Futures, Decolonizing the Anthropocene." *English Language Notes* 55, no. 1–2 (March 1, 2017): 153–62. https://doi.org/10/ggmpbp.

——. "Indigenous Science (Fiction) for the Anthropocene: Ancestral Dystopias and Fantasies of Climate Change Crises." *Environment and Planning E: Nature and Space* 1, no. 1–2 (March 1, 2018): 224–42. https://doi.org/10.1177/2514848618777621.

——. "Our Ancestors' Dystopia Now: Indigenous Conservation and the Anthropocene." In *The Routledge Companion to the Environmental Humanities*, edited by Ursula K. Heise, Jon Christensen and Michelle Niemann, 206–15. New York: Routledge, 2017.

Wilderson, Frank B. *Red, White and Black: Cinema and the Structure of U.S. Antagonisms.* Durham, NC: Duke University Press, 2010.

Willener, Alfred. *The Action-Image of Society: On Cultural Politicization.* London: Tavistock Publications, 1970.

Williams, Bernard. *Truth and Truthfulness.* Princeton, NJ: Princeton University Press, 2002.

Williams, David R., Jourdyn A. Lawrence and Brigette A. Davis. "Racism and Health: Evidence and Needed Research." *Annual Review of Public Health* 40, no. 1 (2019): 105–25. https://doi.org/10/ggbt3m.

Winter, Jay M. *Dreams of Peace and Freedom: Utopian Moments in the Twentieth Century.* New Haven, CT: Yale University Press, 2006.

Wissenburg, Marcel, and David Schlosberg. *Political Animals and Animal Politics.* New York: Palgrave MacMillan, 2018.

Wittgenstein, Ludwig. *Philosophical Investigations,* edited by P. M. S. Hacker and Joachim Schulte. Translated by G. E. M. Anscombe, P. M. S. Hacker and Joachim Schulte. Malden, MA: Wiley-Blackwell, 2009.

Wolf-Meyer, Matthew J. *Theory for the World to Come: Speculative Fiction and Apocalyptic Anthropology.* Minneapolis: University of Minnesota Press, 2019.

Wright, David. "Cultural Capital and the Literary Field." *Cultural Trends* 15, no. 2–3 (2006): 123–39. https://doi.org/10.1080/09548960600712934.

Wright, Erik Olin. *Envisioning Real Utopias.* New York: Verso, 2010.

"How to Be an Anticapitalist Today." *Jacobin,* February 12, 2015. www.jacobinmag.com/2015/12/erik-olin-wright-real-utopias-anticapitalism-democracy.

"Transforming Capitalism through Real Utopias." *American Sociological Review* 78, no. 1 (February 1, 2013): 1–25. https://doi.org/10.1177/0003122412468882.

Young, Iris Marion. *Intersecting Voices: Dilemmas of Gender, Political Philosophy, and Policy.* Princeton, NJ: Princeton University Press, 1997.

Justice and the Politics of Difference. Princeton, NJ: Princeton University Press, 1990.

Yusoff, Kathryn. *A Billion Black Anthropocenes or None.* Minneapolis: University of Minnesota Press, 2018.

Yusoff, Kathryn, and Jennifer Gabrys. "Climate Change and the Imagination." *Wiley Interdisciplinary Reviews: Climate Change* 2, no. 4 (July 1, 2011): 516–34. https://doi.org/10.1002/wcc.117.

Zalasiewicz, Jan. *The Earth after Us: What Legacy Will Humans Leave in the Rocks?* New York: Oxford University Press, 2008.

"The Extraordinary Strata of the Anthropocene." In *Environmental Humanities: Voices from the Anthropocene,* edited by Serpil Oppermann and Serenella Iovino, 115–31. New York: Rowman and Littlefield International, 2017.

Zalasiewicz, Jan, Colin N. Waters, Anthony D. Barnosky et al. "Colonization of the Americas, 'Little Ice Age' Climate, and Bomb-Produced Carbon: Their Role in Defining the Anthropocene." *The Anthropocene Review* 2, no. 2 (August 1, 2015): 117–27. https://doi.org/10.1177/2053019615587056.

Zalasiewicz, Jan, Colin N. Waters, Mark Williams et al. "When Did the Anthropocene Begin? A Mid-twentieth Century Boundary Level Is Stratigraphically Optimal." *Quaternary International,* 383 (October 5, 2015): 196–203. https://doi.org/10.1016/j.quaint.2014.11.045.

Zalasiewicz, Jan, Colin N. Waters, Mark Williams, Colin P. Summerhayes, Martin J. Head and Reinhold Leinfelder. "A General Introduction to the Anthropocene." In *The Anthropocene as a Geological Time Unit: A Guide to the*

Scientific Evidence and Current Debate, edited by Jan Zalasiewicz, Colin N. Waters, Mark Williams and Colin P. Summerhayes, 2–4. Cambridge: Cambridge University Press, 2019.

Zamalin, Alex. *Black Utopia: The History of an Idea from Black Nationalism to Afrofuturism.* New York: Columbia University Press, 2019.

Zerilli, Linda M. G. "'We Feel Our Freedom': Imagination and Judgment in the Thought of Hannah Arendt." *Political Theory* 33, no. 2 (2005): 158–88. https://doi.org/10.2307/30038411.

Index

Lightning Source UK Ltd.
Milton Keynes UK
UKHW012003060123
414970UK00003B/21